ICSA

STUDY TEXT

Pre-Professional Paper 6

Introduction to Accounting

New in this September 2000 edition

- New and updated illustrated questions
- Updated to reflect recent exam questions

FOR EXAMS IN DECEMBER 2000 AND JUNE 2001

BPP Publishing
September 2000

First edition 1993
Sixth edition September 2000

ISBN 0 7517 5130 8 (Previous edition 0 7517 5020 4)

British Library Cataloguing-in-Publication Data
A catalogue record for this book
is available from the British Library

First published by

BPP Publishing Limited
Aldine House, Aldine Place
London W12 8AW

Reprinted in the UK under licence from BPP Publishing Limited by

ICSA Publishing Limited
16 Park Crescent
London W1B 1AH

Printed in Great Britain by The Basingstoke Press Limited

We are grateful to the Institute of Chartered Secretaries and Administrators for permission to reproduce in this text the syllabus of which the Institute holds the copyright.

We are grateful to the Institute of Chartered Secretaries and Administrators, the Association of Accounting Technicians, and the Chartered Institute of Management Accountants for permission to reproduce past examination questions. The suggested answers have been prepared by BPP Publishing Limited.

Page

HOW TO USE THIS STUDY TEXT

Aims of this Study Text

To provide you with the knowledge and understanding, skills and application techniques that you need if you are to be successful in your exams

This Study Text has been carefully written around the official ICSA **Introduction to Accounting** syllabus.

- It is **comprehensive**. We do not omit sections of the syllabus: the examiner may examine any part of the syllabus from any angle- and you do not want to be left high and dry.
- It keeps you **up-to-date** with developments in the subject and the way in which the examiner is designing questions.
- It is **on-target**. We do not include any material which is not examinable. You can therefore rely on the BPP Study Text as the stand-alone source of all your information for the exam, without worrying that any of the material is irrelevant.

To allow you to study in the way that best suits your learning style and the time you have available, by following your personal Study Plan

You may be studying at home on your own until the date of the exam, or you may be attending a full-time course. You may like to read every word, or you may prefer to skim-read and devote the remainder of your time to question practice. Whatever your approach, you will find the BPP Study Text meets your needs in designing and following your personal Study Plan.

To tie in with the rest of the BPP Effective Study Package to ensure you have the best possible chance of passing the exam

The BPP Effective Study Package

Recommended period of use	Elements of the BPP Effective Study Package
3-12 months before exam	**Study Text** Use the Study Text to acquire knowledge, understanding, skills and the ability to use application techniques.

↓

1-3 months before exam	**Practice & Revision Kit** Attempt the tutorial questions and read the helpful checklists which are provided for each topic area in the Kit. Then try the numerous examination questions, for which there are realistic suggested answers.

Settling down to study

By this stage in your career you are probably very experienced at learning and taking exams. But have you ever thought about *how* you learn? Let's have a quick look at the key elements required for effective learning.

Key element of learning	Using the BPP Study Text
Motivation	You can rely on the comprehensiveness and technical quality of BPP material. You've chosen the right Study Text - so you're in pole position to pass your exam!
Clear objectives and standards	Do you want to be a prizewinner or simply achieve a pass? Only you can decide.
Feedback	Work through the examples in this text and do the Exercises and Test your knowledge quizzes. Evaluate your efforts critically - how are you doing?
Study Plan	You need to be honest with yourself about your progress - don't be over-confident, but don't be negative either. Make your Study Plan (see below) and try to stick to it. Focus on the short-term objectives - completing two chapters a week, say - but beware of losing sight of your study objectives.
Practice	Use the Test your knowledge quizzes and Chapter roundups to refresh your memory after you have completed your initial study of each chapter.

These introductory pages let you see exactly what you are up against. But however you study, there are two things you should do.

- **Read through the syllabus and syllabus commentary:** these will help you to identify areas you have already covered, perhaps at a lower level of detail, and areas that are totally new to you.
- **Study the examination paper section,** where we show you the format of the exam and analyse the recent papers **including the one set in June 2000**.

Developing your personal Study Plan

Preparing a Study Plan (and sticking closely to it) is one of the key elements in learning success. First you need to be aware of your style of learning. There are four typical learning styles. Consider yourself in the light of the following descriptions and work out which you fit most closely. You can then plan to follow the key study steps in the sequence suggested on page (viii).

Learning styles	Characteristics
Theorist	Seeks to understand principles before applying them in practice
Reflector	Seeks to observe phenomena, thinks about them and then chooses to act
Activist	Prefers to deal with practical, active problems; does not have much patience with theory
Pragmatist	Prefers to study only if a direct link to practical problems can be seen; not interested in theory for its own sake

Key study steps

We have broken the learning process down into a series of key steps, which you can apply to each chapter in turn. We list them here in the order which seems to work best for **theorists** and **reflectors**. If you are an **activist** or a **pragmatist** you may prefer to use a different sequence. The various options are summarised after the table of steps. Tackle the chapters in the order you find them in the Study Text. Taking into account your individual learning style, follow these key study steps for each chapter.

Key study steps	Activity
Step 1 *Chapter topic list*	Study the list. Each numbered topic is a numbered section in the chapter.
Step 2 *Introduction*	Read through it. It is designed to show you *why* the topics in the chapter need to be studied - how they lead on from previous topics, and how they lead into subsequent ones.
Step 3 *Explanations*	Proceed methodically through the chapter, reading each section thoroughly and making sure you understand. Where a topic has been examined, we state the month and year of examination against the appropriate heading. You should pay particular attention to these topics.
Step 4 *Note taking*	Take brief notes if you wish, avoiding the temptation to copy out too much.
Step 5 *Examples*	Follow each through to its solution very carefully.
Step 6 *Case examples*	Study each one, and try to add flesh to them from your own experience - they are designed to show how the topics you are studying come alive (and often come unstuck) in the real world.
Step 7 *Exercises*	Make a very good attempt at each one in the chapter. These are designed to put your knowledge into practice.
Step 8 *Solutions*	Check yours against ours, and make sure you understand the reasons why they may differ.
Step 9 *Chapter roundup*	Work through it very carefully, to make sure you have grasped the major points it is highlighting.
Step 10 *Test your knowledge quiz*	When you are happy that you have covered the chapter, use the Test your knowledge quiz to check how much you have remembered of the topics covered. The answers are in the paragraphs in the chapter that we refer you to.
Step 11 *Illustrative questions*	Either at this point, or later when you are thinking about revising, make a full attempt at the question(s) suggested at the very end of the chapter. You can find these at the end of the Study Text, along with the answers so you can see how you did.

Learning style approaches

Learning style	Sequence of key study steps in the BPP Study Text
Theorist	1, 2, 3, 5, 6, 7, 8, 9, 10, 11, (4 continuous)
Reflector	
Activist	1, 2, 7/8 (read through), 5, 6, 9, 3, 7/8 (full attempt), 10, 11 (4 continuous)
Pragmatist	7/8 (read through), 2, 5, 6, 9, 1, 3, 7/8 (full attempt), 10, 11 (4 continuous)

Planning your studies

Next you should complete the following checklist.

Am I motivated? (a) ☐

Do I have an objective and a standard that I want to achieve? (b) ☐

Am I a theorist, a reflector, an activist or a pragmatist? (c) ☐

How much time do I have available per week, given: (d) ☐

- the standard I have set myself
- the time I need to set aside later for work on the Practice and Revision Kit
- the other exam(s) I am sitting, and (of course)
- practical matters such as work, travel, exercise, sleep and social life?

Now:

- take the time you have available per week for this Study Text (d), and multiply it by the number of weeks available to give (e). (e) ☐
- divide (e) by the number of chapters to give (f) (f) ☐
- set about studying each chapter in the time represented by (f), following the key study steps in the order suggested by your particular learning style.

This is your personal Study Plan.

Moving on...

However you study, when you are ready to embark on the practice and revision phase of the BPP Effective Study Package, you should still refer back to this Study Text, both as a source of reference (you should find the index particularly helpful for this) and as a refresher (the Chapter roundups and Test your knowledge quizzes help you here).

And remember to keep careful hold of this Study Text - you will find it invaluable in your work.

SYLLABUS

Objective

To provide a fundamental understanding of the principles, role and scope of accounting in relation to the recording of business transactions and the provision of accounting information.

	Covered in Chapter(s)
Accounting principles	
Purpose of accounting	1
Concepts and conventions	2
Users of accounting information	1
The respective roles of financial and management accounting	1, 20
Accounting systems	
Double entry bookkeeping	3, 5, 6, 14
The cash book and bank reconciliation	5, 13
Trial balance	7
Control accounts for sales and purchases ledgers	13
The journal	6, 14
Accounting statements from incomplete information	15
Accounting reports	
The profit and loss account, balance sheet and cash flow statement of sole traders and companies	4, 7, 14, 16, 17
Treatment of accruals and prepayments and other adjustments, including doubtful debts and depreciating accounting	8, 9, 11
Stock valuation	10
Treatment of intangible assets	12
Types of shares and debentures, other fixed interest stocks, capital and revenue reserves and the appropriation of profits and losses	16
Interpretation of financial information	
Elementary ratio analysis in respect of profitability, liquidity, activity and gearing	18, 19
Management accounting	
Cost classification	20
Budgeting and budgetry control	23
Marginal and absorption costing	21, 22
Overhead analysis and pricing	21, 22

THE EXAMINATION PAPER

Paper format

The paper is divided into two sections. Section A comprises three questions worth 30 marks each, and candidates must answer any two of these questions. Section B comprises three questions worth 20 marks each, and again candidates must answer any two of these questions.

Analysis of past papers

June 2000

1 Profit and loss account, appropriation account, balance sheet, cash flow statement for limited company.
2 Journal entries, depreciation, fixed assets.
3 Stock valuation, commenting on different methods.
4 Capital and revenue, purpose of trial balance, liabilities and provisions, concepts.
5 Ratio analysis.
6 Departmental budgeted costs, cost estimate.

December 1999

1 Profit and loss account, appropriation account and balance sheet for limited company.
2 Cash book, sales ledger control account, purchase ledger control account, profit and loss account and balance sheet.
3 Balance sheet and cash flow statement, ratios and their significance.
4 Budgeted profit and loss account by absorption costing and marginal costing.
5 Daily cash and profit figures, bank reconciliation.
6 Suspense account, journal entries, month-end checking routines for errors.

June 1999

1 Trading, profit and loss account, appropriation account and stock adjustments.
2 Incomplete records, profit and loss account and balance sheet.
3 Budget report, redrafting the report using marginal costing.
4 Accounting concepts, management accountants role, absorption costing.
5 Ratio analysis, liquidity ratios and comment.
6 Supplier statement reconciliation and purchase ledger control account.

December 1998

1 Sole trader accounts, writing up cash book.
2 Profitability and investment ratios.
3 Limited company accounts.
4 Marginal and absorption costing.
5 Control accounts and books of prime entry.
6 Ratios.

June 1998

1 Cash budget, trading, profit and loss account.
2 Valuation of stock, calculation of cost of goods sold, calculation of current ratio.
3 Bank reconciliation, suspense account, accounting concepts and conventions.
4 Journal entries, balance sheet, accounting concepts and conventions.
5 Fixed assets, disposal account, accumulated depreciation account, depreciation policy.
6 Overhead absorption, rates and costing.

December 1997

1 Limited company accounts, research and development, sole trader and limited liability company.
2 Ratios.
3 Marginal and absorption costing.
4 Sole trader accounts.
5 Accounting terms.
6 Control accounts, books of prime entry.

June 1997

1 Re-drafting trial balance, correction of errors.
2 Cash flow statement, ratios.
3 Incomplete records, stock valuation.
4 Control accounts, books of prime entry.
5 Marginal and absorption costing.
6 Accounting conventions and adjustments.

December 1996

1 Make or buy decision, break even.
2 Ratio analysis - calculations and limitations.
3 Final accounts from trial balance.
4 Comparing terms.
5 Preparation of cash budget.
6 Accounting treatments, concepts and conventions.

June 1996

1 Ratio analysis, accounting entries.
2 Final accounts from incomplete records.
3 Bank reconciliation.
4 Profit forecast, break even.
5 Accounting concepts, net current assets.
6 Ledger accounting.

STUDY CHECKLIST

This page is designed to help you chart your progress through the Study Text, including the illustrative questions at the back of it. You can tick off each topic as you study and try questions on it. Insert the dates you complete the chapters and questions in the relevant boxes. You will thus ensure that you are on track to complete your study before the exam.

		Text chapters *Date completed*	Illustrative questions *Question numbers*	*Date completed*
	PART A: ACCOUNTING PRINCIPLES			
1	The nature and objectives of accounting		1	
2	Preparing accounts: concepts, conventions and regulations		2	
	PART B: ACCOUNTING SYSTEMS AND REPORTS - RECORDING TRANSACTIONS			
3	Assets, liabilities and the accounting equation		3	
4	An introduction to final accounts		4, 5	
5	Books of prime entry		6	
6	Ledger accounting and double entry		7, 8	
7	From trial balance to financial statements		9	
8	The cost of goods sold, accruals and prepayments		10	
9	Discounts, bad debts and provisions		11	
10	Stocks		12	
11	Fixed assets – depreciation, revaluation and disposal		13 - 15	
12	Intangible fixed assets		16	
	PART C: ACCOUNTING SYSTEMS AND REPORTS – FURTHER ASPECTS			
13	Bank reconciliations and control accounts		17, 18	
14	Correction of errors. Preparation of final accounts		19 - 22	
15	Incomplete records		23, 24	
16	Limited companies		25, 26	
17	Cash flow statements		27	
	PART D: INTERPRETATION OF FINANCIAL INFORMATION			
18	The interpretation of financial statements		28	
19	The operating cycle and working capital ratios		29	
	PART E: MANAGEMENT ACCOUNTING			
20	The management accountant. Classifying costs		30	
21	Absorption costing		31	
22	Marginal costing. Pricing		32, 33	
23	Budgets and budgetary control		34, 35	

Part A

Accounting principles

Chapter 1

THE NATURE AND OBJECTIVES OF ACCOUNTING

This chapter covers the following topics.

1 What is accounting?

2 Why keep accounts?

3 Users of accounting information

4 Management accounting and financial accounting

5 The scope of accounting information

6 The main financial statements

Introduction

The syllabus for the *Introduction to Accounting* paper starts off with a section entitled 'Accounting Principles'. This is because, before you launch into the mechanics of preparing financial statements, it is important that you understand *why* accounting information is necessary and the assumptions on which it is based.

You need to consider the nature of accounting information, its purposes and uses. These are the topics covered in Sections 1 to 3 of this chapter. You may know more about accounting than you realise. Have a go at the first exercise which will encourage you to think about these issues.

You may already be aware that there is a difference between a management accountant and a financial accountant. This topic is covered in Section 4.

Accounting is not an exact science, nor is the information it provides free from drawbacks. It is as well to be aware from the beginning of your studies that there are limitations on the scope and use of accounting information, and this point is explored briefly in Section 5.

Lastly, the chapter introduces you to the main financial statements - the profit and loss account and the balance sheet.

1 WHAT IS ACCOUNTING?

1.1 To set you thinking, attempt the following exercise to assess what you already know about accounting.

Exercise 1

(a) You will often meet with the terms 'an accounting statement' or 'a set of accounts'. Do you know what is meant by these terms?

(b) Who do you think has the task of preparing accounting statements? In an organisation of a reasonable size, would it be one person? One department? Several different departments?

(c) Who are the users of accounting information?

(d) What is the purpose of accounting?

Solution

(a) An accounting statement is any collection of related accounting information. It might be, for example, a profit and loss account or a balance sheet. A set of accounts is a number of accounting statements presented together with the intention of showing an overall view of an organisation's income, expenditure, assets and liabilities.

(b) Most organisations of reasonable size will have at least one dedicated accounts department, staffed by people with detailed knowledge of accounting systems and theory, perhaps gained while acquiring a professional qualification in accountancy. In large organisations there may be several departments, or groups, responsible for preparing accounting information of many different kinds to meet the needs of accounts users.

(c) The users of accounts, as explained in the text of this chapter, include a variety of people and organisations, both internal and external. The extent of their information needs varies widely.

(d) There are many purposes of accounting. You may have thought of: control over the use of resources, knowledge of what the business owes and owns, calculation of profits and losses, cash budgeting, effective financial planning.

1.2 A few definitions will get us started.

Accounting could be defined as the process of collecting, recording, summarising and communicating financial information.

Accounts are the records in which this information is recorded. Keeping the most basic records is described as *bookkeeping.* The profession responsible for the summarising and communicating of financial information is the *accountancy* profession.

2 WHY KEEP ACCOUNTS?

2.1 Accounts have been kept for thousands of years because they help to keep track of money, by showing where it came from and how it has been spent.

2.2 Accounts serve a number of purposes.

(a) They aid the efficient running of a business.
(b) They indicate how successfully managers are performing.
(c) They provide information about the resources and activities of a business.

Consider these purposes in more detail.

2.3 The production of accounting information can itself play an important role in the efficient running of a business. For example, a business needs to pay bills in respect of the goods and services it purchases. It must, therefore, keep a record of such bills so that the correct amounts can be paid at the correct times. Similarly a business needs to keep track of cash and cheques received from customers. Such records form one part of a basic accounting system. Additionally, keeping records of a business's assets (eg its motor vehicles or computers) makes it easier to keep them secure.

2.4 Another reason for keeping accounts arises from the complexity of most modern businesses. Centuries ago, a business enterprise might consist of a single venture with a limited life. For example, a merchant might charter a ship to purchase goods from abroad for sale in his own country. In such cases it was easy to ascertain the merchant's profit: it was simply the amount of cash he had left at the end of the venture. Similarly, a small shop needs to generate enough money to pay for all its proprietor's personal expenses and occasional large purchases (eg replacement till or van). The proprietor can quite easily check that this aim is being met by counting the cash in the till.

2.5 However, modern businesses are often much more complicated. They seldom have a single owner (in fact, some very large enterprises, such as British Telecom, may be owned by millions of shareholders). Frequently the owners are not involved in the day-to-day running of the business but appoint managers to act on their behalf. In addition, there are too many activities and assets for the managers to keep track of simply from personal knowledge and an occasional glance at the bank statement. It is therefore desirable that businesses should produce accounts which will indicate how successfully the managers are performing.

2.6 In 1975 a committee established by the UK accountancy bodies published a discussion paper called *The Corporate Report*. (A corporate report is a report, including accounts, prepared by a business enterprise.) One of the questions which the committee attempted to answer was why businesses produce accounts. They concluded that the fundamental objective of a corporate report is:

> '. . . to communicate economic measurements of, and information about, the resources and performance of the reporting entity useful to those having reasonable rights to such information.'

2.7 In other words, a business should produce information about its activities because there are various groups of people who want or need to know that information. This sounds rather vague: we will look more closely at the classes of people who need information about a business. We need also to think about what information in particular is of interest to the members of each class. Large businesses are usually of interest to a greater variety of people than small businesses, so we will consider the case of a large public company whose shares can be bought and sold on the Stock Exchange.

3 USERS OF ACCOUNTING INFORMATION

User group	Comment
Managers of the company	People appointed by the company's owners to supervise the day-to-day activities of the company need information about the company's current and expected future financial situation. This facilitates efficient management and effective control and planning decisions.
Shareholders of the company, ie the company's owners	Want to assess how effectively management is performing its stewardship function and how much profit they can afford to withdraw from the business for their own use.
Trade contacts, including suppliers who provide goods to the company on credit and customers who purchase the goods or services provided by the company	Suppliers want to know about the company's ability to pay its debts. Customers need to know that the company is a secure source of supply and is in no danger of having to close down.
Providers of finance to the company	Might include a bank which permits the company to operate an overdraft, or provides longer-term finance by granting a loan. Will want to ensure that the company is able to keep up with interest payments, and eventually to repay the amounts advanced.
The Inland Revenue	Wants to know about business profits in order to assess the tax payable by the company.

User Group	Comment
Employees	Should have a right to information about the company's financial situation, because their future careers and the level of their wages and salaries depend on it.
Financial analysts and advisers	Need information for their clients or audience. For example, stockbrokers need information to advise investors in stocks and shares; credit agencies want information to advise potential suppliers; journalists need information for their reading public.
Government and their agencies	Interested in the allocation of resources and in the activities of enterprises. Also require information in order to provide a basis for national statistics.
The public	Want information because enterprises affect them in a variety of ways, eg by providing employment and using local suppliers, or by affecting the environment (pollution).

Exercise 2

It is easy to see how 'internal' people get hold of accounting information. A manager, for example, can just go along to the accounts department and ask the staff there to prepare whatever accounting statements he needs. External users of accounts cannot do this. How, in practice, can a business contact or a financial analyst access accounting information about a company?

Solution

The answer is that limited companies (though not other forms of business such as partnerships) are required to make certain accounting information public. They do so by sending copies of the required information to the Registrar of Companies at Companies House. This information is available, at a fee, to any member of the public who asks for it. Other sources include financial comment in the press and company brochures.

4 MANAGEMENT ACCOUNTING AND FINANCIAL ACCOUNTING

4.1 Accountants try to satisfy the information needs of all the groups mentioned above. Managers of a business need the most information, to help them take their planning and control decisions. They can obtain it through a system of *cost and management accounting*. The preparation of accounting reports for external use is called *financial accounting*. Bookkeeping and costing are the bases of financial and management accounting respectively.

4.2 Management accounting systems produce detailed information often split between different departments within an organisation (sales, production, finance, etc). Although much of the information necessarily deals with past events and decisions, management accountants are also responsible for preparing budgets, helping to set price levels and other decisions about the future activities of a business. They also compare actual performance with budget and try to take corrective action where necessary.

4.3 Financial accountants, however, are usually solely concerned with summarising historical data, often from the same basic records as management accountants, but in a different way. This difference arises partly because external users have different interests from management (and have neither the time nor the need for very detailed information), but also because financial statements are prepared under constraints which do not apply to management accounts produced for internal use. This Study Text serves as an introduction to both financial and management accounting.

4.4 The constraints apply particularly to the accounts of limited companies. The owners of a limited company (the shareholders or members of the company) enjoy limited liability, which means that (as individuals) they are not personally liable to pay the company's debts. If the company's own assets are not sufficient to do so, the company may have to cease trading, but the shareholders are not obliged to make up any shortfall from their own private assets.

4.5 Clearly this system is open to abuse, and one of the safeguards is that limited companies are fenced about with a number of accounting regulations that do not apply to other forms of organisation. For example, they are required by law to prepare financial accounts annually, the minimum content of such accounts being laid down by detailed legal regulations.

4.6 In addition, their annual accounts must, except in the case of some small companies, be audited (ie checked) by an independent person with defined qualifications. The auditor must make a report on the accounts, and will highlight any material areas where they do not comply either with the legal regulations or with other regulations laid down by the accounting profession.

4.7 Different types of financial statements are produced for each external user group. Use the following exercise to develop your understanding of the different information supplied.

Exercise 3

Mark the following statements as true or false.

(a) Shareholders receive annual accounts as prepared in accordance with legal and professional requirements.

(b) The accounts of limited companies are sometimes filed with the Registrar of Companies.

(c) Employees always receive the company's accounts and an employee report.

(d) The Inland Revenue will receive the published accounts and as much supplementary detail as the Inspector of Taxes needs to assess the corporation tax payable on profits.

(e) Banks frequently require more information than is supplied in the published accounts when considering applications for loans and overdraft facilities.

Solution

True

(a) Yes, and, in addition, companies listed on the Stock Exchange have to comply with the regulations in the Stock Exchange's Listing Rules (Yellow Book).

(d) The additional information is usually quite detailed, eg analysis of acquisitions of fixed assets.

(e) Yes, banks may require cash flow and profit forecasts and budgets prepared to show management's estimates of future activity in the business.

False

(b) The accounts of limited companies MUST be filed with the Registrar of Companies and be available for public inspection. In addition, the company itself will often distribute these accounts on request to potential shareholders, the bank and financial analysts. These accounts are all that is usually available to suppliers and customers.

(c) Employees will not necessarily receive company accounts (unless they are shareholders for example), but many companies do distribute the accounts to employees as a matter of policy. Some companies produce employee reports which summarise and expand on matters which are covered in the annual accounts and are of particular interest to them.

Exercise 4

We have already mentioned that a company's auditors must possess a suitable qualification. In practice this means that auditors will be members of one or other of the professional accountancy bodies in the United Kingdom and Ireland. Do you know the names of these bodies? They are often mentioned in the financial press.

Solution

The auditors of a company will usually be either chartered accountants (members of the Institute of Chartered Accountants in England and Wales (ICAEW), the Institute of Chartered Accountants in Ireland (ICAI), or the Institute of Chartered Accountants of Scotland (ICAS)), or certified accountants (members of the Association of Chartered Certified Accountants, the ACCA). The auditors of some public sector organisations, such as local authorities, are members of the Chartered Institute of Public Finance and Accountancy (CIPFA). Qualified management accountants are usually members of the Chartered Institute of Management Accountants (CIMA). However, CIMA members are not authorised to conduct audits. The six organisations are jointly responsible for developing detailed accounting regulations known as Financial Reporting Standards.

5 THE SCOPE OF ACCOUNTING INFORMATION

5.1 Accounting statements are presented in monetary terms. It follows that they will only include items to which a monetary value can be attributed. For example, in the balance sheet of a business monetary values are attributed to assets such as machinery (eg the original cost of the machine). Whereas the flair of a good manager, or the loyalty and commitment of a dedicated workforce, cannot be evaluated in monetary terms and therefore do not appear in the accounts.

5.2 Similarly, there are important factors in the successful running of a business which are non-financial by nature. A manager in a manufacturing business will need a detailed knowledge of his machinery's capabilities, the skills of his production staff and the characteristics of his raw materials. All of these things are important in planning production, but none of them would appear in a set of accounts.

5.3 Subject to these limitations, the range of accounting information which can be prepared is very wide. Accounting statements may cover the following items.

(a) Profit earned by a business, or by each of its departments or divisions, in a period.
(b) Assets and liabilities of a business at a particular date.
(c) Cost of producing and/or selling a particular product or range of products.
(d) Cost of running a particular department or division.
(e) Quantity of a product which must be sold in order for it to pay its way (break even).
(f) Amount of cash coming into and leaving a business over a defined period.
(g) Expected overdraft requirement of a business at defined intervals in the future.

Exercise 5

The above list is far from exhaustive. To ensure you understand the difference between financial and management accountancy, mark each of the above as financial or management statements.

Solution

(a) You could have classified this as both financial and management information. Generally the profit earned by the whole business, included in a historical statement (for example for the past 12 months), will be financial accounting. Forecast information, or information relating to parts of the business, for example departments or divisions, is management accounting.

(b) This usually falls within the scope of financial accounting, although it may be used as an input to management accounting, for example as a basis for a forecast.

(c) Management accounting.

(d) Management accounting.

(e) Management accounting.

(f) Cash flow accounting is financial information when it is a historical statement and usually management accounting when it is a forecast or budget.

(g) Management accounting.

Exercise 6

Try to think of two or three other areas that an accounting statement might cover.

Solution

There are many possibilities. Two that you may have heard of in connection with limited companies' financial accounts are a cash flow statement and a five-year summary of key accounting statistics. Other management accounting examples you might suggest are a forecast of sales revenue (perhaps analysed by product, or by geographical area), or an aged debtors analysis (showing the sums of money owed to the business by its customers and the length of time they have been outstanding).

6 THE MAIN FINANCIAL STATEMENTS

6.1 We end this chapter by looking briefly at the two principal financial statements drawn up by accountants: the balance sheet and the profit and loss account.

6.2 The *balance sheet* is simply a list of all the assets owned by a business and all the liabilities owed by a business as at a particular date. It is a snapshot of the financial position of the business at a particular moment. Assets are the business's resources so, for example, a business may buy buildings to operate from, plant and machinery, stock to sell and cars for its employees. These are all resources which it uses in its operations Additionally, it may have bank balances, cash and amounts of money owed to it. These provide the funds it needs to carry out its operations, and are also assets. On the other hand, it may owe money to the bank or to suppliers. These are liabilities.

6.3 A *profit and loss account* is a record of income generated and expenditure incurred over a given period. The period chosen will depend on the purpose for which the statement is produced. The profit and loss account which forms part of the published annual accounts of a limited company will be made up for the period of a year, commencing from the date of the previous year's accounts. On the other hand, management might want to keep a closer eye on a company's profitability by making up quarterly or monthly profit and loss accounts. The profit and loss account shows whether the business has had more income than expenditure (a profit) or vice versa (a loss). Organisations which are not run for profit (charities, etc) produce a similar statement called an income and expenditure account which shows the surplus of income over expenditure (or a deficit where expenditure exceeds income).

Accruals concept

6.4 It is very important to grasp the principle, which is applied in nearly all accounts, that they are not prepared on a cash basis but on an accruals (or earnings) basis. That is, a sale or purchase is dealt with in the year in which it is made, even if cash changes hands in a later year. This is important because most businesses, even if they do not sell on credit, make purchases on credit. If cash accounting is used, then accounts do not present a true picture of the business's activities in any given period. Accountants call this convention an application of the accruals concept. This is discussed in more detail in Chapter 2, but in the meantime is explained briefly by means of the example below.

Example: accruals concept

6.5 Emma has a business printing and selling T-shirts. In May 20X7 she makes the following purchases and sales.

Invoice date	*Numbers bought/sold*	*Amount*	*Date paid*
Purchases		£	
7.5.X7	20	100	1.6.X5
Sales			
8.5.X7	4	40	1.6.X5
12.5.X7	6	60	1.6.X5
23.5.X7	10	100	1.7.X5

What is Emma's profit for May?

Solution

6.6

	£
Cash basis	
Sales	0
Purchases	0
Profit/loss	0
Accruals basis	
Sales (£40 + £60 + £100)	200
Purchases	100
Profit	100

6.7 Obviously, the accruals basis gives a truer picture than the cash basis. Emma has no cash to show for her efforts until June but her customers are legally bound to pay her and she is legally bound to pay for her purchases.

6.8 Her balance sheet as at 31 May 20X7 would therefore show her assets and liabilities as follows.

	£
Assets	
Debtors (£40 + £60 + £100)	200
Liabilities	
Creditors	100
Net assets	100
Proprietor's capital	100

6.9 *Capital* is a special form of liability, representing the amount owed by the business to its proprietor(s). In Emma's case it represents the profit earned in May, which she, as sole proprietor of the business, is entitled to in full. Usually, however, capital will also include the proprietor's initial investment, introduced as cash and perhaps equipment or other assets.

6.10 For example, if Emma had begun her business on 30 April 20X7 by opening a business bank account and paying in £100, her balance sheet immediately after this transaction would look like this.

	£
Assets	
Bank	100
Proprietor's capital	100

On 31 May 20X7 the balance sheet would look like this.

	£
Assets	
Debtors	200
Bank	100
	300
Liabilities	
Creditors	100
Net assets	200
Proprietor's capital	
Brought forward	100
Profit for the period	100
Carried forward	200

6.11 This simple example shows that both the balance sheet and the profit and loss account are summaries of a great many transactions. In later chapters we will look in detail at the ways in which these transactions are recorded and financial statements prepared.

Exercise 7

By looking at the example of Emma, you may be able to see that there is a simple arithmetical relationship linking capital at the beginning of a period, capital at the end of the period, and profit earned during the period. Can you formulate the relationship?

Solution

The relationship is: opening capital + profit = closing capital. In more complicated examples it would be necessary to make adjustments for new capital introduced during the period, and for any capital withdrawn during the period.

Chapter roundup

- You should now have an understanding of accounting and its main uses.
- Accounting is the process of collecting, recording, summarising and communicating financial information.
- Accounting information is essential to the efficient running of a business. It helps managers to control the use of resources, keep track of the assets and liabilities of the business and plan effectively for the future.
- Accounting information is required by a wide range of interested parties both within and outside of the organisation.
- The scope of accounting information is very wide, but it does not embrace every aspect of an organisation's affairs. The scope of accounting is limited by its restriction to items which have a monetary value.
- The two most important financial statements prepared by accountants are the profit and loss account and the balance sheet. Both are prepared on an accruals basis, not a cash basis.
- In Chapter 2 we will develop your understanding of accountancy by considering the concepts, conventions and regulations used in preparing accounts.

Test your knowledge

1. How has the increasing complexity of modern business contributed to the development of accounting? (see para 2.4)
2. List five categories of people who might want accounting information about a business. How do their information needs differ? (3.1 table)
3. Explain the distinction between financial accounting and management accounting. (4.1-4.3)
4. What safeguards are in place to prevent the abuse of limited liability? (4.5, 4.6)
5. What limitations are there on the scope of accounting information? (5.1, 5.2)
6. Explain briefly:

   (a) What is a balance sheet? (6.2)
   (b) What is a profit and loss account? (6.3)
7. In what sense is the capital of a business a liability of the business? (6.9)

Now try illustrative question 1 at the end of the Study Text

Chapter 2

PREPARING ACCOUNTS: CONCEPTS, CONVENTIONS AND REGULATIONS

This chapter covers the following topics.

Introduction

Accounting practice has developed gradually over a period of centuries. Many of its procedures are operated automatically by people who have never questioned whether alternative methods exist which have equal validity. However, the procedures in common use imply the acceptance of certain concepts which are by no means self-evident; nor are they the only possible concepts which could be used to build up an accounting framework.

Our next step is to look at some of the more important concepts which are taken for granted in preparing accounts. A statement of standard accounting practice (SSAP 2 *Disclosure of accounting policies*) describes four concepts as *fundamental accounting concepts*: they are going concern, prudence, accruals and consistency. These four are also identified as fundamental by companies legislation (the Companies Act 1985), which adds a fifth to the list (the separate valuation principle). There is no universally agreed list of fundamental concepts, and others besides these have been described as fundamental by various authors.

In this chapter we shall single out the following concepts for discussion.

(a) The entity concept
(b) The money measurement concept
(c) The going concern concept
(d) The prudence concept
(e) The accruals or matching concept
(f) The consistency concept
(g) The separate valuation principle
(h) The materiality concept

In the last chapter we saw that one of the limitations of accounting information is that such information is always, by definition, in monetary terms, thus ignoring factors which are not readily quantifiable, but which may nevertheless be important to the success of a business. In Section 2 of this chapter we take the point further and argue that, even when you accept that monetary value is paramount, determining that monetary value is by no means a straightforward uncontroversial task.

In Section 3, we take a look at the regulatory framework within which accounts, particularly those of limited companies, are prepared. Do not feel you have to memorise all the details at this stage, the purpose of the section is to impress upon you the *importance* of this framework, which is to be studied in much more detail in the later stages of your qualification.

1 ACCOUNTING CONCEPTS 6/96 - 6/98, 6/99, 6/00

The entity concept

1.1 This will be discussed more fully in the next chapter. Briefly, the concept is that accountants regard a business as a separate entity, distinct from its owners or managers. The concept applies whether the business is a limited company (and so recognised in law as a separate entity) or a sole proprietorship or partnership (in which case the business is not separately recognised by the law). So, in the example of Emma in the previous chapter, the money she transferred to her business bank account becomes, in accounting terms, a *business* asset (but legally remains a *personal* asset).

1.2 Acceptance of this concept has important practical consequences. Particularly in the case of a small business run by a single individual, the owner's personal affairs and business affairs may appear to be inextricably linked; for example, Emma may conduct her business from home. But in preparing the business accounts it is essential to distinguish her private transactions and keep them separate.

Exercise 1

Suppose that Emma withdraws a number of T-shirts from her stock to give to friends, how would this be reflected in her accounts?

Solution

The correct accounting treatment is to regard her as having purchased the goods from the business, which is a completely separate entity; the subsequent gift to her friends is then a private transaction and is not recorded anywhere in the books of the business. Emma should pay for the T-shirts by taking money from her own purse and putting it into the till, or she should regard the withdrawal as a repayment of capital. Otherwise, the business accounts will give a misleading picture.

The money measurement concept

1.3 In Chapter 1, we stated that accounts deal only with items to which a monetary value can be attributed. This is the money measurement concept. We distinguished between an asset such as a machine (which might be valued at its original purchase cost, its replacement cost, etc) and an asset such as the flair of a manager or the dedication of the workforce.

1.4 Although these latter assets are very hard to quantify in monetary terms, they can be of enormous significance to the success of a business. Recognising their importance, accountants in recent years have tried to suggest ways of 'bringing them on to the balance sheet' by attributing values to them. These methods of 'human resource accounting' are beyond the scope of this book, but you should be aware at least of the problems they attempt to address.

Exercise 2

Perhaps it is too glib to say that monetary values can never be attributed to the skill of the workforce. There is at least one high-profile industry where such valuations are commonplace. Can you think of it? And do you know what the accounting consequences are in that industry?

Solution

The industry referred to is of course the world of sport, particularly football, where transfer fees appear to provide an objective valuation of a player's worth. Many football clubs are run as substantial businesses, some of them with shares quoted on the Stock Exchange. As such, their accounting practices are widely publicised and discussed. In almost all cases, however, they make no attempt to include the value of players on their balance sheet, presumably because such values fluctuate wildly with the form and fitness of the players concerned. Almost invariably transfer fees are therefore shown simply as income or a cost in the profit and loss account.

The going concern concept

1.5 This implies that the business will continue in operational existence for the foreseeable future, and that there is no intention to put the company into liquidation or to make drastic cutbacks to the scale of operations.

1.6 The main significance of the going concern concept is that the assets of the business should not be valued at their 'break-up' value, which is the amount that they would sell for if they were sold off piecemeal and the business were thus broken up.

Example: going concern

1.7 Suppose that Emma acquires a T-shirt-printing machine at a cost of £60,000. The asset has an estimated life of six years, and it is normal to write off the cost of the asset to the profit and loss account over this time. In this case a depreciation cost of £10,000 per annum will be charged. (This topic will be covered in more detail in later chapters.) How does the going concern concept determine the accounting treatment in this scenario?

Solution

1.8 Using the going concern concept, it would be presumed that the business will continue its operations and so the asset will live out its full six years in use. A depreciation charge of £10,000 will be made each year, and the value of the asset in the balance sheet will be its cost less the accumulated amount of depreciation charged to date. After one year, the net book value of the asset would therefore be £(60,000 – 10,000) = £50,000, after two years it would be £40,000, after three years £30,000, etc until it has been written down to a value of 0 after 6 years.

Example continued

1.9 Now suppose that this asset has no other operational use outside the business, and in a forced sale it would only sell for scrap. After one year of operation, its scrap value might be, say, £8,000. What would the net book value be after one year?

Solution

1.10 The net book value of the asset, applying the going concern concept, would be £50,000 after one year, but its immediate sell-off value only £8,000. It might be argued that the asset is over-valued at £50,000 and that it should be written down to its break-up value (ie in the balance sheet it should be shown at £8,000 and the balance of its cost should be treated as an expense). However, provided that the going concern concept is valid, so that the asset will continue to be used and will not be sold, it is appropriate accounting practice to value the asset at its net book value.

Exercise 3

Now try this example yourself.

A retailer commences business on 1 January and buys a stock of 20 washing machines, each costing £100. During the year he sells 17 machines at £150 each. How should the remaining machines be valued at 31 December in the following circumstances?

(a) He is forced to close down his business at the end of the year and the remaining machines will realise only £60 each in a forced sale.

(b) He intends to continue his business into the next year.

Solution

(a) If the business is to be closed down, the remaining three machines must be valued at the amount they will realise in a forced sale, ie 3 × £60 = £180.

(b) If the business is regarded as a going concern, the stock unsold at 31 December will be carried forward into the following year, when the cost of the three machines will be matched against the eventual sale proceeds in computing that year's profits. The three machines will therefore appear in the balance sheet at 31 December at cost, 3 × £100 = £300.

The prudence concept

1.11 This is the concept which states that where alternative procedures, or alternative valuations, are possible, the one selected should be the one which gives the most cautious presentation of the business's financial position or results. For example, you may have wondered why the three washing machines in Exercise 3 were stated in the balance sheet at their cost (£100 each) rather than their selling price (£150 each). This is simply an aspect of the prudence concept: to value the machines at £150 would be to anticipate making a profit before the profit had been realised. (After all, what if you only sold them for £130?)

1.12 The other aspect of the prudence concept is that where a loss is foreseen, it should be anticipated and taken into account immediately. If a business purchases stock for £1,200 but because of a sudden slump in the market only £900 is likely to be realised when the stock is sold, the prudence concept dictates that the stock should be valued at £900. It is not enough to wait until the stock is sold, and then recognise the £300 loss; it must be recognised as soon as it is foreseen.

1.13 A profit can be considered to be a realised profit when it is in one of the following forms.

(a) Cash

(b) Another asset which has a reasonably certain cash value. This includes amounts owing from debtors, provided that there is a reasonable certainty that the debtors will eventually pay up what they owe.

1.14 SSAP 2 describes the prudence concept as follows.

> 'Revenue and profits are not anticipated, but are recognised by inclusion in the profit and loss account only when realised in the form either of cash or of other assets the ultimate cash realisation of which can be assessed with reasonable certainty; provision is made for all known ... expenses and losses whether the amount of these is known with certainty or is a best estimate in the light of the information available.'

1.15 A couple of exercises may help you to understand how the prudence concept is applied in practice.

Exercise 4

(a) A company begins trading on 1 January 20X5 and sells goods worth £100,000 during the year to 31 December. At 31 December there are debts of £15,000 owed to the business by customers. Of these, the company is now doubtful whether £6,000 will ever be paid. What is the effect of this on the company's balance sheet and profit and loss account?

(b) Samson Feeble trades as a carpenter. He has undertaken to make a range of kitchen furniture for a customer at an agreed price of £1,000. At the end of Samson's accounting year the job is unfinished (being two thirds complete) and the following data has been assembled.

	£
Costs incurred in making the furniture to date	800
Further estimated cost to completion of the job	400
Total cost	1,200

The incomplete job represents *work in progress* at the end of the year which is an asset, like stock. Its cost to date is £800, but by the time the job is completed Samson will have made a loss of £200. What is the effect of this on Samson's balance sheet and profit and loss account?

Solution

(a) The company should make a *provision for doubtful debts* of £6,000. Sales for 20X5 will be shown in the profit and loss account at their full value of £100,000, but the provision for doubtful debts would be a cost of £6,000. As there is some uncertainty that the sales will be realised in the form of cash, the prudence concept dictates that the £6,000 should not be included in the profit for the year. Debtors in the balance sheet will be shown at a valuation of £9,000 (£15,000 - £6,000).

(b) The full £200 loss should be charged against profits of the current year. The value of work in progress at the year end should be its *net realisable value*, which is lower than its cost. The net realisable value can be calculated in either of two ways.

	(i)		(ii)
	£		£
Eventual sales value	1,000	Work in progress at cost	800
Less further costs to completion		Less loss foreseen	200
in order to make the sale	400		
Net realisable value	600		600

1.16 Sales revenue should only be 'realised' and so 'recognised' in the trading, profit and loss account as follows.

(a) The sale transaction is for a specific quantity of goods at a known price, so that the sales value of the transaction is known for certain.

(b) The sale transaction has been completed, or else it is certain that it will be completed (eg in the case of long-term contract work, when the job is well under way but not yet completed by the end of an accounting period).

(c) The *critical event* in the sale transaction has occurred. The following events are critical events.

  (i) It becomes virtually certain that cash will eventually be received from the customer.

  (ii) Cash is actually received.

1.17 Usually, revenue is 'recognised' after one of the following has happened.

(a) A cash sale is made.

(b) The customer promises to pay on or before a specified future date, and the debt is legally enforceable.

1.18 The prudence concept is applied here in the sense that revenue should not be anticipated, and included in the trading, profit and loss account, before it is reasonably certain to 'happen'.

Exercise 5

Given that prudence is the main consideration, consider under what circumstances, if any, revenue might be recognised at the following stages of a sale.

(a) Goods have been acquired by the business which it confidently expects to resell very quickly.

(b) A customer places a firm order for goods.

(c) Goods are delivered to the customer.

(d) The customer is invoiced for goods.

(e) The customer pays for the goods.

(f) The customer's cheque in payment for the goods has been cleared by the bank.

Solution

(a) A sale must never be recognised before an order has even been placed. There is no certainty about the value of the sale, nor when it will take place, even if it is virtually certain that goods will be sold.

(b) A sale must never be recognised when the customer places an order. Even though the order is for a specific quantity of goods at a specific price, it is not yet certain that the sale transaction will go through. The customer may cancel the order, or the supplier might be unable to deliver the goods as ordered.

(c) A sale will be recognised on delivery of the goods only in the following circumstances.

(i) The sale is for cash, and so the cash is received at the same time.
(ii) The sale is on credit and the customer accepts delivery (eg by signing a delivery note).

(d) The critical event for a credit sale is usually the dispatch of an invoice to the customer. There is then a legally enforceable debt, payable on specified terms, for a completed sale transaction.

(e) The critical event for a cash sale is when delivery takes place and when cash is received; both take place at the same time.

It is too cautious or 'prudent' to await cash payment for a credit sale transaction before recognising the sale, unless the customer is a high credit risk and there is a serious doubt about his ability or intention to pay.

(f) Again it is over-cautious to wait for clearance of the customer's cheques before recognising sales revenue. Such a precaution is only justified in cases where there is a very high risk of the bank refusing to honour the cheque.

The accruals concept or matching concept

1.19 This concept states that, in computing profit, revenue earned must be matched against the expenditure incurred in earning it. This is illustrated in the example of Emma; profit of £100 was computed by matching the revenue (£200) earned from the sale of 20 T-shirts against the cost (£100) of acquiring them.

1.20 If, however, Emma had only sold 18 T-shirts, it would have been incorrect to charge her profit and loss account with the cost of 20 T-shirts, as she still has two T-shirts in stock. If she intends to sell them in June she is likely to make a profit on the sale. Therefore, only the purchase cost of 18 T-shirts (£90) should be matched with her sales revenue, leaving her with a profit of £90.

1.21 Her balance sheet would therefore look like this.

	£
Assets	
Stock (at cost, ie 2 × £5)	10
Debtors (18 × £10)	180
	190
Liabilities	
Creditors	100
Net assets	90
Proprietor's capital (profit for the period)	90

1.22 In this example, the concepts of going concern and matching are linked. Since the business is assumed to be a going concern, it is possible to carry forward the cost of the unsold T-shirts as a charge against profits of the next period.

Exercise 6

If Emma decided to give up selling T-shirts, how would the two T-shirts in the balance sheet be valued?

Solution

If Emma decided to give up selling T-shirts, then the going concern concept would no longer apply and the value of the two T-shirts in the balance sheet would be a break-up valuation rather than cost. Similarly, if the two unsold T-shirts were now unlikely to be sold at more than their cost of £5 each (say, because of damage or a fall in demand) then they should be recorded on the balance sheet at their net realisable value (ie the likely eventual sales price less any expenses to be incurred to make them saleable, eg paint) rather than cost. This shows the application of the prudence concept.

The accruals concept defined

1.23 The 'accruals' or 'matching' concept is described in SSAP 2 as follows.

> 'Revenues and costs are accrued (that is, recognised as they are earned or incurred, not as money is received or paid), matched with one another so far as their relationship can be established or justifiably assumed, and dealt with in the profit and loss account of the period to which they relate ... Revenue and profits dealt with in the profit and loss account of the period are matched with associated costs and expenses by including in the same account the costs incurred in earning them (so far as these are material and identifiable)'.

1.24 Company legislation gives legal recognition to the accruals concept, stating that: 'all income and charges relating to the financial year to which the accounts relate shall be taken into account, without regard to the date of receipt or payment.' This has the effect, as we have seen, of requiring businesses to take account of sales and purchases when made, rather than when paid for, and also to carry unsold stock forward in the balance sheet rather than to deduct its cost from profit for the period.

The consistency concept

1.25 Accounting is not an exact science. There are many areas in which judgement must be exercised in attributing money values to items appearing in accounts. Over the years certain procedures and principles have come to be recognised as good accounting practice, but within these limits there are often various acceptable methods of accounting for similar items.

1.26 The consistency concept states that in preparing accounts consistency should be observed in two respects.

(a) Similar items within a single set of accounts should be given similar accounting treatment.

(b) The same treatment should be applied from one period to another in accounting for similar items. This enables valid comparisons to be made from one period to the next.

The separate valuation principle

1.27 Company law recognises the same four fundamental accounting concepts as SSAP 2, although it describes them not as concepts but as *accounting principles*. The Act also mentions a fifth principle, which may be called the separate valuation principle. Although it is not described by SSAP 2 as a fundamental accounting concept it has long been recognised as good accounting practice.

1.28 The separate valuation principle states that, in determining the amount to be attributed to an asset or liability in the balance sheet, each component item of the asset or liability must be valued separately. These separate valuations must then be aggregated to arrive at the balance sheet figure. For example, if a company's stock comprises 50 separate items, a valuation must (in theory) be arrived at for each item separately; the 50 figures must then be aggregated and the total is the stock figure which should appear in the balance sheet.

Exercise 7

The following true/false exercise will allow you to ensure that you have understood the concepts and conventions covered so far in this chapter.

Mark the following statements as true or false.

(a) The entity concept is that accountants regard a business as a separate legal entity, distinct from its owners or managers.

(b) Accounts deal only with items to which a monetary value can be attributed.

(c) Where the prudence and accruals concepts conflict, preparers of accounts may follow either.

(d) The accruals, prudence, going concern and consistency concepts are contained in SSAP 2.

Solution

True

(b) Currently this is true, although research is on-going into Human Resource accounting.

(d) Yes. Company law also recognises them as principles and adds a fifth, the separate valuation principle.

False

(a) No. Although it is certainly true that the entity concept is that accountants regard a business as a separate entity, it is not always a legal difference. For example, legally a sole trader is not separate from his business.

(c) Where the prudence and accruals concepts conflict, prudence overrides accruals.

The materiality concept

1.29 Apart from the possibility of downright error, there will be many areas where two different accountants would come up with different figures for the same item. The materiality concept is relevant in this context.

1.30 An item is immaterial if its omission or misstatement would reasonably influence the decisions of a user of the accounts. In preparing accounts it is important to assess what is material and what is not, so that time and money are not wasted in the pursuit of excessive detail.

1.31 Determining whether or not an item is material is a very subjective exercise. There is no absolute measure of materiality. It is common to apply a convenient rule of thumb (for example to define material items as those with a value greater than 5% of the net profit disclosed by the accounts). However, in assessing whether or not an item is material, it is not only the amount of the item which needs to be considered. The context is also important.

(a) If a balance sheet shows fixed assets of £2 million and stocks of £30,000 an error of £20,000 in the fixed asset valuation might not be regarded as material, whereas an error of £20,000 in the stock valuation would be. In other words, the total of which the error forms a part must be considered.

(b) If a business has a bank loan of £50,000 and a £55,000 balance on bank deposit account, it might well be regarded as a material misstatement if these two amounts were displayed on the balance sheet as 'cash at bank £5,000'. In other words, incorrect presentation may amount to material misstatement even if there is no monetary error.

1.32 The assessment of an item as material or immaterial may affect its treatment in the accounts. For example, the profit and loss account of a business will show the expenses incurred by the business grouped under suitable captions (heating and lighting expenses, rent and rates expenses etc); but in the case of very small expenses it may be appropriate to lump them together under a caption such as 'sundry expenses', because a more detailed breakdown would be inappropriate for such immaterial amounts.

Exercise 8

(a) You depreciate your office equipment by 20% each year because it has a useful life, on average, of five years. This year your profitability is down and you think you can squeeze an extra year's life out of your equipment. Is it acceptable not to charge any depreciation this year?

(b) You have recently paid £4.95 for a waste paper bin which should have a useful life of about five years. Should you treat it as a fixed asset?

Solution

(a) No, because of the consistency concept. Once the depreciation policy has been established, it should not be changed without good cause.

(b) No, because of the materiality concept. The cost of the bin is very small. Rather than cluttering up the balance sheet for five years, treat the £4.95 as an expense in this year's profit and loss account.

Clashes between accounting concepts

1.33 Sometimes inconsistencies arise between the different accounting concepts. Consider the following two examples.

(a) Accruals and prudence. The accruals concept requires future income (eg in relation to credit sales) to be accrued. The prudence concept dictates that caution should be exercised, so that if there is doubt about the subsequent receipt, no accrual should be made.

(b) Consistency and prudence. If circumstances change, prudence may conflict with the consistency concept, which requires the same treatment year after year.

1.34 In all situations where prudence conflicts with another accounting concept, prudence must prevail and the other concept must be over-ridden.

2 COST AND VALUES

2.1 A basic principle of accounting (some writers include it in the list of fundamental accounting concepts) is that resources are normally stated in accounts at historical cost, ie at the amount which the business paid to acquire them. An important advantage of this procedure is that the objectivity of accounts is maximised: there is usually objective, documentary evidence to prove the amount paid to purchase an asset or pay an expense.

2.2 In general, accountants prefer to deal with costs, rather than with 'values'. This is because valuations tend to be subjective and to vary according to what the valuation is for. For example, suppose that a company acquires a machine to manufacture its products. The machine has an expected useful life of four years. At the end of two years the company is preparing a balance sheet and has to decide what monetary amount to attribute to the asset.

2.3 Numerous possibilities can be considered.

(a) The original cost (historical cost) of the machine.

(b) Half of the historical cost, on the ground that half of its useful life has expired.

(c) The amount the machine might fetch on the secondhand market.

(d) The amount it would cost to replace the machine with an identical machine.

(e) The amount it would cost to replace the machine with a more modern machine incorporating the technological advances of the previous two years.

(f) The machine's economic value, ie the amount of the profits it is expected to generate for the company during its remaining life.

2.4 All of these valuations have something to commend them, but the great advantage of the first two is that they are based on a figure (the machine's historical cost) which is objectively verifiable. (Some authors regard objectivity, or neutrality, as an accounting concept in its own right.) The subjective judgement involved in the other valuations, particularly (f), is so great as to lessen the reliability of any accounts in which they are used. As we will see in later chapters, method (b), or a variation of it, is the one which would normally be used.

2.5 The method chosen has important consequences for the measurement of profit, as the following example will show.

Example: costs and values

2.6 Brian sets up in business on 1 January 20X7 selling accountancy textbooks. He buys 100 books for £5 each and by 31 December 20X7 he manages to sell his entire stock, all for cash, at a price of £8 each. On 1 January 20X8 he replaces his stock by purchasing another 100 books; by this time the cost of the books has risen to £6 each. Calculate the profit earned by Brian in 20X7.

Solution

2.7 In conventional historical cost accounting, Brian's profit would be computed as follows.

	£
Sale of 100 books (@ £8 each)	800
Cost of 100 books (@ £5 each)	500
Profit for the year	300

2.8 The purchase of the books is stated at their historical cost. Although this is accepted accounting practice, and is the method we will be using almost invariably throughout this book, it involves an anomaly which can be seen if we look at how well off the business is.

2.9 On 1 January 20X7 the assets of the business consist of the 100 books which Brian has purchased as stock. On 1 January 20X8 the business has an identical stock of 100 books, and also has cash of £200 (ie £800 received from customers, less the £600 cost of replacing stock). So despite making a profit of £300, measured in the conventional way, the business appears to be only £200 better off.

2.10 This anomaly could be removed if an alternative accounting convention were used. Suppose that profit was measured as the difference between the selling price of goods and the cost of replacing the goods sold. Brian's profit would then be computed as follows.

	£
Sale of 100 books	800
Cost of replacing 100 books sold @ £6 each	600
Profit for the year	200

2.11 Now the profit for the year is exactly matched by the increase in the company's assets over the year.

Capital maintenance

2.12 The example above leads us on to the important concept of capital maintenance. The capital of a business (also called its net worth) represents the excess of its assets over its liabilities, and, as we saw in the example of Emma in Chapter 1, represents the proprietor's interest in the business. One way of measuring profit would be to measure how well off a business is at the beginning of a period, and compare it with how well off it is at the end of the period; the difference (after allowing for withdrawals of capital and injections of new capital) would be the profit or loss for the period. On this basis, measurement of profit depends on the methods we use to value the assets and liabilities of the business at the beginning and end of the period.

2.13 It is worth looking again at the example of Brian. Using historical cost as our basis of valuation, the value of his business at 1 January 20X7 and 1 January 20X8 is as follows.

	20X7	*20X8*
	£	£
Stocks (at historical cost)	500	600
Cash	0	200
	500	800

2.14 The value of the business has risen by £300 over the year and this is the amount of profit we calculated on the historical cost basis. We can say that the original capital of the business, £500, has been maintained and an addition to capital of £300 has been created.

2.15 Instead of using historical costs, it is theoretically possible to measure capital in physical terms. Brian's physical capital was originally 100 books; on 1 January 20X8, it consists of an identical 100 books plus £200 cash. We can say that Brian's original physical capital has been maintained and an addition to capital of £200 has been created. This is equivalent to the profit we computed on a replacement cost basis.

2.16 A system of accounting based principally on replacement costs, and measuring profit as the increase in physical capital, was used in the UK for some years. It is called *current cost accounting*. The main accounting system has always been, and continues to be, historical cost accounting but current cost accounting was developed as a possible solution to certain problems which arise in periods of rising prices. Theoretical and practical objections to the current cost accounting system led to its withdrawal in the UK.

Accounting in periods of rising prices

2.17 In periods of *inflation*, businessmen and accountants face a number of problems.

Problem	Comment
(a) For businessmen the major difficulty is in decision making.	Successful decisions depend on correct estimates of future events. This is complicated when future costs and prices are affected by inflation. The difficulty is more acute when the effects of the decision extend over a long period of time, but even short-term decisions such as price increases are affected.
(b) Businessmen rely on accounts to show the profit earned by a business, and this is at least partly so that an assessment can be made of how much profit can safely be withdrawn from the business by its owners.	When prices are rising, at least some of the profit shown by historical cost accounts must be ploughed back into the business just to maintain its previous capacity.

Problem	Comment
(c) The accountant must prepare accounts expressed in terms of a monetary unit (eg the £ in the UK).	In times of rising prices the value of the unit is not constant and comparisons between the accounts of the current year with those of previous years may be misleading.
(d) The accountant must cope with difficulties in measuring asset values and profit.	Asset values can become out of date, particularly in the case of fixed assets; for example, a freehold factory purchased 20 years ago will be shown in the accounts at its original cost, even though its value is likely to have increased greatly over the period of ownership. Profit figures are likely to be distorted by increases in the cost of goods purchased during the accounting period because the cost of goods sold is computed in the profit and loss account on the basis of their historical rather than replacement cost.

2.18 Attempts to get round the problems of inflation have a long history in the UK and overseas. One step which has found favour in practice is to prepare *modified* historical cost accounts. This usually means that up-to-date valuations are included in the historical cost balance sheet for some or all of a company's fixed assets, without any other revaluations being made. No attempt is made to tackle the difficulties of profit measurement.

2.19 More active measures have been taken to find alternatives to the historical cost convention. The two alternative systems which have found favour, at different times, in the UK are *current cost accounting* (CCA) and *current purchasing power accounting* (CPP). CCA has already been briefly described. CPP tackles the problems of inflation by attempting to express accounting values in terms of a stable monetary unit.

2.20 For the foreseeable future, historical cost accounting is likely to be the most important system in the UK, despite its inability to reflect the effects of inflation. There are a number of reasons why this is so.

(a) It is easy and cheap. Other methods tend to be far more complicated and onerous to use, particularly for small businesses. Also, there is no agreement on an alternative.

(b) The fact that fixed asset revaluation is permitted or encouraged means that there is less likelihood that a serious understatement of actual value will distort the balance sheet valuation of the business.

(c) It is easy to understand and users are aware of its limitations, so make appropriate allowances. Alternative methods generally involve much more complex concepts.

(d) The figures are easy to obtain and are objective and readily verifiable, being tied to actual transactions. Other methods depend more on valuations and are therefore prone to subjectivity.

Exercise 9

To try and get your mind around the concept of capital maintenance, try to work out the answer to this question. In a period when prices are rising, the profit shown under the historical cost convention will differ from that shown under the current cost convention. In the case of a retail trading company, which of the two profit figures will be higher?

Solution

The profit shown under the historical cost convention will be higher. This is because the value of the resources consumed by the business is measured by their cost at the time they were purchased. Under the current cost convention, the value of these resources is measured by their cost at the (later) time when they were replaced. Given that prices are rising, this cost will be higher and so reported profits will be less.

3 THE REGULATORY FRAMEWORK OF ACCOUNTS

3.1 We have already seen that there is a wide range of accounting concepts in use. There are also different conventions under which accounts can be prepared. It may seem as though almost anything goes. What rules are there to guide us on how accounts should be prepared?

3.2 One important point to grasp is that the answer to this question is very different for a limited company compared with almost any other organisation. The activities of limited companies, including the way they prepare their accounts, are closely regulated. For an unincorporated business, any form of accounting information is adequate if it gives the owner(s) of the business a basis for planning and control, and satisfies the requirements of external users such as the Inland Revenue.

3.3 As far as limited companies are concerned, the regulations on accounts come from four main sources.

(a) Company law enacted by the UK Parliament

(b) Statements of standard accounting practice and financial reporting standards issued by the professional accountancy bodies in the UK and Ireland

(c) International accounting standards

(d) The requirements of the Stock Exchange (these only apply to 'listed' companies, large companies whose shares are bought and sold on the Stock Exchange)

Company law

3.4 Limited companies are required by law to prepare accounts annually for distribution to their shareholders. A copy of these accounts must be lodged with the Registrar of Companies and is available for inspection by any member of the public. For this reason a company's statutory annual accounts are often referred to as its published accounts.

3.5 In 1985, all existing companies legislation was brought together in a number of consolidating Acts, of which by far the most important is the Companies Act 1985 (CA 1985). This was substantially amended on the enactment of the Companies Act 1989 (CA 1989). The 1989 Act repealed parts of the 1985 Act and inserted new sections. This book reflects the 1985 Act *as amended by the 1989 Act*; unless otherwise stated, all statutory references are to the amended Companies Act 1985. Occasionally, where there is no parallel provision, a section number is followed by 'CA 1989' to indicate a section of the new Act itself.

3.6 There are many differences between accounting systems found in the various European Union (EU) member states. For example, in the UK a 'true and fair view' is sought, whereas in West Germany a more 'legal and correct view' is observed. Taxation and accounting principles differ and consolidation practices vary.

3.7 Since the United Kingdom became a member of the EU, it has been obliged to comply with legal requirements decided on by the EU. It does this by enacting UK laws to implement EU directives. For example, the CA 1989 was enacted in part to implement the provisions of the seventh and eighth EU directives, which deal with consolidated accounts and auditors.

3.8 As far as the preparation of accounts is concerned, the overriding requirement of companies legislation is that accounts should show a 'true and fair view'. This is a slippery phrase which is nowhere defined in the Companies Acts. What it certainly does *not* mean is that company accounts are to be exact to the penny in every respect. For one thing, as we shall see later, many of the figures appearing in a set of accounts are arrived at least partly by the exercise of judgement. For another, the amount of time and effort that such a requirement would cost would be out of all proportion to the advantages derived from it: see the discussion earlier in this chapter of the materiality concept.

3.9 The legislation also requires that the accounts of a limited company (except certain small companies) must be *audited*. An audit, for this purpose, may be defined as an 'independent examination of, and expression of opinion on, the financial statements of an enterprise'. This means in practice that a limited company must engage a firm of chartered or certified accountants to conduct an examination of its accounting records and its financial statements in order to form an opinion as to whether the accounts present a 'true and fair view'. At the conclusion of their audit work, the auditors issue a report (addressed to the owners of the company, ie its *members* or *shareholders*) which is published as part of the accounts.

Non-statutory regulation

3.10 Apart from company law, the main regulations affecting accounts in the UK derive from pronouncements issued by the professional accounting bodies (though later we will look briefly at *international* accounting regulations and the regulations of the Stock Exchange).

Six accountancy bodies in the UK are represented on the Consultative Committee of Accountancy Bodies (CCAB). They are as follows.

(a) The Chartered Institute of Management Accountants (CIMA)
(b) The Institute of Chartered Accountants in England and Wales (ICAEW)
(c) The Institute of Chartered Accountants of Scotland (ICAS)
(d) The Institute of Chartered Accountants in Ireland (ICAI)
(e) The Association of Chartered Certified Accountants (ACCA)
(f) The Chartered Institute of Public Finance and Accountancy (CIPFA)

3.11 Through a number of operating arms the CCAB is a major influence on the way in which accounts are prepared. Our main interest at this stage will be in the accounting standards published to lay down prescribed accounting treatments in areas where a variety of approaches might be taken. Clearly the value of accounts would be reduced if users were not able to count on a measure of comparability between them; the aim of accounting standards is to ensure that such comparability exists.

The Accounting Standards Committee (ASC) and the Accounting Standards Board (ASB)

3.12 The ASC was set up in January 1970 with the aim of publishing accounting standards in order to crack down on manipulation of published accounts. This was the beginning of a long line of attempts to protect investors in the wake of accounting scandals.

Exercise 10

You will be aware from your reading that such attempts have not yet been entirely successful. For fun, list a few of the more recent accounting scandals you can think of.

Solution

The list is almost endless, but among the most recent you will certainly have thought of Polly Peck, BCCI, the Maxwell empire and Barings Bank.

3.13 The procedure of the ASC was to publish an *exposure draft* (ED), outlining its proposed accounting treatment for the area under consideration. Comments were invited from interested parties, and in the light of such comments a final document was issued in the form of a *Statement of Standard Accounting Practice* (SSAP). Under the Companies Act 1989, large companies are required to state that their accounts have been prepared in accordance with applicable accounting standards. The ASC issued 25 SSAPs before it was replaced by a successor body on 1 August 1990.

3.14 In response to criticisms of the ASC's ineffectiveness, CCAB appointed a committee under the chairmanship of Sir Ron Dearing to review and make recommendations on the process by which accounting standards are issued. The Committee reported in 1988 and as a result of its recommendations a new standard-setting process was introduced. Under the new system, there are four bodies you need to know about.

(a) The Financial Reporting Council (FRC)
(b) The Accounting Standards Board (ASB)
(c) The Financial Reporting Review Panel (FRRP)
(d) The Urgent Issues Task Force (UITF)

3.15 The *Financial Reporting Council.* The FRC draws its membership from a wide spectrum of accounts preparers and users. Its chairman is appointed by the Government.

3.16 The *Accounting Standards Board.* The FRC operates through two arms: the FRRP (see below) and the ASB. The ASB is, in effect, the successor body to the ASC and is responsible for the issue of accounting standards. Accounting standards issued by the ASB are called *Financial Reporting Standard* (FRSs), of which sixteen have so far been published. Prior to publication, the ASB circulates its proposals in the form of a financial reporting exposure draft (inevitably referred to as a FRED) and invites comments. To avoid chaos, the ASB has 'adopted' those SSAPs still extant, and they therefore remain in force.

3.17 The *Financial Reporting Review Panel.* The FRRP is the second operating arm of the FRC. Its task is to examine accounts published by companies if it appears that Companies Act requirements have been breached - in particular, the requirement that accounts should show a true and fair view. The panel has legal backing: if a public company departs from an accounting standard, the panel may apply to the courts, which may in turn instruct the company to prepare revised accounts.

3.18 The *Urgent Issues Task Force.* The UITF is an offshoot of the ASB. Its role is to assist the ASB in areas where an accounting standard or Companies Act provision already exists, but where unsatisfactory or conflicting interpretations have developed. As its name suggests, the UITF is designed to act quickly (more quickly than the full standard-setting process is capable of) when an authoritative ruling is urgently needed.

International accounting standards

3.19 The International Accounting Standards Committee (IASC) was set up in June 1973 in an attempt to co-ordinate the development of international accounting standards. It includes representatives from many countries throughout the world, including the USA and the UK.

3.20 International standards are not intended to override local regulations. In the UK, however, the ASB expressed their support for international standards by incorporating them within the UK standards. Not every IAS has so far been incorporated in this way.

The Stock Exchange regulations

3.21 The Stock Exchange is a market for stocks and shares, and a company whose securities are traded in this market is known as a 'quoted' or 'listed' company.

3.22 When a share is granted a quotation on The Stock Exchange, it appears on the 'Official List' which is published in London for each business day. The Official List shows the 'official quotation' or price for the share for that particular day; it is drawn up by the Quotations Department of The Stock Exchange, which derives its prices from those actually ruling in this market.

3.23 In order to receive a quotation for its securities, a company must conform with Stock Exchange Listing Rules issued by the Council of The Stock Exchange. The company commits itself to certain procedures and standards, including matters concerning the disclosure of accounting information, which are more extensive than the disclosure requirements of the Companies Acts.

Exercise 11

To ensure you understand which regulations apply to which type of business, fill in the table below with a 'yes' where compliance is required and 'no' where it is not.

Type Of Business	Companies Act	FRSs/SSAPs	IASs	Stock Exchange Listing Rules
Public Listed Company				
Private Limited Company				
Sole Tradership				

Solution

Your table should look like this.

Type Of Business	Companies Act	FRSs/SSAPs	IASs	Stock Exchange Listing Rules
Public Listed Company	YES	YES	NO	YES
Private Limited Company	YES	YES	NO	NO
Sole Tradership	NO	NO	NO	NO

Exercise 12

One of the Stock Exchange's accounting requirements is that listed companies give financial information regularly. How long do you think a listed company can go without providing some sort of accounts?

Solution

Six months. Listed companies are required to publish interim accounts covering the first half of each year as well as accounts covering the whole year. It is common to see statements of six-monthly profit (or loss) figures published by leading companies in the pages of the quality newspapers.

Chapter roundup

- Having completed this chapter you should understand the following points.
- A large number of accounting concepts are at work in the preparation of a set of accounts. To some extent the selection of concepts is an arbitrary exercise, but in fact a large measure of consensus exists among practising accountants.
- Different accounting conventions can lead to different reported results. Of the various possible conventions that could be adopted, the historical cost convention is the only one enjoying wide currency at present. However, you should also be aware of the current cost and current purchasing power conventions.
- Order in this apparent chaos is provided by a comprehensive regulatory framework, based on UK company legislation, accounting standards (both UK and international) and Stock Exchange requirements.

Test your knowledge

1 List the four accounting concepts identified as fundamental by SSAP 2. (see introduction)

2 Briefly re-cap what is meant by: the entity concept (1.1-1.2); the money measurement concept (1.3-1.4); the going concern concept(1.5-1.6); the prudence concept (1.11-1.14); the accruals concept (1.19 - 1.22) and the consistency concept? (1.25-1.26)

3 At what stage is it normal to recognise the revenue arising from a credit sale? (1.16)

4 The separate valuation principle is a provision of SSAP 2. True or false? (1.27)

5 List six possible values that might be attributed in the accounts to a piece of machinery. (2.3)

6 What is the concept of capital maintenance that underlies:

(a) the historical cost convention? (2.13-2.14)
(b) the current cost convention? (2.16-2.19)

7 What is meant by modified historical cost accounts? (2.18)

8 What is the main statute governing the content of limited company accounts in the UK? (3.5)

9 Name the four bodies now responsible for the issue and enforcement of accounting regulations in the UK. (3.14)

Now try illustrative question 2 at the end of the Study Text

Part B

Accounting systems and reports – recording transactions

Chapter 3

ASSETS, LIABILITIES AND THE ACCOUNTING EQUATION

This chapter covers the following topics.

1 The nature of a business: assets and liabilities

2 The accounting equation

3 The business equation

Introduction

Part A of this Study Text gave you a broad overview of the nature and purpose of accounting. Part B should provide you with a understanding of the mechanics of preparing financial accounts.

Up until now, we have used the terms 'business', 'assets' and 'liabilities' without looking too closely at their meaning. This has been possible because the terms are common in everyday speech. From now on we will be examining accounting practice in more detail and it is important to have a thorough understanding of how these terms are used in an accounting context.

Sections 2 and 3 of the chapter introduce two concepts which it is important for you to grasp: the *accounting equation* and the *business equation*. You may already realise that a balance sheet has to balance. You are about to learn why!

Do not rush this chapter. Without an understanding of these essential points you will find it impossible to master more complex aspects later in your studies.

1 THE NATURE OF A BUSINESS: ASSETS AND LIABILITIES

1.1 Try this exercise to set you thinking.

Exercise 1

You may already be familiar with the more technical uses of certain terms. Can you distinguish, for example, between the terms 'an enterprise', 'a business', 'a company' and 'a firm'?

Solution

An 'enterprise' is the most general term, referring to just about any organisation in which people join together to achieve a common end. In the context of accounting it can refer to a multinational conglomerate, a small club, a local authority and so on *ad infinitum.*

A 'business' is also a very general term, but it does not extend as widely as the term 'enterprise': for example, it would not include a charity or a local authority. Any organisation existing to trade and make a profit could be called a business.

A 'company' is an enterprise constituted in a particular legal form, usually involving limited liability for its members. Companies need not be businesses; for example, many charities are constituted as companies.

A 'firm' is a much vaguer term. It is sometimes used loosely in the sense of a business or a company. Some writers, more usefully, try to restrict its meaning to that of an unincorporated business (ie a business not constituted as a company, for example a partnership).

What is a business?

1.2 There are a number of different ways of looking at a business.

(a) A commercial or industrial concern which exists to deal in the manufacture, re-sale or supply of goods and services.

(b) An organisation which uses economic resources to create goods or services which customers will buy.

(c) An organisation providing jobs for people to work in.

(d) A concern that invests money in resources (eg it buys buildings, machinery, it pays employees) in order to make even more money for its owners.

1.3 This last definition introduces the important idea of profit which was briefly discussed in the last chapter. Business enterprises vary in character, size and complexity. They range from very small businesses (the local shopkeeper or plumber) to very large ones (ICI). However the objective of earning profit is common to all of them.

1.4 Profit is the excess of income over expenditure. When expenditure exceeds income, the business is running at a loss. One of the jobs of an accountant is to measure income, expenditure and profit. It is not such a straightforward problem as it may seem and in later chapters we will look at some of the theoretical and practical difficulties involved.

1.5 There are some organisations which do not have a profit motive.

Organisations	Comment
(a) Charities - exist to provide help to the needy.	Must keep expenditure within the level of income or cannot continue in operation.
(b) Public sector organisations - exist to serve the community rather than to make profits.	Include government departments and services (eg the fire service, police force, national health service). Can only spend the money allowed to them by the government. Must be cost-conscious.
(c) Certain clubs and associations - exist to provide services to their members.	To maintain and improve the services they offer, must ensure that income is at least as great as expenditure.

Assets and liabilities

1.6 An *asset* is something valuable which a business owns or has the use of. Examples of assets are factories, office buildings, warehouses, delivery vans, lorries, plant and machinery, computer equipment, office furniture, cash and also goods held in store awaiting sale to customers, and raw materials and components held in store by a manufacturing business for use in production.

1.7 Some assets are held and used in operations for a long time. An office building might be occupied by administrative staff for years; similarly, a machine might have a productive life of many years before it wears out. Other assets are held for only a short time. The owner of a newsagent's shop, for example, will have to sell his newspapers on the same day that he gets them, and weekly newspapers and monthly magazines also have a short shelf life. The more quickly a business can sell the goods it has in store, the more profit it is likely to make.

1.8 A *liability* is something which is owed to somebody else. 'Liabilities' is the accounting term for the debts of a business. Here are some examples of liabilities.

(a) *A bank loan or bank overdraft.* The liability is the amount which must eventually be repaid to the bank.

(b) *Amounts owed to suppliers* for goods purchased but not yet paid for. For example, a boat builder might buy some timber on credit from a timber merchant, which means that the boat builder does not have to pay for the timber until some time after it has been delivered. Until the boat builder pays what he owes, the timber merchant will be his creditor for the amount owed.

(c) *Taxation owed to the government.* A business pays tax on its profits but there is a gap in time between when a company declares its profits and becomes liable to pay tax, and the time when the tax bill must eventually be paid.

Exercise 2

Attempt to classify the following items as long-term assets ('fixed assets'), short-term assets ('current assets') or liabilities.

(a) A personal computer used in the accounts department of a retail store
(b) A personal computer on sale in an office equipment shop
(c) Wages due to be paid to staff at the end of the week
(d) A van for sale in a motor dealer's showroom
(e) A delivery van used in a grocer's business
(f) An amount owing to a leasing company for the acquisition of a van

Solution

(a) Fixed asset
(b) Current asset
(c) Liability
(d) Current asset
(e) Fixed asset
(f) Liability

Note that the same item can be categorised differently in different businesses.

The business as a separate entity

1.9 So far we have spoken of assets and liabilities 'of a business'. In the previous chapter, it was pointed out that in accounting terms, a business is always a separate entity; but there are two aspects to this question: the strict legal position and the convention adopted by accountants.

1.10 Many businesses are carried on in the form of *limited companies*. The owners of a limited company are its shareholders, who may be few in number (as with a small, family-owned company) or very numerous (eg in the case of a large public company (BT) whose shares are quoted on the Stock Exchange).

1.11 The law recognises a company as a legal entity, quite separate from its owners. A company may, in its own name, acquire assets, incur debts, and enter into contracts. If a company's assets become insufficient to meet its liabilities, the company as a separate entity might become 'bankrupt', but the owners of the company could not usually be required to pay the debts from their own private resources: the debts are not debts of the shareholders, but of the company. This is *limited liability*: the liability of shareholders to the company is *limited* to the amount the company asks for their shares on issue.

1.12 The case is different, in law, when a business is carried on not by a company, but by an individual (a sole trader) or by a group of individuals (a partnership). Suppose that Fiona Middleton sets herself up in business as a hairdresser trading under the business name 'Fiona's Salon'. The law recognises no distinction between Fiona Middleton, the individual, and the business known as 'Fiona's Salon'. Any debts of the business which cannot be met from business assets must be met from Fiona's private resources.

Exercise 3

Fill in the missing words to make sure you understand the entity concept and how the law differs from accounting practice.

The entity concept regards a business as a ______ entity, distinct from its____ . The concept applies to ____ businesses. However, the law only recognises a ____ as a legal entity separate from its _____________. The liability of shareholders to the company is _____ to the amount the company asks them to pay for their shares.

Solution

The missing words are:

separate; owners; all; company; owners; limited.

1.13 The crucial point which must be understood at the outset is that the convention adopted in preparing accounts (the *entity concept*) is *always* to treat a business as a separate entity from its owner(s). This applies whether or not the business is recognised in law as a separate entity, so it applies whether the business is carried on by a company or by a sole trader.

1.14 This idea is the basis of a fundamental rule of accounting, which is that the assets and liabilities of a business must always be equal. This known as the accounting equation.

2 THE ACCOUNTING EQUATION 12/99

2.1 We will begin our discussion of the preparation of financial accounts by illustrating how to account for a business's transactions from the time that trading first begins. Our example will illustrate the 'accounting equation'.

Example: the accounting equation

2.2 On 1 July 20X6, Courtney Spice decided to open up a stall in the market, to sell herbs and spices. She had £2,500 to put into her business.

2.3 When the business is set up, an 'accountant's picture' can be drawn of what it owns and what it owes.

The business begins by owning the cash that Courtney has put into it, £2,500. Does it owe anything? The answer is yes.

The business is a separate entity in accounting terms. It has obtained its assets, in this example cash, from its owner, Courtney Spice. It therefore owes this amount of money to its owner. If Courtney changed her mind and decided not to go into business after all, the business would be dissolved by the 'repayment' of the cash by the business to Courtney.

2.4 The money put into a business by its owners is *capital*. In accounting, capital is an investment of money (funds) with the intention of earning a return. A business proprietor invests capital with the intention of earning profit. As long as that money is invested, accountants will treat the capital as money owed to the proprietor by the business.

2.5 When Courtney Spice sets up her business:

Capital invested	=	£2,500
Cash	=	£2,500

Capital invested is a form of liability, because it is an amount owed by the business to its owner(s). Adapting this to the idea that liabilities and assets are always equal amounts, we can state the accounting equation as follows.

Assets	=	*Capital*	+	*Liabilities*

For Courtney Spice, as at 1 July 20X6:

£2,500 (cash)	=	£2,500	+	£0

Example continued

2.6 Courtney Spice uses some of the money invested to purchase a market stall from Noel Jarvis, who is retiring. The cost of the stall is £1,800.

She also purchases some herbs and spices, at a cost of £650.

This leaves £50 in cash, after paying for the stall and goods for resale, out of the original £2,500. Courtney keeps £30 in the bank and draws out £20 in small change. She is now ready for her first day of market trading on 3 July 20X6.

2.7 The assets and liabilities of the business have now altered, and at 3 July, before trading begins, the state of her business is as follows.

Assets	£	=	*Capital*	+	*Liabilities*
Stall	1,800	=	£2,500	+	£0
Herbs and spices	650				
Cash at bank	30				
Cash in hand	20				
	2,500				

The stall and the herbs and spices are physical items, but they must be given a money value. As explained in the last chapter, this money value will usually be their historical cost.

Profit introduced into the accounting equation

2.8 Let us now suppose that on 3 July Courtney has a very successful day. She is able to sell all of her herbs and spices, for £900. All of her sales are for cash.

Since Courtney has sold goods costing £650 to earn revenue of £900, we can say that she has earned a profit of £250 on the day's trading.

Profits belong to the owners of a business. In this case, the £250 belongs to Courtney Spice. However, so long as the business retains the profits, and does not pay anything out to its owners, the retained profits are accounted for as an addition to the proprietor's capital.

Assets		=	*Capital*		+	*Liabilities*
	£			£		
Stall	1,800		Original investment	2,500		
Herbs and spices	0					
Cash in hand and at bank (30+20+900)	950		Retained profit	250		
	2,750			2,750	+	£0

2.9 We can re-arrange the accounting equation to help us to calculate the capital balance.

Assets – liabilities	=	Capital, which is the same as
Net assets	=	Capital

2.10 At the beginning and then at the end of 3 July 20X6 Courtney Spice's financial position was as follows.

	Net Assets	Capital
(a) At the beginning of the day:	£(2,500 – 0) = £2,500 =	£2,500
(b) At the end of the day:	£(2,750 – 0) = £2,750 =	£2,750

There has been an increase of £250 in net assets, which is the amount of profits earned during the day.

Drawings

2.11 Drawings are amounts of money taken out of a business by its owner.

Since Courtney Spice has made a profit of £250 from her first day's work, she feels justified in drawing some of the profits out of the business. After all, business owners, like everyone else, need income for living expenses. We will suppose that Courtney pays herself £180 in 'wages'.

2.12 The payment of £180 is probably regarded by Courtney as a fair reward for her day's work, and she might think of the sum as being in the nature of wages. However, the £180 is not an expense to be deducted before the figure of net profit is arrived at. In other words, it would be incorrect to calculate the net profit earned by the business as follows.

	£
Profit on sale of flowers etc	250
Less 'wages' paid to Courtney	180
Net profit earned by business (incorrect)	70

2.13 This is because any amounts paid by a business to its proprietor are treated by accountants as withdrawals of profit (the usual term is appropriations of profit), and not as expenses incurred by the business. In the case of Courtney's business, the true position is that the net profit earned is the £250 surplus on sale of flowers.

	£
Net profit earned by business	250
Less profit withdrawn by Courtney	180
Net profit retained in the business	70

2.14 Profits are capital as long as they are retained in the business. Once they are appropriated, they are no longer capital. When they are paid out, the business suffers a reduction in capital (drawings).

2.15 The drawings are taken in cash, and so the business loses £180 of its cash assets. After the drawings have been made, the accounting equation would be restated.

(a) *Assets*		=	*Capital*		+	*Liabilities*
	£			£		
Stall	1,800		Original investment	2,500		
Herbs and spices	0		Retained profit	70		
Cash (950-180)	770					
	2,570			2,570	+	£0

(b) Alternatively	*Net assets*		*Capital*
	£(2,570 – 0)	=	£2,570

The increase in net assets since trading operations began is now only £(2,570 – 2,500) = £70, which is the amount of the retained profits.

3 THE BUSINESS EQUATION

12/99

3.1 The business equation gives a definition of profits earned. The preceding example has attempted to show that the amount of profit earned can be related to the increase in the net assets of the business, and the drawings of profits by the proprietor.

3.2 The business equation is:

$$P = I + D - C_i$$

where

P represents profit

I represents the increase in net assets, after drawings have been taken out by the proprietor

D represents drawings

C_i represents the amount of extra capital introduced into the business during the period. This is a negative figure in the equation, because when a business is given new capital, perhaps in the form of extra money paid in by the proprietor himself, there will be an increase in the net assets of the business without any profits being earned. This means, say, that if a proprietor puts an extra £5,000 into his business the profit from the transaction, according to the business equation would be P = £5,000 + 0 – £5,000 = £0.

3.3 In our example of Courtney Spice's business on 3 July 20X6, after drawings have been taken:

Profit = £70 + £180 – £0
= £250

Example continued

3.4 The next market day is on 10 July, and Courtney purchases more herbs and spices for cash, at a cost of £740. She is not feeling well, because of a heavy cold, and so she accepts the offer of help for the day from her cousin Bianca. Bianca will be paid a wage of £40 at the end of the day.

Trading on 10 July is again very brisk, and Courtney and Bianca sell all their goods for £1,100 cash. Courtney pays Bianca her wage of £40 and draws out £200 for herself.

Required

(a) State the accounting equation before trading began on 10 July.

(b) State the accounting equation at the end of 10 July, after paying Bianca:

(i) But before drawings are taken out.
(ii) After drawings have been made.

(c) State the business equation to compute profits earned on 10 July.

You are reminded that the accounting equation for the business at the end of transactions for 3 July is given in Paragraph 2.15(a).

Solution

3.5 (a) After the purchase of the goods for £740.

Assets		=	*Capital*	+	*Liabilities*
	£				
Stall	1,800				
Goods	740				
Cash (770 – 740)	30				
	2,570	=	£ 2,570	+	£0

(b) (i) On 10 July, all the goods are sold for £1,100 cash, and Bianca is paid £40. The profit for the day is £320.

	£	£
Sales		1,100
Less cost of goods sold	740	
Bianca's wage	40	
		780
Profit		320

Assets		=	*Capital*		+	*Liabilities*
	£			£		
Stall	1,800		At beginning of 10 July	2,570		
Goods	0		Profits earned on 10 July	320		
Cash (30+ 1,100 – 40)	1,090					
	2,890			2,890	+	£0

(ii) After Courtney has taken drawings of £200 in cash, retained profits will be only £(320 - 200) = £120.

Assets		=	*Capital*		+	*Liabilities*
	£			£		
Stall	1,800		At beginning of 10 July	2,570		
Goods	0		Retained profits for 10 July	120		
Cash (1,090 – 200)	890					
	2,690			2,690	+	£0

(c) The increase in net assets on 10 July, after drawings have been taken, is as follows.

	£
Net assets at end of 10 July	2,690
Net assets at beginning of 10 July	2,570
Increase in net assets	120

The business equation is:

$$P = I + D - C_i$$
$$= £120 + £200 - £0$$
$$= £320$$

This confirms the calculation of profit made in b(i).

Tutorial note. It is very important you should understand the principles described so far. Do not read on until you are confident that you understand the solution to this example.

Creditors and debtors

3.6 A *creditor* is a person to whom a business owes money and is therefore a liability of a business.

A trade creditor is a person to whom a business owes money for debts incurred in the course of trading operations, and in an examination question, this term might refer to debts still outstanding which arise from the purchase from suppliers of materials, components or goods for resale.

3.7 A business does not always pay immediately for goods or services it buys. It is a common business practice to make purchases on credit, with a promise to pay within 30 days, or two months or three months of the date of the bill or 'invoice' for the goods. For example, if A buys goods costing £2,000 on credit from B, B might send A an invoice for £2,000, dated say 1 March, with credit terms that payment must be made within 30 days. If A then delays payment until 31 March, B will be a creditor of A between 1 and 31 March, for £2,000.

3.8 Just as a business might buy goods on credit, so too might it sell goods to customers on credit. A customer who buys goods without paying cash for them straight away is a *debtor*. For example, suppose that C sells goods on credit to D for £6,000 on terms that the debt must be settled within two months of the invoice date 1 October. If D does not pay the £6,000 until 30 November, D will be a debtor of C for £6,000 from 1 October until 30 November.

3.9 A debtor is an asset of a business. When the debt is finally paid, the debtor 'disappears' as an asset, to be replaced by 'cash at bank and in hand'.

Example continued

3.10 The example of Courtney Spice's market stall is continued by looking at the following transactions in the week to 17 July 20X6. (See Paragraph 3.5 (b)(ii) for the situation as at the end of 10 July.)

(a) Courtney Spice realises that she is going to need more money in the business and so she makes the following arrangements.

  (i) She invests immediately a further £250 of her own capital.

  (ii) She persuades her Uncle Felix to lend her £500 immediately. Uncle Felix tells her that she can repay the loan whenever she likes, but in the meantime, she must pay him interest of £5 per week each week at the end of the market day. They agree that it will probably be quite a long time before the loan is eventually repaid.

(b) She decides that she can afford to buy a second hand van to pick up herbs and spices from her supplier and bring them to her stall in the market. She finds a car dealer, Laurie Loader, who agrees to sell her a van on credit for £700. Courtney agrees to pay for the van after 30 days' trial use.

(c) During the week to 17 July, Courtney's Uncle Grant telephones her to ask whether she would be interested in selling him some spice racks and herb chopping boards as presents for his friends. Courtney tells him that she will look for a supplier. After some investigations, she buys what Uncle Grant has asked for, paying £300 in cash to the supplier. Uncle Grant accepts delivery of the goods and agrees to pay £350 to Courtney for them, but he asks if she can wait until the end of the month for payment. Courtney agrees.

(d) The next market day approaches, and Courtney buys herbs and spices costing £800. Of these purchases £750 are paid in cash, with the remaining £50 on seven days' credit. Courtney decides to use Bianca's services again as an assistant on market day, at an agreed wage of £40.

(e) For the third market day running, on 17 July, Courtney succeeds in selling all her goods earning revenue of £1,250 (all in cash). She decides to take out drawings of £240 for her week's work. She also pays Bianca £40 in cash. She decides to make the interest payment to her Uncle Felix the next time she sees him.

(f) We shall ignore any van expenses for the week, for the sake of relative simplicity.

Required

(a) State the accounting equation in each case.

  (i) After Courtney and Uncle Felix have put more money into the business and after the purchase of the van

  (ii) After the sale of goods to Uncle Grant

  (iii) After the purchase of goods for the weekly market

  (iv) At the end of the day's trading on 17 July, and after drawings have been appropriated out of profit

(b) State the business equation showing profit earned during the week ended 17 July.

Solution

3.11 There are a number of different transactions to account for here. This solution deals with them one at a time in chronological order. (In practice, it would be possible to do one set of calculations which combines the results of all the transactions, but we shall defer such 'shortcut' methods until later.)

(a) (i) *The addition of Courtney's extra capital and Uncle Felix's loan*

An investment analyst might define the loan of Uncle Felix as a capital investment on the grounds that it will probably be for the long term. Uncle Felix is not the owner of the business, however, even though he has made an investment of a loan in it. He would only become an owner if Courtney offered him a partnership in the business, and she has not done so. To the business, Uncle Felix is a long-term creditor, and it is more appropriate to define his investment as a liability of the business and not as business capital.

The accounting equation after £(250 + 500) = £750 cash is put into the business as follows.

Assets		=	*Capital*		+	*Liabilities*	
	£			£			£
Stall	1,800		As at end of 10 July	2,690		Loan	500
Goods	0		Additional capital put in	250			
Cash (890+750)	1,640						
	3,440	=		2,940	+		500

The purchase of the van (cost £700) is on credit.

Assets		=	*Capital*		+	*Liabilities*	
	£			£			£
Stall	1,800		As at end of 10 July	2,690		Loan	500
Van	700		Additional capital	250		Creditor	700
Cash	1,640						
	4,140	=		2,940	+		1,200

(ii) *The sale of goods to Uncle Grant on credit (£350) which cost the business £300 (cash paid)*

Assets		=	*Capital*		+	*Liabilities*	
	£			£			
Stall	1,800		As at end of 10 July	2,690		Loan	500
Van	700		Additional capital	250		Creditor	700
Debtors	350		Profit on sale to				
Cash(1,640 – 300)	1,340		Uncle Grant	50			
	4,190	=		2,990	+		1,200

(iii) *After the purchase of goods for the weekly market (£750 paid in cash and £50 of purchases on credit)*

Assets		=	*Capital*		+	*Liabilities*	
	£			£			£
Stall	1,800		As at end of 10 July	2,690		Loan	500
Van	700					Creditor for	
						car	700
Goods	800		Additional capital	250		Creditor	
						for goods	50
Debtors	350		Profit on sale to				
Cash(1,340 – 750)	590		Uncle Grant	50			
	4,240	=		2,990	+		1,250

(iv) *After market trading on 17 July*

Sales of goods costing £800 earned revenues of £1,250. Bianca's wages were £40 (paid), Uncle Felix's interest charge is £5 (not paid yet) and drawings out of profits were £240 (paid). The profit for 17 July may be calculated as follows, taking the full £5 of interest as a cost on that day.

	£	£
Sales		1,250
Cost of goods sold	800	
Wages	40	
Interest	5	
		845
Profit earned on 17 July		405
Profit on sale of goods to Uncle Grant		50
Profit for the week		455
Drawings appropriated out of profits		240
Retained profit		215

Assets		= *Capital*		+ *Liabilities*	
	£		£		£
Stall	1,800	As at end of 10 July	2,690	Loan	500
Van	700	Additional capital	250	Creditor for van	700
Goods	0			Creditor for goods	50
Debtors	350				
Cash (590+ 1,250 – 40 – 240)	1,560	Profits retained	215	Creditor for interest payment	5
	4,410		3,155		1,255

(b) The increase in the net assets of the business during the week was as follows.

	£
Net assets as at the end of 17 July £(4,410 – 1,255)	3,155
Net assets as at the end of 10 July (Paragraph 3.5(b)(ii))	2,690
Increase in net assets	465

The business equation for the week ended 17 July is as follows.

(Remember that extra capital of £250 was invested by the proprietor.)

$$P = I + D - C_i$$
$$= £465 + £240 - £250$$
$$= £455$$

This confirms the calculation of profit above in (a)(iv).

Exercise 4

Calculate the profit for the year ended 31 December 20X1 from the following information.

	1 January 20X1		*31 December 20X1*	
	£	£	£	£
Assets				
Property	20,000		20,000	
Machinery	6,000		9,000	
Debtors	4,000		8,000	
Cash	1,000		1,500	
		31,000		38,500
Liabilities				
Overdraft	6,000		9,000	
Creditors	5,000		3,000	
		(11,000)		(12,000)
Net assets		20,000		26,500

Drawings during the year	£4,500
Additional capital introduced by the proprietor during the year	£5,000

Solution

The increase in net assets during the year was £(26,500 - 20,000) = £6,500.

$$P = I + D - C_i$$
$$= £6,500 + £4,500 - £5,000$$
$$= £6,000$$

Chapter roundup

- A *business* owns assets and owes liabilities. It is important to keep business assets and liabilities separate from the personal assets and liabilities of the proprietor(s).
- *Assets* are items belonging to a business and based on the running of the business. They may be fixed (such as machinery or office premises), or current (such as stock, debtors and cash).
- *Liabilities* are sums of money owed by a business to outsiders such as a bank or a trade creditor.
- The assets of a business are always equal to its liabilities (including capital).
- The accounting equation and the business equation are useful introductory concepts in accounting for the following reasons.
  - The accounting equation emphasises the equality between assets and liabilities (including capital as a liability).
  - The business equation emphasises the inter-relationship between profits, net assets, appropriations of profit (drawings) and new capital investment.
- You should now be aware, for example, that when business transactions are accounted for, it should be possible to do two things as follows.
  - Restate the assets and liabilities of the business after the transactions have taken place.
  - State the profit or loss, if any, arising as a result of the transactions.
- In practice, the accounting equation and business equation are rarely used to state assets and liabilities and profit.
  - The assets and liabilities of a business at any moment in time are shown in a balance sheet. This is very similar to the accounting equation.
  - The profit (or loss) earned by a business during a given period of time is shown in a trading, profit and loss account.

  These will be described in the following chapter.

Test your knowledge

1. What is meant by profit? (see para 1.4)
2. List as many organisations as you can which do not have profit as their main objective. (1.5, table)
3. Briefly explain the legal distinction between a sole trader and a limited company (1.10 - 1.12)
4. In what sense can a proprietor's capital be regarded as a liability of the business? (2.4)
5. What is the accounting equation? (2.5)
6. What are drawings? (2.11)
7. What is the business equation? (3.2)
8. Distinguish between a debtor and a creditor. (3.6, 3.9)

Now try illustrative question 3 at the end of the Study Text

Chapter 4

AN INTRODUCTION TO FINAL ACCOUNTS

This chapter covers the following topics.

1 The balance sheet

2 The trading, profit and loss account

3 Capital and revenue expenditure

Introduction

In Chapter 3 you were introduced to the idea of the accounting equation. If you understand this, you should now have little difficulty in getting to grips with the balance sheet. You should already have some idea of what is meant by the profit and loss account. In this chapter you will see this in more detail.

A *balance sheet* is a statement of the liabilities, capital and assets of a business at a given moment in time. It is like a 'snapshot' photograph, since it captures on paper a still image, frozen at a single moment in time, of something which is dynamic and continually changing. Typically, a balance sheet is prepared to show the liabilities, capital and assets as at the end of the accounting period to which the financial accounts relate.

A balance sheet is therefore very similar to the accounting equation. In fact, the only two differences between a balance sheet and an accounting equation are as follows.

(a) The manner or format in which the liabilities and assets are presented
(b) The extra detail which is usually contained in a balance sheet

The details shown in a balance sheet will not be described in full in this chapter. Instead, we will make a start in this chapter, and add more detail in later chapters as we go on to look at other ideas and methods in accounting.

The *profit and loss account* has been mentioned several times. It is a statement which matches the revenue earned in a period with the costs incurred in earning it. It is usual to distinguish between a gross profit (sales revenue less the cost of goods sold) and a net profit (being the gross profit less the expenses of selling, distribution, administration, etc).

There is a fair amount to learn before you will be able to prepare these statements yourself, although you will be surprised how quickly you will be in that enviable position. It is important to introduce the financial statements now so you can see what you are aiming at. Keep them in your mind as you tackle the 'nuts and bolts' of ledger accounting in the next few chapters.

Common sense may tell you that, if you spend money on something which you could use in the business over the next twenty years, it would be misleading to charge all the expenses in the first year. This is the principle behind the important distinction between *capital and revenue expenditure* which is explored in Section 3 of the chapter.

1 THE BALANCE SHEET

1.1 A balance sheet is divided into two halves, and shown in one of two ways.

(a) Capital and liabilities in one half and assets in the other
(b) Capital in one half and net assets in the other

1.2 In other words, a balance sheet can be presented in the following ways.

(a) Either

NAME OF BUSINESS
BALANCE SHEET AS AT (DATE)

	£
Assets (item by item)	X
	X
	X
	£
Capital	X
Liabilities (item by item)	X
	X

(b) Or

NAME OF BUSINESS
BALANCE SHEET AS AT (DATE)

	£
Assets	X
Less liabilities	X
Net assets	X
Capital	X

Method (a) puts capital and liabilities in the same half of the balance sheet, whereas method (b) shows capital on its own, and nets off liabilities against assets in the other half. This Study Text generally uses method (b), which is the method approved in CA 85.

1.3 In either form of presentation, the total value in one half of the balance sheet will equal the total value in the other half. You should readily understand this from the accounting equation.

1.4 Since each half of the balance sheet has an equal value, one half balances the other. However, the equal value of the two halves is not the origin of the term balance sheet. A balance sheet is so called because it is a statement of the outstanding balances on the ledger accounts for the capital, liabilities and assets of the business, at a given moment in time. Ledger accounts are described in a later chapter.

1.5 Capital, liabilities and assets are usually shown in some detail in a balance sheet. The following paragraphs describe the sort of detail we might expect to find.

Capital (sole trader)

1.6 The proprietor's capital is usually analysed into its component parts.

	£	£
Capital as at the beginning of the accounting period (ie capital 'brought forward')		X
Add additional capital introduced during the period		X
		X
Add profit earned during the period	X	
Less drawings	(X)	
Retained profit for the period		X
Capital as at the end of the accounting period (ie capital 'carried forward')		X

1.7 'Brought forward' means 'brought forward from the previous period', and 'carried forward' means 'carried forward to the next period'. The carried forward amount at the end of one period is also the brought forward amount of the next period. The word 'down' is sometimes used instead of 'forward'.

Liabilities

1.8 The various types of liabilities should be itemised separately. In addition, a distinction is made between current liabilities and long-term liabilities.

Current liabilities

1.9 These are debts of the business that must be paid within a fairly short period of time. By convention, a 'fairly short period of time' has come to be accepted as one year. In the accounts of limited companies, the Companies Act 1985 requires use of the term 'creditors: amounts falling due within one year' rather than 'current liabilities' although they mean the same thing.

The following are examples of current liabilities.

(a) Loans repayable within one year

(b) A bank overdraft (see Paragraph 1.10)

(c) Trade creditors

(d) Bills of exchange which are payable by the business

(e) Taxation payable

(f) 'Accrued charges'

Accrued charges are expenses already built up by the business, for which no invoice has yet been received, or for which the date of payment by standing order has not yet arrived. An example of accrued charges is the cost of gas or electricity. If a business ends its accounting year on 31 December, but does not expect its next quarterly gas bill until the end of January, there will be two months of accrued gas charges, ie charges for which no invoice has been received and no debt is yet 'officially' payable, to record in the balance sheet as a liability. Accruals will be described more fully in a later chapter.

Long-term liabilities ('deferred liabilities')

1.10 A long-term liability is a debt which is not payable within the 'short term' and so any liability which is not current must be long-term. Therefore an overdraft is usually classed as 'short term', even though a business may run an overdraft for years.

1.11 Just as 'short-term' by convention means one year or less, 'long-term' means more than one year. In the accounts of limited companies, the Companies Act 1985 requires use of the term: 'Creditors: amounts falling due after more than one year'.

1.12 Examples of long-term liabilities are as follows.

(a) Loans which are not repayable for more than one year, such as a bank loan, or a loan from an individual to a business.

(b) A mortgage loan, which is a loan specifically secured against a freehold property. (If the business fails to repay the loan, the lender then has 'first claim' on the property, and is entitled to repayment from the proceeds from the enforced sale of the property.)

(c) Debentures or debenture loans. These are common with limited companies. Debentures are securities issued by a company at a fixed rate of interest. They are repayable on agreed terms by a specified date in the future. Holders of debentures are therefore lenders of money to a company. Their interests, including security for the loan, are protected by the terms of a trust deed.

Assets

1.13 Assets in the balance sheet are divided into two groups.

(a) Fixed assets

(i) Tangible fixed assets
(ii) Intangible fixed assets
(iii) Investments (long term)

(b) Current assets

Fixed assets

1.14 A fixed asset is an asset acquired for continuing use within the business, with a view to earning income or making profits from its use, either directly or indirectly. A fixed asset is not acquired for sale to a customer.

(a) In a manufacturing industry, a production machine would be a fixed asset, because it makes goods which are then sold.

(b) In a service industry, equipment used by employees giving service to customers would be classed as fixed assets (eg the equipment used in a garage, and furniture in a hotel).

(c) Less obviously, factory premises, office furniture, computer equipment, company cars, delivery vans or pallets in a warehouse are all fixed assets.

1.15 A further condition is that the asset must have a 'life' in use of more than one year (strictly, more than one 'accounting period' which might be more or less than one year).

1.16 A *tangible* fixed asset is a physical asset, ie one that can be touched. It has a real, 'solid' existence. All of the examples of fixed assets mentioned above are tangible.

An *intangible* fixed asset is an asset which does not have a physical existence. It cannot be 'touched'. The idea of intangible assets might well puzzle you at the moment, and a description of them will be deferred until a later chapter.

An *investment* might also be a fixed asset. Investments are commonly found in the published accounts of large limited companies. A large company A might invest in another company B by purchasing some of the shares or debentures of B. These investments would earn income for A in the form of interest or dividends paid out by B. If the investments are purchased by A with a view to holding on to them for more than one year, they would be classified as fixed assets of A.

In this chapter, we shall restrict our attention to tangible fixed assets.

Fixed assets and depreciation

1.17 Fixed assets are held and used by a business for a number of years, but they wear out or lose their usefulness in the course of time. Every tangible fixed asset has a limited life. The only exception is land held freehold or on a very long leasehold.

1.18 The accounts of a business try to recognise that the cost of a fixed asset is gradually consumed as the asset wears out. This is done by gradually writing off the asset's cost in the profit and loss account over several accounting periods. For example, in the case of a machine costing £1,000 and expected to wear out after ten years, it might be appropriate to reduce the balance sheet value by £100 each year. This process is known as depreciation.

1.19 If a balance sheet were drawn up four years, say, after the asset was purchased, the amount of depreciation which would have accumulated would be 4 × £100 = £400. The machine would then appear in the balance sheet as follows.

	£
Machine at original cost	1,000
Less accumulated depreciation	400
Net book value*	600

* ie the value of the asset in the books of account, net of depreciation. After ten years the asset would be fully depreciated and would appear in the balance sheet with a net book value of zero.

Current assets

1.20 Current assets are one of the following.

(a) Items owned by the business with the intention of turning them into cash within one year

(b) Cash, including money in the bank, owned by the business

These assets are 'current' in the sense that they are continually flowing through the business.

1.21 The definition in (a) above needs explaining further. Let us suppose that a trader, Roy Evans, runs a business selling motor cars, and purchases a showroom which he stocks with cars for sale. He obtains the cars from a manufacturer, and pays for them in cash on delivery.

(a) If he sells a car in a cash sale, the goods are immediately converted into cash. The cash might then be used to buy more cars for re-sale.

(b) If he sells a car in a credit sale, the car will be given to the customer, who then becomes a debtor of the business. Eventually, the debtor will pay what he owes, and Roy Evans will receive cash. Once again, the cash might then be used to buy more cars for sale.

1.22 Current assets can be identified in this example as follows.

(a) The cars (goods) held in stock for re-sale are current assets, because Roy Evans intends to sell them within one year, in the normal course of trade.

(b) Any debtors are current assets, if they are expected to pay what they owe within one year.

(c) Cash is a current asset.

1.23 The transactions described above could be shown as a cash cycle.

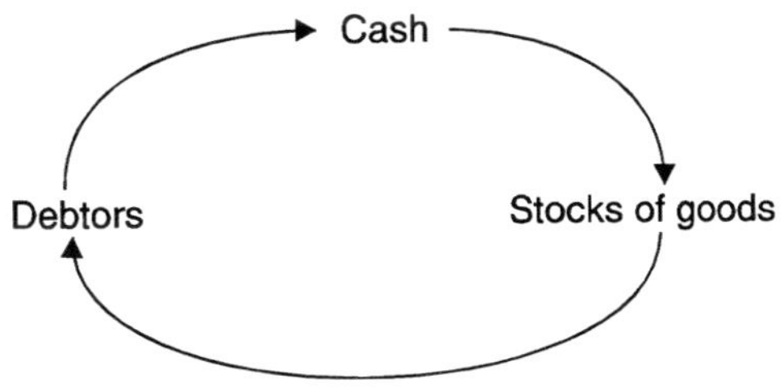

1.24 Cash is used to buy goods which are sold. Sales on credit create debtors, but eventually cash is earned from the sales. Some, perhaps most, of the cash will then be used to replenish stocks.

1.25 The main items of current assets are therefore shown below.

(a) Stocks
(b) Debtors
(c) Cash

1.26 It is important to realise that cars are current assets of Roy Evans because he is in the business of buying and selling them, ie he is a car trader. If he also has a car which he keeps and uses for business purposes, this car would be a fixed asset. The distinction between a fixed asset and a current asset is not what the asset is physically, but for what purpose it is obtained and used by the business.

1.27 There are some other categories of current assets.

(a) *Short-term investments.* These are stocks and shares of other businesses, currently owned, but with the intention of selling them in the near future. For example, if a business has a lot of spare cash for a short time, its managers might decide to 'have a flutter' on the stock exchange, and buy shares in, say, BT, ICI or Powergen. The shares will later be sold when the business needs the cash again. If share prices rise in the meantime, the business will make a profit from its short-term investment.

(b) *Prepayments.* These are amounts of money already paid by the business for benefits which have not yet been enjoyed but will be enjoyed within the next accounting period. Suppose, for example, that a business pays an annual insurance premium of £240 to insure its premises against fire and theft, and that the premium is payable annually in advance on 1 December. Now, if the business has an accounting year end of 31 December it will pay £240 on 1 December, but only enjoy one month's insurance cover by the end of the year. The remaining 11 months' cover (£220 cost, at £20 per month) will be enjoyed in the next year. The prepayment of £220 would therefore be shown in the balance sheet of the business, at 31 December, as a current asset.

A prepayment might be thought of as a form of debtor. In the example above, at 31 December the insurance company still owes the business 11 months' worth of insurance cover.

Trade debtors and other debtors

1.28 Although it is convenient to think of debtors as customers who buy goods on credit, it is more accurate to say that a debtor is anyone who owes the business money.

1.29 A distinction can be made between two groups of debtors.

(a) Trade debtors, ie customers who still owe money for goods or services bought on credit in the course of the trading activities of the business.

(b) Other debtors, ie anyone else owing money to the business (eg a tax refund).

Example: balance sheet preparation

1.30 We shall now look at how the various types of assets and liabilities are shown in the balance sheet of a business. You might like to attempt to prepare a balance sheet yourself before reading the solution which follows.

Exercise 1

You are required to prepare a balance sheet for the Ted Hills Hardware Store as at 31 December 20X6, given the information below.

	£
Capital as at 1 January 20X6	47,600
Profit for the year to 31 December 20X6	8,000
Freehold premises, net book value at 31 December 20X6	50,000
Motor vehicles, net book value at 31 December 20X6	9,000
Fixtures and fittings, net book value at 31 December 20X6	8,000
Long-term loan (mortgage)	25,000
Bank overdraft*	2,000
Goods held in stock for resale	16,000
Debtors	500
Cash in hand*	100
Creditors	1,200
Taxation payable	3,500
Drawings	4,000
Accrued costs of rent	600
Prepayment of insurance	300

* A shop might have cash in its cash registers, but an overdraft at the bank.

Solution

TED HILLS BALANCE SHEET
AS AT 31 DECEMBER 20X6

	£	£
Fixed assets at net book value		
Freehold premises		50,000
Fixtures and fittings		8,000
Motor vehicles		9,000
		67,000
Current assets		
Stocks	16,000	
Debtors	500	
Prepayment	300	
Cash	100	
	16,900	
Current liabilities		
Bank overdraft	2,000	
Creditors	1,200	
Taxation payable	3,500	
Accrued costs	600	
	7,300	
Net current assets		9,600
		76,600
Long-term liabilities		
Loan		(25,000)
		51,600
Capital		
Capital as at 1 January 20X6		47,600
Profit for the year		8,000
		55,600
Less drawings		(4,000)
		51,600

The order of items in the balance sheet

1.31 By convention, a balance sheet lists liabilities and assets in a particular order. This order is not compulsory, nor will you find that it is used all the time; however, you should try to get into the habit of using the conventional order of items yourself.

1.32 The format most commonly used is the vertical balance sheet in one of four formats.

(a) Net assets above and capital below

(b) Fixed assets and net current assets above, with capital and long-term liabilities below

(c) Assets above and liabilities (including capital) below

(d) Capital and liabilities above, with assets below

As you will appreciate, there is no hard and fast rule about the order of items in a vertical balance sheet, except that the Companies Act 1985 requires (a) to be used for the published accounts of most limited companies. This format is therefore one in particular you should try to familiarise yourself with and use as a matter of habit.

Order of items within categories

1.33 Note the following points.

(a) *Fixed assets* are listed in a descending order of 'length of useful life'. Property has a longer life than fixtures and fittings, which in turn perhaps have a longer life than motor vehicles. This is why the fixed assets are listed in the order shown in Exercise 1 above.

(b) *Current assets* are listed in descending order of the length of time it might be before the asset will be converted into cash. Broadly speaking, stocks will convert into debtors, and debtors will convert into cash, and so stock, debtors and cash will be listed in that order. Prepayments, because they are similar to debtors, should be listed after debtors and before cash.

Working capital, or net current assets 6/96

1.34 The 'working' capital of a business is the difference between its current assets and current liabilities, ie working capital is the amount of net current assets. In the balance sheet above, the Ted Hills Hardware Store has net current assets of £(16,900 – 7,300) = £9,600. This is a figure which is shown separately when a balance sheet is prepared in a vertical format.

1.35 The balance sheet of the Ted Hills Hardware Store could be arranged in either of the following ways, using formats (a) and (b) above.

Method (a)
TED HILLS BALANCE SHEET
AS AT 31 DECEMBER 20X6

	£	£
Fixed assets at net book value		
Freehold premises		50,000
Fixtures and fittings		8,000
Motor vehicles		9,000
		67,000
Current assets		
Stocks	16,000	
Debtors	500	
Prepayment	300	
Cash	100	
	16,900	
Less *current liabilities*		
Bank overdraft	2,000	
Creditors	1,200	
Taxation payable	3,500	
Accrued costs	600	
	7,300	
Net current assets		9,600
		76,600
Less *long-term liabilities*		
Loan		25,000
		51,600
Capital		
Capital as at 1 January 20X6		47,600
Profit for the year		8,000
		55,600
Less drawings		4,000
		51,600

Method (b)
TED HILLS BALANCE SHEET
AS AT 31 DECEMBER 20X6

	£	£
Fixed assets at net book value		
Freehold premises		50,000
Fixtures and fittings		8,000
Motor vehicles		9,000
		67,000
Current assets		
Stocks	16,000	
Debtors	500	
Prepayment	300	
Cash	100	
	16,900	
Less *current liabilities*		
Bank overdraft	2,000	
Creditors	1,200	
Taxation payable	3,500	
Accrued costs	600	
	7,300	
		9,600
		76,600
Capital		
Capital as at 1 January 20X6		47,600
Profit for the year		8,000
		55,600
Less drawings		4,000
		51,600
Long-term liabilities		
Loan		25,000
		76,600

Method (a) is now the format of balance sheet we recommend that you use unless examination questions specify otherwise.

2 THE TRADING, PROFIT AND LOSS ACCOUNT 6/98, 6/99 – 6/00

2.1 The trading, profit and loss account is a statement showing in detail how the profit (or loss) of a period has been made. The owners and managers of a business obviously want to know how much profit or loss has been made, but there is only a limited information value in the profit figure alone.

2.2 In order to exercise financial control effectively, managers need to know how much income has been earned, what various items of costs have been, and whether the performance of sales or the control of costs appears to be satisfactory. This is the basic reason for preparing the trading, profit and loss account.

2.3 There are two parts to the statement, a trading account and a profit and loss account.

(a) *The trading account*. This shows the gross profit for the accounting period. Gross profit is the difference between (i) and (ii) below.

(i) The value of sales (excluding value added tax)
(ii) The purchase cost or production cost of the goods sold

In the retail business, the cost of the goods sold is their purchase cost from the suppliers. In a manufacturing business, the production cost of goods sold is the cost of raw materials in the finished goods, plus the cost of the labour required to make the goods, and often plus an amount of production 'overhead' costs.

(b) *The profit and loss account*. This shows the net profit of the business. The net profit is calculated by adding (i) and (ii), then deducting (iii).

(i) The gross profit
(ii) Any other income from sources other than the sale of goods
(iii) Other expenses of the business which are not included in the cost of goods sold

Detail in the profit and loss account

2.4 Income from other sources will include the following.

(a) Dividends or interest received from investments.

(b) Profits on the sale of fixed assets.

(c) Bad debts written off in a previous accounting period which were unexpectedly recovered in the current period (see Paragraph 2.5(a)(vii) below).

2.5 Other business expenses that will appear in the profit and loss account are as follows.

(a) *Selling and distribution expenses*. These are expenses associated with the process of selling and delivering goods to customers. They include the following items.

(i) The salaries of a sales director and sales management.

(ii) The salaries and commissions of salesmen.

(iii) The travelling and entertainment expenses of salesmen.

(iv) Marketing costs (eg advertising and sales promotion expenses).

(v) The costs of running and maintaining delivery vans.

(vi) Discounts allowed to customers for early payment of their debt. For example, a business might sell goods to a customer for £100 and offer a discount of 5% for payment in cash. If the customer takes the discount, the accounts of the business would not record the sales value at £95; they would instead record sales at the full £100, with a cost for discounts allowed of £5. Discounts are described more fully in Chapter 9.

(vii) Bad debts written off. Sometimes debtors fail to pay what they owe, and a business might have to decide at some stage of chasing after payment that there is now no prospect of ever being paid. The debt has to be written off as 'bad'. The amount of the debt written off is charged as an expense in the profit and loss account. Bad debts will be described more fully in Chapter 9.

(b) *Administration expenses*. These are the expenses of providing management and administration for the business.

(i) The salaries of directors, management and office staff
(ii) Rent and rates
(iii) Insurance
(iv) Telephone and postage
(v) Printing and stationery
(vi) Heating and lighting

(c) *Finance expenses*. These include, for example, the following.

(i) Interest on a loan
(ii) Bank overdraft interest

As far as possible, you should try to group items of expenses (selling and distribution, administration and finance) but this is not something that you should worry about unnecessarily at this stage.

Example: trading, profit and loss account

2.6 On 1 June 20X5, Jock Heiss commenced trading as an ice cream salesman, selling ice creams from a van which he drove around the streets of his town.

(a) He rented the van at a cost of £1,000 for three months. Running expenses for the van averaged £300 per month.

(b) He hired a part time helper at a cost of £100 per month.

(c) He borrowed £2,000 from his bank, and the interest cost of the loan was £25 per month.

(d) His main business was to sell ice cream to customers in the street, but he also did some special catering arrangements for business customers, supplying ice creams for office parties. Sales to these customers were usually on credit.

(e) For the three months to 31 August 20X5, his total sales were as follows.

(i) Cash sales £8,900
(ii) Credit sales £1,100

(f) He purchased his ice cream from a local manufacturer, Floors Ltd. The cost of purchases in the three months to 31 August 20X5 was £6,200, and at 31 August he had sold every item of stock. He still owed £700 to Floors Ltd for unpaid purchases on credit.

(g) One of his credit sale customers has gone bankrupt, owing Jock £250. Jock has decided to write off the debt in full, with no prospect of getting any of the money owed.

(h) He used his own home for his office work. Telephone and postage expenses for the three months to 31 August were £150.

(i) During the period he paid himself £300 per month.

Required

Prepare a trading, profit and loss account for the three months 1 June to 31 August 20X5.

Solution

2.7 A trading, profit and loss account can be presented in either a horizontal format or a vertical format. However the vertical format is most common in practice and that will be the format used for the rest of this Study Text.

JOCK HEISS
TRADING, PROFIT AND LOSS ACCOUNT
FOR THE THREE MONTHS ENDED 31 AUGUST 20X5

	£	£
Sales		10,000
Less cost of sales		6,200
Gross profit		3,800
Wages	300	
Van rental	1,000	
Van expenses	900	
Bad debt written off	250	
Telephone and postage	150	
Interest charges	75	
		2,675
Net profit (transferred to the balance sheet)		1,125

Notes

(a) Drawings are appropriations of profit, not expenses, and so are not included in the profit and loss account. They would be deducted from capital in the balance sheet.

(b) Cost of sales is £6,200, even though £700 is still unpaid. Floors Ltd will be a creditor for £700 in the balance sheet.

3 CAPITAL AND REVENUE EXPENDITURE 12/99, 6/00

3.1 Capital expenditure is expenditure which results in the acquisition of fixed assets, or an improvement in their earning capacity.

(a) Capital expenditure is not charged as an expense in the profit and loss account, although a depreciation charge will usually be made to write off the capital expenditure gradually over time. Depreciation charges are expenses in the profit and loss account.

(b) Capital expenditure on fixed assets results in the appearance of a fixed asset in the balance sheet of the business.

3.2 Revenue expenditure is expenditure which is incurred for either of the following reasons.

(a) For the purpose of the trade of the business. This includes expenditure classified as selling and distribution expenses, administration expenses and finance charges.

(b) To maintain the existing earning capacity of fixed assets.

3.3 Revenue expenditure is charged to the profit and loss account of a period, provided that it relates to the trading activity and sales of that particular period. For example, if a business buys ten widgets for £200 (£20 each) and sells eight of them during an accounting period, it will have two widgets left in stock at the end of the period. The full £200 is revenue expenditure but only £160 is a cost of goods sold during the period. The remaining £40 (cost of two units) will be included in the balance sheet in the stock of goods held - ie as a current asset valued at £40.

3.4 Suppose that a business purchases a building for £30,000. It then adds an extension to the building at a cost of £10,000. The building needs to have a few broken windows mended, its floors polished and some missing roof tiles replaced. These cleaning and maintenance jobs cost £900.

In this example, the original purchase (£30,000) and the cost of the extension (£10,000) are capital expenditures, because they are incurred to acquire and then improve a fixed asset. The other costs of £900 are revenue expenditure, because these merely maintain the building and thus the 'earning capacity' of the building.

Capital income and revenue income

3.5 Capital income is the proceeds from the sale of non-trading assets (ie proceeds from the sale of fixed assets, including fixed asset investments). The profits (or losses) from the sale of fixed assets are included in the profit and loss account of a business, for the accounting period in which the sale takes place.

3.6 Revenue income is income derived from the following sources.

(a) The sale of trading assets
(b) Interest and dividends received from investments held by the business

Capital transactions

3.7 The categorisation of capital and revenue items given above does not mention raising additional capital from the owner(s) of the business, or raising and repaying loans. These are transactions which result in one of the following happening.

(a) Add to the cash assets of the business, thereby creating a corresponding liability (capital or loan).

(b) When a loan is repaid, reduce the liabilities (loan) and the assets (cash) of the business

None of these transactions would be reported through the profit and loss account.

Why is the distinction between capital and revenue items important?

3.8 Revenue expenditure results from the purchase of goods and services.

(a) They are used fully in the accounting period in which they are purchased, and so are a cost or expense in the trading, profit and loss account.

(b) They result in a current asset as at the end of the accounting period because the goods or services have not yet been consumed or made use of. The current asset would be shown in the balance sheet and is not yet a cost or expense in the trading, profit and loss account.

3.9 Capital expenditure results in the purchase or improvement of fixed assets, which are assets that will provide benefits to the business in more than one accounting period, and which are not acquired with a view to being resold in the normal course of trade. The cost of purchased fixed assets is not charged in full to the trading, profit and loss account of the period in which the purchase occurs. Instead, the fixed asset is gradually depreciated over a number of accounting periods.

3.10 Since revenue items and capital items are accounted for in different ways, the correct and consistent calculation of profit for any accounting period depends on the correct and consistent classification of items as revenue or capital.

Exercise 2

State whether each of the following items should be classified as 'capital' or 'revenue' expenditure or income for the purpose of preparing the trading, profit and loss account and the balance sheet of the business.

(a) The purchase of leasehold premises.

(b) The annual depreciation of leasehold premises.

(c) Solicitors' fees in connection with the purchase of leasehold premises.

(d) The costs of adding extra storage capacity to a mainframe computer used by the business.

(e) Computer repairs and maintenance costs.

(f) Profit on the sale of an office building.

(g) Revenue from sales by credit card.

(h) The cost of new machinery.

(i) Customs duty charged on the machinery when imported into the country.

(j) The 'carriage' costs of transporting the new machinery from the supplier's factory to the premises of the business purchasing the machinery.

(k) The cost of installing the new machinery in the premises of the business.

(l) The wages of the machine operators.

Solution

(a) Capital expenditure.

(b) Depreciation of a fixed asset is a revenue expenditure.

(c) The legal fees associated with the purchase of a property may be added to the purchase price and classified as capital expenditure. The cost of the leasehold premises in the balance sheet of the business will then include the legal fees.

(d) Capital expenditure (enhancing an existing fixed asset).

(e) Revenue expenditure.

(f) Capital income (net of the costs of sale).

(g) Revenue income.

(h) Capital expenditure.

(i) If customs duties are borne by the purchaser of the fixed asset, they may be added to the cost of the machinery and classified as capital expenditure.

(j) Similarly, if carriage costs are paid for by the purchaser of the fixed asset, they may be included in the cost of the fixed asset and classified as capital expenditure.

(k) Installation costs of a fixed asset are also added to the fixed asset's cost and classified as capital expenditure.

(l) Revenue expenditure.

Chapter roundup

- The purpose of this chapter has been to introduce in broad outline the characteristics of the balance sheet and the trading, profit and loss account. In the next chapters, we shall go on to consider in detail some of the techniques and principles applied to prepare the trading, profit and loss account.
- A balance sheet is a statement of the financial position of a business at a given moment in time.
- A trading, profit and loss account is a financial statement showing in detail how the profit or loss of a period has been made.
- A distinction is made in the balance sheet between long-term liabilities and current liabilities, and between fixed assets and current assets.
- 'Current' means 'within one year'. Current assets are expected to be converted into cash within one year. Current liabilities are debts which are payable within one year.
- Fixed assets are those acquired for long-term use within the business. They are normally valued at cost less depreciation.
- Capital expenditure is expenditure which results in the acquisition of fixed assets or an improvement in their earning capacity.
- Revenue expenditure is incurred for one of the following reasons.
  - For the purpose of the trade of the business.
  - To maintain the existing earning capacity of fixed assets.

Test your knowledge

1 What are the component parts of the item 'proprietor's capital' in a balance sheet? (see para 1.6)

2 Give two examples of long-term liabilities. (1.12)

3 What are the main items of current assets in a balance sheet? (1.25)

4 What is the 'working capital' of a business? (1.34)

5 What is the difference between gross profit and net profit? (2.3)

6 Identify a source of income other than the sale of goods. (2.4)

7 What items might be included in selling and distribution expenses? (2.5)

8 What is the distinction between capital expenditure and revenue expenditure? (3.1, 3.2)

Now try illustrative questions 4 and 5 at the end of the Study Text

Chapter 5

BOOKS OF PRIME ENTRY

This chapter covers the following topics.

1 The role of source documents

2 The need for books of prime entry

3 Sales and purchase day books

4 Cash books

Introduction

From your studies of the first two chapters, you should have grasped some important points about the nature and purpose of accounting. You should have realised that most organisations exist to provide products and services in the ultimate hope of making a surplus or profit for their owners, which they do by receiving payment in money for goods and services provided. The role of the accounting system is to record these monetary effects and create information about them.

You should also understand the basic principles underlying the balance sheet and profit and loss account and have an idea of what they look like.

We now turn our attention to the process by which a business transaction works its way through to the financial statements.

It is usual to record a business transaction on a *document*. Such documents include invoices, orders, credit notes and goods received notes, all of which will be discussed in Section 1 of this chapter. In terms of the accounting system these are known as *source documents*. The information on them is processed by the system by, for example, aggregating (adding together) or classifying.

Records of source documents are kept in 'books of prime entry', which, as the name suggests, are the first stage at which a business transaction enters into the accounting system. The various types of books of prime entry are discussed in Sections 2 to 4.

In the next chapter we consider what happens to transactions after the books of prime entry stage.

1 THE ROLE OF SOURCE DOCUMENTS

1.1 Whenever a business transaction takes place, involving sales or purchases, receiving or paying money, or owing or being owed money, it is usual for the transaction to be recorded on a document. These documents are the source of all the information recorded by a business.

1.2 Documents used to record the business transactions in the 'books of account' of the business include the following.

(a) *Sales order*. A customer writes out an order or signs an order for goods or services he wishes to buy.

(b) *Purchase order*. A business makes an order from another business for the purchase of goods or services, such as material supplies.

(c) *Invoices* and *credit notes*. These are discussed further below.

1.3 An *invoice* relates to a sales order or a purchase order.

(a) When a business sells goods or services on credit to a customer, it sends out an invoice. The details on the invoice should match up with the details on the sales order. The invoice is a request for the customer to pay what he owes.

(b) When a business buys goods or services on credit it receives an invoice from the supplier. The details on the invoice should match up with the details on the purchase order.

1.4 The invoice is primarily a demand for payment, but it is used for other purposes as well, as we shall see. As it has several uses, an invoice is often produced on multi-part stationery, or photocopied, or carbon-copied. The top copy will go to the customer and other copies will be used by various people within the business.

What does an invoice show?

1.5 Most invoices are numbered, so that the business can keep track of all the invoices it sends out. Information usually shown on an invoice includes the following.

(a) Name and address of the seller and the purchaser.

(b) Date of the sale.

(c) Description of what is being sold.

(d) Quantity and unit price of what has been sold (eg 20 pairs of shoes at £25 a pair).

(e) Details of trade discount, if any (eg 10% reduction in cost if buying over 100 pairs of shoes).

(f) Total amount of the invoice including (in the UK) details of any VAT.

(g) Sometimes, the date by which payment is due, and other terms of sale.

The credit note

1.6 Suppose that Student Supplies sent out its invoice for 450 rulers, but the typist accidentally typed in a total due of £162.10, instead of £62.10. The county council has been *overcharged* by £100. What is Student Supplies to do?

1.7 Alternatively, suppose that when the primary school received the rulers, it found that they had all been broken in the post and that it was going to send them back. Although the county council has received an invoice for £62.10, it has no intention of paying it, because the rulers were useless. Again, what is Student Supplies to do?

1.8 The answer is that the supplier (in this case, Student Supplies) sends out a *credit note*. A credit note is sometimes printed in red to distinguish it from an invoice. Otherwise, it will be made out in much the same way as an invoice, but with less detail and 'Credit Note Number' instead of 'Invoice Number'.

1.9 Other documents sometimes used in connection with sales and purchases are:

(a) Debit notes.
(b) Goods received notes.

1.10 A debit note might be issued instead of raising an invoice to adjust an invoice already issued. This is also commonly achieved by issuing a revised invoice after raising a credit or debit note purely for internal purposes (ie to keep the records straight).

1.11 More commonly, a debit note is issued to a supplier as a means of formally requesting a credit note.

1.12 Goods received notes (GRNs) are filled in to record a receipt of goods, most commonly in a warehouse. They may be used in addition to suppliers' advice notes. Often the accounts department will require to see the relevant GRN before paying a supplier's invoice. Even where GRNs are not routinely used, the details of a consignment from a supplier which arrives without an advice note must always be recorded.

2 THE NEED FOR BOOKS OF PRIME ENTRY 6/97, 12/98

2.1 We have seen that in the course of business, source documents are created. The details on these source documents need to be summarised, as otherwise the business might forget to ask for some money, or forget to pay some, or even accidentally pay something twice. In other words, it needs to keep records of source documents - of transactions - so that it can keep tabs on what is going on.

2.2 Such records are made in books of prime entry. The main books of prime entry which we need to look at are as follows.

(a) Sales day book
(b) Purchase day book
(c) Sales returns day book
(d) Purchases returns day book
(e) Journal (described in the next chapter)
(f) Cash book
(g) Petty cash book

2.3 It is worth bearing in mind that, for convenience, this chapter describes books of prime entry as if they are actual books. Nowadays, books of prime entry are often not books at all, but rather files hidden in the memory of a computer. However, the principles remain the same whether they are manual or computerised.

3 SALES AND PURCHASE DAY BOOKS 12/97, 12/98

The sales day book

3.1 The sales day book is used to keep a list of all invoices sent out to customers each day. An extract from a sales day book might look like this.

SALES DAY BOOK

Date	*Invoice*	*Customer*	*Sales ledger folio*	*Total amount invoiced*
20X0				£
Jan 10	247	Jones & Co	SL14	105.00
	248	Smith Ltd	SL 8	86.40
	249	Alex & Co	SL 6	31.80
	250	Enor College	SL 9	1,264.60
				1,487.80

3.2 The column called 'sales ledger folio' is a reference to the sales ledger. It means, for example, that the sale to Jones & Co for £105 is also recorded on page 14 of the sales ledger.

3.3 Most businesses 'analyse' their sales. For example, suppose that the business sells boots and shoes, and that the sale to Smith was entirely boots, the sale to Alex was entirely shoes, and the other two sales were a mixture of both.

3.4 Then the sales day book might look like this.

SALES DAY BOOK

Date	*Invoice*	*Customer*	*Sales ledger folio*	*Total amount invoiced*	*Boot sales*	*Shoe sales*
20X0				£	£	£
Jan 10	247	Jones & Co	SL 14	105.00	60.00	45.00
	248	Smith Ltd	SL 8	86.40	86.40	
	249	Alex & Co	SL 6	31.80		31.80
	250	Enor College	SL 9	1,264.60	800.30	464.30
				1,487.80	946.70	541.10

3.5 This sort of analysis gives the managers of the business useful information which helps them to decide how best to run the business.

The purchase day book

3.6 A business also keeps a record in the purchase day book of all the invoices it receives.

3.7 An extract from a purchase day book might look like this.

PURCHASE DAY BOOK

Date	*Supplier*	*Purchase ledger folio*	*Total amount invoiced*	*Purchases*	*Electricity etc*
20X8			£	£	£
Mar 15	Cook & Co	PL 31	315.00	315.00	
	W Butler	PL 46	29.40	29.40	
	EEB	PL 42	116.80		116.80
	Show Fair Ltd	PL 12	100.00	100.00	
			561.20	444.40	116.80

3.8 You should note the following points.

(a) The 'purchase ledger folio' is a reference to the purchase ledger just as the sales ledger folio was to the sales ledger. We will see the purpose of this in the next chapter.

(b) There is no 'invoice number' column, because the purchase day book records other people's invoices, which have all sorts of different numbers.

(c) Like the sales day book, the purchase day book analyses the invoices which have been sent in. In this example, three of the invoices related to goods which the business intends to re-sell (called simply 'purchases') and the fourth invoice was an electricity bill.

The sales returns day book

3.9 When customers return goods for some reason, the returns are recorded in the sales return day book. An extract from the sales returns day book might look like this:

SALES RETURNS DAY BOOK

Date	*Customer and goods*	*Sales ledger folio*	*Amount*
20X8			£
30 April	Owen Plenty		
	3 pairs 'Texas' boots	SL 82	135.00

3.10 Not all sales returns day books analyse what goods were returned, but it makes sense to keep as complete a record as possible.

The purchase returns day book

3.11 There are no prizes for guessing that the purchase returns day book is kept to record goods which the business sends back to its suppliers. The business might expect a cash refund from the supplier. In the meantime, however, it might issue a debit note to the supplier, indicating the amount by which the business expects its total debt to the supplier to be reduced.

3.12 An extract from the purchase returns day book might look like this:

PURCHASE RETURNS DAY BOOK

Date	*Supplier and goods*	*Purchase ledger folio*	*Amount*
20X8			£
29 April	Boxes Ltd		
	300 cardboard boxes	PL 123	46.60

4 CASH BOOKS

12/98, 12/99

The cash book

4.1 The cash book is also a day book, which is used to keep a cumulative record of money received and money paid out by the business. The cash book deals with money paid into and out of the business *bank* account. This could be money received on the business premises in notes, coins and cheques. There are also receipts and payments made by bank transfer, standing order, direct debit and, in the case of bank interest and charges, directly by the bank.

4.2 Some cash, in notes and coins, is usually kept on the business premises in order to make occasional payments for odd items of expense. This cash is usually accounted for separately in a *petty cash book* (which we will look at shortly).

4.3 The best way to see how the cash book works is to follow through an example.

Example: cash book

4.4 At the beginning of 1 September, Robin Plenty had £900 in the bank.

4.5 During 1 September 20X7, Robin Plenty had the following receipts and payments.

(a) Cash sale - receipt of £80
(b) Payment from credit customer Hay £400 less discount allowed £20
(c) Payment from credit customer Been £720
(d) Payment from credit customer Seed £150 less discount allowed £10
(e) Cheque received for cash to provide a short-term loan from Len Dinger £1,800
(f) Second cash sale - receipts of £150
(g) Cash received for sale of machine £200
(h) Payment to supplier Kew £120
(i) Payment to supplier Hare £310
(j) Payment of telephone bill £400
(k) Payment of gas bill £280
(l) £100 in cash withdrawn from bank for petty cash
(m) Payment of £1,500 to Hess for new plant and machinery

4.6 If you look through these transactions, you will see that seven of them are receipts and six of them are payments.

4.7 The receipts part of the cash book for 1 September would look like this.

CASH BOOK (RECEIPTS)

Date	*Narrative*	*Folio*	*Total*
20X7			£
1 Sept	Balance b/d*		900
	Cash sale		80
	Debtor: Hay		380
	Debtor: Been		720
	Debtor: Seed		140
	Loan: Len Dinger		1,800
	Cash sale		150
	Sale of fixed asset		200
			4,370
2 Sept	Balance b/d*		1,660

* 'b/d' = brought down (ie brought forward)

4.8 You should note the following points.

(a) There is space so that the receipts can be analysed under various headings - for example, 'receipts from debtors', 'cash sales' and 'other receipts'.

(b) The cash received in the day amounted to £3,470. Added to the £900 at the start of the day, this comes to £4,370. But this is not, of course, the amount to be carried forward to the next day, because first we have to subtract all the payments made during 1 September.

4.9 The payments part of the cash book for 1 September would look like this.

CASH BOOK (PAYMENTS)

Date	*Narrative*	*Folio*	*Total*
20X7			£
1 Sept	Creditor: Kew		120
	Creditor: Hare		310
	Telephone		400
	Gas bill		280
	Petty cash		100
	Machinery purchase		1,500
	Balance c/d		1,660
			4,370

4.10 As you can see, this is very similar to the receipts part of the cash book. The only points to note are as follows.

(a) The analysis would be under headings like 'payments to creditors', 'payments into petty cash', 'wages' and 'other payments'.

(b) Payments during 1 September totalled £2,710. We know that the total of receipts was £4,370. That means that there is a balance of £4,370 - £2,710 = £1,660 to be 'carried down' to the start of the next day. As you can see this 'balance carried down' is noted at the end of the payments column, so that the receipts and payments totals show the same figure of £4,370 at the end of 1 September. And if you look to the receipts part of this example, you can see that £1,660 has been brought down ready for the next day.

4.11 With analysis columns completed, the cash book given in the examples above might look as follows.

CASH BOOK (RECEIPTS)

Date	Narrative	Folio	Total	Debtors	Cash sales	Other
			£	£	£	£
20X7						
1 Sept	Balance b/d		900			
	Cash sale		80		80	
	Debtor - Hay		380	380		
	Debtor - Been		720	720		
	Debtor - Seed		140	140		
	Loan - Len Dinger		1,800			1,800
	Cash sale		150		150	
	Sale of fixed asset		200			200
			4,370	1,240	230	2,000

CASH BOOK (PAYMENTS)

Date	Narrative	Folio	Total	Creditors	Petty cash	Wages	Other
			£	£	£	£	£
20X7							
1 Sept	Creditor - Kew		120	120			
	Creditor - Hare		310	310			
	Telephone		400				400
	Gas bill		280				280
	Petty cash		100		100		
	Machinery purchase		1,500				1,500
	Balance c/d		1,660				
			4,370	430	100	-	2,180

Bank statements

4.12 Weekly or monthly, a business will receive a bank statement. Bank statements should be used to check that the amount shown as a balance in the cash book agrees with the amount on the bank statement, and that no cash has 'gone missing'. This agreement or 'reconciliation' of the cash book with a statement is the subject of Chapter 13.

Petty cash book

4.13 Most businesses keep a small amount of cash on the premises to make occasional small payments in cash - eg to pay the milkman, to buy a few postage stamps, to pay the office cleaner, to pay for some bus or taxi fares, etc. This is often called the cash float or petty cash account. The cash float can also be the resting place for occasional small receipts, such as cash paid by a visitor to make a phone call, or take some photocopies.

4.14 There are usually more payments than receipts, and petty cash must be 'topped up' from time to time with cash from the business bank account.

4.15 Under what is called the imprest system, the amount of money in petty cash is kept at an agreed sum or 'float' (say £100). Expense items are recorded on vouchers as they occur, so that at any time:

	£
Cash still held in petty cash	57
Plus voucher payments	43
Must equal the agreed sum or float	100

The total float is made up regularly (to £100, or whatever the agreed sum is) by means of a cash payment from the bank account into petty cash. The amount of the 'top-up' into petty cash will be the total of the voucher payments since the previous top-up.

4.16 The format of a petty cash book is much the same as for the cash book, with analysis columns (chiefly for expenditure items, such as travel, postage, cleaning, etc).

4.17 Try the following exercise on books of prime entry.

Exercise

State which books of prime entry the following transactions would be entered into.

(a) Your business pays A Brown (a supplier) £450.00.
(b) You send D Smith (a customer) an invoice for £650.
(c) Your accounts manager asks you for £12 urgently in order to buy some envelopes.
(d) You receive an invoice from A Brown for £300.
(e) You pay D Smith £500.
(f) F Jones (a customer) returns goods to the value of £250.
(g) You return goods to J Green to the value of £504.
(h) F Jones pays you £500.

Solution

(a) Cash book
(b) Sales day book
(c) Petty cash book
(d) Purchases day book
(e) Cash book
(f) Sales returns day book
(g) Purchase returns day book
(h) Cash book

4.18 Another book of prime entry is the *journal* which is considered in the next chapter.

Chapter roundup

- Business transactions are recorded on source documents. These include the following.
  - Sales orders
  - Purchase orders
  - Invoices
  - Credit notes
- These transactions are recorded in books of prime entry of which there are seven.
  - Sales day book
  - Sales returns day book
  - Purchase day book
  - Purchase returns day book
  - Cash book
  - Petty cash book
  - Journal
- Most businesses keep petty cash on the premises which is topped up from the main bank account. Under the imprest system the petty cash is kept at an agreed sum.
- You should be aware of which transactions go in a given book of prime entry.

Test your knowledge

1 Name four pieces of information normally shown on an invoice. (see para 1.5)
2 Name the seven books of prime entry. (2.2)
3 What information is summarised in the sales day book? (3.1 - 3.4)
4 What is the purchase returns day book used for? (3.11)
5 What is the difference between the cash book and the petty cash book? (4.1, 4.2)
6 Describe how the imprest system works. (4.15)

Now try illustrative question 6 at the end of the Study Text

Chapter 6

LEDGER ACCOUNTING AND DOUBLE ENTRY

This chapter covers the following topics.

1 The nominal ledger

2 Double entry bookkeeping

3 The journal

4 Day book analysis

5 The imprest system

6 The sales and purchase ledgers

Introduction

In earlier chapters we looked at the theory of preparing accounts for the proprietor(s) of a business, by presenting a profit and loss account for a given period of time and a balance sheet as at the end of that period. We have also seen, by means of the accounting equation and the business equation, that it would be possible to prepare a statement of the affairs of a business at any time we like, and that a profit and loss account and a balance sheet could be drawn up on any date, relating to any period of time. A business is continually making transactions, buying and selling etc, and do not want to prepare a profit and loss account and a balance sheet on completion of every individual transaction. To do so is a time-consuming and cumbersome task.

A business should keep records of the transactions that it makes, the assets it acquires and liabilities it incurs, and when the time comes to prepare a profit and loss account and a balance sheet, the relevant information can be taken from those records.

The records of transactions, assets and liabilities are kept as follows.

(a) In chronological order, and dated so that transactions can be related to a particular period of time.

(b) Built up in cumulative totals. For example, a business may build up the total of its sales:

(i) day by day (eg total sales on Monday, total sales on Tuesday)
(ii) week by week
(iii) month by month
(iv) year by year

We have already seen the first step in this process, which is to list all the transactions in various books of prime entry. Now we must turn our attention to the method used to summarise these records.

This chapter introduces *double entry bookkeeping*. This is the cornerstone of accounts preparation, and is surprisingly simple.

1 THE NOMINAL LEDGER

6/96

1.1 The nominal ledger is an accounting record which summarises the financial affairs of a business. It contains details of assets, liabilities and capital, income and expenditure and so profit and loss. It consists of a large number of different accounts, each account having its own purpose or 'name' and an identity or code. There may be various subdivisions, whether for convenience, ease of handling, confidentiality, security, or to meet the needs of computer software design.

1.2 The nominal ledger is sometimes called the 'general ledger'.

1.3 Examples of accounts in the nominal ledger include the following.

(a) Plant and machinery at cost (fixed asset)
(b) Motor vehicles at cost (fixed asset)
(c) Plant and machinery, provision for depreciation (liability)
(d) Motor vehicles, provision for depreciation (liability)
(e) Proprietor's capital (liability)
(f) Stocks - raw materials (current asset)
(g) Stocks - finished goods (current asset)
(h) Total debtors (current asset)
(i) Total creditors (current liability)
(j) Wages and salaries (expense item)
(k) Rent and rates (expense item)
(l) Advertising expenses (expense item)
(m) Bank charges (expense item)
(n) Motor expenses (expense item)
(o) Telephone expenses (expense item)
(p) Sales (income)
(q) Total cash or bank overdraft (current asset or liability)

The format of a ledger account

1.4 If a ledger account is kept in an actual book rather than as a computer record, it looks like this.

ADVERTISING EXPENSES

Date	*Narrative*	*Folio*	£	*Date*	*Narrative*	*Folio*	£
20X6							
15 April	JFK Agency for quarter to 31 March	PL 348	2,500				

Only one entry in the account is shown here, because the example is introduced simply to illustrate the general format of a ledger account.

1.5 There are two sides to the account, and an account heading on top, and so it is convenient to think in terms of 'T' accounts.

(a) On top of the account is its name.
(b) There is a left hand side, or debit side.
(c) There is a right hand side, or credit side.

NAME OF ACCOUNT

DEBIT SIDE	£	CREDIT SIDE	£

2 DOUBLE ENTRY BOOKKEEPING 6/96, 12/99

2.1 As we have seen, since the total of liabilities plus capital is always equal to total assets, any transaction which changes the amount of total assets must also change the total liabilities plus capital, and vice versa. Alternatively, a transaction might use up assets of a certain value to obtain other assets of the same value. For example, if a business pays £50 in cash for some goods, its total assets will be unchanged, but as the amount of cash falls by £50, the value of goods in stocks rises by the same amount.

2.2 Ledger accounts, with their debit and credit sides, are kept in a way which allows the two-sided nature of business transactions to be recorded. This system of accounting was first used in Venice in 1494 AD and it is known as the 'double entry' system of bookkeeping, so called because every transaction is recorded twice in the accounts. This is sometimes referred to as the concept of duality.

2.3 Double entry bookkeeping is not entirely standardised, and there are some variations found in practice in the way that business transactions are recorded. In this text, double entry bookkeeping will be explained according to a given set of well practised 'rules'. Variations in these rules that are made in the accounting systems of some businesses may be mentioned from time to time. However, if you learn the system as described here, you should be able to adapt your knowledge to any (minor) differences which either might appear in an examination question, or you might come across in your practical experience.

The rules of double entry bookkeeping

2.4 The basic rule which must always be observed is that *every* financial transaction gives rise to two accounting entries, one a debit and the other a credit. The total value of debit entries in the nominal ledger is therefore always equal at any time to the total value of credit entries. Which account receives the credit entry and which receives the debit depends on the nature of the transaction.

(a) An increase in an expense (eg a purchase of stationery) or an increase in an asset (eg a purchase of office furniture) is a *debit*.

(b) An increase in income (eg a sale) or an increase in a liability (eg buying goods on credit) is a *credit*.

(c) A decrease in an asset (eg making a cash payment) is a *credit*.

(d) A decrease in a liability (eg paying a creditor) is a *debit*.

2.5 Students coming to the subject for the first time often have difficulty in knowing where to begin. A good starting point is the cash account, ie the nominal ledger account in which receipts and payments of cash are recorded. The rule to remember about the cash account is as follows.

(a) A cash *payment* is a *credit* entry in the cash account. Here the asset is decreasing. Cash may be paid out, for example, to pay an expense (such as rates) or to purchase an asset (such as a machine). The matching debit entry is therefore made in the appropriate expense account or asset account.

(b) A cash *receipt* is a *debit* entry in the cash account. Here the asset is increasing. Cash might be received, for example, by a retailer who makes a cash sale. The credit entry would then be made in the sales account.

Example: double entry for cash transactions

2.6 In the cash book of a business, the following transactions have been recorded.

(a) A cash sale (ie a receipt) of £2
(b) Payment of a rent bill totalling £150
(c) Buying some goods for cash at £100

(d) Buying some shelves for cash at £200

2.7 How would these four transactions be posted to the ledger accounts? For that matter, which ledger accounts should they be posted to? Don't forget that each transaction will be posted twice, in accordance with the rule of double entry.

Solution

2.8 (a) The two sides of the transaction are:

(i) Cash is received (debit entry in the cash account).
(ii) Sales increase by £2 (credit entry in the sales account).

CASH ACCOUNT

	£		£
Sales a/c	2		

SALES ACCOUNT

	£		£
		Cash a/c	2

(Note how the entry in the cash account is cross-referenced to the sales account and vice-versa. This enables a person looking at one of the accounts to trace where the other half of the double entry can be found.)

(b) The two sides of the transaction are:

(i) Cash is paid (credit entry in the cash account).
(ii) Rent expense increases by £150 (debit entry in the rent account).

CASH ACCOUNT

	£		£
		Rent a/c	150

RENT ACCOUNT

	£		£
Cash a/c	150		

(c) The two sides of the transaction are:

(i) Cash is paid (credit entry in the cash account).
(ii) Purchases increase by £100 (debit entry in the purchases account).

CASH ACCOUNT

	£		£
		Purchases a/c	100

PURCHASES ACCOUNT

	£		£
Cash a/c	100		

(d) The two sides of the transaction are:

(i) Cash is paid (credit entry in the cash account).
(ii) Assets - in this case, shelves - increase by £200 (debit entry in shelves account).

CASH ACCOUNT

	£		£
		Shelves a/c	200

SHELVES (ASSET) ACCOUNT

	£		£
Cash a/c	200		

2.9 If all four of these transactions related to the same business, the cash account of that business would end up looking as follows.

CASH ACCOUNT

	£		£
Sales a/c	2	Rent a/c	150
		Purchases a/c	100
		Shelves a/c	200

Credit transactions

2.10 Not all transactions are settled immediately in cash. A business might purchase goods or fixed assets from its suppliers on credit terms, so that the suppliers would be creditors of the business until settlement was made in cash. Equally, the business might grant credit terms to its customers who would then be debtors of the business. Clearly no entries can be made in the cash book when a credit transaction occurs, because initially no cash has been received or paid. Where then can the details of the transactions be entered?

2.11 The solution to this problem is to use debtors and creditors accounts instead. A debtor is someone who owes money to the business. A creditor is someone to whom the business owes money.

Example: credit transactions

2.12 Recorded in the sales day book and the purchase day book are the following transactions.

(a) The business sells goods on credit to a customer Mr A for £2,000.
(b) The business buys goods on credit from a supplier B Ltd for £100.

2.13 How and where are these transactions posted in the ledger accounts?

Solution

2.14 (a)

DEBTORS ACCOUNT

	£		£
Sales a/c	2,000		

SALES ACCOUNT

	£		£
		Debtors account	2,000

(b)

CREDITORS ACCOUNT

	£		£
		Purchases a/c	100

PURCHASES ACCOUNT

	£		£
Creditors a/c	100		

When cash is paid to creditors or by debtors

2.15 What happens when a credit transaction is eventually settled in cash? Suppose that, in the example above, the business paid £100 to B Ltd one month after the goods were acquired. The two sides of this new transaction are:

(a) Cash is paid (credit entry in the cash account).
(b) The amount owing to creditors is reduced (debit entry in the creditors account).

CASH ACCOUNT

	£		£
		Creditors a/c (B Ltd)	100

CREDITORS ACCOUNT

	£		£
Cash a/c	100		

2.16 If we now bring together the two parts of this example, the original purchase of goods on credit and the eventual settlement in cash, we find that the accounts appear as follows.

CASH ACCOUNT

	£		£
		Creditors a/c	100

PURCHASES ACCOUNT

	£		£
Creditors a/c	100		

CREDITORS ACCOUNT

	£		£
Cash a/c	100	Purchases a/c	100

2.17 The two entries in the creditors account cancel each other out, indicating that no money is owing to creditors any more. We are left with a credit entry of £100 in the cash account and a debit entry of £100 in the purchases account. These are exactly the entries which would have been made to record a *cash* purchase of £100 (compare example above). This is what we would expect: after the business has paid off its creditors it is in exactly the position of a business which has made cash purchases of £100, and the accounting records reflect this similarity.

2.18 Similar reasoning applies when a customer settles his debt. In the example above when Mr A pays his debt of £2,000 the two sides of the transaction are:

(a) Cash is received (debit entry in the cash account).
(b) The amount owed by debtors is reduced (credit entry in the debtors account).

CASH ACCOUNT

	£		£
Debtors a/c	2,000		

DEBTORS ACCOUNT

	£		£
		Cash a/c	2,000

2.19 The accounts recording this sale to, and payment by, Mr A now appear as follows.

CASH ACCOUNT

	£		£
Debtors a/c	2,000		

SALES ACCOUNT

	£		£
		Debtors a/c	2,000

DEBTORS ACCOUNT

	£		£
Sales a/c	2,000	Cash a/c	2,000

2.20 The two entries in the debtors account cancel each other out; while the entries in the cash account and sales account reflect the same position as if the sale had been made for cash (see above).

2.21 Now try the following exercises.

Exercise 1

See if you can identify the debit and credit entries in the following transactions.

(a) Bought a machine on credit from A, cost £8,000.
(b) Bought goods on credit from B, cost £500.
(c) Sold goods on credit to C, value £1,200.
(d) Paid D (a creditor) £300.
(e) Collected £180 from E, a debtor.
(f) Paid wages £4,000.
(g) Received rent bill of £700 from landlord G.
(h) Paid rent of £700 to landlord G.
(i) Paid insurance premium £90.

Solution

			£	£
(a)	DEBIT	Machine account (fixed asset)	8,000	
	CREDIT	Creditors (A)		8,000
(b)	DEBIT	Purchases account	500	
	CREDIT	Creditors (B)		500
(c)	DEBIT	Debtors (C)	1,200	
	CREDIT	Sales		1,200
(d)	DEBIT	Creditors (D)	300	
	CREDIT	Cash		300
(e)	DEBIT	Cash	180	
	CREDIT	Debtors (E)		180
(f)	DEBIT	Wages account	4,000	
	CREDIT	Cash		4,000
(g)	DEBIT	Rent account	700	
	CREDIT	Creditors (G)		700
(h)	DEBIT	Creditors (G)	700	
	CREDIT	Cash		700
(i)	DEBIT	Insurance costs	90	
	CREDIT	Cash		90

Exercise 2

See whether you can record the ledger entries for the following transactions. Ron Knuckle set up a business selling keep fit equipment, trading under the name of Buy Your Biceps Shop. He put £7,000 of his own money into a business bank account (transaction A) and in his first period of trading, the following transactions occurred.

Transaction		£
B	Paid rent of shop for the period	3,500
C	Purchased equipment (stocks) on credit	5,000
D	Raised loan from bank	1,000
E	Purchase of shop fittings (for cash)	2,000
F	Sales of equipment: cash	10,000
G	Sales of equipment: on credit	2,500
H	Payments to trade creditors	5,000
I	Payments from debtors	2,500
J	Interest on loan (paid)	100
K	Other expenses (all paid in cash)	1,900
L	Drawings	1,500

All stocks purchased during the period were sold, and so there were no closing stocks of equipment.

Try to do as much of this exercise as you can by yourself before reading the solution.

Solution

Clearly, there should be an account for cash, debtors, creditors, purchases, a shop fittings account, sales, a loan account and a proprietor's capital account. It is also useful to keep a separate *drawings account* until the end of each accounting period. Other accounts should be set up as they seem appropriate and in this exercise, accounts for rent, bank interest and other expenses would seem appropriate.

The cash account is a good place to start, if possible. You should notice that cash transactions include the initial input of capital by Ron Knuckle, subsequent drawings, the payment of rent, the loan from the bank, the interest, some cash sales and cash purchases, and payments to creditors and by debtors. (The transactions are identified below by their reference, to help you to find them.)

CASH

	£		£
Capital - Ron Knuckle (A)	7,000	Rent (B)	3,500
Bank loan (D)	1,000	Shop fittings (E)	2,000
Sales (F)	10,000	Trade creditors (H)	5,000
Debtors (I)	2,500	Bank loan interest (J)	100
		Other expenses (K)	1,900
		Drawings (L)	1,500
			14,000
		Balancing figure - the amount of cash left over after payments have been made	
			6,500
	20,500		20,500

CAPITAL (RON KNUCKLE)

	£		£
		Cash (A)	7,000

BANK LOAN

	£		£
		Cash (D)	1,000

PURCHASES

	£		£
Trade creditors (C)	5,000		

TRADE CREDITORS

	£		£
Cash (H)	5,000	Purchases (C)	5,000

RENT

	£		£
Cash (B)	3,500		

FIXED ASSETS

	£		£
Cash (E)	2,000		

SALES

	£		£
		Cash (F)	10,000
		Debtors (G)	2,500
			12,500

DEBTORS

	£		£
Sales (G)	2,500	Cash (I)	2,500

BANK LOAN INTEREST

	£		£
Cash (J)	100		

OTHER EXPENSES

	£		£
Cash (K)	1,900		

DRAWINGS ACCOUNT

	£		£
Cash (L)	1,500		

(a) If you want to make sure that this solution is complete, you should go through the transactions A to L and tick off each of them twice in the ledger accounts, once as a debit and once as a credit. When you have finished, all transactions in the 'T' account should be ticked, with only totals left over.

(b) In fact, there is an easier way to check that the solution to this sort of problem does 'balance' properly, which we will meet in the next chapter.

3 THE JOURNAL

6/98, 12/99, 6/00

3.1 You may remember that one of the books of prime entry from the previous chapter was the journal. The journal keeps a record of unusual movements between accounts. It is used to record any double entries made which do not arise from the other books of prime entry. For example, journal entries are made when errors are discovered and need to be corrected.

3.2 Whatever type of transaction is being recorded, the following is the usual format of a journal entry.

Date	*Folio*	*Debit*	*Credit*
		£	£
Account to be debited		X	
Account to be credited			X
(Narrative to explain the transaction)			

(Remember: in due course, the ledger accounts will be written up to include the transactions listed in the journal.)

3.3 A narrative explanation must accompany each journal entry. It is required for audit and control, to indicate the purpose and authority of every transaction which is not first recorded in a book of prime entry.

Examples: journal entries

3.4 Some examples might help to illustrate the format. Note that an examination question might ask you to 'journalise' transactions which would not in practice be recorded in the journal at all. If you are faced with such a problem, you should simply record the debit and credit entries for every transaction you can recognise, giving some supporting narrative to each transaction.

3.5 The following is a summary of the transactions of Yve's hairdressing business of which Fred Brown is the sole proprietor.

1 January	Put in cash of £2,000 as capital
	Purchased brushes and combs for cash £50
	Purchased hair dryers from Z Ltd on credit £150
30 January	Paid three months rent to 31 March £300
	Collected and paid in takings £600
31 January	Gave Mrs X a perm, highlights etc on credit £80.

Show the transactions by means of journal entries.

Solution

3.6 JOURNAL

			£	£
1 January	DEBIT	Cash	2,000	
	CREDIT	Fred Brown - capital account		2,000
	Initial capital introduced			
1 January	DEBIT	Brushes and combs account	50	
	CREDIT	Cash		50
	The purchase for cash of brushes and combs as fixed assets			
1 January	DEBIT	Hair dryer account	150	
	CREDIT	Sundry creditors account *		150
	The purchase on credit of hair dryers as fixed assets			
30 January	DEBIT	Rent account	300	
	CREDIT	Cash		300
	The payment of rent to 31 March			
30 January	DEBIT	Cash	600	
	CREDIT	Sales (or takings account)		600
	Cash takings			
31 January	DEBIT	Debtors account	80	
	CREDIT	Sales account (or takings account)		80
	The provision of a hair-do on credit			

* *Note.* Creditors who have supplied fixed assets are included amongst sundry creditors, as distinct from creditors who have supplied raw materials or goods for resale, who are trade creditors. It is quite common to have separate 'total creditors' accounts, one for trade creditors and another for sundry other creditors.

The correction of errors

3.7 The journal is most commonly used to record corrections to errors that have been made in writing up the nominal ledger accounts. Errors corrected by the journal must be capable of correction by means of a double entry in the ledger accounts.

3.8 There are several types of error which can occur. They are looked at in some detail in Chapter 14 of this text, along with the method of using journal entries to correct them.

4 DAY BOOK ANALYSIS

4.1 In the previous chapter, we used the following example of four transactions entered into the sales day book.

SALES DAY BOOK

Date	*Invoice*	*Customer*	*Sales ledger folios*	*Total amount invoiced*	*Boot sales*	*Shoe sales*
20X0			£	£	£	
Jan 10	247	Jones & Co	SL 14	105.00	60.00	45.00
	248	Smith Ltd	SL 8	86.40	86.40	
	249	Alex & Co	SL 6	31.80		31.80
	250	Enor College	SL 9	1,264.60	800.30	464.30
				1,487.80	946.70	541.10

4.2 We have already seen that in theory these transactions are posted to the ledger accounts as follows:

DEBIT	Total debtors account	£1,487.80	
CREDIT	Sales account		£1,487.80

4.3 But a total sales account is not very informative, particularly if the business sells lots of different products. So, using our example, the business might open up a 'sale of shoes' account and a 'sale of boots' account, then at the end of the day, the ledger account postings are:

		£	£
DEBIT	Debtors account	1,487.80	
CREDIT	Sale of shoes account		541.10
	Sale of boots account		946.70

4.4 That is why the analysis of sales is kept. Exactly the same reasoning lies behind the analyses kept in other books of prime entry.

5 THE IMPREST SYSTEM

5.1 In the last chapter, we saw how the petty cash book was used to operate the imprest system for petty cash. It is now time to see how the double entry works in the imprest system.

5.2 Suppose a business starts off a cash float on 1.3.20X7 with £250. This will be a payment from cash at bank to petty cash, ie:

DEBIT	Petty cash	£250	
CREDIT	Cash at bank		£250

5.3 Suppose further that five payments were made out of petty cash during March 20X7. The petty cash book might look as follows.

Receipts	*Date*	*Narrative*	*Total*	*Payments* *Postage*	*Travel*
£			£	£	£
250.00	1.3.X7	Cash			
	2.3.X7	Stamps	12.00	12.00	
	8.3.X7	Stamps	10.00	10.00	
	19.3.X7	Travel	16.00		16.00
	23.3.X7	Travel	5.00		5.00
	28.3.X7	Stamps	11.50	11.50	
250.00			54.50	33.50	21.00

5.4 At the end of each month (or at any other suitable interval) the total payments (credits) in the petty cash book are posted to ledger accounts. For March 20X7, £33.50 would be debited to postage account, and £21.00 to travel account. The cash float would need to be topped up by a payment of £54.50 from the main cash book, ie:

		£	£
DEBIT	Petty cash	54.50	
CREDIT	Cash		54.50

5.5 So the rules of double entry have been satisfied, and the petty cash book for the month of March 20X7 will look like this.

Receipts	*Date*	*Narrative*	*Total*	*Payments* *Postage*	*Travel*
£			£	£	£
250.00	1.3.X7	Cash			
	2.3.X7	Stamps	12.00	12.00	
	8.3.X7	Stamps	10.00	10.00	
	19.3.X7	Travel	16.00		16.00
	23.3.X7	Travel	5.00		5.00
	28.3.X7	Stamps	11.50	11.50	
	31.3.X7	Balance c/d	195.50		
250.00			250.00	33.50	21.00

195.50	1.4.X7	Balance b/d
54.50	1.4.X7	Cash

5.6 As you can see, the cash float is back up to £250 on 1.4.X7, ready for more payments to be made.

6 THE SALES AND PURCHASE LEDGERS

Impersonal accounts and personal accounts

6.1 The accounts in the nominal ledger (ledger accounts) relate to types of income, expense, asset, liability - sales, rent, rates, debtors, creditors, etc - rather than to the person to whom the money is paid or from whom it is received. They are therefore called *impersonal* accounts. However, there is also a need for *personal* accounts, most commonly for debtors and creditors, and these are contained in the sales ledger and purchase ledger.

6.2 Personal accounts include details of transactions which have already been summarised in ledger accounts (eg sales invoices are recorded in sales and total debtors, payments to creditors in the cash and creditors accounts). The personal accounts do not therefore form part of the double entry system, as otherwise transactions would be recorded twice over (ie two debits and two credits for each transaction). They are *memorandum* accounts only.

The sales ledger

6.3 The sales day book provides a chronological record of invoices sent out by a business to credit customers. For many businesses, this might involve very large numbers of invoices per day or per week. The same customer might appear in several different places in the sales day book, for invoices sent out at different times. So at any point in time, a customer may owe money on several unpaid invoices.

6.4 In addition to keeping a chronological record of invoices, a business should also keep a record of how much money each individual credit customer owes, and what this total debt consists of. The need for a *personal account* for each customer is a practical one.

(a) A customer might telephone, and ask how much he currently owes. Staff must be able to tell him.

(b) It is a common practice to send out statements to credit customers at the end of each month, showing how much they still owe, and itemising new invoices sent out and payments received during the month.

(c) The managers of the business will want to keep a check on the credit position of an individual customer, and to ensure that no customer is exceeding his credit limit.

(d) Most important is the need to match payments received against debts owed. If a customer makes a payment, the business must be able to set off the payment against the customer's debt and establish how much he still owes on balance.

6.5 Sales ledger accounts are written up as follows.

(a) When entries are made in the sales day book (invoices sent out), they are subsequently also made in the *debit side* of the relevant customer account in the sales ledger.

(b) Similarly, when entries are made in the cash book (payments received), or in the sales returns day book, they are also made in the *credit side* of the relevant customer account.

6.6 Each customer account is given a reference or code number, and it is that reference which is the 'sales ledger folio' in the *sales day book*. We say that amounts are *posted* from the sales day book to the sales ledger.

6.7 Here is an example of how a sales ledger account is laid out.

ENOR COLLEGE

A/c no: SL 9

		£		£
Balance b/f		250.00		
10.1.X0	Sales - SDB 48			
	(invoice no 250)	1,264.60	Balance c/d	1,514.60
		1,514.60		1,514.60
11.1.X0	Balance b/d	1,514.60		

6.8 The debit side of this personal account, then, shows amounts owed by Enor College. When Enor pays some of the money it owes it will be entered into the cash book (receipts) and subsequently 'posted' to the credit side of the personal account. For example, if the college paid £250 on 10.1.20X0, it would appear as follows.

ENOR COLLEGE

A/c no: SL 9

		£		£
Balance b/f		250.00	10.1.X0 Cash	250.00
10.1.X0	Sales - SDB 48			
	(invoice no 250)	1,264.60	Balance c/d	1,264.60
		1,514.60		1,514.60
11.1.X0	Balance b/d	1,264.60		

6.9 The opening balance owed by Enor College on 11.1.X0 is now £1,264.60 instead of £1,514.60, because of the £250 receipt which came in on 10.1.X0.

The purchase ledger (bought ledger)

6.10 The purchase ledger, like the sales ledger, consists of a number of personal accounts. These are separate accounts for each individual supplier, and they enable a business to keep a continuous record of how much it owes each supplier at any time.

6.11 After entries are made in the purchase day book, cash book, or purchase returns day book - ie after entries are made in the books of prime entry - they are also made in the relevant supplier account in the purchase ledger. Again we say that the entries in the purchase day book are *posted* to the suppliers' personal accounts in the purchase ledger.

6.12 Here is an example of how a purchase ledger account is laid out.

COOK & CO

A/c no: SL 31

	£		£
Balance c/d	515.00	Balance b/f	200.00
		15 Mar 20X8	
		Invoice received	
		PDB 37	315.00
	515.00		515.00
		16 March 20X8	
		Balance b/d	515.00

6.13 The credit side of this personal account, then, shows amounts owing to Cook & Co. If the business paid Cook & Co some money, it would be entered into the cash book (payments) and subsequently be posted to the debit side of the personal account. For example, if the business paid Cook & Co £100 on 15 March 20X8, it would appear as follows:

COOK & CO

A/c no: SL 31

		£			£
15.3.X8	Cash	100.00		Balance b/f	200.00
			15.3.X8	Invoice received PDB 37	
	Balance c/d	415.00			315.00
		515.00			515.00
			16.3.X8	Balance b/d	415.00

6.14 The opening balance owed to Cook & Co on 16.3.X8 is now £415.00 instead of £515.00 because of the £100 payment made on 15.3.X8.

6.15 The roles of the sales day book and purchases day book are very similar, with one book dealing with invoices sent out and the other with invoices received. The sales ledger and purchases ledger also serve similar purposes, with one consisting of personal accounts for credit customers and the other consisting of personal accounts for credit suppliers.

Chapter roundup

- Double entry bookkeeping is based on the same idea as the accounting equation. Every accounting transaction alters the make-up of a business's assets and liabilities. The equality of assets and liabilities is always preserved and so it follows that each transaction must have two equal but opposite effects.
- In a system of double entry bookkeeping every accounting event must be entered in ledger accounts both as a debit and as an equal but opposite credit. The principal accounts are contained in a ledger called the nominal ledger.
- Some accounts in the nominal ledger represent the total of very many smaller balances. For example, the debtors accounts represents all the balances owed by individual customers of the business, while the creditors account represents all amounts owed by the business to its suppliers.
- To keep track of individual customer and supplier balances, it is common to maintain subsidiary ledgers (called the sales ledger and the purchase ledger respectively). Each account in these ledgers represents the balance owed by or to an individual customer or supplier. These subsidiary ledgers are kept purely for reference and are therefore known as *memorandum* records. They do *not* normally form part of the double entry system.
- The rules of double entry bookkeeping are best learnt by considering the cash book. In the cash book a *credit* entry indicates a payment made by the business; the matching debit entry is then made in an account denoting an expense paid, an asset purchased or a liability settled. A *debit* entry in the cash book indicates cash received by the business; the matching credit entry is then made in an account denoting revenue received, a liability created or an asset sold.

Test your knowledge

1 Give six examples of nominal ledger accounts. (see para 1.3)

2 What is the double entry to record a cash sale of £50? (2.8(a))

3 What is the double entry to record a purchase of office chairs for £1,000? (2.8(d))

4 What is the double entry to record a credit sale? (2.14(a))

5 Name one reason for making a journal entry. (3.1, 3.7)

6 What is the difference between the creditors account in the nominal ledger and the purchase ledger? (6.1)

Now try illustrative questions 7 and 8 at the end of the Study Text

Chapter 7

FROM TRIAL BALANCE TO FINANCIAL STATEMENTS

This chapter covers the following topics.

1 The trial balance

2 The trading, profit and loss account

3 The balance sheet

4 Balancing accounts and preparing financial statements

Introduction

In the previous chapter you learned the principles of double entry and how to post to the ledger accounts. The next step in our progress towards the financial statements is the trial balance.

Before transferring the relevant balances at the year end to the profit and loss account and putting closing balances carried forward into the balance sheet, it is usual to test the accuracy of double entry bookkeeping records by preparing a trial balance. This is done by taking all the balances on every account. Because of the self-balancing nature of the system of double entry, the total of the debit balances will be exactly equal to the total of the credit balances.

In very straightforward circumstances, where no complications arise and where the records are complete, it is possible to prepare accounts directly from a trial balance. This is covered in Section 4.

Exam questions at all levels in financial accounting sometimes involve preparation of final accounts from trial balance. Last but not least, you may end up having to do it in 'real life'.

1 THE TRIAL BALANCE 6/97, 6/00

1.1 Imagine that an examination question has given you a list of transactions, and has asked you to post them to the relevant ledger accounts. You do it as quickly as possible and find that you have a little time left over at the end of the examination. How do you check that you have posted all the debit and credit entries properly?

There is no foolproof method, but a technique which shows up the more obvious mistakes is to prepare a *trial balance*.

The first step

1.2 Before you draw up a trial balance, you must have a collection of ledger accounts. For the sake of convenience, we will use the accounts of Ron Knuckle, which we drew up in the previous chapter.

CASH

	£		£
Capital - Ron Knuckle (A)	7,000	Rent	3,500
Bank loan	1,000	Shop fittings	2,000
Sales	10,000	Trade creditors	5,000
Debtors	2,500	Bank loan interest	100
		Incidental expenses	1,900
		Drawings	1,500
			14,000
		Balancing figure - the amount of cash left over after payments have been made	6,500
	20,500		20,500

CAPITAL (RON KNUCKLE)

	£		£
		Cash	7,000

BANK LOAN

	£		£
		Cash	1,000

PURCHASES

	£		£
Trade creditors	5,000		

TRADE CREDITORS

	£		£
Cash	5,000	Purchases	5,000

RENT

	£		£
Cash	3,500		

SHOP FITTINGS

	£		£
Cash	2,000		

SALES

	£		£
		Cash	10,000
		Debtors	2,500
			12,500

DEBTORS

	£		£
Sales	2,500	Cash	2,500

BANK LOAN INTEREST

	£		£
Cash	100		

OTHER EXPENSES

	£		£
Cash	1,900		

DRAWINGS ACCOUNT

	£		£
Cash	1,500		

1.3 The next step is to 'balance' each account.

Balancing ledger accounts

1.4 At the end of an accounting period, a balance is struck on each account in turn. This means that all the debits on the account are totalled and so are all the credits. If the total debits exceed the total credits there is said to be a debit balance on the account; if the credits exceed the debits then the account has a credit balance.

1.5 In our simple example, there is very little balancing to do.

(a) Both the trade creditors account and the debtors account balance off to zero.
(b) The cash account has a debit balance of £6,500.
(c) The total on the sales account is £12,500, which is a credit balance.

Otherwise, the accounts have only one entry each, so there is no totalling to do to arrive at the balance on each account.

Collecting the balances

1.6 If the basic principle of double entry has been correctly applied throughout the period it will be found that the credit balances equal the debit balances in total. This can be illustrated by collecting together the balances on Ron Knuckle's accounts.

	Debit	*Credit*
	£	£
Cash	6,500	
Capital		7,000
Bank loan		1,000
Purchases	5,000	
Trade creditors	-	-
Rent	3,500	
Shop fittings	2,000	
Sales		12,500
Debtors	-	-
Bank loan interest	100	
Other expenses	1,900	
Drawings	1,500	
	20,500	20,500

1.7 This list of balances is called the trial balance. It does not matter in what order the various accounts are listed, because the trial balance is not a document that a company *has* to prepare. It is just a method used to test the accuracy of the double entry bookkeeping methods.

What if the trial balance shows unequal debit and credit balances?

1.8 If the two columns of the trial balance are not equal, there must be an error in recording the transactions in the accounts. A trial balance, however, will not disclose the following types of errors.

(a) The complete omission of a transaction, because neither a debit nor a credit is made.

(b) The posting of a debit or credit to the correct side of the ledger, but to a wrong account.

(c) Compensating errors (eg an error of £100 is exactly cancelled by another £100 error elsewhere).

(d) Errors of principle, eg cash received from debtors being debited to the debtors account and credited to cash, instead of the other way round.

Example: trial balance

1.9 As at 30.3.20X7, your business has the following balances on its ledger accounts.

Accounts	*Balance*
	£
Bank loan	12,000
Cash	11,700
Capital	13,000
Rates	1,880
Trade creditors	11,200
Purchases	12,400
Sales	14,600
Sundry creditors	1,620
Debtors	12,000
Bank loan interest	1,400
Other expenses	11,020
Vehicles	2,020

On 31.3.X7, the business made the following transactions.

(a) Bought materials for £1,000, half for cash and half on credit.
(b) Made £1,040 sales, £800 of which was for credit.
(c) Paid wages to shop assistants of £260 in cash.

You are required to draw up a trial balance showing the balances as at the end of 31.3.X7.

Solution

1.10 First it is necessary to put the original balances into a trial balance - ie decide which are debit and which are credit balances.

Account	*Dr*	*Cr*
	£	£
Bank loan		12,000
Cash	11,700	
Capital		13,000
Rates	1,880	
Trade creditors		11,200
Purchases	12,400	
Sales		14,600
Sundry creditors		1,620
Debtors	12,000	
Bank loan interest	1,400	
Other expenses	11,020	
Vehicles	2,020	
	52,420	52,420

1.11 Now we must take account of the effects of the three transactions which took place on 31.3.X7.

			£	£
(a)	DEBIT	Purchases	1,000	
	CREDIT	Cash		500
		Trade creditors		500
(b)	DEBIT	Cash	240	
		Debtors	800	
	CREDIT	Sales		1,040
(c)	DEBIT	Other expenses	260	
	CREDIT	Cash		260

1.12 When these figures are included in the trial balance, it becomes:

Account	*Dr*	*Cr*
	£	£
Bank loan		12,000
Cash (11,700 – 500 + 240 – 260)	11,180	
Capital		13,000
Rates	1,880	
Trade creditors (11,200 + 500)		11,700
Purchases (12,400 + 1,000)	13,400	
Sales (14,600 + 1,040)		15,640
Sundry creditors		1,620
Debtors (12,000 + 800)	12,800	
Bank loan interest	1,400	
Other expenses (11,020 + 260)	11,280	
Vehicles	2,020	
	53,960	53,960

2 THE TRADING, PROFIT AND LOSS ACCOUNT 2/97, 6/98, 6/99, 12/99, 6/00

2.1 The first step in the process of preparing the financial statements is to open up another ledger account, called the trading, profit and loss account, which we introduced in chapter 4. In it a business summarises its results for the period by gathering together all the ledger account balances relating to income and expenses. This account is still part of the double entry system, so the basic rule of double entry still applies: every debit must have an equal and opposite credit entry.

2.2 This trading, profit and loss account we have opened up is not the financial statement we are aiming for, even though it has the same name. The difference between the two is not very great, because they contain the same information. However, the financial statement lays it out differently and may be much less detailed.

2.3 So what do we do with this new ledger account? The first step is to look through the ledger accounts and identify which ones relate to income and expenses. In the case of Ron Knuckle, the income and expense accounts consist of purchases, rent, sales, bank loan interest, and other expenses.

2.4 The balances on these accounts are transferred to the new trading, profit and loss account. For example, the balance on the purchases account is £5,000 DR. To balance this to zero, we write in £5,000 CR. To comply with the rule of double entry, there has to be a debit entry somewhere, so we write £5,000 DR in the trading, profit and loss account. Now the balance on the purchases account has been moved to the trading, profit and loss account.

2.5 If we do the same thing with all the income and expense accounts of Ron Knuckle, the result is as follows.

PURCHASES

	£		£
Trade creditors	5,000	Trading, P & L a/c	5,000

RENT

	£		£
Cash	3,500	Trading, P & L a/c	3,500

SALES

	£		£
Trading, P & L a/c	12,500	Cash	10,000
		Debtors	2,500
	12,500		12,500

BANK LOAN INTEREST

	£		£
Cash	100	Trading, P & L a/c	100

OTHER EXPENSES

	£		£
Cash	1,900	Trading, P & L a/c	1,900

TRADING, PROFIT AND LOSS ACCOUNT

	£		£
Purchases	5,000	Sales	12,500
Rent	3,500		
Bank loan interest	100		
Other expenses	1,900		

(Note that the trading, profit and loss account has not yet been balanced off but we will return to that later.)

2.6 If you look at the items we have gathered together in the trading, profit and loss account, they should strike a chord in your memory. They are the same items that we need to draw up the trading, profit and loss account in the form of a financial statement. With a little rearrangement they could be presented as follows.

RON KNUCKLE: TRADING, PROFIT AND LOSS ACCOUNT

	£	£
Sales		12,500
Cost of sales (= purchases in this case)		(5,000)
Gross profit		7,500
Expenses		
Rent	3,500	
Bank loan interest	100	
Other expenses	1,900	
		(5,500)
Net profit		2,000

3 THE BALANCE SHEET 12/97, 6/98, 6/99, 12/99, 6/00

3.1 Look back at the ledger accounts of Ron Knuckle. Now that we have dealt with those relating to income and expenses, which ones are left? The answer is that we still have to find out what to do with cash, capital, bank loan, trade creditors, shop fittings, debtors and the drawings account.

3.2 Are these the only ledger accounts left? No: don't forget there is still the last one we opened up, called the trading, profit and loss account. The balance on this account represents the profit earned by the business, and if you go through the arithmetic, you will find that it has a credit balance - a profit - of £2,000. (Not surprisingly, this is the figure that is shown in the trading profit and loss account financial statement.)

3.3 These remaining accounts must also be balanced and ruled off, but since they represent assets and liabilities of the business (not income and expenses) their balances are not transferred to the trading profit and loss account. Instead they are *carried down* in the books of the business. This means that they become opening balances for the next accounting period and indicate the value of the assets and liabilities at the end of one period and the beginning of the next.

3.4 The conventional method of ruling off a ledger account at the end of an accounting period is illustrated by the bank loan account in Ron Knuckle's books.

BANK LOAN ACCOUNT

	£		£
Balance carried down (c/d)	1,000	Cash (D)	1,000
		Balance brought down (b/d)	1,000

3.5 Ron Knuckle therefore begins the new accounting period with a credit balance of £1,000 on this account. A credit balance brought down denotes a liability. An asset would be represented by a debit balance brought down.

3.6 One further point is worth noting before we move on to complete this example. You will remember that a proprietor's capital comprises any cash introduced by him, plus any profits made by the business, less any drawings made by him. At the stage we have now reached, these three elements are contained in different ledger accounts: cash introduced of £7,000 appears in the capital account; drawings of £1,500 appear in the drawings account; and the profit made by the business is represented by the £2,000 credit balance on the trading profit and loss account. It is convenient to gather together all these amounts into one capital account, in the same way as we earlier gathered together income and expense accounts into one trading and profit and loss account.

3.7 If we go ahead and gather the three amounts together, the results are as follows.

DRAWINGS

	£		£
Cash	1,500	Capital a/c	1,500

TRADING, PROFIT AND LOSS ACCOUNT

	£		£
Purchases	5,000	Sales	12,500
Rent	3,500		
Bank loan interest	100		
Other expenses	1,900		
Capital a/c	2,000		
	12,500		12,500

CAPITAL

	£		£
Drawings	1,500	Cash	7,000
Balance c/d	7,500	Trading, P & L a/c	2,000
	9,000		9,000
		Balance b/d	7,500

3.8 A re-arrangement of these balances will complete Ron Knuckle's simple balance sheet:

RON KNUCKLE
BALANCE SHEET AT END OF FIRST TRADING PERIOD

	£
Fixed assets	
Shop fittings	2,000
Current assets	
Cash	6,500
Total assets	8,500
Liabilities	
Bank loan	(1,000)
Net assets	7,500
Proprietor's capital	7,500

3.9 When a balance sheet is drawn up for an accounting period which is not the first one, then it ought to show the capital at the start of the accounting period and the capital at the end of the accounting period. This will be illustrated in the next example.

3.10 In an examination question, you might not be given the ledger accounts - you might have to draw them up in the first place. That is the case with the following exercise - see if you can do it by yourself before looking at the solution.

4 BALANCING ACCOUNTS AND PREPARING FINANCIAL STATEMENTS 12/96

4.1 The exercise which follows is by far the most important in this text so far. It uses all the accounting steps from entering up ledger accounts to preparing the financial statements, and is set out in a style which you might well find in an examination. It is very important that you try the question by yourself: if you do not, you will be missing out a vital part of this text.

Exercise

A business is established with capital of £2,000, and this amount is paid into a business bank account by the proprietor. During the first year's trading, the following transactions occurred:

	£
Purchases of goods for resale, on credit	4,300
Payments to trade creditors	3,600
Sales, all on credit	5,800
Payments from debtors	3,200
Fixed assets purchased for cash	1,500
Other expenses, all paid in cash	900

The bank has provided an overdraft facility of up to £3,000.

Prepare the ledger accounts, a trading, profit and loss account for the year and a balance sheet as at the end of the year.

Solution

The first thing to do is to open ledger accounts so that the transactions can be entered up. The relevant accounts which we need for this example are: cash; capital; trade creditors; purchases; fixed assets; sales; debtors; other expenses.

The next step is to work out the double entry bookkeeping for each transaction. Normally you would write them straight into the accounts, but to make this example easier to follow, they are first listed below.

(a)	Establishing business (£2,000)	DR	Cash	CR	Capital
(b)	Purchases (£4,300)	DR	Purchases	CR	Creditors
(c)	Payments to creditors (£3,600)	DR	Creditors	CR	Cash
(d)	Sales (£5,800)	DR	Debtors	CR	Sales
(e)	Payments by debtors (£3,200)	DR	Cash	CR	Debtors
(f)	Fixed assets (£1,500)	DR	Fixed assets	CR	Cash
(g)	Other (cash) expenses (£900)	DR	Other expenses	CR	Cash

So far, the ledger accounts will look like this.

CASH

	£		£
Capital	2,000	Creditors	3,600
		Fixed assets	1,500
Debtors	3,200	Other expenses	900

CAPITAL

	£		£
		Cash	2,000

CREDITORS

	£		£
Cash	3,600	Purchases	4,300

PURCHASES

	£		£
Creditors	4,300		

FIXED ASSETS

	£		£
Cash	1,500		

SALES

	£		£
		Debtors	5,800

DEBTORS

	£		£
Sales	5,800	Cash	3,200

OTHER EXPENSES

	£		£
Cash	900		

The next thing to do is to balance all these accounts. It is at this stage that you could, if you wanted to, draw up a trial balance to make sure the double entries are accurate. There is not very much point in this simple example, but if you did draw up a trial balance, it would look like this.

	Dr	*Cr*
	£	£
Cash		800
Capital		2,000
Creditors		700
Purchases	4,300	
Fixed assets	1,500	
Sales		5,800
Debtors	2,600	
Other expenses	900	
	9,300	9,300

After balancing the accounts, the trading, profit and loss account should be opened. Into it should be transferred all the balances relating to income and expenses (ie purchases, other expenses, and sales). At this point, the ledger accounts will be:

CASH

	£		£
Capital	2,000	Trade creditors	3,600
Debtors	3,200	Fixed assets	1,500
Balance c/d	800	Other expenses	900
	6,000		6,000
		Balance b/d	800*

* A credit balance b/d means that this cash item is a liability, not an asset. This indicates a bank overdraft of £800, with cash income of £5,200 falling short of payments of £6,000 by this amount.

CAPITAL

	£		£
Balance c/d	2,600	Cash	2,000
		P & L a/c	600
	2,600		2,600

TRADE CREDITORS

	£		£
Cash	3,600	Stores (purchases)	4,300
Balance c/d	700		
	4,300		4,300
		Balance b/d	700

PURCHASES ACCOUNT

	£		£
Trade creditors	4,300	Trading a/c	4,300

FIXED ASSETS

	£		£
Cash	1,500	Balance c/d	1,500
Balance b/d	1,500		

SALES

	£		£
Trading a/c	5,800		5,800

DEBTORS

	£		£
Sales	5,800	Cash	3,200
		Balance c/d	2,600
	5,800		5,800
Balance b/d	2,600		

OTHER EXPENSES

	£		£
Cash	900	P & L a/c	900

TRADING, PROFIT AND LOSS ACCOUNT

	£		£
Purchases account	4,300	Sales	5,800
Gross profit c/d	1,500		
	5,800		5,800
Other expenses	900	Gross profit b/d	1,500
Net profit (transferred to capital account)	600		
	1,500		1,500

So the trading, profit and loss account financial statement will be:

TRADING, PROFIT AND LOSS ACCOUNT
FOR THE ACCOUNTING PERIOD

	£
Sales	5,800
Cost of sales (purchases)	(4,300)
Gross profit	1,500
Expenses	900
Net profit	600

Listing and then rearranging the balances on the ledger accounts gives the balance sheet as:

BALANCE SHEET AS AT THE END OF THE PERIOD

	£	£
Fixed assets		1,500
Current assets		
Debtors	2,600	
Current liabilities		
Bank overdraft	800	
Trade creditors	700	
	1,500	
Net current assets		1,100
		2,600

Capital	
At start of period	£
	2,000
Net profit for period	600
At end of period	2,600

4.2 In an examination you do not need to spell out your answer in such detail. The detail is given here to help you to work through the example properly, and you may wish to do things this way yourself until you get more practised in accounting techniques and are confident enough to take short cuts.

Chapter roundup

- At suitable intervals, the entries in each ledger accounts are totalled and a balance is struck. Balances are usually collected in a trial balance which is then used as a basis for preparing a profit and loss account and a balance sheet.
- A trial balance can be used to test the accuracy of the double entry accounting records. It works by listing the balances on ledger accounts, some of which will be debits and some credits, to see if they balance off to zero.
- A profit and loss ledger account is opened up to gather all items relating to income and expenses. When rearranged, the items make up the profit and loss account financial statement.
- The balances on all remaining ledger accounts (including the profit and loss account) can be listed and rearranged to form the balance sheet.

Test your knowledge

1 What is the purpose of a trial balance? (see para 1.1)

2 Give four circumstances in which a trial balance might balance although some of the balances are wrong. (1.8)

3 What is the difference between the ledger account and the financial statement both called the trading, profit and loss account? (2.1, 2.2)

4 What is the difference between balancing off an expense account and balancing off a liability account? (3.3)

Now try illustrative question 9 at the end of the Study Text

Chapter 8

THE COST OF GOODS SOLD, ACCRUALS AND PREPAYMENTS

This chapter covers the following topics.

1 The accounting treatment of stocks, carriage costs and returns

2 Accruals and prepayments

Introduction

When we looked at the trading, profit and loss account near the start of this text, we defined profit as the value of sales less the cost of sales and expenses. This definition might seem simple enough; however, it is not always immediately clear how much are the cost of sales or expenses. A variety of difficulties can arise in measuring them: some of these problems can be dealt with fairly easily, whereas others are less obvious to solve. The purpose of this chapter is to describe some of these problems and their solutions.

In this chapter, we shall consider unsold goods in stock at the beginning and end of an accounting period, carriage costs, writing off or writing down stock values, and the accounting treatment of accruals and prepayments. Their common feature is that they are applications of the accruals concept or matching concept described in Chapter 2.

We also deal with goods returned by customers or to suppliers. They are treated as a deduction from sales or purchases.

1 THE ACCOUNTING TREATMENT OF STOCKS, CARRIAGE COSTS AND RETURNS 6/98, 6/99

Unsold goods in stock at the end of an accounting period

1.1 Goods might be unsold at the end of an accounting period and so still be held in stock at the end of the period. The purchase cost of these goods should not be included in the cost of sales of the period.

Example: closing stock

1.2 Suppose that Perry P Louis, trading as the Umbrella Shop, ends his financial year on 30 September each year. On 1 October 20X4 he had no goods in stock. During the year to 30 September 20X5, he purchased 30,000 umbrellas costing £60,000 from umbrella wholesalers and suppliers. He resold the umbrellas for £5 each, and sales for the year amounted to £100,000 (20,000 umbrellas). At 30 September there were 10,000 unsold umbrellas left in stock, valued at £2 each.

What was Perry P Louis's gross profit for the year?

Solution

1.3 Perry P Louis purchased 30,000 umbrellas, but only sold 20,000. Purchase costs of £60,000 and sales of £100,000 do not represent the same quantity of goods.

The gross profit for the year should be calculated by 'matching' the sales value of the 20,000 umbrellas sold with the cost of those 20,000 umbrellas. The cost of sales in this example is therefore the cost of purchases minus the cost of goods in stock at the year end.

	£	£
Sales (20,000 units)		100,000
Purchases (30,000 units)	60,000	
Less closing stock (10,000 units @ £2)	20,000	
Cost of sales (20,000 units)		40,000
Gross profit		60,000

Example continued

1.4 We shall continue the example of the Umbrella Shop into its next accounting year, 1 October 20X5 to 30 September 20X6. Suppose that during the course of this year, Perry P Louis purchased 40,000 umbrellas at a total cost of £95,000. During the year he sold 45,000 umbrellas for £230,000. At 30 September 20X6 he had 5,000 umbrellas left in stock, which had cost £12,000.

What was his gross profit for the year?

Solution

1.5 In this accounting year, he purchased 40,000 umbrellas to add to the 10,000 he already had in stock at the start of the year. He sold 45,000, leaving 5,000 umbrellas in stock at the year end. Once again, gross profit should be calculated by matching the value of 45,000 units of sales with the cost of those 45,000 units.

The cost of sales is the value of the 10,000 umbrellas in stock at the beginning of the year, plus the cost of the 40,000 umbrellas purchased, less the value of the 5,000 umbrellas in stock at the year end.

	£	£
Sales (45,000 units)		230,000
Opening stock (10,000 units) *	20,000	
Add purchases (40,000 units)	95,000	
	115,000	
Less closing stock (5,000 units)	12,000	
Cost of sales (45,000 units)		103,000
Gross profit		127,000

*Taken from the closing stock value of the previous accounting year, see paragraph 1.3.

The cost of goods sold

1.6 The cost of goods sold is found by applying the following formula.

	£
Opening stock value	X
Add cost of purchases (or, in the case of a manufacturing company, the cost of production)	X
	X
Less closing stock value	(X)
Equals cost of goods sold	X

In other words, to match 'sales' and the 'cost of goods sold', it is necessary to adjust the cost of goods manufactured or purchased to allow for increases or reduction in stock levels during the period.

1.7 You should learn the above formula, because it is fundamental among the principles of accounting.

Test your knowledge of the formula with the following example.

Example: cost of goods sold and variations in stock levels

1.8 On 1 January 20X6, the Grand Union Food Stores had goods in stock valued at £6,000. During 20X6 its proprietor, who ran the shop, purchased supplies costing £50,000. Sales turnover for the year to 31 December 20X6 amounted to £80,000. The cost of goods in stock at 31 December 20X6 was £12,500.

Calculate the gross profit for the year.

Solution

1.9 GRAND UNION FOOD STORES
TRADING ACCOUNT FOR THE YEAR ENDED 31 DECEMBER 20X6

	£	£
Sales		80,000
Opening stocks	6,000	
Add purchases	50,000	
	56,000	
Less closing stocks	12,500	
Cost of goods sold		43,500
Gross profit		36,500

The cost of carriage inwards and outwards

1.10 'Carriage' refers to the cost of transporting purchased goods from the supplier to the premises of the business which has bought them. Someone has to pay for these delivery costs: sometimes the supplier pays, and sometimes the purchaser pays. When the purchaser pays, the cost to the purchaser is carriage inwards. When the supplier pays, the cost to the supplier is known as carriage outwards.

1.11 The cost of carriage inwards is usually added to the cost of purchases, and is therefore included in the trading account.

The cost of carriage outwards is a selling and distribution expense in the profit and loss account.

Example: carriage inwards and carriage outwards

1.12 Gwyn Tring, trading as Clickety Clocks, imports and resells cuckoo clocks and grandfather clocks. He must pay for the costs of delivering the clocks from his supplier in Switzerland to his shop in Wales.

He resells the clocks to other traders throughout the country, paying the costs of carriage for the consignments from his business premises to his customers.

On 1 July 20X5, he had clocks in stock valued at £17,000. During the year to 30 June 20X6 he purchased more clocks at a cost of £75,000. Carriage inwards amounted to £2,000. Sales for the year were £162,100. Other expenses of the business amounted to £56,000 excluding carriage outwards which cost £2,500. Gwyn Tring took drawings of £20,000 from the business during the course of the year. The value of the goods in stock at the year end was £15,400.

Required

Prepare the trading, profit and loss account of Clickety Clocks for the year ended 30 June 20X6.

Solution

1.13 CLICKETY CLOCKS
TRADING, PROFIT AND LOSS ACCOUNT FOR THE YEAR ENDED 30 JUNE 20X6

	£	£
Sales		162,100
Opening stock	17,000	
Purchases	75,000	
Carriage inwards	2,000	
	94,000	
Less closing stock	15,400	
Cost of goods sold		78,600
Gross profit		83,500
Carriage outwards	2,500	
Other expenses	56,000	
		58,500
Net profit (transferred to balance sheet)		25,000

Note: The figure for drawings is a 'red herring'. It is an appropriation of profit and so is not included in the trading, profit and loss account.

Goods written off or written down

1.14 A trader might be unable to sell all the goods that he purchases, because a number of things might happen to the goods before they can be sold. For example, goods might:

(a) Be lost or stolen.

(b) Be damaged, and so become worthless (such damaged goods might be thrown away).

(c) Become obsolete or out of fashion. These might have to be thrown away, or possibly sold off at a very low price in a clearance sale.

1.15 When goods are lost, stolen or thrown away as worthless, the business will make a loss on those goods because their 'sales value' will be nil.

Similarly, when goods lose value because they have become obsolete or out of fashion, the business will make a loss if their clearance sales value is less than their cost. For example, if goods which originally cost £500 are now obsolete and could only be sold for £150, the business would suffer a loss of £350.

1.16 If, at the end of an accounting period, a business still has goods in stock which are either worthless or worth less than their original cost, the value of the stocks should be written down to either (a) or (b).

(a) Nothing, if they are worthless.
(b) Their net realisable value, if this is less than their original cost.

This means that the loss will be reported as soon as the loss is foreseen, even if the goods have not yet been thrown away or sold off at a cheap price. This is an application of another concept - the prudence concept - which we will look at again in Chapter 10.

1.17 The costs of stock written off or written down should not usually cause any problems in calculating the gross profit of a business, because the cost of goods sold will include the cost of stocks written off or written down, as the following example shows.

Example: stocks written off and written down

1.18 Lucas Wagg, trading as Fairlock Fashions, ends his financial year on 31 March. At 1 April 20X5 he had goods in stock valued at £8,800. During the year to 31 March 20X6, he purchased goods costing £48,000. Fashion goods which cost £2,100 were still held in stock at 31 March 20X6, and Lucas Wagg believes that these could only now be sold at a sale price of £400. The goods still held in stock at 31 March 20X6 (including the fashion goods) had an original purchase cost of £7,600. Sales for the year were £81,400.

Required

Calculate the gross profit of Fairlock Fashions for the year ended 31 March 20X6.

Solution

1.19 Initial calculation of closing stock values:

STOCK COUNT

	At cost	*Realisable value*	*Amount written down*
	£	£	£
Fashion goods	2,100	400	1,700
Other goods (balancing figure)	5,500	5,500	-
	7,600	5,900	1,700

FAIRLOCK FASHIONS
TRADING ACCOUNT FOR THE YEAR ENDED 31 MARCH 20X6

	£	£
Sales		81,400
Value of opening stock	8,800	
Purchases	48,000	
	56,800	
Less closing stock	5,900	
Cost of goods sold		50,900
Gross profit		30,500

Note: If the fashion goods had a saleable value of at least their cost, the closing stock figures could have been £7,600; cost of goods sold £49,200; and gross profit £32,200. Therefore, writing down the closing stocks figure for the fashion goods has decreased gross profit by £1,700 (the amount written down).

Returns inwards and outwards

1.20 In Chapter 5 you were introduced to the idea of the goods being returned, either to suppliers or by customers.

1.21 Goods returned by customers are called sales returns or returns inwards. Goods returned to suppliers are called purchases returns or returns outwards.

1.22 The accounting treatment for returns is set out in the following proforma trading account.

PROFORMA LIMITED
TRADING ACCOUNT FOR THE YEAR ENDED 31 DECEMBER 20X7

	£	£
Sales		X
Less returns inwards		(X)
		X
Cost of sales		
Opening stock	X	
Purchases	X	
	X	
Less returns outwards	(X)	
	X	
Less closing stock	(X)	
		(X)
Gross profit		X

2 ACCRUALS AND PREPAYMENTS

Introduction

2.1 Expenses might not be paid for during the period to which they relate. For example, if a business rents a shop for £20,000 per annum, it might pay the full annual rent on, say, 1 April each year. Now if we were to calculate the profit of the business for the first six months of the year 20X7, the correct charge for rent in the profit and loss account would be £10,000 even though the rent payment would be £20,000 in that period. Similarly, the rent charge in a profit and loss account for the business in the second six months of the year would be £10,000, even though no rent payment would be made in that six month period.

2.2 Accruals or accrued expenses are expenses which are charged against the profit for a particular period, even though they have not yet been paid for. Prepayments are payments which have been made in one accounting period, but should not be charged against profit until a later period, because they relate to that later period.

2.3 Accruals and prepayments might seem difficult at first, but the following examples might help to clarify the principle involved, that expenses should be matched against the period to which they relate.

Example: accruals

2.4 Horace Goodrunning, trading as Goodrunning Motor Spares, ends his financial year on 28 February each year. His telephone was installed on 1 April 20X6 and he receives his telephone account quarterly at the end of each quarter. He pays it promptly as soon as it is received. On the basis of the following data, you are required to calculate the telephone expense to be charged to the profit and loss account for the year ended 28 February 20X7.

Goodrunning Motor Spares - telephone expense for the three months ended:

	£
30.6.20X6	23.50
30.9.20X6	27.20
31.12.20X6	33.40
31.3.20X7	36.00

Solution

2.5 The telephone expenses for the year ended 28 February 20X7 are:

	£
1 March - 31 March 20X6 (no telephone)	0.00
1 April - 30 June 20X6	23.50
1 July - 30 September 20X6	27.20
1 October - 31 December 20X6	33.40
1 January - 28 February 20X7 (two months)	24.00
	108.10

The charge for the period 1 January - 28 February 20X7 is two-thirds of the quarterly charge received on 31 March. As at 28 February 20X7, no telephone bill has been received for the quarter, because it is not due for another month. However, it would be inappropriate to ignore the telephone expenses for January and February, and so an accrued charge of £24 should be made, being two-thirds of the quarter's bill of £36.

The accrued charge will also appear in the balance sheet of the business as at 28 February 20X7, as a current liability, in order to complete the double entry.

Exercise 1

Ratsnuffer is a business dealing in pest control. Its owner, Roy Dent, employs a team of eight who were paid £12,000 per annum each in the year to 31 December 20X5. At the start of 20X6 he raised salaries by 10% to £13,200 per annum each.

On 1 July 20X6, he hired a trainee at a salary of £8,400 per annum.

He pays his work force on the first working day of every month, one month in arrears, so that his employees receive their salary for January on the first working day in February, etc.

Required

(a) Calculate the cost of salaries which would be charged in the profit and loss account of Ratsnuffer for the year ended 31 December 20X6.

(b) Calculate the amount actually paid in salaries during the year (ie the amount of cash received by the work force).

(c) State the amount of accrued charges for salaries which would appear in the balance sheet of Ratsnuffer as at 31 December 20X6.

Solution

(a) *Salaries cost in the profit and loss account*

	£
Cost of 8 employees for a full year at £13,200 each	105,600
Cost of trainee for a half year	4,200
	109,800

(b) *Salaries actually paid in 20X6*

	£
December 20X5 salaries paid in January (8 employees × £1,000 per month)	8,000
Salaries of 8 employees for January - November 20X6 paid in February - December (8 employees × £1,100 per month × 11 months)	96,800
Salaries of trainee (for July - November paid in August - December 20X6: 5 months × £700 per month)	3,500
Salaries actually paid	108,300

(c) *Accrued salaries costs as at 31 December 20X6*
(ie costs charged in the P & L account, but not yet paid)

	£
8 employees x 1 month x £1,100 per month	8,800
1 trainee x 1 month x £700 per month	700
	9,500

(d) *Summary*

	£
Accrued wages costs as at 31 December 20X5 (paid January 20X6)	8,000
Add salaries cost for 20X6 (P & L account)	109,800
	117,800
Less salaries paid	108,300
Equals accrued wages costs as at 31 December 20X6	9,500

Example: prepayments

2.6 The Square Wheels Garage pays fire insurance annually in advance on 1 June each year. The firm's financial year end is 28 February. From the following record of insurance payments you are required to calculate the charge to profit and loss for the financial year to 28 February 20X8.

	Insurance paid
	£
1.6.20X6	600
1.6.20X7	700

2.7 Insurance cost for:

	£
(a) The 3 months, 1 March - 31 May 20X7 (3/12 × £600)	150
(b) The 9 months, 1 June 20X7 - 28 February 20X8 (9/12 × £700)	525
Insurance cost for the year, charged to the P & L account	675

At 28 February 20X8 there is a prepayment for fire insurance, covering the period 1 March - 31 May 20X8. This insurance premium was paid on 1 June 20X7, but only nine months worth of the full annual cost is chargeable to the accounting period ended 28 February 20X8. The prepayment of £175 (3/12 × £700) as at 28 February 20X8 will appear as a current asset in the balance sheet of the Square Wheels Garage as at that date.

In the same way, there was a prepayment of £150 (3/12 × £600) in the balance sheet one year earlier as at 28 February 20X7.

Summary	£
Prepaid insurance premiums as at 28 February 20X7	150
Add insurance premiums paid 1 June 20X7	700
	850
Less insurance costs charged to the P & L account for the year ended 28 February 20X8	675
Equals prepaid insurance premiums as at 28 February 20X8	175

Exercise 2

The Batley Print Shop rents a photocopying machine from a supplier for which it makes a quarterly payment as follows:

(a) Three months rental in advance.
(b) A further charge of 2 pence per copy made during the quarter just ended.

The rental agreement began on 1 August 20X4 and the first six quarterly bills were as follows.

Bills dated and received	*Rental*	*Costs of copies taken*	*Total*
	£	£	£
1 August 20X4	2,100	0	2,100
1 November 20X4	2,100	1,500	3,600
1 February 20X5	2,100	1,400	3,500
1 May 20X5	2,100	1,800	3,900
1 August 20X5	2,700	1,650	4,350
1 November 20X5	2,700	1,950	4,650

The bills are paid promptly, as soon as they are received.

(a) Calculate the charge for photocopying expenses for the year to 31 August 20X4 and the amount of prepayments and/or accrued charges as at that date.

(b) Calculate the charge for photocopying expenses for the following year to 31 August 20X5, and the amount of prepayments and/or accrued charges as at that date.

Solution

(a) *Year to 31 August 20X4*	£
One months' rental (1/3 x £2,100) *	700
Accrued copying charges (1/3 x £1,500) **	500
Photocopying expense (P & L account)	1,200

* From the quarterly bill dated 1 August 20X4
** From the quarterly bill dated 1 November 20X4

There is a prepayment for 2 months' rental (£1,400) as at 31 August 20X4, and an accrual of £500 for copying charges (as calculated above).

(b) *Year to 31 August 20X5*

	£	£
Rental from 1 September 20X4 - 31 July 20X5 (11 months at £2,100 per quarter or £700 per month)		7,700
Rental from 1 August – 31 August 20X5 (1/3 × £2,700)		900
Rental charge for the year		8,600
Copying charges		
1 September - 31 October 20X4 (2/3 × £1,500)	1,000	
1 November 20X4 – 31 January 20X5	1,400	
1 February - 30 April 20X5	1,800	
1 May - 31 July 20X5	1,650	
Accrued charges for August 20X5 (1/3 × £1,950)	650	
		6,500
Total photocopying expenses (P & L account)		15,100

There is a prepayment for 2 months' rental (£1,800) as at 31 August 20X5, and an accrual of £650 for copying charges (as calculated above).

Summary of year 1 September 20X4 - 31 August 20X5

	Rental charges £	*Copying costs* £
Prepayments as at 31.8.20X4	1,400	
Accrued charges as at 31.8.20X4		(500)
Bills received during the year		
1 November 20X4	2,100	1,500
1 February 20X5	2,100	1,400
1 May 20X5	2,100	1,800
1 August 20X5	2,700	1,650
Prepayment as at 31.8.20X5	(1,800)	
Accrued charges as at 31.8.20X5		650
Charge to the P & L account for the year	8,600	6,500
Balance sheet items as at 31 August 20X5		
Prepaid rental (current asset)	1,800	
Accrued copying charges (current liability)		650

Further example: accruals

2.8 Suppose that Willie Woggle opens a shop on 1 May 20X6 to sell hiking and camping equipment. The rent of the shop is £12,000 per annum, payable quarterly in arrears (with the first payment on 31 July 20X6). Willie decides that his accounting period should end on 31 December each year.

2.9 The rent account as at 31 December 20X6 will record only two rental payments (on 31 July and 31 October) and there will be two months' accrued rental expenses for November and December 20X6, (£2,000), since the next rental payment is not due until 31 January 20X7.

The charge to the P & L account for the period to 31 December 20X6 will be for 8 months' rent (May-December inclusive) and so it follows that the total rental cost should be £8,000.

2.10 So far, the rent account appears as follows.

RENT ACCOUNT

		£			£
20X6			*20X6*		
31 July	Cash	3,000			
31 Oct	Cash	3,000	31 Dec	P & L account	8,000

2.11 To complete the picture, the accruals of £2,000 have to be put in, not only to balance the account, but also to have an opening balance of £2,000 ready for next year. So the accrued rent of £2,000 is debited to the rent account as a balance to be carried down, and credited to the rent account as a balance brought down.

RENT ACCOUNT

		£			£
20X6			*20X6*		
31 July	Cash	3,000			
31 Oct	Cash	3,000			
31 Dec	Balance c/d (accruals)	2,000	31 Dec	P & L account	8,000
		8,000			8,000
			20X7		
			1 Jan	Balance b/d	2,000

2.12 The rent account for the *next* year to 31 December 20X7, assuming no increase in rent in that year, would be as follows.

RENT ACCOUNT

		£			£
20X7			*20X7*		
31 Jan	Cash	3,000	1 Jan	Balance b/d	2,000
30 Apr	Cash	3,000			
31 Jul	Cash	3,000			
31 Oct	Cash	3,000			
31 Dec	Balance c/d (accruals)	2,000	31 Dec	P & L account	12,000
		14,000			14,000
			20X8		
			1 Jan	Balance b/d	2,000

2.13 Here, you will see that for a full year, a full twelve months' rental charges are taken as an expense to the P & L account.

Further example: prepayments

2.14 Prepayments are expenses which have been paid (or for which an invoice demanding payment has been received) but which relate to a future accounting period, and so should be an expense in the P & L account of that future period.

2.15 Suppose that Terry Trunk commences business as a landscape gardener on 1 September 20X5. He immediately decides to join his local trade association, the Confederation of Luton Gardeners, for which the annual membership subscription is £180, payable annually in advance. He paid this amount on 1 September. Terry decides that his account period should end on 30 June each year.

In the first period to 30 June 20X6 (10 months), a full year's membership will have been paid, but only ten twelfths of the subscription should be charged to the period (ie 10/12 × £180 = £150). There is a prepayment of two months of membership subscription - ie 2/12 × £180 = £30.

2.16 It is therefore necessary to recognise the prepayment in the ledger account for subscriptions. This is done in much the same way as accounting for accruals, by using the balance carried down/brought down technique.

CREDIT	Subscriptions account with prepayment as a balance c/d		£30
DEBIT	Subscriptions account with the same balance b/d	£30	

The remaining expenses in the subscriptions account should then be taken to the P & L account. The balance on the account will appear as a current asset (prepaid subscriptions) in the balance sheet as at 30 June 20X6.

SUBSCRIPTIONS ACCOUNT

		£			£
20X5			*20X6*		
1 Sept	Cash	180	30 Jun	P & L account	150
			30 Jun	Balance c/d (prepayment)	30
		180			180
20X6					
1 Jul	Balance b/d	30			

2.17 The subscription account for the next year, assuming no increase in the annual charge and that Terry Trunk remains a member of the association, will be:

SUBSCRIPTIONS ACCOUNT

		£			£
20X6			*20X7*		
1 Jul	Balance b/d	30	30 Jun	P & L account	180
1 Sep	Cash	180	30 Jun	Balance c/d (prepayment)	30
		210			210
20X7					
1 Jul	Balance b/d	30			

2.18 Again, we see here for a full accounting year, the charge to the P & L account is for a full year's subscriptions.

Chapter roundup

- This chapter has illustrated how the amount of profit is calculated when:
  - There are opening or closing stocks of goods in hand
  - There is carriage inwards and/or carriage outwards
  - Stocks are written off or written down in value
  - There are accrued charges
  - There are prepayments of expenses
- The cost of goods sold is calculated by adding the value of opening stock in hand to the cost of purchases and subtracting the value of closing stock.
- Accrued expenses are expenses which relate to an accounting period but have not yet been paid for. They are a charge against the profit for the period and they are shown in the balance sheet as at the end of the period as a current liability.
- Prepayments are expenses which have already been paid but relate to a future accounting period. They are not charged against the profit of the current period, and they are shown in the balance sheet at the end of the period as a current asset.
- Accruals and prepayments are aspects of the accruals concept which is one of the fundamental concepts in accounting.

Test your knowledge

1 How is the cost of goods sold calculated? (see para 1.6)

2 Distinguish between carriage inwards and carriage outwards. (1.10)

3 How is carriage inwards treated in the trading, profit and loss account? (1.11)

4 Give three reasons why goods purchased might have to be written off. (1.14)

5 If a business has paid rates of £1,000 for the year to 31 March 20X9, what is the prepayment in the accounts for the year to 31 December 20X8? (2.1)

6 Define an accrual. (2.2)

Now try illustrative question 10 at the end of the Study Text

Chapter 9

DISCOUNTS, BAD DEBTS AND PROVISIONS

This chapter covers the following topics.

1 Discounts

2 Accounting for bad and doubtful debts

Introduction

As a general rule, for the purpose of accounting (as distinct from the legal aspects of the law of contract), sales and purchases are treated as follows.

(a) A sale takes place at one of two points in time (this is called *revenue recognition*).

 (i) *Cash sales.* The sale occurs when the goods or services are given in exchange for an immediate payment (in notes and coins, or by cheque or credit card).

 (ii) *Credit sales.* The sale occurs when the business making the sale sends out an invoice for the goods or services supplied.

(b) The purchase of goods or services by a business also takes place at one of two points in time.

 (i) *Purchases for cash.* The purchase occurs when the goods and cash exchange hands.

 (ii) *Purchases on credit.* The purchase normally occurs when the business receives the goods, accompanied by an invoice from the supplier.

The accounting problems discussed in this chapter are concerned with sales or purchases on credit. With credit transactions, the point in time when a sale or purchase is recognised in the accounts of the business is not the same as the point in time when cash is eventually received or paid for the sale or purchase. There is a gap in time between the sale or purchase and the eventual cash settlement, and it is possible that something might happen during that time which results in the amount of cash eventually paid (if any) being different from the original value of the sale or purchase on the invoice.

We shall consider three such 'happenings'.

(a) Discounts allowed by the supplier for goods purchased by the business.

(b) Discounts allowed to customers for goods sold by the business.

(c) Bad debts, which arise when the business decides that a credit customer will never pay the money he owes.

1 DISCOUNTS

Types of discount

1.1 A discount is a reduction in the price of goods below the amount at which those goods would normally be sold to other customers of the supplier. A distinction must be made between the following types of discounts.

 (a) Trade discount
 (b) Cash discount, or settlement discount

1.2 *Trade discount* is a reduction in the cost of goods owing to the nature of the trading transaction. It usually results from buying goods in bulk. For example:

(a) A customer might be quoted a price of £1 per unit for a particular item, but a lower price of, say, 95 pence per unit if the item is bought in quantities of, say, 100 units or more at a time.

(b) An important customer or a regular customer might be offered a discount on all the goods he buys, regardless of the size of each individual order, because the total volume of his purchases over time is so large.

1.3 *Cash discount* is a reduction in the amount payable to the supplier, in return for immediate payment in cash, rather than purchase on credit. For example, a supplier might charge £1,000 for goods, but offer a discount of, say, 5% if the goods are paid for immediately in cash.

1.4 *Settlement discount* is similar to cash discount. It is a discount on the price of the goods purchased for credit customers who pay their debts promptly. For example, a supplier might charge £1,000 to a credit customer for goods purchased, but offer a discount of, say, 5% for payment within ten days of the invoice date.

Accounting for trade discount

1.5 Trade discount is a reduction in the amount of money demanded from a customer.

(a) If trade discount is received by a business for goods purchased from a supplier, the amount of money demanded from the business by the supplier will be net of discount (ie it will be the normal sales value less the discount).

(b) Similarly, if a trade discount is given by a business for goods sold to a customer, the amount of money demanded by the business will be after deduction of the discount.

1.6 Trade discount should therefore be accounted for as follows.

(a) Trade discount received should be deducted from the gross cost of purchases. In other words, the cost of purchases in the trading account will be stated at gross cost minus discount (ie it will be stated at the invoiced amount).

(b) Trade discount allowed should be deducted from the gross sales price, so that sales for the period will be reported in the trading account at their invoice value.

Cash discounts and settlement discounts received

1.7 When a business is given the opportunity to take advantage of a cash discount or a settlement discount for prompt payment, the decision as to whether or not to take the discount is a matter of financing policy, not of trading policy.

1.8 Suppose that A buys goods from B, on the understanding that A will be allowed a period of credit before having to pay for the goods. The terms of the transaction might be as follows.

(a) Date of sale: 1 July 20X6

(b) Credit period allowed: 30 days

(c) Invoice price of the goods: £2,000 (the invoice will be issued at this price when the goods are delivered)

(d) Cash discount offered: 4% discount for prompt payment

1.9 A has the choice between:

(a) Holding on to his money for 30 days and then paying the full £2,000.

(b) Paying £2,000 less 4% (£1,920) now.

This is a financing decision about whether it is worthwhile for A to save £80 by paying its debts sooner, or whether it can employ its cash more usefully for 30 days, and pay the debt at the latest acceptable moment.

1.10 If A decides to take the cash discount, he will pay £1,920, instead of the invoiced amount £2,000. The cash discount received (£80) will be accounted for in the books of A as follows.

(a) In the trading account, the cost of purchases will be at the invoiced price of £2,000. When the invoice for £2,000 is received by A, it will be recorded in his books of account at that price, and the subsequent financing decision about accepting the cash discount is ignored.

(b) In the profit and loss account, the cash discount received is shown as though it were income received. There is no expense in the P & L account from which the cash discount can be deducted, and so there is no alternative other than to show the discount received as income.

1.11 In our example, we would have:

	£
Cost of purchase from B by A (trading account)	2,000
Discount received (income in the P & L account)	(80)
Net cost	1,920

Settlement discounts received are accounted for in exactly the same way as cash discounts received.

Cash discounts and settlement discounts allowed

1.12 The same principle is applied in accounting for cash discounts or settlement discounts allowed to customers. Goods are sold at a trade price, and the offer of a discount on that price is a matter of financing policy for the business and not a matter of trading policy.

1.13 Suppose that X sells goods to Y at a price of £5,000. Y is allowed 60 days' credit before payment, but is also offered a settlement discount of 2% for payment within 10 days of the invoice date.

X will issue an invoice to Y for £5,000 when the goods are sold. X has no idea whether or not Y will take advantage of the discount. In trading terms, and in terms of the amount charged in the invoice to Y, Y is a debtor for £5,000.

1.14 If Y subsequently decides to take the discount, he will pay £5,000 less 2% - ie £4,900 - ten days later. The discount allowed (£100) will be accounted for by X as follows.

(a) In the trading account, sales will be valued at their full invoice price, £5,000.
(b) In the profit and loss account, the discount allowed will be shown as an expense.

1.15 In our example, we would have:

	£
Sales (trading account)	5,000
Discounts allowed (P & L account)	(100)
Net sales	4,900

Cash discounts allowed are accounted for in exactly the same way as settlement discounts allowed.

Exercise 1

You are required to prepare the trading, profit and loss account of Seesaw Timber Merchants for the year ended 31 March 20X6, given the following information.

	£
Goods in stock, 1 April 20X5	18,000
Purchases at gross cost	120,000
Trade discounts received	4,000
Cash and settlement discounts received	1,500
Goods in stock, 31 March 20X6	25,000
Cash sales	34,000
Credit sales at invoice price	150,000
Cash and settlement discounts allowed	8,000
Selling expenses	32,000
Administrative expenses	40,000
Drawings by proprietor, Tim Burr	22,000

Solution

SEESAW TIMBER MERCHANTS
TRADING, PROFIT AND LOSS ACCOUNT
FOR THE YEAR ENDED 31 MARCH 20X6

	£	£
Sales (note 1)		184,000
Opening stocks	18,000	
Purchases (note 2)	116,000	
	134,000	
Less closing stocks	25,000	
Cost of goods sold		109,000
Gross profit		75,000
Discounts received		1,500
		76,500
Expenses		
Selling expenses	32,000	
Administrative expenses	40,000	
Discounts allowed	8,000	
		80,000
Net loss transferred to balance sheet (note 3)		(3,500)

Notes

1 £(34,000 + 150,000)
2 £(120,000 - 4,000)
3 Drawings are not an expense, but an appropriation of profit.

Recording discounts in the cash book

1.16 Discounts allowed and received are recorded in a column in the cash book on the receipts and payments side respectively.

1.17 Discounts allowed on sales are shown in a separate column which has nothing to do with the actual monies received; it is a *memorandum* column. The discounts allowed column is required to show why the full amount of a debt has not been received from a customer. A list of the debts owed to the company will be recorded in the sales ledger. The discount allowed will be posted to the sales ledger thus clearing the total debt.

1.18 Similarly discounts received from suppliers are recorded in a separate column on the payments side of the cash book. Again this is a memorandum column showing why the full amount owed has not been paid to the supplier.

1.19 Examples of discount columns in cash books are given in Chapter 13 on control accounts, where it will be made clear how the discounts are posted.

2 ACCOUNTING FOR BAD AND DOUBTFUL DEBTS *6/00*

2.1 Customers who buy goods on credit might fail to pay for them, perhaps out of dishonesty or perhaps because they have gone bankrupt and cannot pay. Customers in another country might be prevented from paying by the unexpected introduction of foreign exchange control restrictions by their country's government during the credit period.

For one reason or another, a business might decide to give up expecting payment and to write the debt off as a 'lost cause'.

Writing off bad debts

2.2 If Alfred's Mini-Cab Service sends an invoice for £300 to a customer who subsequently does a 'moonlight flit' from his office premises, never to be seen or heard of again, the debt of £300 must be written off. It might seem sensible to record the business transaction as:

Sales £(300 – 300) = £0.

2.3 However, bad debts written off are accounted for as follows.

(a) Sales are shown at their invoice value in the trading account. The sale has been made, and gross profit should be earned. The subsequent failure to collect the debt is a separate matter, which is reported in the P & L account.

(b) Bad debts written off are shown as an expense in the profit and loss account.

2.4 In our example of Alfred's Mini-Cab Service:

	£
Sale (in the trading account)	300
Bad debt written off (expense in the P & L account)	300
Net profit on this transaction	0

2.5 Obviously, when a debt is written off, the value of the debtor as a current asset falls to zero. If the debt is expected to be uncollectable, its 'net realisable value' is nil, and so it has a zero balance sheet value.

Bad debts written off: ledger accounting entries

2.6 For bad debts written off, there is a bad debts account. The double-entry bookkeeping is fairly straightforward, but there are two separate transactions to record.

(a) When it is decided that a particular debt will not be paid, the customer is no longer called an outstanding debtor, and becomes a bad debt. We therefore:

DEBIT Bad debts account (expense)
CREDIT Debtors account

(b) At the end of the accounting period, the balance on the bad debts account is transferred to the P & L ledger account (like all other expense accounts):

DEBIT P & L account
CREDIT Bad debts account.

Example: bad debts written off

2.7 At 1 October 20X5 a business had total outstanding debts of £8,600. During the year to 30 September 20X6:

(a) Credit sales amounted to £44,000.

(b) Payments from various debtors amounted to £49,000.

(c) Two debts, for £180 and £420, were declared bad and the customers are no longer purchasing goods from the company. These are to be written off.

Required

Prepare the debtors account and the bad debts account for the year.

Solution

2.8

DEBTORS

	£		£
Opening balance b/f	8,600	Cash	49,000
Sales	44,000	Bad debts	180
		Bad debts	420
		Closing balance c/d	3,000
	52,600		52,600
Opening balance b/d	3,000		

BAD DEBTS

	£		£
Debtors	180	P & L a/c: bad debts written off	600
Debtors	420		
	600		600

2.9 In the sales ledger, the personal accounts of the customers whose debts are bad will be taken off the ledger. The business should then take steps to ensure that it does not sell goods on credit to those customers again.

Bad debts written off and subsequently paid

2.10 A bad debt which has been written off might occasionally be unexpectedly paid. The only accounting problem to consider is when a debt written off as bad in one accounting period is subsequently paid in a later accounting period. The amount paid should be recorded as additional income in the profit and loss account of the period in which the payment is received.

2.11 For example, a trading, profit and loss account for the Blacksmith's Forge for the year to 31 December 20X5 could be prepared as shown below from the following information.

	£
Stocks of goods in hand, 1 January 20X5	6,000
Purchases of goods	122,000
Stocks of goods in hand, 31 December 20X5	8,000
Cash sales	100,000
Credit sales	70,000
Discounts allowed	1,200
Discounts received	5,000
Bad debts written off	9,000
Debts paid in 20X5 which were previously written off as bad in 20X4	2,000
Other expenses	31,800

BLACKSMITH'S FORGE
TRADING, PROFIT AND LOSS ACCOUNT FOR THE YEAR ENDED 31.12.20X5

	£	£
Sales		170,000
Opening stock	6,000	
Purchases	122,000	
	128,000	
Less closing stock	8,000	
Cost of goods sold		120,000
Gross profit		50,000
Add: discounts received		5,000
debts paid, previously written off as bad		2,000
		57,000
Expenses		
Discounts allowed	1,200	
Bad debts written off	9,000	
Other expenses	31,800	
		42,000
Net profit		15,000

A provision for doubtful debts

2.12 When bad debts are written off, specific debts owed to the business are identified as unlikely ever to be collected.

However, because of the risks involved in selling goods on credit, and it might be accepted that a certain percentage of outstanding debts at any time are unlikely to be collected. Although it might be estimated that, say, 5% of debts will turn out bad, the business will not know until later which *specific* debts are bad.

2.13 Suppose that a business commences operations on 1 July 20X4, and in the twelve months to 30 June 20X5 makes sales of £300,000 (all on credit) and writes off bad debts amounting to £6,000. Cash received from customers during the year is £244,000, so that at 30 June 20X5, the business has outstanding debtors of £50,000.

	£
Credit sales during the year	300,000
Add debtors at 1 July 20X4	0
Total debts owed to the business	300,000
Less cash received from credit customers	244,000
	56,000
Less bad debts written off	6,000
Debtors outstanding at 30 June 20X5	50,000

Now, some of these outstanding debts might turn out to be bad. The business does not know on 30 June 20X5 which specific debts in the total £50,000 owed will be bad, but it might guess (from experience perhaps) that 5% of debts will eventually be found to be bad.

2.14 When a business expects bad debts amongst its current debtors, but does not yet know which specific debts will be bad, it can make a *provision* for doubtful debts as a prudent precaution. The business will be more likely to avoid claiming profits which subsequently fail to materialise because some debts turn out to be bad.

2.15 (a) When a provision is first made, the amount of this initial provision is charged as an expense in the profit and loss account of the business, for the period in which the provision is created.

(b) When a provision already exists, but is subsequently increased in size, the amount of the *increase* in provision is charged as an expense in the profit and loss account, for the period in which the increased provision is made.

(c) When a provision already exists, but is subsequently reduced in size, the amount of the *decrease* in provision is recorded as an item of 'income' in the profit and loss account, for the period in which the reduction in provision is made.

2.16 The balance sheet, as well as the profit and loss account of a business, must be adjusted to show a provision for doubtful debts. *The value of debtors in the balance sheet must be shown after deducting the provision for doubtful debts.* This is because the net realisable value of all the debtors of the business is estimated to be less than their 'sales value'. After all, this is the reason for making the provision in the first place.

2.17 In the example above (in paragraph 2.13) the newly created provision for doubtful debts at 30 June 20X5 will be 5% of £50,000 = £2,500. This means that although total debtors are £50,000, eventual payment of only £47,500 is expected.

(a) In the P & L account, the newly created provision of £2,500 will be shown as an expense.

(b) In the balance sheet, debtors will be shown as:

	£
Total debtors at 30 June 20X5	50,000
Less provision for doubtful debts	2,500
	47,500

Provision for doubtful debts: ledger accounting entries

2.18 The provision account is opened by the following entries:

DEBIT	Doubtful debts account (expense)
CREDIT	Provision for doubtful debts

When preparing a balance sheet, the credit balance on the provision account is deducted from the total debit balances in the debtors ledger (as in 2.17 (b) above).

2.19 *In subsequent years*, adjustments may be needed to the amount of the provision. The procedure to be followed then is as follows.

(a) Calculate the new provision required.

(b) Compare it with the existing balance on the provision account (ie the balance b/f from the previous accounting period).

(c) Calculate increase or decrease required.

(i) If a higher provision is required now:

CREDIT	Provision for doubtful debts
DEBIT	P & L account

with the amount of the increase.

(ii) If a lower provision is needed now than before:

DEBIT	Provision for doubtful debts
CREDIT	P & L account

with the amount of the decrease.

Example: accounting entries for provision for doubtful debts

2.20 Alex Gullible has total debtors' balances outstanding at 31 December 20X2 of £28,000. He believes that about 1% of these balances will not be collected and wishes to make an appropriate provision. Before now, he has not made any provision for doubtful debts at all.

On 31 December 20X3 his debtors balances amount to £40,000. His experience during the year has convinced him that a provision of 5% should be made.

What accounting entries should Alex make on 31 December 20X2 and 31 December 20X3, and what figures for debtors will appear in his balance sheets as at those dates?

Solution

2.21 *At 31 December 20X2*

Provision required = 1% × £28,000
= £280

Alex will make the following entries.

DEBIT	P & L account (doubtful debts)	£280	
CREDIT	Provision for doubtful debts		£280

In the balance sheet debtors will appear as follows under current assets.

	£
Sales ledger balances	28,000
Less provision for doubtful debts	280
	27,720

At 31 December 20X3

Following the procedure described above, Alex will calculate as follows.

	£
Provision required now (5% × £40,000)	2,000
Existing provision	(280)
∴ Additional provision required	1,720

He will make the following entries.

DEBIT	P & L account (doubtful debts)	£1,720	
CREDIT	Provision for doubtful debts		£1,720

The provision account will by now appear as follows.

PROVISION FOR DOUBTFUL DEBTS

		£			£
20X2			*20X2*		
31 Dec	Balance c/d	280	31 Dec	P & L account	280
20X3			*20X3*		
31 Dec	Balance c/d	2,000	1 Jan	Balance b/d	280
			31 Dec	P & L account	1,720
		2,000			2,000
			20X4		
			1 Jan	Balance b/d	2,000

For the balance sheet debtors will be valued as follows.

	£
Sales ledger balances	40,000
Less provision for doubtful debts	2,000
	38,000

2.22 In practice, it is unnecessary to show the total debtors balances and the provision as separate items in the balance sheet. A balance sheet would normally show only the net figure (£27,720 in 20X2, £38,000 in 20X3). However, it might be good examination practice at this stage in your studies to show the provision in the balance sheet, so that the examiner/marker can check that you have got your accounting procedures correct.

Example: provision for doubtful debts

2.23 Corin Flakes owns and runs the Aerobic Health Foods Shop in Dundee. He commenced trading on 1 January 20X1, selling health foods to customers, most of whom make use of a credit facility that Corin offers. (Customers are allowed to purchase up to £200 of goods on credit but must repay a certain proportion of their outstanding debt every month.)

This credit system gives rise to a large number of bad debts, and Corin Flake's results for his first three years of operations are as follows.

Year to 31 December 20X1	
Gross profit	£27,000
Bad debts written off	£8,000
Debts owed by customers as at 31 December 20X1	£40,000
Provision for doubtful debts	2½% of outstanding debtors
Other expenses	£20,000
Year to 31 December 20X2	
Gross profit	£45,000
Bad debts written off	£10,000
Debts owed by customers as at 31 December 20X2	£50,000
Provision for doubtful debts	2½% of outstanding debtors
Other expenses	£28,750
Year to 31 December 20X3	
Gross profit	£60,000
Bad debts written off	£11,000
Debts owed by customers as at 31 December 20X3	£30,000
Provision for doubtful debts	3% of outstanding debtors
Other expenses	£32,850

Required

For each of these three years, prepare the profit and loss account of the business, and state the value of debtors appearing in the balance sheet as at 31 December.

Solution

2.24 AEROBIC HEALTH FOOD SHOP
PROFIT AND LOSS ACCOUNTS FOR THE YEARS ENDED 31 DECEMBER

	20X1		*20X2*		*20X3*	
	£	£	£	£	£	£
Gross profit		27,000		45,000		60,000
Reduction in provision for doubtful debts*						350
						60,350
Expenses:						
Bad debts written off	8,000		10,000		11,000	
Increase in provision for doubtful debts*	1,000		250		-	
Other expenses	20,000		28,750		32,850	
		29,000		39,000		43,850
Net(loss)/profit		(2,000)		6,000		16,500

*At 1 January 20X1 when Corin began trading the provision for doubtful debts was nil. At 31 December 20X1 the provision required was 2½% of £40,000 = £1,000. The increase in the provision is therefore £1,000. At 31 December 20X2 the provision required was 2½% of £50,000 = £1,250. The 20X1 provision must therefore be increased by £250. At 31 December 20X3 the provision required is 3% × £30,000 = £900. The 20X2 provision is therefore reduced by £350.

VALUE OF DEBTORS IN THE BALANCE SHEET

	As at 31.12.20X1	*As at 31.12.20X2*	*As at 31.12.20X3*
	£	£	£
Total value of debtors	40,000	50,000	30,000
Less provision for doubtful debts	1,000	1,250	900
Balance sheet value	39,000	48,750	29,100

2.25 Now try the following exercise on provision for doubtful debts for yourself.

Exercise 2

Horace Goodrunning fears that his business will suffer an increase in defaulting debtors in the future and so he decides to make a provision for doubtful debts of 2% of outstanding debtors at the balance sheet date from 28 February 20X6. On 28 February 20X8, Horace decides that the provision has been over-estimated and he reduces it to 1% of outstanding debtors. Outstanding debtors balances at the various balance sheet dates are as follows.

	£
28.2.20X6	15,200
28.2.20X7	17,100
28.2.20X8	21,400

You are required to show extracts from the following accounts for each of the three years above.

(a) Debtors
(b) Provision for doubtful debts
(c) Profit and loss

Show how debtors would appear in the balance sheet at the end of each year.

Solution

The entries for the three years are denoted by (a), (b) and (c) in each account.

DEBTORS (EXTRACT)

			£	£
(a)	28.2.20X6	Balance	15,200	
(b)	28.2.20X7	Balance	17,100	
(c)	28.2.20X8	Balance	21,400	

PROVISION FOR DOUBTFUL DEBTS

			£			£
(a)	28.2.20X6	Balance c/d		28.2.20X6	Profit and loss	304
		(2% of 15,200)	304			
			304			304
(b)	28.2.20X7	Balance c/d		1.3.20X6	Balance b/d	304
		(2% of 17,100)	342	28.2.20X7	Profit and loss (note (i))	38
			342			342
(c)	28.2.20X8	Profit and loss (note (ii))	128	1 .3.20X7	Balance b/d	342
	28.2.20X8	Balance c/d				
		(1% of 21,400)	214			
			342			342
				1.3.20X8	Balance b/d	214

PROFIT AND LOSS (EXTRACT)

		£
28.2.20X6	Provision for doubtful debts	304
28.2.20X7	Provision for doubtful debts	38
28.2.20X8	Provision for doubtful debts	(128)

Notes

(i) The increase in the provision is £(342 - 304) = £38
(ii) The decrease in the provision is £(342 - 214) = £128
(iii) We calculate the net debtors figure for inclusion in the balance sheet as follows.

	20X6	*20X7*	*20X8*
	£	£	£
Current assets			
Debtors	15,200	17,100	21,400
Less provision for doubtful debts	304	342	214
	14,896	16,758	21,186

Other provisions

2.26 A provision for doubtful debts is not the only type of provision you will come across in accounting. Companies legislation defines a provision as 'any amount written off or retained by way of providing for depreciation, renewals or diminution in value of assets or retained by way of providing for any known liability of which the amount cannot be determined with substantial accuracy'.

2.27 For most businesses, by far the largest provision in their accounts is the provision for depreciation which is described in Chapter 11.

You should now try to use what you have learned to attempt a solution to the following exercise, which involves preparing a trading, profit and loss account and balance sheet.

Exercise 3

The financial affairs of Newbegin Tools prior to the commencement of trading were as follows.

NEWBEGIN TOOLS
BALANCE SHEET AS AT 1 AUGUST 20X5

	£	£
Fixed assets		
Motor vehicle	2,000	
Shop fittings	3,000	
		5,000
Current assets		
Stocks	12,000	
Cash	1,000	
	13,000	
Current liabilities		
Bank overdraft	2,000	
Trade creditors	4,000	
	6,000	
Net current assets		7,000
		12,000
Financed by		
Capital		12,000

At the end of six months the business had made the following transactions.

(a) Goods were purchased on credit at a gross amount of £10,000.

(b) Trade discount received was 2% on this gross amount and there was a settlement discount received of 5% on settling debts to suppliers of £8,000. These were the only payments to suppliers in the period.

(c) Closing stocks of goods were valued at £5,450.

(d) Cash sales and credit sales together totalled £27,250.

(e) Outstanding debtors balances at 31 January 20X6 amounted to £3,250 of which £250 were to be written off.

(f) A further provision for doubtful debts is to be made amounting to 2% of the remaining outstanding debtors.

(g) Cash payments were made in respect of the following expenses.

		£
(i)	Stationery, postage and wrapping	500
(ii)	Telephone charges	200
(iii)	Electricity	600
(iv)	Cleaning and refreshments	150

(h) Cash drawings by the proprietor, Alf Newbegin, amounted to £6,000.

(i) The outstanding overdraft balance as at 1 August 20X5 was paid off. Interest charges and bank charges on the overdraft amounted to £40.

Alf Newbegin knew the balance of cash on hand at 31 January 20X6 but he wanted to know if the business had made a profit for the six months that it had been trading, and so he asked his friend, Harry Oldhand, if he could tell him.

Prepare the trading, profit and loss account of Newbegin Tools for the six months to 31 January 20X6 and a balance sheet as at that date.

Solution

The trading, profit and loss account should be fairly straightforward.

NEWBEGIN TOOLS
TRADING AND PROFIT AND LOSS ACCOUNT
FOR THE SIX MONTHS ENDED 31 JANUARY 20X6

	£	£
Sales		27,250
Opening stocks	12,000	
Purchases (note (a))	9,800	
	21,800	
Less closing stocks	5,450	
Cost of goods sold		16,350
Gross profit		10,900
Discounts received (note (b))		400
		11,300
Electricity (note (c))	600	
Stationery, postage and wrapping	500	
Bad debts written off	250	
Provision for doubtful debts (note (d))	60	
Telephone charges	200	
Cleaning and refreshments	150	
Interest and bank charges	40	
		1,800
Net profit		9,500

Notes

(a) Purchases at cost £10,000 less 2% trade discount.

(b) 5% of £8,000 = £400

(c) Expenses are grouped into sales and distribution expenses (here assumed to be electricity, stationery and postage, bad debts and provision for doubtful debts) administration expenses (here assumed to be telephone charges and cleaning) and finance charges.

(d) 2% of £3,000 = £60.

The preparation of a balance sheet is not so easy, because we must calculate the value of creditors and cash in hand.

(a) *Creditors as at 31 January 20X6*

The amount owing to creditors is the sum of the amount owing at the beginning of the period, plus the cost of purchases during the period (net of all discounts), less the payments already made for purchases. If you think carefully about this, you might see that this calculation is logical. What is still owed is the total amount of costs incurred less payments already made.

	£
Creditors as at 1 August 20X5	4,000
Add purchases during the period, net of trade discount	9,800
	13,800
Less settlement discounts received	(400)
	13,400
Less payments to creditors during the period*	(7,600)
	5,800

* £8,000 less cash discount of £400.

(b) *Cash at bank and in hand at 31 January 20X6*

This too requires a fairly lengthy calculation. You need to identify cash payments received and cash payments made.

		£
(i)	*Cash received from sales*	
	Total sales in the period	27,250
	Add debtors as at 1 August 20X5	0
		27,250
	Less unpaid debts as at 31 January 20X6	3,250
	Cash received	24,000
(ii)	*Cash paid*	
	Trade creditors (see (a))	7,600
	Stationery, postage and wrapping	500
	Telephone charges	200
	Electricity	600
	Cleaning and refreshments	150
	Bank charges and interest	40
	Bank overdraft repaid	2,000
	Drawings by proprietor	6,000
		17,090

Note. It is easy to forget some of these payments, especially drawings.

		£
(iii)	Cash in hand at 1 August 20X5	1,000
	Cash received in the period	24,000
		25,000
	Cash paid in the period	(17,090)
	Cash at bank and in hand as at 31 January 20X6	7,910

(c) When bad debts are written off, the value of outstanding debtors must be reduced by the amount written off. This is because the debtors are no longer expected to pay, and it would be misleading and absurd to show them in the balance sheet as current assets of the business for which cash payment is expected within one year. Debtors in the balance sheet will be valued at £3,000 (£3,250 – bad debt £250) less the provision for doubtful debts of £60 - ie at £2,940.

(d) Fixed assets should be depreciated. However, in this exercise depreciation has been ignored.

NEWBEGIN TOOLS
BALANCE SHEET AS AT 31 JANUARY 20X6

	£	£
Fixed assets		
Motor vehicles	2,000	
Shop fittings	3,000	
		5,000
Current assets		
Stocks	5,450	
Debtors	2,940	
Cash	7,910	
		16,300
		21,300
Current liabilities		
Trade creditors		(5,800)
		15,500
Capital		
Capital at 1 August 20X5		12,000
Net profit for the period		9,500
		21,500
Less drawings		6,000
Capital at 31 January 20X6		15,500

The bank overdraft has now been repaid and is therefore not shown.

Chapter roundup

- In this chapter, the following terms were defined.
    - *Trade discount* is a reduction in the catalogue price of an article, given by a wholesaler or manufacturer to a retailer. It is often given in return for bulk purchase orders.
    - *Cash discount* is a reduction in the amount payable for the purchase of goods or services in return for payment in cash rather than taking credit.
    - *Settlement discount* is a reduction in the amount payable for the purchase of goods or services in return for prompt payment within an agreed credit period.
    - *Bad debts* are specific debts owed to a business which it decides are never going to be paid.
    - *Doubtful debts* are debts which might become bad in the future but are not yet bad.
    - A *provision* is an amount written off to provide for depreciation or the fall in value of an asset, or to provide for any known liability of uncertain value. The amount is written off by:
        - Charging the amount of the extra provision as an expense in the P & L account, and also
        - Reducing the value of the asset in the balance sheet by the amount of the provision.
- We looked at the accounting treatment of each of these items.
    - *Trade discounts received* are deducted from the cost of purchases. *Cash and settlement discounts received* are included as 'other income' of the period in the profit and loss account. Similarly, cash and settlement discounts allowed are shown as expenses in the profit and loss account.
    - *Bad debts written off* are an expense in the profit and loss account.
- An *increase* in the provision for doubtful debts is an expense in the profit and loss account whereas a decrease in the provision for doubtful debts is shown as 'other income' in the P & L account.
- *Debtors* are valued in the balance sheet after deducting any provision for doubtful debts.

Test your knowledge

1 When is a cash sale recorded? (see introduction)

2 When is a purchase on credit recorded? (introduction)

3 Define a trade discount. (1.2)

4 How does cash discount differ from settlement discount? (1.4)

5 Explain how cash discount allowed is accounted for. (1.14-1.15)

6 What is the double entry to record a bad debt written off? (2.6)

7 If a doubtful debts provision is increased, what is the effect on the P & L account? (2.15)

Now try illustrative question 11 at the end of the Study Text

Chapter 10

STOCKS

This chapter covers the following topics.

1 Accounting for opening and closing stocks

2 Stocktaking

3 Valuing stocks

Introduction

Stock is one of the most important assets in a company's balance sheet. As we have seen it also affects the profit and loss account.

In an earlier chapter, we saw that in order to calculate gross profit it is necessary to work out the cost of goods sold, and in order to calculate the cost of goods sold it is necessary to have values for the opening stock (ie stock in hand at the beginning of the accounting period) and closing stock (ie stock in hand at the end of the accounting period).

You should remember that the trading part of a profit and loss account includes:

	£
Opening stock	X
Plus purchases	X
Less closing stock	(X)
Equals cost of goods sold	X

However, just writing down this formula hides three basic problems.

(a) How do you manage to get a precise count of stock in hand at any one time?
(b) Even once it has been counted, how do you value the stock?
(c) Assuming the stock is given a value, how does the double entry bookkeeping for stock work?

The purpose of this chapter is to answer all three of these questions. In order to make the presentation a little easier to follow, it is convenient to tackle the last question first.

1 ACCOUNTING FOR OPENING AND CLOSING STOCKS 6/98, 6/99

Ledger accounting for stocks

1.1 It has already been shown that purchases are introduced to the trading account by means of the double entry:

DEBIT	Trading account	£X	
CREDIT	Purchases account		£X

1.2 But what about opening and closing stocks? How are their values accounted for in the double entry bookkeeping system? The answer is that a stock account must be kept. This stock account is only ever used at the end of an accounting period, when the business counts up and values the stock in hand, in a stocktake.

(a) When a stocktake is made, the business will have a value for its closing stock, and the double entry is:

DEBIT	Stock account (closing stock value)	£X	
CREDIT	Trading account		£X

However, rather than show the closing stock as a 'plus' value in the trading account (eg by adding it to sales) it is usual to show it as a 'minus' figure in arriving at cost of sales. This is illustrated in the formula in the introduction. The debit balance on stock account represents an asset, which will be shown as part of current assets in the balance sheet.

(b) Closing stock at the end of one period becomes opening stock at the start of the next period. The stock account remains unchanged until the end of the next period, when the value of opening stock is taken to the trading account; ie

DEBIT	Trading account	£X	
CREDIT	Stock account (value of opening stock)		£X

1.3 Partly as an example of how this ledger accounting for stocks works, and partly as revision on ledger accounting in general, try the following exercise. It is an example from an earlier part of this text which has had a closing stocks figure added.

Exercise

A business is established with capital of £2,000 and this amount is paid into a business bank account by the proprietor. During the first year's trading, the following transactions occurred:

	£
Purchases of goods for resale, on credit	4,300
Payments to trade creditors	3,600
Sales, all on credit	4,000
Payments from debtors	3,200
Fixed assets purchased for cash	1,500
Other expenses, all paid in cash	900

The bank has provided an overdraft facility of up to £3,000.

All 'other expenses' relate to the current year.

Closing stocks of goods are valued at £1,800. (As this is the first year of the business, there are no opening stocks.)

Ignore depreciation and drawings.

Required

Prepare the ledger accounts, a trading, profit and loss account for the year and a balance sheet as at the end of the year.

Solution

CASH

	£		£
Capital	2,000	Trade creditors	3,600
Debtors	3,200	Fixed assets	1,500
Balance c/d	800	Other expenses	900
	6,000		6,000
		Balance b/d	800

CAPITAL

	£		£
Balance c/d	2,600	Cash	2,000
		P & L a/c	600
	2,600		2,600
		Balance b/d	2,600

TRADE CREDITORS

	£		£
Cash	3,600	Purchases	4,300
Balance c/d	700		
	4,300		4,300
		Balance b/d	700

PURCHASES ACCOUNT

	£		£
Trade creditors	4,300	Trading a/c	4,300

FIXED ASSETS

	£		£
Cash	1,500	Balance c/d	1,500
Balance b/d	1,500		

SALES

	£		£
Trading a/c	4,000	Debtors	4,000

DEBTORS

	£		£
Sales	4,000	Cash	3,200
		Balance c/d	800
	4,000		4,000
Balance b/d	800		

OTHER EXPENSES

	£		£
Cash	900	P & L a/c	900

TRADING, PROFIT AND LOSS ACCOUNT

	£		£
Purchases account	4,300	Sales	4,000
Gross profit c/d	1,500	Closing stock (stock account)	1,800
	5,800		5,800
Other expenses	900	Gross profit b/d	1,500
Net profit (transferred to capital account)	600		
	1,500		1,500

Alternatively, closing stock could be shown as a minus value on the debit side of the trading account, instead of a credit entry, giving purchases £4,300 less closing stock £1,800 equals cost of goods sold £2,500.

STOCK ACCOUNT

	£		£
Trading account (closing stock)	1,800	Balance c/d	1,800
Balance b/d	1,800		

BALANCE SHEET AS AT THE END OF THE PERIOD

	£	£
Fixed assets		1,500
Current assets		
Goods in stock	1,800	
Debtors	800	
	2,600	
Current liabilities		
Bank overdraft	800	
Trade creditors	700	
	1,500	
Net assets		1,100
		2,600
Capital		
At start of period		2,000
Profit for period		600
		2,600

Make sure you can see what has happened here. The balance on the stock account was £1,800, which appears in the balance sheet as a current asset. As it happens, the £1,800 closing stock was the only entry in the stock account - there was no figure for opening stock.

If there had been, it would have been eliminated by transferring it as a debit balance to the trading account, ie:

DEBIT Trading account (with value of opening stock)
CREDIT Stock account (with value of opening stock)

The debit in the trading account would then have increased the cost of sales, ie opening stock is added to purchases in calculating cost of sales. Again, this is illustrated in the formula: opening stock + purchases – closing stock = cost of sales.

1.4 So if we can establish the value of stocks on hand, the above paragraphs and exercise show us how to account for that value. That takes care of one of the problems noted in the introduction of this chapter. But now another of those problems becomes apparent - how do we establish the value of stocks on hand? The first step must be to establish how much stock is held.

2 STOCKTAKING

2.1 Business trading is a continuous activity, but accounting statements must be drawn up at a particular date. In preparing a balance sheet it is necessary to 'freeze' the activity of a business so as to determine its assets and liabilities at a given moment. This includes establishing the quantities of stocks on hand, which can create problems.

2.2 The continuous nature of trading activity means that stock movements will not necessarily cease during the time that the physical stocktake is in progress. Two possible solutions are as follows.

(a) Close down the business while the count takes place.
(b) Keep detailed records of stock movements during the course of the stocktake.

2.3 Closing down the business for a short period for a stocktake (eg over a weekend or at Christmas) is considerably easier than trying to keep detailed records of stock movements during a stocktake. So most businesses prefer that method unless they happen to keep detailed records of stock movements anyway (for example, because they wish to keep strict control on stock movements).

2.4 In more complicated cases, where a business holds considerable quantities of varied stock, an alternative approach to establishing stock quantities is to maintain continuous stock records. This means that a card is kept for every item of stock, showing receipts and issues from the stores, and a running total. A few stock items are counted each day to make sure their record cards are correct - this is called a 'continuous' stocktake because it is spread out over the year rather than completed in one stocktake at a designated time.

2.5 One obstacle is overcome once a business has established how much stock is on hand. However another of the problems noted in the introduction immediately raises its head. What value should the business place on those stocks?

3 VALUING STOCKS 6/97, 6/98, 6/00

The basic rule

3.1 There are several methods which, in theory, might be used for the valuation of stock items.

(a) Stocks might be valued at their expected selling price.

(b) Stocks might be valued at their expected selling price, less any costs still to be incurred in getting them ready for sale and then selling them. This amount is referred to as the *net realisable value (NRV)* of the stocks.

(c) Stocks might be valued at their historical cost (ie the cost at which they were originally bought).

(d) Stocks might be valued at the amount it would cost to replace them. This amount is referred to as the current replacement cost of stocks.

3.2 Current replacement costs are not used in the type of accounts dealt with in this syllabus.

3.3 The use of selling prices in stock valuation is ruled out because this would create a profit for the business before the stock has been sold.

3.4 A simple example might help to explain this. Suppose that a trader buys two items of stock, each costing £100. He can sell them for £140 each, but in the accounting period we shall consider, he has only sold one of them. The other is closing stock in hand.

3.5 Since only one item has been sold, you might think it is common sense that profit ought to be £40. But if closing stock is valued at selling price, profit would be £80 - ie profit would be taken on the closing stock as well.

	£	£
Sales		140
Opening stock	-	
Purchases (2 × 100)	200	
	200	
Less closing stock (at selling price)	140	
Cost of sale		60
Profit		80

This would contradict the accounting concept of prudence - because a profit is being claimed before the item has actually been sold.

3.6 The same objection *usually* applies to the use of NRV in stock valuation. Say that the item purchased for £100 requires £5 of further expenditure in getting it ready for sale and then selling it (eg £5 of processing and distribution costs). If its expected selling price is £140, its NRV is £(140 – 5) = £135. To value it at £135 in the balance sheet would still be to anticipate a £35 profit.

3.7 We are left with historical cost as the normal basis of stock valuation. The only time when historical cost is not used is in the exceptional cases where the prudence concept requires a lower value to be used.

3.8 Staying with the example in Paragraph 3.6, suppose that the market in this kind of product suddenly slumps and the item's expected selling price is only £90. The item's NRV is then £(90 – 5) = £85 and the business has in effect made a loss of £15 (£100 – £85). The prudence concept requires that losses should be recognised as soon as they are foreseen. This can be achieved by valuing the stock item in the balance sheet at its NRV of £85.

3.9 The argument developed above suggests that the rule to follow is that stocks should be valued at cost, or if lower, net realisable value. The accounting treatment of stock is governed by an accounting standard, SSAP 9 *Stocks and long-term contracts*. SSAP 9 states that *stock should be valued at the lower of cost and net realisable value*. This is an important rule and one which you should learn by heart.

Applying the basic valuation rule

3.10 If a business has many stock items on hand the comparison of cost and NRV should theoretically be carried out for each item separately. It is not sufficient to compare the total cost of all stock items with their total NRV. An example will show why.

3.11 Suppose a company has four items of stock on hand at the end of its accounting period. Their cost and NRVs are as follows.

Stock item	*Cost*	*NRV*	*Lower of cost/NRV*
	£	£	£
1	27	32	27
2	14	8	8
3	43	55	43
4	29	40	29
	113	135	107

3.12 It would be incorrect to compare total costs (£113) with total NRV (£135) and to state stocks at £113 in the balance sheet. The company can foresee a loss of £6 on item 2 and this should be recognised. If the four items are taken together in total the loss on item 2 is masked by the anticipated profits on the other items. By performing the cost/NRV comparison for each item separately the prudent valuation of £107 can be derived. This is the value which should appear in the balance sheet.

3.13 However, for a company with large amounts of stock this procedure may be impracticable. In this case it is acceptable to group similar items into categories and perform the comparison of cost and NRV category by category, rather than item by item.

3.14 So have we now solved the problem of how a business should value its stocks? It seems that all the business has to do is to choose the lower of cost and net realisable value. This is true as far as it goes, but there is one further problem, perhaps not so easy to foresee: for a given item of stock, what was the cost?

Determining the purchase cost

3.15 Stock may be raw materials or components bought from suppliers, finished goods which have been made by the business but not yet sold, or work in the process of production, but only part-completed (this type of stock is called work in progress or WIP). It will simplify matters, however, if we think about the historical cost of purchased raw materials and components, which ought to be their purchase price.

3.16 A business may be continually purchasing consignments of a particular component. As each consignment is received from suppliers they are stored in the appropriate bin or on the appropriate shelf or pallet, where they will be mingled with previous consignments. When the storekeeper issues components to production he will simply pull out from the bin the nearest components to hand, which may have arrived in the latest consignment or in an earlier consignment or in several different consignments. Our concern is to devise a pricing technique, a rule of thumb which we can use to attribute a cost to each of the components issued from stores.

3.17 There are several techniques which are used in practice.

(a) *FIFO (first in, first out).* Using this technique, we assume that components are used in the order in which they are received from suppliers. The components issued are deemed to have formed part of the oldest consignment still unused and are costed accordingly.

(b) *Average cost.* As purchase prices change with each new consignment, the average price of components in the bin is constantly changed. Each component in the bin at any moment is assumed to have been purchased at the average price of all components in the bin at that moment.

(c) *LIFO (last in, first out).* This involves the opposite assumption, that components issued to production originally formed part of the most recent delivery, while older consignments lie in the bin undisturbed.

(d) *Standard cost.* A pre-determined standard cost is applied to all stock items. If this standard price differs from prices actually paid during the period it will be necessary to write off the difference as a 'variance' in the profit and loss account.

(e) *Replacement cost.* The arbitrary assumption is made that the cost at which a stock unit was purchased is the amount it would cost to replace it. This is often (but not necessarily) the unit cost of stocks purchased in the next consignment *following* the issue of the component to production. For this reason, a method which produces similar results to replacement costs is called NIFO (next in, first out).

3.18 Any or all of these methods might provide a suitable basis for valuing stocks. But it is worth mentioning here that if you are preparing *financial* accounts you would normally expect to use FIFO or average costs for the balance sheet valuation of stock. SSAP 9 specifically discourages the use of LIFO and replacement costs. (CA 85 allows any method the directors think appropriate, so long as, under the historical cost accounting rules, stock is stated at production cost or purchase price.) You should note furthermore that terms such as LIFO and FIFO refer to *valuation techniques* only. The actual components can be used in any order.

3.19 To illustrate the various pricing methods, the following transactions will be used in each case.

TRANSACTIONS DURING MAY 20X3

	Quantity Units	*Unit cost* £	*Total cost* £	*Market value per unit on date of transactions* £
Opening balance 1 May	100	2.00	200	
Receipts 3 May	400	2.10	840	2.11
Issues 4 May	200			2.11
Receipts 9 May	300	2.12	636	2.15
Issues 11 May	400			2.20
Receipts 18 May	100	2.40	240	2.35
Issues 20 May	100			2.35
Closing balance 31 May	200			2.38
			1,916	

'Receipts' mean goods received into store and 'issues' represent the issue of goods from store.

The problem is to put a valuation on the:

(a) Issues of materials.
(b) Closing stock.

How would issues and closing stock be valued using:

(a) FIFO?

(b) LIFO?
(c) Average cost?
(d) Standard cost?

FIFO (first in, first out)

3.20 FIFO assumes that materials are issued out of stock in the order in which they were delivered into stock, ie issues are priced at the cost of the earliest delivery remaining in stock.

The cost of issues and closing stock value in the example, using FIFO would be as follows (note that o/s stands for opening stock).

Date of issue	*Quantity*	*Value issued*	*Cost of issues*	
	Units	£	£	£
4 May	200	100 o/s at £2	200	
		100 at £2.10	210	
				410
11 May	400	300 at £2.10	630	
		100 at £2.12	212	
				842
20 May	100	100 at £2.12		212
Cost of materials issued				1,464
Closing stock value	200	100 at £2.12	212	
		100 at £2.40	240	
				452
				1,916

Note that the cost of materials issued plus the value of closing stock equals the cost of purchases plus the value of opening stock (£1,916).

LIFO (last in, first out)

3.21 LIFO assumes that materials are issued out of stock in the reverse order to which they were delivered, ie most recent deliveries are issued before earlier ones, and are priced accordingly.

3.22 The following table shows a method of calculating the cost of issues and the closing stock value under the LIFO method.

	Opening stock in units	*Purchases in units 3 May*	*9 May*	*18 May*
Issues	100	400	300	100
4 May		(200)		
11 May		(100)	(300)	
20 May				(100)
Closing stock	100	100	-	-

			£	£
Issues	4 May	200 @ £2.10		420
	11 May	300 @ £2.12	636	
		100 @ £2.10	210	
				846
	20 May	100 @ £2.40		240
Cost of materials issued				1,506
Closing stock valuation:		100 @ £2.00	200	
		100 @ £2.10	210	
				410
				1,916

Again, note that the cost of materials issued plus the value of closing stock equals the cost of purchases plus the value of opening stock (£1,916).

Average cost

3.23 There are various ways in which average costs may be used in pricing stock issues. The most common (cumulative weighted average pricing) is illustrated below.

3.24 The cumulative weighted average pricing method calculates a weighted average price for all units in stock. Issues are priced at this average cost, and the balance of stock remaining would have the same unit valuation.

A new weighted average price is calculated whenever a new delivery of materials into store is received. This is the key feature of cumulative weighted average pricing.

3.25 In our example, issue costs and closing stock values would be as follows.

Date	*Received* Units	*Issued* Units	*Balance* Units	*Total stock value* £	*Unit cost* £	*Price of issue* £
Opening stock			100	200	2.00	
3 May	400			840	2.10	
			500	1,040	2.08 *	
4 May		200		(416)	2.08 **	416
			300	624	2.08	
9 May	300			636	2.12	
			600	1,260	2.10 *	
11 May		400		(840)	2.10 **	840
			200	420	2.10	
18 May	100			240	2.40	
			300	660	2.20 *	
20 May		100		(220)	2.20 **	220
Cost of materials issued						1,476
Closing stock value			200	440	2.10	440
						1,916

* A new unit cost of stock is calculated whenever a new receipt of materials occurs.

** Whenever stocks are issued, the unit value of the items issued is the current weighted average cost per unit at the time of the issue.

For this method too, the cost of materials issued plus the value of closing stock equals the cost of purchases plus the value of opening stock (£1,916).

Standard cost pricing

3.26 Under the standard costing method, all issues are at pre-determined standard price.

3.27 Let us assume in our example that the standard price applied is £2 per unit.

Date of issue	*Quantity issued* Units	*Valuation* £
4 May	200 × £2	400
11 May	400 × £2	800
20 May	100 × £2	200
Cost of materials issued		1,400
Closing stock	200 × £2	400
		1,800

3.28 Under this method the standard cost of the materials issued plus the value of closing stock differs from the combined value of opening stock plus purchases by an amount called the *materials price variance.* If actual costs exceed standard cost, this adjustment will result in a decrease in profit (in this example profit would be reduced by £116). If actual costs are less than standard costs, the adjustment will result in an increase in profit. In this example we have:

	£
Standard cost of issues plus closing stock	1,800
Purchase price of goods plus value of opening stock	1,916
Materials price variance	116

At the end of an accounting period this variance will be taken as an adjustment to the profit and loss account to reconcile actual costs paid.

Summary

3.29

	Issue cost	*Closing stock*	*Variance*	*Total*
FIFO	*1,464*	*452*	-	*1,916*
LIFO	*1,506*	*410*	-	*1,916*
Average cost	*1,476*	*440*	-	*1,916*
Standard cost	*1,400*	*400*	*116*	*1,916*

Stock valuations and profit

3.30 In the previous descriptions of FIFO, LIFO, average costing and so on, the example used raw materials as an illustration. Each method of valuation produced different costs both of closing stocks and also of material issues. Since raw material costs affect the cost of production, and the cost of production works through eventually into the cost of sales, it follows that different methods of stock valuation will provide different profit figures. An example may help to illustrate this point.

Example: stock valuations and profit

3.31 On 1 November 20X2 a company held 300 units of finished goods item No 9639 in stock. These were valued at £12 each. During November 20X2 three batches of finished goods were received into store from the production department as follows:

Date	*Units received*	*Production cost per unit*
10 November	400	£12.50
20 November	400	£14
25 November	400	£15

Goods sold out of stock during November were as follows:

Date	*Units sold*	*Sale price per unit*
14 November	500	£20
21 November	500	£20
28 November	100	£20

What was the profit from selling stock item 9639 in November 20X2, applying the following principles of stock valuation.

(a) FIFO
(b) LIFO
(c) Cumulative weighted average costing

Ignore administration, sales and distribution costs.

Solution

3.32 (a) FIFO:

Date	Issue costs	Issue cost Total £	Closing stock £
14 November	300 units × £12 plus		
	200 units × £12.50	6,100	
21 November	200 units × £12.50 plus		
	300 units × £14	6,700	
28 November	100 units × £14	1,400	
Closing stock	400 units × £15		6,000
		14,200	6,000

(b) LIFO

14 November	400 units × £12.50 plus		
	100 units × £12	6,200	
21 November	400 units × £14 plus		
	100 units × £12	6,800	
28 November	100 units × £15	1,500	
Closing stock	300 units × £15 plus		
	100 units × £12		5,700
		14,500	5,700

(c) Cumulative weighted average costs:

			Unit cost £	Balance in stock £	Total cost of issues £	Closing stock £
1 November	Opening stock	300	12.000	3,600		
10 November		400	12.500	5,000		
		700	12.286	8,600		
14 November		500	12.286	6,143	6,143	
		200	12.286	2,457		
20 November		400	14.000	5,600		
		600	13.428	8,057		
21 November		500	13.428	6,714	6,714	
		100	13.428	1,343		
25 November		400	15.000	6,000		
		500	14.686	7,343		
28 November		100	14.686	1,469	1,469	
30 November		400	14.686	5,874	14,326	5,874

(d)

Profit:	FIFO £	LIFO £	Weighted average £
Opening stock	3,600	3,600	3,600
Cost of production	16,600	16,600	16,600
	20,200	20,200	20,200
Closing stock	6,000	5,700	5,874
Cost of sales	14,200	14,500	14,326
Sales (1,100 × £20)	22,000	22,000	22,000
Profit	7,800	7,500	7,674

3.33 Different stock valuations have produced different cost of sales figures, and therefore different profits. In our example opening stock values are the same, therefore the difference in the amount of profit under each method is the same as the difference in the valuations of closing stock.

3.34 The profit differences are only temporary. In our example, the opening stock in December 20X2 will be £6,000, £5,700 or £5,874, depending on the stock valuation used. Different opening stock values will affect the cost of sales and profits in December, so that in the long run inequalities in costs of sales each month will even themselves out.

Chapter roundup

- The quantity of stocks held at the year end is established by means of a physical count of stock in an annual stocktaking exercise, or by a 'continuous' stocktake.
- The value of these stocks is then calculated, taking the lower of cost and net realisable value (NRV) for each separate item or group of stock items.
- In order to arrive at cost, some rule of thumb must be adopted. The possibilities include FIFO, LIFO, average costs and standard costs. Remember that in *financial* accounts FIFO or average cost should normally be used. These are the two methods which you need to know for the purposes of your examination.
- NRV is the selling price less all costs to completion and less selling costs.
- Cost comprises purchase costs and costs of production.
- The value of closing stocks is accounted for in the nominal ledger by debiting a stock account and crediting the trading account at the end of an accounting period. The stock will therefore always have a debit balance at the end of a period, and this balance will be shown in the balance sheet as a current asset for stocks.
- Opening stocks brought forward in the stock account are transferred to the trading account, and so at the end of the accounting year, the balance on the stock account ceases to be the opening stock value b/f, and becomes instead the closing stock value c/f.

Test your knowledge

1 When is a stock account used? (see para 1.2)

2 How is closing stock incorporated in financial statements? (1.2)

3 What is 'continuous' stocktaking? (2.4)

4 Define net realisable value. (3.1)

5 Why is stock not valued at expected selling price? (3.3 - 3.5)

6 Give five methods of pricing a stock item at historical cost. (3.17)

Now try illustrative question 12 at the end of the Study Text

Chapter 11

FIXED ASSETS - DEPRECIATION, REVALUATION AND DISPOSAL

This chapter covers the following topics.

Introduction

You should by now be familiar with the distinction between fixed and current assets, a fixed asset being one bought for ongoing use in the business. If you are unsure of this look back to Chapter 3 to refresh your memory.

Fixed assets might be held and used by a business for a number of years, but they wear out or lose their usefulness in the course of time. Every tangible fixed asset has a limited life. The only exception is land held freehold or very long leasehold.

The accounts of a business try to recognise that the cost of a fixed asset is gradually consumed as the asset wears out. This is done by gradually writing off the asset's cost in the profit and loss account over several accounting periods. For example, in the case of a machine costing £1,000 and expected to wear out after ten years, it might be appropriate to reduce the balance sheet value by £100 each year. This process is known as depreciation and is the subject of Section 1 of this chapter.

Occasionally, particularly in the case of land or buildings, the market value of a fixed asset will rise with time. The asset may then be *revalued*. The accounting treatment of revaluations and the effect on depreciation are considered in Section 2. Section 3 deals with disposals of fixed assets. A profit may arise on the sale of a fixed asset if too much depreciation has been charged.

Fixed assets are valuable and need to be controlled. This is discussed in Section 4. Depreciation is covered in a Financial Reporting Standard (FRS 15), which you will need to know about for your exam. The standard is fairly straightforward and is discussed in Section 5.

1 DEPRECIATION *6/98, 6/00*

1.1 This section is a detailed look at depreciation and how it is calculated. Depreciation is also discussed in section 5 when we will see how FRS 15 affects the use of depreciation.

1.2 A fixed asset is acquired for use within a business with a view to earning profits. Its life extends over more than one accounting period, and so it earns profits over more than one period.

1.3 With the exception of land held on freehold or very long leasehold, every fixed asset eventually wears out over time. Machines, cars and other vehicles, fixtures and fittings, and even buildings do not last for ever. When a business acquires a fixed asset, it will have some idea about how long its useful life will be, and it might decide on one of the following policies.

(a) Use the fixed asset until it becomes completely worn out, useless, and worthless.
(b) Sell the fixed asset at the end of its useful life, as second-hand or scrap.

1.4 Since a fixed asset has a cost, and a limited useful life, and its value eventually declines, it follows that a charge should be made in the trading, profit and loss account to reflect the use that is made of the asset by the business. This charge is called *depreciation*.

Definition of depreciation

1.5 Suppose that a business buys a machine for £40,000. Its expected life is four years, and at the end of that time it is expected to be worthless.

1.6 Since the fixed asset is used to make profits for four years, it would be reasonable to charge the cost of the asset over those four years (perhaps by charging £10,000 per annum) so that at the end of the four years the total cost of £40,000 would have been charged against profits.

1.7 Indeed, one way of defining depreciation is to describe it as a means of spreading the cost of a fixed asset over its useful life, and so matching the cost against the full period during which it earns profits for the business. Depreciation charges are an example of the application of the accruals concept to calculate profits.

1.8 Depreciation has two important aspects.

(a) Depreciation is a *measure of the wearing out* or depletion of a fixed asset through use, time or obsolescence.

(b) Depreciation charges should be *spread fairly* over a fixed asset's life, and so allocated to the accounting periods which are expected to benefit (ie make profits) from the asset's use.

The total charge for depreciation: the depreciable amount

1.9 The total amount to be charged over the life of a fixed asset ('the depreciable amount') is usually its cost less any expected 'residual' sales value or disposal value at the end of the asset's life.

(a) A fixed asset costing £20,000 which has an expected life of five years and an expected residual value of nil should be depreciated by £20,000 in total over the five year period.

(b) A fixed asset costing £20,000 which has an expected life of five years and an expected residual value of £3,000 should be depreciated by £17,000 in total over the five year period.

Depreciation in the accounts of a business

1.10 When a fixed asset is depreciated, two things must be accounted for.

(a) The *charge for depreciation* is a *cost or expense* of the accounting period. We shall charge depreciation as an expense in the profit and loss account.

(b) At the same time, the fixed asset is wearing out and diminishing in value, and so the value of the fixed asset in the balance sheet must be reduced by the amount of depreciation charged. The balance sheet value of the fixed asset will be its '*net book value*' which is its cost less accumulated depreciation in the books of account.

1.11 The amount of depreciation deducted from the cost of a fixed asset to arrive at its net book value will build up (or 'accumulate') over time, as more depreciation is charged in each successive accounting period. This accumulated depreciation is a 'provision' because it provides for the fall in value of the fixed asset. The term 'provision for depreciation' refers to the 'accumulated depreciation' of a fixed asset.

1.12 For example, a fixed asset costing £40,000 has an expected life of four years and an estimated residual value of nil, so it is depreciated by £10,000 per annum.

	Depreciation charge for the year (P & L a/c) (A)	*Accumulated depreciation at end of year* (B)	*Cost of the asset* (C)	*Net book value at end of year* (C-B)
	£	£	£	£
At beginning of its life	-	-	40,000	40,000
Year 1	10,000	10,000	40,000	30,000
Year 2	10,000	20,000	40,000	20,000
Year 3	10,000	30,000	40,000	10,000
Year 4	10,000	40,000	40,000	0
	40,000			

At the end of year 4, the full £40,000 of depreciation charges have been made in the profit and loss accounts of the four years. The net book value of the fixed asset is now nil. In theory (although perhaps not in practice) the business will no longer use the fixed asset, which would now need replacing.

Methods of depreciation

1.13 There are several different methods of depreciation. Of these, the ones you need to know about are:

- Straight line method
- Reducing balance method
- Sum of the digits method
- Revaluation method
- Machine hour method

The straight line method

1.14 This is the most commonly used method. The total depreciable amount is charged in equal instalments to each accounting period over the expected useful life of the asset. (In this way, the net book value of the fixed asset declines at a steady rate, or in a 'straight line' over time.)

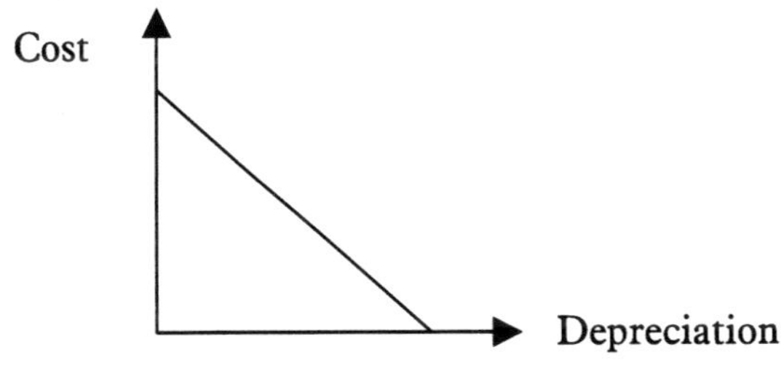

1.15 The annual depreciation charge is calculated as:

$$\frac{\text{Cost of asset minus residual value}}{\text{Expected useful life of the asset}}$$

Example: straight line depreciation

1.16 (a) A fixed asset costing £20,000 with an estimated life of 10 years and no residual value would be depreciated at the rate of:

$$\frac{£20{,}000}{10 \text{ years}} = £2{,}000 \text{ per annum}$$

(b) A fixed asset costing £60,000 has an estimated life of 5 years and a residual value of £7,000. The annual depreciation charge using the straight line method would be:

$$\frac{£(60{,}000 - 7{,}000)}{5 \text{ years}} = £10{,}600 \text{ per annum}$$

The net book value of the fixed asset would be:

	After 1 year	*After 2 years*	*After 3 years*	*After 4 years*	*After 5 years*
	£	£	£	£	£
Cost of the asset	60,000	60,000	60,000	60,000	60,000
Accumulated depreciation	10,600	21,200	31,800	42,400	53,000
Net book value	49,400	38,800	28,200	17,600	7,000 *

* ie its estimated residual value.

1.17 Since the depreciation charge per annum is the same amount every year with the straight line method, it is often convenient to state that depreciation is charged at the rate of x per cent per annum on the cost of the asset. In the example in paragraph 1.16(a) above, the depreciation charge per annum is 10% of cost (ie 10% of £20,000 = £2,000).

Examination questions often describe straight line depreciation in this way.

1.18 The straight line method of depreciation is a fair allocation of the total depreciable amount between the different accounting periods, provided that it is reasonable to assume that the business enjoys equal benefits from the use of the asset in every period throughout its life.

Assets acquired in the middle of an accounting period

1.19 A business can purchase new fixed assets at any time during the course of an accounting period, and so it might seem fair to charge an amount for depreciation in the period when the purchase occurs which reflects the limited amount of use the business has had from the asset in that period.

Example: assets acquired in the middle of an accounting period

1.20 Suppose that a business which has an accounting year which runs from 1 January to 31 December purchases a new fixed asset on 1 April 20X1, at a cost of £24,000. The expected life of the asset is 4 years, and its residual value is nil. What should be the depreciation charge for 20X1?

Solution

1.21 The annual depreciation charge will be $\frac{24{,}000}{4 \text{ years}} = £6{,}000$ per annum

However, since the asset was acquired on 1 April 20X1, the business has only benefited from the use of the asset for 9 months instead of a full 12 months. It would therefore seem fair to charge depreciation in 20X1 of only

$$\frac{9}{12} \times £6{,}000 = £4{,}500$$

1.22 In practice, many businesses ignore the niceties of part-year depreciation, and charge a full year's depreciation on fixed assets in the year of their purchase and/or disposal, regardless of the time of year they were acquired.

The reducing balance method

1.23 The **reducing balance method** of depreciation calculates the annual depreciation charge as a fixed percentage of the net book value of the asset, as at the end of the previous accounting period.

1.24 For example, suppose that a business purchases a fixed asset at a cost of £10,000. Its expected useful life is 3 years and its estimated residual value is £2,160. The business wishes to use the reducing balance method to depreciate the asset, and calculates that the rate of depreciation should be 40% of the reducing (net book) value of the asset. (The method of deciding that 40% is a suitable annual percentage is a problem of mathematics, not financial accounting, and is not described here.)

The total depreciable amount is £(10,000 – 2,160) = £7,840.

The depreciation charge per annum and the net book value of the asset as at the end of each year will be as follows:

	£	*Accumulated depreciation* £	
Asset at cost	10,000		
Depreciation in year 1 (40%)	4,000	4,000	
Net book value at end of year 1	6,000		
Depreciation in year 2 (40% of reducing balance)	2,400	6,400	(4,000 + 2,400)
Net book value at end of year 2	3,600		
Depreciation in year 3 (40%)	1,440	7,840	(6,400 + 1,440)
Net book value at end of year 3	2,160		

1.25 You should note that with the reducing balance method, the annual charge for depreciation is higher in the earlier years of the asset's life, and lower in the later years. In the example above, the annual charges for years 1, 2 and 3 are £4,000, £2,400 and £1,440 respectively. The reducing balance method might therefore be used when it is considered fair to allocate a greater proportion of the total depreciable amount to the earlier years and a lower proportion to later years, on the assumption that the benefits obtained by the business from using the asset decline over time.

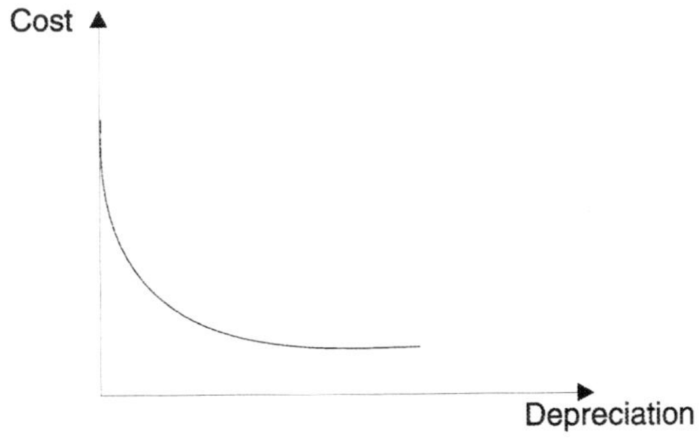

Sum of the digits method

1.26 This is a variant of the reducing balance method, but it is based on the estimated useful life of an asset. If an asset has an estimated useful life of five years, then the digits 1, 2, 3, 4 and 5 are added together, giving a total of 15. Depreciation of 5/15, 4/15, 3/15 and so on of the cost of the asset (less any residual value), will be charged in the respective years.

Example: sum of the digits method

1.27 A van cost £20,000 and is expected to be sold for £4,000 after four years. Calculate the depreciation to be provided in each of the years 1 to 4 using the sum of the digits method.

Solution

1.28

		£
Year 1	Cost	20,000
	Depreciation at 4/10 of £16,000	6,400
	Net book value	13,600
Year 2	Depreciation at 3/10 of £16,000	4,800
	Net book value	8,800
Year 3	Depreciation at 2/10 of £16,000	3,200
	Net book value	5,600
Year 4	Depreciation at 1/10 of £16,000	1,600
	Net book value	4,000

Revaluation method

1.29 This is used when depreciation is charged on a value other than cost, ie a revalued amount. Revaluations are dealt with in Section 2 of this chapter.

The machine hour method of depreciation

1.30 As the name of this method implies, it is a method of depreciation which might be considered suitable for plant and machinery, where it is assumed that the fixed asset wears out through use rather than over time. Instead of calculating a depreciation charge relating to a period of time, depreciation is calculated according to the number of hours of use made of the machine by the business during the course of the period.

1.31 The life of the asset is estimated in hours (or miles or other conventional units) and each unit is given a money value for depreciation purposes. The rate of depreciation is calculated as:

$$\frac{\text{Cost of asset minus estimated residual value}}{\text{Expected useful life of the asset in hours of used time}}$$

Example: the machine hour method

1.32 A business purchases a machine at a cost of £45,000. Its estimated useful life is 8,000 hours of running time, and its estimated residual value is £5,000.

The rate of depreciation by the machine hour method will be:

$$\frac{\pounds(45{,}000 - 5{,}000)}{8{,}000 \text{ hours}} = \pounds 5 \text{ per machine hour}$$

1.33 Suppose that the actual use of the machine each year is:

	Hours
Year 1	3,000
Year 2	1,500
Year 3	2,500
Year 4	1,000
	8,000

We can calculate the annual depreciation charge and net book value of the machine as at the end of each year as follows.

Year	Depreciation charge in the P & L account of the year £	Accumulated depreciation as at end of the year £	Fixed asset at cost £	Net book value as at end of the year £
Start of life			45,000	45,000
Year 1 (3,000 × £5)	15,000	15,000	45,000	30,000
Year 2 (1,500 × £5)	7,500	22,500	45,000	22,500
Year 3 (2,500 × £5)	12,500	35,000	45,000	10,000
Year 4 (1,000 × £5)	5,000	40,000	45,000	5,000
	40,000			

1.34 This method is sometimes modified so as to base each year's depreciation on the number of units produced by the machine in that year, rather than on the number of hours in which the machine is active. In this case the depreciation method is referred to as the units of output method.

Example: provision for depreciation

1.35 Brian Box set up his own computer software business on 1 March 20X6. He purchased a computer system on credit from a manufacturer, at a cost of £16,000. The system has an expected life of three years and a residual value of £2,500. Using the straight line method of depreciation, the fixed asset account, provision for depreciation account and P & L account (extract) and balance sheet (extract) would be as follows, for each of the next three years, 28 February 20X7, 20X8 and 20X9.

FIXED ASSET - COMPUTER EQUIPMENT

	Date		£	Date		£
(a)	1.3.X6	Creditor	16,000	28.2.X7	Balance c/d	16,000
(b)	1.3.X7	Balance b/d	16,000	28.2.X8	Balance c/d	16,000
(c)	1.3.X8	Balance b/d	16,000	28.2.X9	Balance c/d	16,000
(d)	1.3.X9	Balance b/d	16,000			

In theory, the fixed asset has now lasted out its expected useful life. However, until it is sold off or scrapped, the asset will still appear in the balance sheet at cost (less accumulated depreciation) and it should remain in the ledger account for computer equipment until it is eventually disposed of.

PROVISION FOR DEPRECIATION

	Date		£	Date		£
(a)	28.2.X7	Balance c/d	4,500	28.2.X7	P & L account	4,500
(b)	28.2.X8	Balance c/d	9,000	1.3.X7	Balance b/d	4,500
				28.2.X8	P & L account	4,500
			9,000			9,000
(c)	28.2.X9	Balance c/d	13,500	1.3.X8	Balance b/d	9,000
				28.2.X9	P & L account	4,500
			13,500			13,500
				1.3.X9	Balance b/d	13,500

The annual depreciation charge is $\frac{(£16,000 - 2,500)}{3 \text{ years}} = £4,500$ pa

At the end of three years, the asset is fully depreciated down to its residual value. If it continues to be used by Brian Box, it will not be depreciated any further (unless its estimated value is reduced).

P & L ACCOUNT (EXTRACT)

	Date		£
(a)	28 Feb 20X7	Provision for depreciation	4,500
(b)	28 Feb 20X8	Provision for depreciation	4,500
(c)	28 Feb 20X9	Provision for depreciation	4,500

BALANCE SHEET (EXTRACT) AS AT 28 FEBRUARY

	20X7	*20X8*	*20X9*
	£	£	£
Computer equipment at cost	16,000	16,000	16,000
Less accumulated depreciation	4,500	9,000	13,500
Net book value	11,500	7,000	2,500

Example: provision for depreciation with assets acquired part-way through the year

1.36 Brian Box prospers in his computer software business, and before long he purchases a car for himself, and later for his chief assistant Bill Ockhead. Relevant data is as follows.

	Date of purchase	*Cost*	*Estimated life*	*Estimated residual value*
Brian Box car	1 June 20X6	£20,000	3 years	£2,000
Bill Ockhead car	1 June 20X7	£8,000	3 years	£2,000

The straight line method of depreciation is to be used.

1.37 Prepare the motor vehicles account and provision for depreciation of motor vehicle account for the years to 28 February 20X7 and 20X8. (You should allow for the part-year's use of a car in computing the annual charge for depreciation.)

Calculate the net book value of each of the motor vehicles as at 28 February 20X8.

Solution

1.38 (a) (i) Brian Box car Annual depreciation $\frac{£(20,000 - 2,000)}{3 \text{ years}}$ = £6,000 pa

Monthly depreciation £500

Depreciation 1 June 20X6 - 28 February 20X7 (9 months) £4,500

1 March 20X7 - 28 February 20X8 £6,000

(ii) Bill Ockhead car Annual depreciation $\frac{£(8,000 - 2,000)}{3 \text{ years}}$ = £2,000 pa

Depreciation 1 June 20X7 - 28 February 20X8 (9 months) £1,500

(b) MOTOR VEHICLES

Date		£	*Date*		£
1 Jun 20X6	Creditors (or cash)		28 Feb 20X7	Balance c/d	20,000
	(car purchase)	20,000			
1 Mar 20X7	Balance b/d	20,000			
1 Jun 20X7	Creditors (or cash)		28 Feb 20X8	Balance c/d	28,000
	(car purchase)	8,000			
		28,000			28,000
1 Mar 20X8	Balance b/d	28,000			

PROVISION FOR DEPRECIATION OF MOTOR VEHICLES

Date		£	*Date*		£
28 Feb 20X7	Balance c/d	4,500	28 Feb 20X7	P & L account	4,500
			1 Mar 20X7	Balance b/d	4,500
28 Feb 20X8	Balance c/d	12,000	28 Feb 20X8	P & L account (6,000+1,500)	7,500
		12,000			12,000
			1 March 20X8	Balance b/d	12,000

BALANCE SHEET (WORKINGS) AS AT 28 FEBRUARY 20X8

	Brian Box car		*Bill Ockhead car*		*Total*
	£	£	£	£	£
Asset at cost		20,000		8,000	28,000
Accumulated depreciation:					
Year to:					
28 Feb 20X7	4,500		-		
28 Feb 20X8	6,000		1,500		
		10,500		1,500	12,000
Net book value		9,500		6,500	16,000

Applying a depreciation method consistently

1.39 It is up to the business concerned to decide which method of depreciation to apply to its fixed assets. Once that decision has been made, however, it should not be changed - the chosen method of depreciation should be applied consistently from year to year. This is an instance of the consistency concept, which we looked at in Chapter 2.

1.40 Similarly, it is up to the business to decide what a sensible life span for a fixed asset should be. Again, once that life span has been chosen, it should not be changed unless something unexpected happens to the fixed asset.

1.41 It is permissible for a business to depreciate different categories of fixed assets in different ways. For example, if a business owns three cars, then each car would normally be depreciated in the same way (eg by the straight line method) but another category of fixed asset, say, photocopiers, might be depreciated using a different method (eg by the machine hour method).

Exercise 1

A lorry bought for a business cost £17,000. It is expected to last for five years and then be sold for scrap for £2,000. Usage over the five years is expected to be:

Year 1	200 days
Year 2	100 days
Year 3	100 days
Year 4	150 days
Year 5	40 days

Required

Work out the depreciation to be charged each year under the following methods.

(a) The straight line method
(b) The reducing balance method (using a rate of 35%)
(c) The machine hour method

Solution

(a) Under the straight line method, depreciation for each of the five years is:

$$\text{Annual depreciation} = \frac{£17,000 - 2,000}{5} = £3,000$$

(b) Under the reducing balance method, depreciation for each of the five years is:

Year	*Depreciation*		
1	35% x £17,000	=	£5,950
2	35% x (£17,000 – £5,950) = 35% x £11,050	=	£3,868
3	35% x (£11,050 – £3,868) = 35% x £7,182	=	£2,514
4	35% x (£7,182 – £2,514) = 35% x £4,668	=	£1,634
5	Balance to bring book value down to £2,000 = £4,668 – £1,634 - £2,000	=	£1,034
			£15,000

(c) Under the machine hour method, depreciation for each of the five years is calculated as follows.

Total usage (days) = 200 + 100 + 100 + 150 + 40 = 590 days

$$\text{Depreciation per day} = \frac{£17,000 - 2,000}{590} = £25.42$$

Year	*Usage (days)*	*Depreciation (£) (days x £25.42)*
1	200	5,084.00
2	100	2,542.00
3	100	2,542.00
4	150	3,813.00
5	40	1,016.80
		14,997.80

(The answer does not come to exactly £15,000 because of the rounding carried out at the 'depreciation per day' stage of the calculation.)

A fall in the value of a fixed asset

1.42 When the 'market' value of a fixed asset falls so that it is worth less than the amount of its net book value, and the fall in value is expected to be permanent, the asset should be written down to its new low market value. The charge in the profit and loss account for the diminution in the value of the asset during the accounting period should then be:

	£
Net book value at the beginning of the period	X
Less: new reduced value	(X)
Equals: the charge for the diminution in the asset's value in the period.	X

Example: fall in asset value

1.43 A business purchased a leasehold property on 1 January 20X1 at a cost of £100,000. The lease has a 20 year life. After 5 years' use, on 1 January 20X6, the business decides that since property prices have fallen sharply, the leasehold is now worth only £60,000, and that the value of the asset should be reduced in the accounts of the business.

The leasehold was being depreciated at the rate of 5% per annum on cost.

1.44 Before the asset is reduced in value, the annual depreciation charge is:

$$\frac{£100,000}{20 \text{ years}} = £5,000 \text{ per annum } (= 5\% \text{ of } £100,000)$$

After 5 years, the accumulated depreciation would be £25,000, and the net book value of the leasehold £75,000, which is £15,000 more than the new asset value. This £15,000 should be written off as a charge for depreciation or fall in the asset's value in year 5, so that the total charge in year 5 is:

	£
Net book value of the leasehold after 4 years (£100,000 – 20,000)	80,000
Revised asset value at end of year 5	60,000
Charge against profit in year 5	20,000

An alternative method of calculation is:

	£
'Normal' depreciation charge per annum	5,000
Further fall in value, from net book value at end of year 5 to revised value	15,000
Charge against profit in year 5	20,000

1.45 The leasehold has a further 15 years to run, and its value is now £60,000. From year 6 to year 20, the annual charge for depreciation will be:

$$\frac{£60,000}{15 \text{ years}} = £4,000 \text{ per annum}$$

Depreciation is not a cash expense

1.46 Depreciation spreads the cost of a fixed asset (less its estimated residual value) over the asset's life. The cash payment for the fixed asset will be made when, or soon after, the asset is purchased. Annual depreciation of the asset in subsequent years is not a cash expense - rather it allocates costs to those later years for a cash payment that has occurred previously.

1.47 For example, suppose a business purchased some shop fittings for £6,000 on 1 July 20X5 and paid for them in cash on that date.

Subsequently, depreciation may be charged at £600 pa for ten years. So each year £600 is deducted from profits and the net book value of the fittings goes down, but no actual cash is being paid. The cash was all paid on 1 July 20X5. So annual depreciation is not a cash expense, but rather an allocation of the original cost to later years.

2 REVALUATION OF FIXED ASSETS 6/98, 6/00

2.1 Largely because of inflation, it is now quite common for the market value of certain fixed assets to go up, in spite of getting older. The most obvious example of rising market values is land and buildings (both freehold and leasehold).

A business which owns fixed assets which are rising in value is not obliged to revalue those assets in its balance sheet. However, in order to give a more 'true and fair view' of the position of the business, it might be decided that some fixed assets should be revalued upwards; otherwise the total value of the assets of the business might seem unrealistically low. When fixed assets are revalued, depreciation should be charged on the revalued amount.

Example: the revaluation of fixed assets

2.2 When Ira Vann commenced trading as a car hire dealer on 1 January 20X1, he purchased business premises freehold at a cost of £50,000.

For the purpose of accounting for depreciation, he decided that:

(a) The freehold land part of the business premises was worth £20,000. This would not be depreciated.

(b) The building part of the business premises was worth the remaining £30,000. This would be depreciated by the straight-line method to a nil residual value over 30 years.

After five years of trading on 1 January 20X6, Ira decides that his business premises are now worth £150,000, divided into:

	£
Land	75,000
Building	75,000
	150,000

He estimates that the building still has a further 25 years of useful life remaining.

Calculate the annual charge for depreciation in each of the 30 years of its life, and the balance sheet value of the land and building as at the end of each year.

Solution

2.3 *Before the revaluation*, the annual depreciation charge is £1,000 per annum on the building. This charge is made in each of the first five years of the asset's life.

The net book value of the asset will decline by £1,000 per annum, to:

(a) £49,000 as at 31.12.X1
(b) £48,000 as at 31.12.X2
(c) £47,000 as at 31.12.X3
(d) £46,000 as at 31.12.X4
(e) £45,000 as at 31.12.X5

2.4 *When the revaluation takes place*, the amount of the revaluation is:

	£
New asset value	150,000
Net book value as at end of 20X5	45,000
Amount of revaluation	105,000

The asset will be revalued by £105,000 to £150,000. If you remember the accounting equation, that the total value of assets must be equalled by the total value of capital and liabilities you should recognise that if assets go up in value by £105,000, capital or liabilities must also go up by the same amount. Since the increased value benefits the owners of the business, the amount of the revaluation is added to capital.

2.5 *After the revaluation*, depreciation will be charged on the building at a new rate of:

$$\frac{£75,000}{25 \text{ years}} = £3,000 \text{ per annum}$$

The net book value of the property will then fall by £3,000 per annum over 25 years, from £150,000 as at 1 January 20X6 to only £75,000 at the end of the 25 years - ie the building part of the property value will have been fully depreciated.

2.6 The consequence of an upwards revaluation is therefore a higher annual depreciation charge.

3 FIXED ASSET DISPOSALS

The disposal of fixed assets — *6/98, 6/00*

3.1 Fixed assets are not purchased by a business with the intention of reselling them in the normal course of trade. However, they might be sold off at some stage during their life. A business might decide to sell off a fixed asset long before its useful life has ended (perhaps because it is now surplus to requirements).

3.2 When fixed assets are disposed of, there will be a profit or loss on disposal. Since it is a capital item being sold, the profit or loss will be a capital gain or a capital loss. These gains or losses are reported in the profit and loss account of the business (and not as a trading profit in the trading account). They are commonly referred to as 'profit on disposal of fixed assets' or 'loss on disposal'.

3.3 Examination questions on the disposal of fixed assets usually ask for ledger accounts to be prepared, showing the entries in the accounts to record the disposal. Before we look at the ledger accounting for disposals, we had better look at the principles behind calculating the profit (or loss) on disposing of assets.

The principles behind calculating the profit or loss on disposal

3.4 The profit or loss on the disposal of a fixed asset is the difference between (a) and (b) below.

(a) The net book value of the asset at the time of its sale.
(b) Its net sale price (the price minus any costs of making the sale).

A profit is made when the sale price exceeds the net book value, and a loss is made when the sale price is less than the net book value.

Example: disposal of a fixed asset

3.5 A business purchased a fixed asset on 1 January 20X1 for £25,000. It had an estimated life of six years and an estimated residual value of £7,000. The asset was eventually sold after three years on 1 January 20X4 to another trader who paid £17,500 for it.

What was the profit or loss on disposal, assuming that the business uses the straight line method for depreciation?

Solution

3.6 Annual depreciation $= \dfrac{\text{£}(25{,}000 - 7{,}000)}{6 \text{ years}}$

$= \text{£}3{,}000$ per annum

	£
Cost of asset	25,000
Less accumulated depreciation (three years)	9,000
Net book value at date of disposal	16,000
Sale price	17,500
Profit on disposal	1,500

This profit will be shown in the profit and loss account of the business, where it will be an item of other income added to the gross profit brought down from the trading account.

Second example: disposal of a fixed asset

3.7 A business purchased a machine on 1 July 20X1 at a cost of £35,000. The machine had an estimated residual value of £3,000 and a life of eight years. The machine was sold for £18,600 on 31 December 20X4, the last day of the accounting year of the business. To make the sale, the business had to incur dismantling costs and costs of transporting the machine to the buyer's premises. These amounted to £1,200.

The business uses the straight line method of depreciation. What was the profit or loss on disposal of the machine?

Solution

3.8 Annual depreciation $\dfrac{\text{£}(35{,}000 - 3{,}000)}{8 \text{ years}} = \text{£}4{,}000$ per annum

It is assumed that in 20X1 only one-half year's depreciation was charged, because the asset was purchased six months into the year.

	£	£
Fixed asset at cost		35,000
Depreciation in 20X1 (6 months)	2,000	
20X2, 20X3 and 20X4	12,000	
Accumulated depreciation		14,000
Net book value at date of disposal		21,000
Sale price	18,600	
Costs incurred in making the sale	(1,200)	
Net sale price		17,400
Loss on disposal		(3,600)

This loss will be shown as an expense in the profit and loss account of the business. It is a capital loss, not a trading loss, and it should not therefore be shown in the trading account.

3.9 It is customary in ledger accounting to record the disposal of fixed assets in a *disposal of fixed assets* account.

(a) The profit or loss on disposal is the difference between the following items.

(i) The sale price of the asset (if any)
(ii) The net book value of the asset at the time of sale

(b) The relevant items which must appear in the disposal of fixed assets account are therefore:

(i) Value of the asset (at cost, or revalued amount*)
(ii) Accumulated depreciation up to the date of sale
(iii) Sale price of the asset

*To simplify the explanation of the rules, we will assume now that the fixed assets disposed of are valued at cost.

(c) The ledger accounting entries are as follows.

(i) DEBIT Disposal of fixed asset account
CREDIT Fixed asset account

with the cost of the asset disposed of.

(ii) DEBIT Provision for depreciation account
CREDIT Disposal of fixed asset account

with the accumulated depreciation on the asset as at the date of sale.

(iii) DEBIT Debtor account or cash book
CREDIT Disposal of fixed asset account

with the sale price of the asset. The sale is therefore not recorded in a sales account, but in the disposal of fixed asset account itself.

(iv) The balance on the disposal account is the profit or loss on disposal and the corresponding double entry is recorded in the P & L account itself.

Example: disposal of assets: ledger accounting entries

3.10 A business has £110,000 worth of machinery at cost. Its policy is to make a provision for depreciation at 20% per annum straight line. The total provision now stands at £70,000. The business now sells for £19,000 a machine which it purchased exactly two years ago for £30,000.

Show the relevant ledger entries.

Solution

3.11 PLANT AND MACHINERY ACCOUNT

	£		£
Balance b/d	110,000	Plant disposals account	30,000
		Balance c/d	80,000
	110,000		110,000
Balance b/d	80,000		

PLANT AND MACHINERY DEPRECIATION PROVISION

	£		£
Plant disposals (20% of £30,000 for 2 years)	12,000	Balance b/d	70,000
Balance c/d	58,000		
	70,000		70,000
		Balance b/d	58,000

PLANT DISPOSALS

	£		£
Plant and machinery account	30,000	Depreciation provision	12,000
Profit and loss a/c (profit on sale)	1,000	Cash	19,000
	31,000		31,000

Check:

	£
Asset at cost	30,000
Accumulated depreciation at time of sale	12,000
Net book value at time of sale	18,000
Sale price	19,000
Profit on sale	1,000

Example continued

3.12 Taking the example above assume that, instead of the machine being sold for £19,000, it was exchanged for a new machine costing £60,000, a credit of £19,000 being received upon exchange. In other words £19,000 is the trade-in price of the old machine. Now what are the relevant ledger account entries?

Solution

3.13 PLANT AND MACHINERY ACCOUNT

	£		£
Balance b/d	110,000	Plant disposal	30,000
Cash (60,000 - 19,000)	41,000	Balance c/d	140,000
Plant disposals	19,000		
	170,000		170,000
Balance b/d	140,000		

The new asset is recorded in the fixed asset account at cost £(41,000 + 19,000) = £60,000.

PLANT AND MACHINERY DEPRECIATION PROVISION

	£		£
Plant disposals (20% of £30,000 for 2 years)	12,000	Balance b/d	70,000
Balance c/d	58,000		
	70,000		70,000
		Balance b/d	58,000

PLANT DISPOSALS

	£		£
Plant and machinery	30,000	Depreciation provision	12,000
Profit transferred to P & L	1,000	Plant and machinery	19,000
	31,000		31,000

Exercise 2

A business purchased two widget-making machines on 1 January 20X5 at a cost of £15,000 each. Each had an estimated life of five years and a nil residual value. The straight line method of depreciation is used.

Owing to an unforeseen slump in market demand for widgets, the business decided to reduce its output of widgets, and switch to making other products instead. On 31 March 20X7, one widget-making machine was sold (on credit) to a buyer for £8,000.

Later in the year, however, it was decided to abandon production of widgets altogether, and the second machine was sold on 1 December 20X7 for £2,500 cash.

Prepare the machinery account, provision for depreciation of machinery account and disposal of machinery account for the accounting year to 31 December 20X7.

Solution

MACHINERY ACCOUNT

		£			£
20X7			*20X7*		
1 Jan	Balance b/f	30,000	31 Mar	Disposal of machinery account	15,000
			1 Dec	Disposal of machinery account	15,000
		30,000			30,000

PROVISION FOR DEPRECIATION OF MACHINERY

		£			£
20X7			*20X7*		
31 Mar	Disposal of machinery account*	6,750	1 Jan	Balance b/f	12,000
1 Dec	Disposal of Machinery account **	8,750	31 Dec	P& L account ***	3,500
		15,500			15,500

* Depreciation at date of disposal £6,000 + £750

** Depreciation at date of disposal £6,000 + £2,750

*** Depreciation charge for the year = £750 + £2,750

DISPOSAL OF MACHINERY

20X7		£	20X7		£
31 Mar	Machinery account	15,000	31 Mar	Debtor account (sale price)	8,000
			31 Mar	Provision for depreciation	6,750
1 Dec	Machinery account	15,000	1 Dec	Cash (sale price)	2,500
			1 Dec	Provision for depreciation	8,750
			31 Dec	P & L account (loss on disposal)	4,000
		30,000			30,000

You should be able to calculate that there was a loss on the first disposal of £250, and on the second disposal of £3,750, giving a total loss of £4,000.

Workings

1 At 1 January 20X7, accumulated depreciation on the machines will be

$$2 \text{ machines} \times 2 \text{ years} \times \frac{£15,000}{5} \text{ per machine pa} = £12,000,$$

or £6,000 per machine

2 Monthly depreciation is $\frac{£3,000}{12}$ = £250 per machine per month

3 The machines are disposed of in 20X7.

(a) On 31 March - after 3 months of the year.
Depreciation for the year on the machine = 3 months × £250 = £750.

(b) On 1 December - after 11 months of the year.
Depreciation for the year on the machine = 11 months × £250 = £2,750

4 THE FIXED ASSETS REGISTER

4.1 Nearly all but the smallest organisations keep a fixed assets register. This is a listing of all fixed assets owned by the organisation, broken down perhaps by department, location or asset type.

4.2 A fixed assets register is maintained primarily for internal purposes. It does not record rights over or obligations towards third parties but shows an organisation's investment in capital equipment. A fixed asset register is also part of the *internal control system*. Fixed assets registers or ledgers are sometimes called *real accounts,* to distinguish them from *impersonal accounts* such as 'rent' in the nominal ledger and *personal accounts* such as 'A Detta' in the sales ledger. They tend to include very few transactions and for this reason they are separated from those accounts that are more heavily used.

Data kept in a fixed assets register

4.3 Details held about each fixed asset might include the following.

(a) The organisation's internal reference number (for physical identification purposes)
(b) Manufacturer's serial number (for maintenance purposes)
(c) Description of asset
(d) Location of asset
(e) Department which 'owns' asset
(f) Purchase date (for calculation of depreciation)
(g) Cost
(h) Depreciation method and estimated useful life (for calculation of depreciation)
(i) Net book value (or written down value)

4.4 The main events giving rise to entries in a fixed asset register or 'inputs' in the case of a computerised one, would be:

(a) Purchase of an asset.
(b) Sale of an asset.

(c) Loss or destruction of an asset.
(d) Transfer of assets between departments.
(e) Revision of estimated useful life of an asset.
(f) Scrapping of an asset.
(g) Revaluation of an asset.

4.5 'Outputs' from a fixed assets register would be made:

(a) To enable reconciliations to be made to the nominal ledger.
(b) To enable depreciation charges to be posted to the nominal ledger.
(c) For physical verification/audit purposes.

Layout of fixed assets register

4.6 The layout of a fixed assets register and the degree of detail included will depend on the organisation in question. With a hand-written fixed assets register, the details are usually recorded in columns spread across two pages facing each other. The column headings will typically reflect the details outlined in paragraph 4.3 above. For the layout of a computerised fixed assets register, look ahead to paragraph 4.14.

Control

4.7 It is important, both from the point of view of external reporting (ie the audit) and for internal purposes, that there are controls over fixed assets. The fixed assets register has already been mentioned. Four further points should be made in this context.

(a) *Purchase* of fixed assets, which can involve a great deal of capital expenditure, must be authorised and must only be made by a responsible official.

  (i) The purchaser should obtain several quotations.

  (ii) The person authorising the expenditure should not be the same as the person who is using the asset.

(b) Procedures should exist and be enforced for *disposal* of fixed assets to ensure that the sales proceeds are not misappropriated.

(c) The fixed assets register must reconcile with the nominal ledger.

(d) The fixed assets register must reconcile with the physical presence of capital items.

The first two points are self explanatory. The second two will be examined in more detail.

The fixed assets register and the nominal ledger

4.8 Generally, the fixed assets register is not integrated with the nominal ledger. The entry typically lists the nominal ledger accounts (cost account, accumulated depreciation account and depreciation expense account) to which the relevant amounts must be posted and also contains other details not required in those nominal ledger accounts. In other words, the fixed assets register is not part of the double entry and is there for memorandum and control purposes.

4.9 The fixed assets register must therefore be reconciled to the nominal ledger to make sure that all additions, disposals and depreciation provisions and charges have been posted. For example, the total of all the 'cost' figures in the fixed assets register for motor vehicles should equal the balance on the 'motor vehicles cost' account in the nominal ledger, and the same goes for accumulated depreciation.

The fixed assets register and the fixed assets

4.10 It is possible that the fixed assets register may not reconcile with the fixed assets actually present, for the following reasons.

(a) An asset has been stolen or damaged and this has not been noticed or not recorded.

(b) A fixed asset may have suffered excessive wear and tear, or have become obsolete or damaged and need to be written off but the appropriate entries have not been made.

(c) New assets have been purchased but not yet recorded in the register because the register has not been kept up to date.

(d) Errors have been made in entering details in the register.

(e) Improvements and modifications made to the fixed asset have not been recorded in the register.

4.11 It is important therefore that the company:

(a) Physically inspects all the items in the fixed assets register.
(b) Keeps the fixed assets register up to date.

The nature of the inspection will obviously vary between organisations. A large company might carry out a fixed asset inspection of, for example, 25% of assets by value each year, aiming to cover all categories every four years. A small company might be able to inspect all its fixed assets very quickly, although this 'inspection' will probably not always be formally recorded.

Dealing with discrepancies

4.12 As mentioned in 4.10 above, some assets may require an adjustment in their expected life due to excessive wear and tear or damage. The proper authority to change any estimations as to the life of an asset must have the correct authorisation, and the information should be communicated to the accounts department who will need to make the right adjustments in the journal, the register and the ledger.

4.13 When discrepancies are discovered, the appropriate action must be taken. It may be possible to resolve the discrepancy by updating the fixed assets register and/or nominal ledger to reflect the new position. It may not be possible for the person who discovers the discrepancy to resolve it himself. For example, if a fixed asset has to be revalued downwards due to wear and tear or obsolescence, he may have to refer the matter to his superior who has more experience and judgement in such matters.

Example: Extract from a computerised fixed assets register

4.14 Most fixed assets registers will be computerised. On the next page is an extract from a fixed asset register showing one item as it might appear when the details are printed out.

FASSET HOLDINGS PLC

Asset Code: 938		Next depreciation: 539.36
A	Description:	1 × Seisha Laser printer YCA40809 office publisher
B	Date of purchase:	25/05/X6
C	Cost:	1618.25
D	Accumulated depreciation:	584.35
E	Depreciation %:	33.33%
F	Depreciation type:	straight line
G	Date of disposal:	NOT SET
H	Sale proceeds:	0.00
I	Accumulated depreciation account:	55Q O/EQPT DEP CHARGE
J	Depreciation expense account:	34F DEPN O/EQPT
K	Depreciation period:	standard
L	Comments:	electronic office
M	Residual value:	0.00
N	Cost account:	65C O/E ADDITIONS

5 FRS 15 TANGIBLE FIXED ASSETS

5.1 FRS 15 *Tangible fixed assets* was published in February 1999. It goes into a lot more detail than the Companies Act 1985.

5.2 FRS 15 replaced SSAP 12, *Accounting for depreciation*.

Objective

5.3 FRS 15 deals with accounting for the initial measurement, valuation and depreciation of tangible fixed assets. It also sets out the information that should be disclosed to enable readers to understand the impact of the accounting policies adopted in relation to these issues.

Initial measurement

5.4 A tangible fixed asset should initially be measured at cost.

Cost is purchase price and any costs directly attributable to bringing the asset into working condition for its intended use.

5.5 Examples of directly attributable costs include the following.

- Acquisition costs, eg stamp duty, import duties
- Cost of site preparation and clearance
- Initial delivery and handling costs
- Installation costs
- Professional fees eg legal fees
- The estimated cost of dismantling and removing the asset and restoring the site, to the extent that it is recognised as a provision.

Depreciation

5.6 The Companies Act 1985 requires that all fixed assets having a limited economic life should be depreciated. FRS 15 gives a useful discussion of the purpose of depreciation and supplements the statutory requirements in important ways. Depreciation is defined in FRS 15 as 'the measure of the cost or revalued amount of the economic benefits of the tangible fixed assets that have been consumed during the period. Consumption includes the wearing out, using up or other reduction in the useful economic life of a tangible fixed asset, whether arising from use, passing of time or obsolescence through either changes in technology or demand for the goods and services produced by the asset'.

5.7 The need to depreciate fixed assets arises from the accruals concept. If money is expended in purchasing an asset then the amount expended must at some time be charged against profits. If the asset is one which contributes to an enterprise's revenue over a number of accounting periods it would be inappropriate to charge any single period (for example the period in which the asset was acquired) with the whole of the expenditure. Instead, some method must be found of spreading the cost of the asset over its useful economic life.

5.8 This view of depreciation as a process of *allocation* of the cost of an asset over several accounting periods is the view adopted by FRS 15. It is worth mentioning here two common *misconceptions* about the purpose and effect of depreciation.

(a) It is sometimes thought that the net book value (NBV) of an asset is equal to its net realisable value and that the object of charging depreciation is to reflect the fall in value of an asset over its life. This misconception is the basis of a common, but incorrect, argument which says that freehold properties (say) need not be depreciated in times when property values are rising. It is true that historical cost balance sheets often give a misleading impression when a property's NBV is much below its market value, but in such a case it is open to a business to incorporate a revaluation into its books. This is a separate problem from that of allocating the property's cost over successive accounting periods.

(b) Another misconception is that depreciation is provided so that an asset can be replaced at the end of its useful life. This is not the case.

(i) If there is no intention of replacing the asset, it could then be argued that there is no need to provide for any depreciation at all.

(ii) If prices are rising, the replacement cost of the asset will exceed the amount of depreciation provided.

5.9 FRS 15 contains no detailed guidance on the calculation of depreciation or the suitability of the various depreciation methods, merely stating the following two general principles.

> 'The depreciable amount of a tangible fixed asset should be allocated on a systematic basis over its useful economic life. The depreciation method used should reflect as fairly as possible the pattern in which the asset's economic benefits are consumed by the entity. The depreciation charge for each period should be recognised as an expense in the profit and loss account unless it is permitted to be included in the carrying amount of another asset.'

> 'A variety of methods can be used to allocate the depreciable amount of a tangible fixed asset on a systematic basis over its useful economic life. The method chosen should result in a depreciation charge throughout the asset's useful economic life and not just towards the end of its useful economic life or when the asset is falling in value.'

Factors affecting depreciation

5.10 FRS 15 states that the following factors need to be considered in determining the useful economic life, residual value and depreciation method of an asset.

(a) The expected usage of the asset by the entity, assessed by reference to the asset's expected capacity or physical output.

(b) The expected physical deterioration of the asset through use or passing of time; this will depend upon the repair and maintenance programme of the entity both when the asset is in use and when it is idle.

(c) Economic or technological obsolescence, for example arising from changes or improvements in production, or a change in the market demand for the product or service output of that asset.

(d) Legal or similar limits on the use of the asset, such as the expiry dates of related leases.

5.11 Neither the Companies Act nor FRS 15 prescribes which method should be used. Management must exercise its judgement. Furthermore, FRS 15 states:

> 'The useful economic life of a tangible fixed asset should be reviewed at the end of each reporting period and revised if expectations are significantly different from previous estimates. If a useful economic life is revised, the carrying amount of the tangible fixed asset at the date of revision should be depreciated over the revised remaining useful economic life.'

5.12 Therefore, if it becomes clear that the original estimate of an asset's useful life was incorrect, it should be revised. Normally, no adjustment should be made in respect of the depreciation charged in previous years; instead the remaining net book value of the asset should be depreciated over the new estimate of its remaining useful life.

5.13 FRS 15 also states that a change from one method of providing deprecation to another is permissible only on the grounds that the new method will give a fairer presentation of the results and of the financial position. Such a change does not, however, constitute a change of accounting policy; the carrying amount of the tangible fixed asset is depreciated using the revised method over the remaining useful economic life, beginning in the period in which the change is made.

5.14 Many companies carry fixed assets in their balance sheets at revalued amounts, particularly in the case of freehold buildings. When this is done, the depreciation charge should be calculated on the basis of the revalued amount (not the original cost).

Disclosure requirements of FRS 15

5.15 The following information should be disclosed separately in the financial statements for each class of tangible fixed assets.

(a) The depreciation methods used.

(b) The useful economic lives or the depreciation rates used.

(c) Total depreciation charged for the period.

(d) Where material, the financial effect of a change during the period in either the estimate of useful economic lives or the estimate of residual values.

(e) The cost or revalued amount at the beginning of the financial period and at the balance sheet date.

(f) The cumulative amount of provisions for depreciation or impairment at the beginning of the financial period and at the balance sheet date.

(g) A reconciliation of the movements, separately disclosing additions, disposals, revaluations, transfers, depreciation, impairment losses, and reversals of past impairment losses written back in the financial period.

(h) The net carrying amount at the beginning of the financial period and at the balance sheet date.

5.16 Where there has been a change in the depreciation method used, the effect, if material, should be disclosed in the period of change. The reasons for the change should also be disclosed.

Exercise 3

Annette Book is the financial controller of a medium-sized publishing company. The managing director, Eddie Torial, is a man of sound literary judgement and marketing instinct, but has no accountancy training. Annette has received from him the following note.

'I understand that we have to provide 'depreciation' on all our fixed assets except land. This is going to come out of our profit, so there has to be a reason for it. Could you answer the following questions?

(a) Why do we provide depreciation?
(b) What exactly is net book value? (I think I know roughly what it is.)
(c) Why do we sometimes use the reducing balance method and not the straight line method?'

Required

Write Annette's reply to Eddie, addressing each of the above queries.

Solution

To: Eddie Torial, Managing director
From: Annette Book
Date: 5 March 20X7
Subject: Depreciation

(a) The accounts of a business try to recognise that the cost of a fixed asset is gradually consumed as the asset wears out. This is done by gradually writing off the asset's cost in the profit and loss account over several accounting periods. This process is known as depreciation, and is an example of the matching concept. FRS 15 *Tangible fixed assets* requires that depreciation should be allocated to charge against income a fair proportion of cost or valuation of the asset to each accounting period expected to benefit from its use.

With regard to the matching principle, it is fair that the profits should be reduced by the depreciation charge; this is not an arbitrary exercise. Depreciation is not, as is sometimes supposed, an attempt to set aside funds to purchase new fixed assets when required. Depreciation is not generally provided on freehold land because if does not 'wear out' (unless it is held for mining etc).

(b) In simple terms the net book value of an asset is the cost of an asset less the 'accumulated depreciation', that is all depreciation charged so far. It should be emphasised that the main purpose of charging depreciation is to ensure that profits are fairly reported. Thus depreciation is concerned with the profit and loss account rather than the balance sheet. In consequence the net book value figure in the balance sheet can be quite arbitrary. In particular, it does not necessarily bear any relation to the market value of an asset and is of little use for planning and decision making.

An obvious example of the disparity between net book value and market value is found in the case of buildings, which may be worth more than ten times as much as their net book value.

(c) The reducing balance method of depreciation is used instead of the straight line method when it is considered fair to allocate a greater proportion of the total depreciable amount to the earlier years and a lower proportion to the later years on the assumption that the benefits obtained by the business from using the asset decline over time.

In favour of this method it may be argued that it links the depreciation charge to the costs of maintaining and running the asset. In the early years these costs are low and the depreciation charge is high, while in later years this is reversed.

Chapter roundup

- The cost of a fixed asset, less its estimated residual value, is allocated fairly between accounting periods by means of depreciation. The provision for depreciation is:
  - Charged against profit.
  - Deducted from the value of the fixed asset in the balance sheet.
- Depreciation is an example of the matching concept and also the prudence concept - a fixed asset does not last forever and must be written off.
- There are several different methods of depreciation, but the straight line method and the reducing balance method are most commonly used in practice. You also need to know how to use the machine hour method of depreciation. Every method described in this chapter allocates the total depreciable amount between accounting periods, although in different ways.
- When a fixed asset is revalued, depreciation is charged on the revalued amount.
- When a fixed asset is sold, there is likely to be a profit or loss on disposal. This is the difference between the net sale price of the asset and its net book value at the time of disposal.
- You should also know how to handle the double entry bookkeeping for providing for depreciation, and for the disposal of fixed assets.
- You should be aware of the basic provisions of FRS 15 *Tangible fixed assets.*
- Most organisations keep a fixed assets register. This is a listing of all fixed assets owned by the organisation broken down perhaps by department, location or asset type. This must be kept up to date.
- Discrepancies between the fixed assets register and the fixed assets present and between the fixed assets register and the nominal ledger must be investigated and either resolved or referred to the appropriate person.

Test your knowledge

1 Define a fixed asset. (see para 1.2)

2 What does depreciation measure? (1.8)

3 What is an asset's net book value? (1.10)

4 Give three common depreciation methods. (1.13)

5 How should a permanent fall in the value of a fixed asset be accounted for? (1.42 - 1.45)

6 Define (in accounting terms) the profit or loss which arises on disposal of a fixed asset. (3.4)

7 What details about a fixed asset might be included in a fixed assets register? (4.3)

8 Why might the fixed assets register not reconcile with the fixed assets? (4.10)

9 Define depreciation according to FRS 15 (5.6)

Now try illustrative questions 13 to 15 at the end of the Study Text

Chapter 12

INTANGIBLE FIXED ASSETS

This chapter covers the following topics.

Introduction

Intangible fixed assets are fixed assets which have a value to the business because they have been paid for, but which do not have any physical substance. The most significant of such intangible assets are goodwill and deferred development costs.

The concept of goodwill might be familiar to you already, from common everyday knowledge. Goodwill is created by good relationships between a business and its customers, for example:

(a) By building up a reputation (by word of mouth perhaps) for high quality products or high standards of service.

(b) By responding promptly and helpfully to queries and complaints from customers.

(c) Through the personality of the staff and their attitudes to customers.

In many companies, especially those which produce food or 'scientific' products such as medicines or 'high technology' products, the expenditure on *research and development* is considerable. When R & D is a large item of cost its accounting treatment may have a significant influence on the profits of a business and its balance sheet valuation. Due to this, attempts have been made to standardise the treatment and these are discussed in Section 2 of this chapter.

1 GOODWILL

1.1 The value of goodwill to a business might be extremely significant. However, goodwill is not usually valued in the accounts of a business at all, and we should not normally expect to find an amount for goodwill in its balance sheet. For example, the welcoming smile of the bar staff may contribute more to a pub's profits than the fact that a new electronic cash register has recently been acquired; even so, whereas the cash register will be recorded in the accounts as a fixed asset, the value of staff would be ignored for accounting purposes. (This is an example of the 'money measurement' concept.)

1.2 On reflection, this omission of goodwill from the accounts of a business might be easy to understand.

(a) The goodwill is inherent in the business but it has not been paid for, and it does not have an 'objective' value. We can guess at what such goodwill is worth, but such guesswork would be a matter of individual opinion, and not based on hard facts.

(b) Goodwill changes from day to day. One act of bad customer relations might damage goodwill and one act of good relations might improve it. Staff with a favourable personality might retire or leave to find another job, to be replaced by staff who need time to find their feet in the job, etc. Since goodwill is continually changing in value, it cannot realistically be recorded in the accounts of the business.

Purchased goodwill

1.3 There is one exception to the general rule that goodwill has no objective valuation. This is when a business is sold. People wishing to set up in business have a choice of how to do it - they can either buy their own fixed assets and stock and set up their business from scratch, or they can buy up an existing business from a proprietor willing to sell it. When a buyer purchases an existing business, he will have to purchase not only its fixed assets and stocks (and perhaps take over its creditors and debtors too) but also the goodwill of the business.

1.4 For example, suppose that Tony Tycoon agrees to purchase the business of Clive Dunwell for £30,000. Clive's business has net fixed assets valued at £14,000 and net current assets of £11,000, all of which are taken over by Tony. Tony will be paying more for the business than its tangible assets are worth, because he is purchasing the goodwill of the business too. The balance sheet of Tony's business when it begins operations (assuming that he does not change the value of the tangible fixed and current assets) will be:

TONY TYCOON
BALANCE SHEET AS AT THE START OF BUSINESS

	£
Intangible fixed asset: goodwill	5,000
Tangible fixed assets: net book value	14,000
Net current assets	11,000
Net assets	30,000
Capital	30,000

1.5 Purchased goodwill is shown in this balance sheet because it has been paid for. It has no tangible substance, and so it is an intangible fixed asset.

Purchased goodwill has been defined as 'the excess of the price paid for a business over the fair market value of the individual assets and liabilities acquired'.

Exercise

To make sure that you understand goodwill, try a solution to the following quick exercise.

Toad goes into business with £10,000 capital and agrees to buy Thrush's shoe-repair shop in the centre of a busy town for £6,500. Thrush's recent accounts show net assets of £3,500, which Toad values at £4,000.

Required

Prepare the balance sheet of Toad's business:

(a) Before he purchases Thrush's business.
(b) After the purchase.

Solution

(a) Toad's balance sheet before the purchase is:

	£
Cash	10,000
Proprietor's capital	10,000

(b) Thrush's valuation of the assets to be acquired is irrelevant to Toad who sees the situation thus:

	£
Consideration (cash to be paid)	6,500
Less net assets acquired (at Toad's valuation)	4,000
Difference (= goodwill)	2,500

Toad must credit his cash book with the £6,500 paid. He can only debit sundry assets with £4,000. A further debit of £2,500 is thus an accounting necessity and he must open up a goodwill account.

Toad's balance sheet immediately after the transfer would therefore be:

	£
Goodwill	2,500
Sundry assets	4,000
Cash (£10,000 - £6,500)	3,500
	10,000
Proprietor's capital	10,000

(Normally one would have more detail as to the breakdown of the sundry assets into fixed assets, current assets etc, but this is not relevant to the illustration. The main point is that the sundry assets acquired are tangible whereas the goodwill is not.)

This exercise highlights the difference between 'internally generated' goodwill, which (as in Thrush's case above) is not shown in the books and 'purchased' goodwill, which is. The purchased goodwill in this case is simply Thrush's internally generated goodwill, which has changed hands, bought by Toad at a price shown in Toad's accounts.

The accounting treatment of purchased goodwill

1.6 Once purchased goodwill appears in the accounts of a business, we must decide what to do with it. Purchased goodwill is basically a premium paid for the acquisition of a business as a going concern: indeed, it is often referred to as a 'premium on acquisition'. When a purchaser agrees to pay such a premium for goodwill, he does so because he believes that the true value of the business is worth more to him than the value of its tangible assets.

1.7 One major reason why he might think so is that the business will earn good profits over the next few years, and so he will pay a premium now to get the business, in the expectation of getting his money back later. However, he pays for the goodwill at the time of purchase, and the value of the goodwill will eventually wear off.

1.8 Goodwill, it was suggested earlier, is a continually changing thing. A business cannot last forever on its past reputation; it must create new goodwill as time goes on. Even goodwill created by a favourable location might suddenly disappear - for example, a newsagent's shop by a bus stop will lose its location value if the bus route is axed by the local transport authorities.

1.9 Since goodwill wears off, and is basically unstable anyway, it would be inadvisable to keep purchased goodwill indefinitely in the accounts of a business. The treatment of goodwill is the subject of an accounting standard, FRS10 *Goodwill and intangible assets*.

1.10 FRS 10 requires that goodwill should be capitalised and shown in the balance sheet as an intangible fixed asset. It is then amortised over its expected useful economic life. There is a rebuttable presumption that this does not exceed 20 years, although it may be longer than this in limited cases.

1.11 The gradual 'write-off' approach is based on the idea that goodwill has a limited life and is a cost to be offset against future profits. Consistent with this approach is the fact that if goodwill is presumed to last longer than twenty years, an annual impairment review must be carried out to ensure that the presumption is still appropriate.

How is the value of purchased goodwill decided?

1.12 When a business is sold, there is likely to be some purchased goodwill in the selling price. But how is the amount of this purchased goodwill decided?

This is not really a problem for accountants, who must simply record the goodwill in the accounts of the new business. The value of the goodwill is a matter for the purchaser and seller to agree upon in fixing the purchase/sale price. However, two methods of valuation are worth mentioning here.

(a) The seller and buyer agree on a price without specifically quantifying the goodwill. The purchased goodwill will then be the difference between the price agreed and the value of the tangible assets in the books of the new business.

(b) However, the calculation of goodwill often precedes the fixing of the purchase price and becomes a central element of negotiation. There are many ways of arriving at a value for goodwill and most of them are related to the profit record of the business in question. Some of these ways are illustrated below.

1.13 For an illustration of a few possible methods, let us suppose that a business being sold on 31.12.X3 has recently generated profits as follows:

Year ending 31.12.X1 - £4,000
Year ending 31.12.X2 - £5,000
Year ending 31.12.X3 - £7,000
Capital employed £20,000

Goodwill might be valued at:

(a) twice the final year's profit - ie 2 × £7,000 = $\underline{£14,000}$

or

(b) twice the average profit for the past three years

$$\text{ie } 2 \times \frac{£4,000 + £5,000 + £7,000}{3} = \underline{£10,667}$$

or perhaps

(c) three times the average profit for the past two years

$$\text{ie } 3 \times \frac{£5,000 + £7,000}{2} = \underline{£18,000}$$

(d) Alternatively the 'super profits' approach could be used. This relates the profit to the capital employed in one of a number of ways. Let us assume that in this particular business a reasonable return on capital employed would be 10% and that a reasonable salary for the proprietor would be £4,000. For the year 20X3 the return on the proprietor's funds, in excess of the salary that he could earn elsewhere, is therefore £3,000.

We could say:

(i) The £3,000 represents a 10% return on the assets of the business; the assets must therefore be:

$$\frac{100}{10} \times £3,000 = \underline{£30,000}$$

Of the £30,000 we know that £20,000 exists in tangible form (net assets employed). Therefore the remaining £10,000 must be intangible, ie goodwill is £10,000.

In other words as well as our 10% return on tangible assets (£20,000 × 10% = £2,000) our intangible asset, goodwill, earns us a further £1,000 (£10,000 × 10%) which is the 'super profit'.

(ii) We could regard the intangible asset as having limited life and purchase, say seven years 'super profits'.

Goodwill would therefore be 7 × £1,000 = $\underline{£7,000}$

Many other variations are possible. A formula may be agreed between vendor and purchaser in advance or there may be much haggling to reach agreement. The goodwill element of the purchase price is of course additional to the value of tangible assets acquired.

1.14 Any attempt to quantify goodwill in financial terms is purely arbitrary. Using the above methods we have calculated goodwill as high as £18,000 and as low as £7,000. Neither of these figures is the 'correct' figure because there is no correct figure; once a basis for the calculation has been agreed (eg two years purchase of average profits for the past three years) then a figure can be arrived at, but selection of the basis is entirely subjective. In practice, examination questions will always tell you the basis on which goodwill is to be calculated, and it will usually be some version of methods (a) to (c) above. The 'super profits' concept is generally considered rather old-fashioned, but it is mentioned for completeness.

1.15 No matter how goodwill is calculated within the total agreed purchase price, the goodwill shown by the purchaser in his accounts will be the difference between the purchase consideration and his own valuation of the tangible net assets acquired. If A values his tangible net assets at £40,000, goodwill is agreed at £21,000 and B agrees to pay £61,000 for the business but values the tangible net assets at only £38,000, then the goodwill in B's books will be £61,000 – £38,000 = £23,000.

2 DEFERRED DEVELOPMENT COSTS 12/97

2.1 This is the other intangible fixed asset you should know about. Large companies may spend significant amounts of money on research and development (R & D) activities. Obviously, any amounts so expended must be credited to cash and debited to an account for research and development expenditure. The accounting problem is how to treat the debit balance on R & D account at the balance sheet date.

2.2 There are two possibilities.

(a) The debit balance may be classified as an expense and transferred to the profit and loss account. This is referred to as 'writing off' the expenditure.

(b) The debit balance may be classified as an asset and included in the balance sheet. This is referred to as 'capitalising' or 'carrying forward' or 'deferring' the expenditure.

2.3 The argument for writing off R & D expenditure is that it is an expense just like rates or wages and its accounting treatment should be the same. This argument is based on the prudence concept.

2.4 The argument for carrying forward R & D expenditure is based on the accruals or matching concept. If R & D activity eventually leads to new or improved products which generate revenue, the costs should be carried forward to be matched against that revenue in future accounting periods.

2.5 Like goodwill, R & D expenditure is the subject of an accounting standard, SSAP 13 *Accounting for research and development*. SSAP 13 (and the Companies Act 1985) requires that *research* expenditure should always be written off in the period in which it is incurred. This is because the advantages derived from general research activities are too remote to justify carrying the expenditure forward.

2.6 Development expenditure is different. It usually relates to a specific project (eg the development of a new product) which can be profitably exploited in the foreseeable future. Provided the viability of the project has been carefully assessed, there is a strong argument for capitalising the development costs associated with it.

2.7 SSAP 13 allows companies to capitalise development expenditure in their accounts, provided that certain criteria are satisfied. Broadly, it is permissible to carry forward such expenditure in the circumstances described above. Even so, a company is never *obliged* to do so; it is always open to a company to take the most prudent view and write off development expenditure in the same way as research expenditure.

2.8 If a company capitalises development expenditure, it will appear in the balance sheet as an intangible asset. Like capitalised goodwill, it must be depreciated (amortised). The process of amortisation should begin when the development project is brought into commercial production.

2.9 Be sure to attempt illustrative question 16, which illustrates the accounting entries required in respect of goodwill and development expenditure.

Chapter roundup

- Intangible fixed assets are those which have a value to the business but which do not have any physical substance. The most significant intangible assets are goodwill and deferred development expenditure.
- If a business has goodwill, it means that the value of the business as a going concern is greater than the value of its separate tangible assets. The valuation of goodwill is extremely subjective and fluctuates constantly. For this reason, goodwill is not normally shown as an asset in the balance sheet.
- The exception to this rule is when someone purchases a business as a going concern. In this case the purchaser and vendor will fix an agreed price which includes an element in respect of goodwill. The way in which goodwill is then valued is not an accounting problem, but a matter of agreement between the two parties.
- Purchased goodwill must be retained in the balance sheet as an intangible asset. It must be amortised over its estimated useful economic life, which would in normal circumstances be 20 years or less.
- Expenditure on research activities must always be written off in the period in which it is incurred.
- Expenditure on development activities may also be written off in the same way. But if the criteria laid down by SSAP 13 are satisfied, such expenditure *may* be capitalised as an intangible asset. It must then be amortised, beginning from the time when the development project is brought into commercial production.

Test your knowledge

1 Why is it unusual to record goodwill as an asset in the accounts? (see para 1.2)

2 What is purchased goodwill? (1.3, 1.5)

3 What method of accounting for purchased goodwill is dictated by FRS10? (1.10)

4 How is the amount of purchased goodwill calculated? (1.15)

5 What is the required accounting treatment for expenditure on research? (2.5)

6 In what circumstances may development expenditure be capitalised? (2.6, 2.7)

Now try illustrative question 16 at the end of the Study Text

Part C

Accounting systems and reports – further aspects

Chapter 13

BANK RECONCILIATIONS AND CONTROL ACCOUNTS

This chapter covers the following topics.

1 Bank reconciliations

2 Control accounts

Introduction

Errors can easily be made in the recording of transactions and the preparation of accounts.

In this chapter and the next chapter we will look at the methods which can be used to detect and deal with errors.

1 BANK RECONCILIATIONS 6/96, 6/98, 12/99

Introduction

1.1 The cash book of a business is the record of how much cash the business believes that it has in the bank. In the same way, you yourself might keep a private record of how much money you think you have in your own personal account at your bank, perhaps by making a note in your cheque book of income received and the cheques you write. If you do keep such a record you will know that when your bank sends you a bank statement from time to time the amount it shows as being the balance in your account is rarely exactly the same as your own calculation.

1.2 Why might your own estimate of your bank balance be different from the amount shown on your bank statement? There are three common explanations.

(a) *Errors*. Errors in calculation, or recording income and payments, are more likely to have been made by yourself than by the bank, but it is conceivable that the bank has made a mistake.

(b) *Bank charges or bank interest*. The bank might deduct charges for interest on an overdraft or for its services, which you are not informed about until you receive the bank statement.

(c) *Timing differences*

(i) There might be some cheques that you have received and paid into the bank, but which have not yet been 'cleared' and added to your account. So although your own records show that some cash has been added to your account, this has not yet been acknowledged by the bank.

(ii) Similarly, you might have made some payments by cheque, and reduced the balance in your account accordingly in the record that you keep, but the person who receives the cheque might not bank it for a while. Even when it is banked, it takes a day or two for the banks to process it and for the money to be deducted from your account.

1.3 If you do keep a personal record of your cash position at the bank, and if you do check your periodic bank statements against what you think you should have in your account, you will be doing exactly the same thing that the bookkeepers of a business do when they make a bank reconciliation. A bank reconciliation is a comparison of a bank statement (probably sent monthly by the bank) with the cash book. Differences between the balance on the bank statement and the balance in the cash book should be identified and satisfactorily explained.

1.4 If a customer has money in his account, the bank owes him that money, and the customer is therefore a creditor of the bank (hence the phrase 'to be in credit' means to have money in your account). This means that if a business has £8,000 cash in the bank, it will have a debit balance in its own cash book, but the bank statement, if it reconciles exactly with the cash book, will state that there is a credit balance of £8,000. The bank's records are a 'mirror image' of the customer's own records, with debits and credits reversed.

What to look for when doing a bank reconciliation

1.5 The cash book and bank statement will rarely agree at a given date. If you are doing a bank reconciliation, you may have to look for the following items.

(a) *Corrections and adjustments to the cash book*

(i) Payments made into the account or from the account by way of standing order, which have not yet been entered in the cash book.

(ii) Dividends received (on investments held by the business), paid directly into the bank account but not yet entered in the cash book.

(iii) Bank interest and bank charges, not yet entered in the cash book.

(b) *Items reconciling the correct cash book balance to the bank statement*

(i) Cheques drawn (ie paid) by the business and credited in the cash book, which have not yet been presented to the bank, or 'cleared' and so do not yet appear on the bank statement.

(ii) Cheques received by the business, paid into the bank and debited in the cash book, but which have not yet been cleared and entered in the account by the bank, and so do not yet appear on the bank statement.

Example: bank reconciliation (1)

1.6 At 30 September 20X6, the balance in the cash book of Wordsworth Ltd was £805.15. A bank statement on 30 September 20X6 showed Wordsworth Ltd to be in credit by £1,112.30.

On investigation of the difference between the two sums, it was established that:

(a) The cash book had been undercast by £90.00 on the debit side.
(b) Cheques paid in not yet credited by the bank amounted to £208.20.
(c) Cheques drawn not yet presented to the bank amounted to £425.35.

Required

(a) Show the correction to the cash book.

(b) Prepare a statement reconciling the balance per the bank statement to the balance per the cash book.

Solution

1.7 (a)

	£
Cash book balance brought forward	805.15
Add correction of undercast	90.00
Corrected balance	895.15

(b)

	£	£
Balance per bank statement		1,112.30
Add		
Cheques paid in, recorded in the cash book, but not yet credited to the account by the bank	208.20	
Less		
Cheques drawn by the company but not yet presented to the company's bank	425.35	
		(217.15)
Balance per cash book		895.15

Example: bank reconciliation (2)

1.8 On 30 June 20X0, Abigail's cash book showed that she had an overdraft of £300 on her current account at the bank. A bank statement as at the end of June 20X0 showed that she was in credit with the bank by £65.

On checking the cash book with the bank statement you find the following.

(a) Cheques drawn, amounting to £500, had been entered in the cash book but had not been presented.

(b) Cheques received, amounting to £400, had been entered in the cash book, but had not been credited by the bank.

(c) On instructions from Abigail the bank had transferred interest of £60 from her deposit account to her current account, recording the transfer on 5 July 20X0. This amount had, however, been credited in the cash book as on 30 June 20X0.

(d) Bank charges of £35 shown in the bank statement had not been entered in the cash book.

(e) The payments side of the cash book had been undercast by £10.

(f) Dividends received amounting to £200 had been paid directly to the bank and had not been entered in the cash book.

(g) A cheque for £50 drawn on deposit account had been shown in the cash book as drawn on current account.

(h) A cheque issued to Jones for £25 was replaced when out of date. It was entered again in the cash book, no other entry being made. Both cheques were included in the total of unpresented cheques shown above.

Required

(a) Indicate the appropriate adjustments in the cash book.

(b) Prepare a statement reconciling the amended balance with that shown in the bank statement.

Solution

1.9 (a) The errors to correct are given in notes (c) (e) (f) (g) and (h) of the problem. Bank charges (note (d)) also call for an adjustment.

	Item	Adjustments in cash book Debit (ie add to cash balance) £	Credit (ie deduct from cash balance) £
(b)	Cash book incorrectly credited with interest on 30 June. It should have been debited with the receipt	60	
(c)	Debit cash book (current a/c) with transfer of interest from deposit a/c (note 1)	60	
(d)	Bank charges		35
(e)	Undercast on payments (credit) side of cash book		10
(f)	Dividends received should be debited in the cash book	200	
(g)	Cheque drawn on deposit account, not current account. Add cash back to current account	50	
(h)	Cheque paid to Jones is out of date and so cancelled. Cash book should now be debited, since previous credit entry is no longer valid (note 2)	25	
		395	45
	Cash book: balance on current account as at 30 June 20X0		(300)
	Adjustments and corrections:		
	Debit entries (adding to cash)	395	
	Credit entries (reducing cash balance)	(45)	
	Net adjustments		350
	Corrected balance in the cash book		50

Notes

1 Item (c) is rather complicated. The transfer of interest from the deposit to the current account was presumably given as an instruction to the bank on or before 30 June 20X0. Since the correct entry is to debit the current account (and credit the deposit account) the correction in the cash book should be to debit the current account with 2 × £60 = £120, to cancel out the incorrect credit entry in the cash book and then to make the correct debit entry. However, the bank does not record the transfer until 5 July, and so it will not appear in the bank statement.

2 Item (h). Two cheques have been paid to Jones, but one is now cancelled. Since the cash book is credited whenever a cheque is paid, it should be debited whenever a cheque is cancelled. The amount of cheques drawn but not yet presented should be reduced by the amount of the cancelled cheque.

(b) BANK RECONCILIATION STATEMENT AT 30 JUNE 20X0

	£	£
Balance per bank statement		65
Add: outstanding lodgements		
(ie cheques paid in but not yet credited)	400	
deposit interest not yet credited	60	
		460
		525
Less: unpresented cheques	500	
less cheque to Jones cancelled	25	
		475
Balance per corrected cash book		50

1.10 Notice that in preparing a bank reconciliation it is good practice to begin with the balance shown by the bank statement and end with the balance shown by the cash book. It is this corrected cash book balance which will appear in the balance sheet as 'cash at bank'. But examination questions sometimes ask for the reverse order: as always, read the question carefully.

Exercise 1

From the information given below relating to PWW Ltd you are required:

(a) To make such additional entries in the cash at bank account of PWW Ltd as you consider necessary to show the correct balance at 31 October 20X2.

(b) To prepare a statement reconciling the correct balance in the cash at bank account as shown in (a) above with the balance at 31 October 20X2 that is shown on the bank statement from Z Bank plc.

CASH AT BANK ACCOUNT IN THE LEDGER OF PWW LIMITED

20X2		£	*20X2*		£
October			*October*		
1	Balance b/d	274	1	Wages	3,146
8	Q Manufacturing	3,443	1	Petty cash	55
8	R Cement	1,146	8	Wages	3,106
11	S Ltd	638	8	Petty cash	39
11	T & Sons	512	15	Wages	3,029
11	U & Co	4,174	15	Petty cash	78
15	V plc	1,426	22	A & Sons	929
15	W Electrical	887	22	B Ltd	134
22	X and Associates	1,202	22	C & Company	77
26	Y Ltd	2,875	22	D & E	263
26	Z Ltd	982	22	F Ltd	1,782
29	ABC plc	1,003	22	G Associates	230
29	DEE Corporation	722	22	Wages	3,217
29	GHI Ltd	2,461	22	Petty cash	91
31	Balance c/d	14	25	H & Partners	26
			26	J Sons & Co Ltd	868
			26	K & Co	107
			26	L, M & N	666
			28	O Ltd	112
			29	Wages	3,191
			29	Petty cash	52
			29	P & Sons	561
		21,759			21,759
			31	Balance b/d	14

Z BANK PLC - STATEMENT OF ACCOUNT WITH PWW LIMITED

20X2		*Payments*	*Receipts*		*Balance*
October		£	£		£
1					1,135
1	cheque	55			
1	cheque	3,146			
1	cheque	421		O/D	2,487
2	cheque	73			
2	cheque	155		O/D	2,715
6	cheque	212		O/D	2,927
8	sundry credit		4,589		
8	cheque	3,106			
8	cheque	39		O/D	1,483
11	sundry credit		5,324		3,841
15	sundry credit		2,313		
15	cheque	78			
15	cheque	3,029			3,047
22	sundry credit		1,202		
22	cheque	3,217			
22	cheque	91			941
25	cheque	1,782			
25	cheque	134		O/D	975
26	cheque	929			
26	sundry credit		3,857		
26	cheque	230			1,723
27	cheque	263			
27	cheque	77			1,383
29	sundry credit		4,186		
29	cheque	52			
29	cheque	3,191			
29	cheque	26			
29	dividends on investments		2,728		
29	cheque	666			4,362
31	bank charges	936			3,426

Solution

(a)

CASH BOOK

		£			£
31 Oct	Dividends received	2,728	31 Oct	Balance b/d (overdraft)	14
			31 Oct	Bank charges	936
			31 Oct	Balance c/d	1,778
		2,728			2,728
31 Oct	Balance b/d	1,778			

(b) BANK RECONCILIATION STATEMENT
AT 31 OCTOBER 20X2

	£
Balance per bank statement	3,426
Less unpresented cheques	1,648
Balance per cash book	1,778

Workings

1 Payments in the cash book but not on the bank statement
£(868 + 107 + 112 + 561) £1,648

2 Bank charges, not in the cash book £936

3 Receipts recorded by bank statement but not in cash book:
dividends on investments £2,728

2 CONTROL ACCOUNTS 6/97, 12/97, 12/98, 6/99, 12/99

2.1 A control account is an account in which a record is kept of the total value of a number of similar but individual items. Control accounts are used chiefly for debtors and creditors.

(a) A debtors control account (also called a sales ledger control account) is an account in which records are kept of transactions involving all debtors in total. The balance on the debtors control account at any time will be the total amount due to the business at that time from its debtors.

(b) A creditors control account (also called a purchase ledger control account) is an account in which records are kept of transactions involving all creditors in total, and the balance on this account at any time will be the total amount owed by the business at that time to its creditors.

2.2 Although control accounts are used mainly in accounting for debtors and creditors, they can also be kept for other items, such as wages and salaries. The first important idea to remember, however, is that a control account is an account which keeps a total record for a collective item (eg debtors) which in reality consists of many individual items (eg individual debtors).

2.3 A control account is an (impersonal) ledger account which will appear in the nominal ledger. Before we look at the reasons for having control accounts, we will first look at how they are made up.

Control accounts and personal accounts

2.4 The personal accounts of individual debtors are kept in the sales ledger, and the amount owed by each debtor will be a balance on his personal account. The amount owed by all the debtors together will be a balance on the debtors control account.

2.5 At any time the balance on the debtors control account should be equal to the sum of the individual balances on the personal accounts in the sales ledger.

2.6 For example, if a business has three debtors, A who owes £80, B who owes £310 and C who owes £200, the debit balances on the various accounts would be:

Sales ledger (personal accounts)	£
A	80
B	310
C	200
Nominal ledger - debtors control account	590

2.7 The three entries of £80, £310 and £200 were first entered into the sales day book. They were also recorded in the three personal accounts of A, B and C in the sales ledger, but remember that this is not part of the double entry system. Later, the total of £590 was posted from the sales day book into the debtors (control) account.

Example: accounting for debtors

2.8 In the following example, folio numbers will be used to show the cross-referencing between accounts. Numbers beginning:

(a) SDB, refer to a page in the sales day book.
(b) SL, refer to a particular account in the sales ledger.
(c) NL, refer to a particular account in the nominal ledger.
(d) CB, refer to a page in the cash book.

2.9 At 1 July 20X2, the Outer Business Company had no debtors at all. During July, the following transactions affecting credit sales and customers occurred.

(a) July 3: invoiced A Arnold for the sale on credit of hardware goods: £100.

(b) July 11: invoiced B Bagshaw for the sale on credit of electrical goods: £150.

(c) July 15: invoiced C Cloning for the sale on credit of hardware goods: £250.

(d) July 10: received payment from A Arnold of £90, in settlement of his debt in full, having taken a permitted discount of £10 for payment within seven days.

(e) July 18: received a payment of £72 from B Bagshaw in part settlement of £80 of his debt. A discount of £8 was allowed for payment within seven days of invoice.

(f) July 28: received a payment of £120 from C Cloning, who was unable to claim any discount.

Account numbers are as follows:

SL 4	Personal account: A Arnold
SL 9	Personal account: B Bagshaw
SL 13	Personal account: C Cloning
NL 6	Debtors control account
NL 7	Discount allowed
NL 21	Sales: hardware
NL 22	Sales: electrical

2.10 The accounting entries would be as follows.

SALES DAY BOOK — SDB 35

Date	*Name*	*Folio*	*Total*	*Hardware*	*Electrical*
20X2			£	£	£
July					
3	A Arnold	SL 4 Dr	100.00	100.00	
11	B Bagshaw	SL 9 Dr	150.00		150.00
15	C Cloning	SL13 Dr	250.00	250.00	
			500.00	350.00	150.00
			NL 6 Dr	NL 21 Cr	NL 22 Cr

CASH BOOK EXTRACT
DEBIT SIDE - JULY 20X2 — CB 23

Date	*Narrative*	*Folio*	*Total*	*Discount*	*Debtors*
20X2			£	£	£
July					
10	A Arnold	SL 4 Cr	90.00	10.00	100.00
18	B Bagshaw	SL 9 Cr	72.00	8.00	80.00
28	C Cloning	SL13 Cr	120.00		120.00
			282.00	18.00	300.00
				NL 7 Dr	NL 6 Cr

The personal accounts in the sales ledger are memorandum accounts, because they are not a part of the double entry system.

MEMORANDUM SALES LEDGER
ARNOLD — A/c no: SL 4

Date	*Narrative*	*Folio*	£	*Date*	*Narrative*	*Folio*	£
20X2				*20X2*			
July				July			
3	Sales	SDB 35	100.00	10	Cash	CB 23	90.00
					Discount	CB 23	10.00
			100.00				100.00

B BAGSHAW

A/c no: SL 9

Date	*Narrative*	*Folio*	£	*Date*	*Narrative*	*Folio*	£
20X2				*20X2*			
July				July			
11	Sales	SDB 35	150.00	18	Cash	CB 23	72.00
					Discount	CB 23	8.00
				31	Balance	c/d	70.00
			150.00				150.00
Aug							
1	Balance	b/d	70.00				

C CLONING

A/c no: SL 13

Date	*Narrative*	*Folio*	£	*Date*	*Narrative*	*Folio*	£
20X2				*20X2*			
July				July			
15	Sales	SDB 35	250.00	28	Cash	CB 23	120.00
				31	Balance	c/d	130.00
			250.00				250.00
Aug							
1	Balance	b/d	130.00				

In the nominal ledger, the accounting entries can be made from the books of prime entry to the ledger accounts, in this example at the end of the month.

NOMINAL LEDGER (EXTRACT)
DEBTORS CONTROL

A/c no: NL 6

Date	*Narrative*	*Folio*	£	*Date*	*Narrative*	*Folio*	£
20X2				*20X2*			
July				July			
31	Sales	SDB 35	500.00	31	Cash and discount	CB 23	300.00
				31	Balance	c/d	200.00
			500.00				500.00
Aug							
1	Balance	b/d	200.00				

Note. At 31 July the closing balance on the debtors control account (£200) is the same as the total of the individual balances on the personal accounts in the sales ledger (£0 + £70 + £130).

DISCOUNT ALLOWED

A/c no: NL 7

Date	*Narrative*	*Folio*	£	*Date*	*Narrative*	*Folio*	£
20X2							
July							
31	Debtors	CB 23	18.00				

SALES - HARDWARE

A/c no: NL 21

Date	*Narrative*	*Folio*	£	*Date*	*Narrative*	*Folio*	£
				20X2			
				July			
				31	Debtors	SDB 35	350.00

SALES - ELECTRICAL

A/c no: NL 22

Date	*Narrative*	*Folio*	£	*Date*	*Narrative*	*Folio*	£
				20X2			
				July			
				31	Debtors	SDB 35	150.00

Accounting for creditors

2.11 The entries for creditors are the same as for debtors, except that balances owed to creditors appear on the credit side of accounts in the purchases ledger and of the creditors control account, and the credit side of the cash book is used to record cash payments.

Entries in control accounts

2.12 Typical entries in the control accounts are listed below. Folio reference Jnl indicates that the transaction is first lodged in the journal before posting to the control account and other accounts indicated. References SRDB and PRDB are to sales returns and purchase returns day books.

SALES LEDGER (DEBTORS) CONTROL

	Folio	£		*Folio*	£
Opening debit balances	b/d	7,000	Opening credit balances		
Sales	SDB	52,390	(if any)	b/d	200
Dishonoured bills or	Jnl	1,000	Cash received	CB	52,250
Cheques			Discounts allowed	CB	1,250
Cash paid to clear credit			Returns inwards from		
Balances	CB	110	debtors	SRDB	800
Closing credit balances	c/d	120	Bad debts	Jnl	300
			Closing debit balances	c/d	5,820
		60,620			60,620
Debit balances b/d		5,820	Credit balances b/d		120

Note. Opening credit balances are unusual in the debtors control account. They represent debtors to whom the business owes money, probably as a result of the over payment of debts or for advance payments of debts for which no invoices have yet been sent.

BOUGHT LEDGER (CREDITORS) CONTROL

	Folio	£		*Folio*	£
Opening debit balances			Opening credit balances	b/d	8,300
(if any)	b/d	70	Purchases and other		
Cash paid	CB	29,840	expenses	PDB	31,000
Discounts received	CB	30	Cash received clearing		
Returns outwards to	PRDB		debit balances	CB	20
Suppliers		60	Closing debit balances		
Closing credit balances	c/d	9,400	(if any)	c/d	80
		39,400			39,400
Debit balances	b/d	80	Credit balances	b/d	9,400

Note. Opening debit balances in the creditors control account would represent suppliers who owe the business money, perhaps because debts have been overpaid or because debts have been prepaid before the supplier has sent an invoice.

2.13 Posting from the journal to the memorandum sales or bought ledgers and to the nominal ledger may be effected as in the following example, where C Cloning has returned goods with a sales value of £50.

Journal entry	*Folio*	*Dr*	*Cr*
		£	£
Sales	NL 21	50	
To debtors' control	NL 6	-	50
To C Cloning (memorandum)	SL 13	-	50

Return of electrical goods inwards.

2.14 The following flowchart may help you to see how the debtors ledger and debtors (control) account are used.

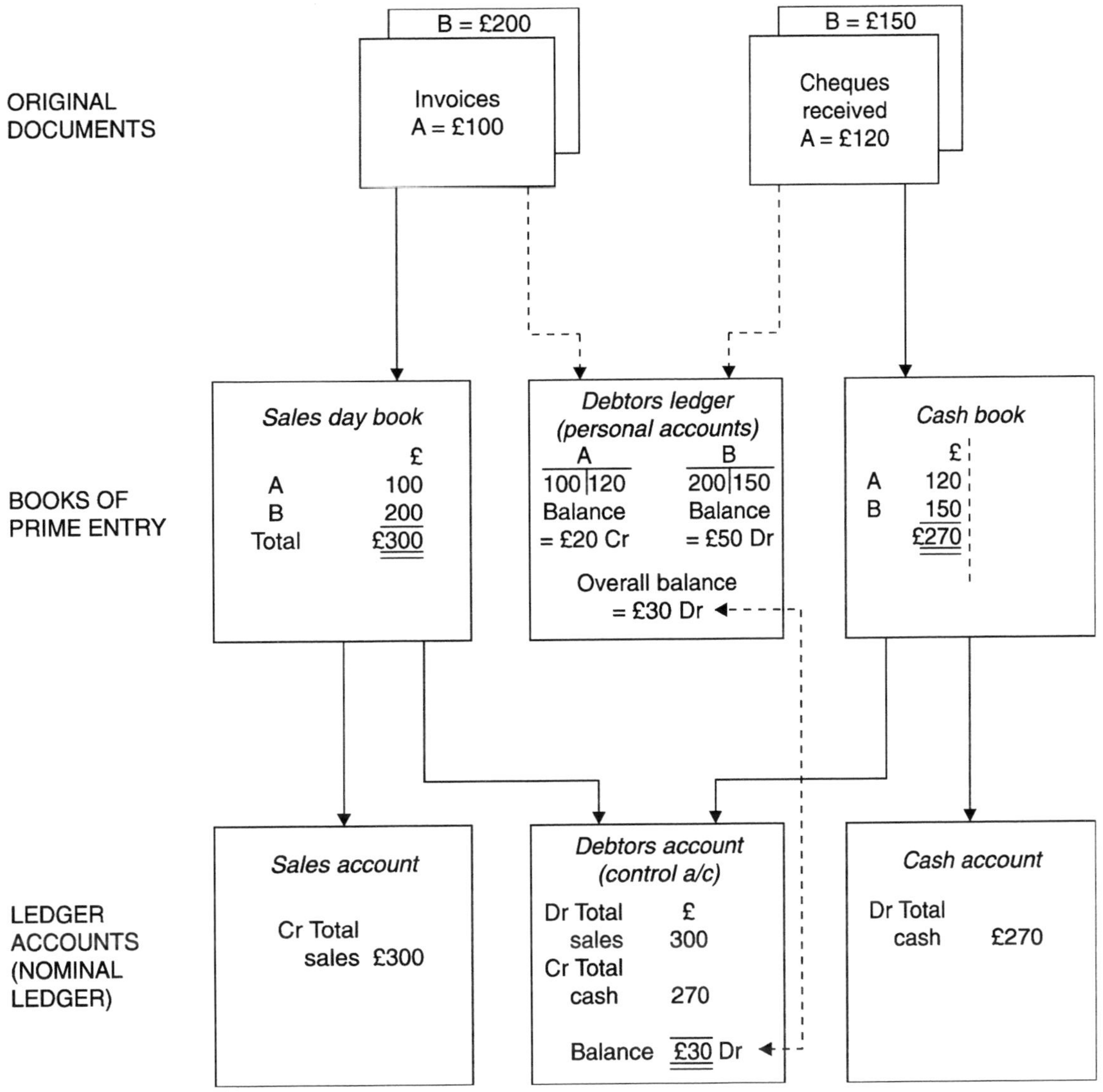

Notes

(a) The debtors ledger is not part of the double entry system (it is not used to post the ledger accounts).

(b) Nevertheless, the total balance on the debtors ledger (ie all the personal account balances added up) should equal the balance on the debtors account (the debtors control account).

(c) This diagram implies that the memorandum accounts (sales or purchase ledger) are written up from the original invoices rather than from the sales day book. The other treatment is also possible in practice.

2.15 See now whether you can do the following exercise.

Exercise 2

On examining the books of Exports Ltd, you ascertain that on 1 October 20X8 the debtors' ledger balances were £8,024 debit and £57 credit, and the creditors' ledger balances on the same date £6,235 credit and £105 debit.

For the year ended 30 September 20X9 the following particulars are available.

	£
Sales	63,728
Purchases	39,974
Cash received from debtors	55,212
Cash paid to creditors	37,307
Discount received	1,475
Discount allowed	2,328
Returns inwards	1,002
Returns outwards	535
Bad debts written off	326
Cash received in respect of debit balances in creditors' ledger	105
Amount due from customer as shown by debtors' ledger, offset against amount due to the same firm as shown by creditors' ledger (settlement by contra)	434
Cash received in respect of debt previously written off as bad	94
Allowances to customers on goods damaged in transit	212

On 30 September 20X9 there were no credit balances in the debtors' ledger except those outstanding on 1 October 20X8, and no debit balances in the creditors' ledger.

You are required to write up the following accounts recording the above transactions bringing down the balances as on 30 September 20X9.

(a) Debtors control account
(b) Creditors control account

Solution

(a)

DEBTORS CONTROL (OR TOTAL) ACCOUNT

		£			£
20X8			*20X8*		
Oct 1	Balances b/f	8,024	Oct 1	Balances b/f	57
20X9			*20X9*		
Sept 30	Sales	63,728	Sept 30	Cash received from debtors	55,212
	Balances c/f	57		Discount allowed	2,328
				Returns	1,002
				Bad debts written off	326
				Transfer creditors control account	434
				Allowances on goods damaged	212
				Balances c/f	12,238
		71,809			71,809
Oct 1	Balances b/f	12,238	Oct 1	Balances c/f	57

(b)

CREDITORS CONTROL (OR TOTAL) ACCOUNT

		£			£
20X8			*20X8*		
Oct 1	Balances b/f	105	Oct 1	Balances b/f	6,235
20X9			*20X9*		
Sept 30	Cash paid to creditors	37,307	Sept 30	Purchases	39,974
	Discount received	1,475		Cash	105
	Returns outwards	535			
	Transfer debtors control account	434			
	Balances c/f	6,458			
		46,314			46,314
			Oct 1	Balances b/f	6,458

Note. The double entry in respect of cash received for the bad debt previously written off is:

DEBIT	Cash	£94	
CREDIT	Profit and loss account		£94

Reasons for having control accounts

2.16 The reasons for having control accounts are as follows.

(a) They provide a check on the accuracy of entries made in the personal accounts in the sales ledger and purchase ledger. It is very easy to make a mistake in posting entries, because there might be hundreds of entries to make. Figures might get transposed. Some entries might be omitted altogether, so that an invoice or a payment transaction does not appear in a personal account as it should. By doing the comparisons (i) and (ii) it is possible to identify the fact that errors have been made.

   (i) The total balance on the debtors control account with the total of individual balances on the personal accounts in the sales ledger.

   (ii) The total balance on the creditors control account with the total of individual balances on the personal accounts in the purchase ledger.

(b) The control accounts could also assist in the location of errors, where postings to the control accounts are made daily or weekly, or even monthly. If a clerk fails to record an invoice or a payment in a personal account, or makes a transposition error, it would be a formidable task to locate the error or errors at the end of a year, say, given the hundreds or thousands of transactions during the year. By using the control account, a comparison with the individual balances in the sales or purchase ledger can be made for every week or day of the month, and the error found much more quickly than if control accounts did not exist.

(c) Where there is a separation of clerical (bookkeeping) duties, the control account provides an *internal check*. The person posting entries to the control accounts will act as a check on a different person whose job it is to post entries to the sales and purchase ledger accounts.

(d) To provide debtors and creditors balances more quickly for producing a trial balance or balance sheet. A single balance on a control account is obviously extracted more simply and quickly than many individual balances in the sales or purchase ledger. This means also that the number of accounts in the double entry bookkeeping system can be kept down to a manageable size, since the personal accounts are memorandum accounts only and the control accounts instead provide the accounts required for a double entry system.

2.17 However, particularly in computerised systems, it may be feasible to use sales and purchase ledgers without the need for operating separate control accounts. In such a system, the sales or purchase ledger printouts produced by the computer constitute the list of individual balances as well as providing a total balance which represents the control account balance.

Balancing and agreeing control accounts with sales and purchase (bought) ledgers

2.18 The control accounts should be balanced regularly (at least monthly), and the balance on the account agreed with the sum of the individual debtors' or creditors' balances extracted from the sales or bought ledgers respectively. It is one of the sad facts of an accountant's life that more often than not the balance on the control account does not agree with the sum of balances extracted, for one or more of the following reasons.

(a) An incorrect amount may be posted to the control account because of a miscast of the total in the book of prime entry (ie adding up incorrectly the total value of invoices or payments). The nominal ledger debit and credit postings will then balance, but the control account balance will not agree with the sum of individual balances extracted from the (memorandum) sales ledger or purchase ledger. A journal entry must then be made in the nominal ledger to correct the control account and the corresponding sales or expense account.

(b) A transposition error may occur in posting an individual's balance from the book of prime entry to the memorandum ledger, eg the sale to C Cloning of £250 might be posted to his account as £520. This means that the sum of balances extracted from the memorandum ledger must be corrected. No accounting entry would be required to do this, except to alter the figure in C Cloning's account.

(c) A transaction may be recorded in the control account and not in the memorandum ledger, or vice versa. This requires an entry in the ledger that has been missed out which means a double posting if the control account has to be corrected, and a single posting if it is the individual's balance in the memorandum ledger that is at fault.

(d) The sum of balances extracted from the memorandum ledger may be incorrectly extracted or miscast. This would involve simply correcting the total of the balances.

Example: agreeing control account balances with the sales and bought ledgers

2.19 Reconciling the control account balance with the sum of the balances extracted from the (memorandum) sales ledger or bought ledger should be done in two stages.

(a) Correct the total of the balances extracted from the memorandum ledger. (The errors must be located first of course.)

	£	£
Sales ledger total		
Original total extracted		15,320
Add difference arising from transposition error (£95 written as £59)		36
		15,356
Less		
Credit balance of £60 extracted as a debit balance (£60 × 2)	120	
Overcast of list of balances	90	
		210
		15,146

(b) Bring down the balance before adjustments on the control account, and adjust or post the account with correcting entries.

DEBTORS CONTROL

	£		£
Balance before adjustments	15,091	Petty cash - posting omitted	10
		Returns inwards – individual posting omitted from control Account	35
Undercast of total invoices issued in sales day book	100	Balance c/d (now in agreement with the corrected total of individual balances in (a))	15,146
	15,191		15,191
Balance b/d	15,146		

Reconciling bought ledger accounts with suppliers' statements 6/99

2.20 Another important control over the bought ledger (memorandum) is a comparison of the individual accounts with the suppliers' statements.

2.21 Most suppliers will send a customer a statement of account every month. This usually consists of the balance brought forward from the previous month, additional invoices sent out during the month, payments received and the balance carried forward at the end of the month.

2.22 The statement can then be compared with the supplier's account in the (memorandum) bought ledger to ensure that all invoices are accounted for. A reconciliation can be drawn up in a similar way to a bank reconciliation.

Chapter roundup

- A bank reconciliation requires a comparison between the bank balance recorded in the books of a business and the balance appearing on the bank statement. The comparison may reveal errors or omissions in the records of the business, which should be corrected by appropriate adjustments in the cash book.
- Once the cash book has been corrected it should be possible to reconcile its balance with the bank statement balance by taking account of timing differences, ie payments made and cheques received which are recorded in the cash book but have not yet cleared to the bank statement.
- The two most important control accounts are those for debtors and creditors. They are part of the double entry system. Cash books and day books are totalled periodically (say once a month) and the appropriate totals are posted to the control accounts.
- The individual entries in cash and day books will have been entered one by one in the appropriate personal accounts contained in the sales ledger and the purchase ledger. These personal accounts are not part of the double entry system: they are memorandum only.
- At suitable intervals the balances on personal accounts are extracted from the ledgers, listed and totalled. The total of the outstanding balances can then be reconciled to the balance on the appropriate control account and any errors located and corrected.

Test your knowledge

1 Name four common reasons for differences between the bank balance per the cash book and the balance per the bank statement. (see para 1.2)

2 Show the standard layout of a bank reconciliation. (1.7(b))

3 Name three accounting items for which control accounts may be used in the nominal ledger. (2.2)

4 Why might the balance on a control account not agree with the total of the ledger account balances? (2.18)

Now try illustrative questions 17 and 18 at the end of the Study Text

Chapter 14

CORRECTION OF ERRORS. PREPARATION OF FINAL ACCOUNTS

This chapter covers the following topics.

1 Types of error in accounting
2 The correction of errors
3 Preparation of final accounts

Introduction

You are nearly in a position to prepare the final accounts of a sole trader.

This chapter continues the subject of errors in accounts. You have already learned about errors which arise in the context of the cash book or the sales and purchase ledgers and debtors and creditors control accounts. Here we deal with errors that may be corrected by means of the journal or a suspense account.

1 TYPES OF ERROR IN ACCOUNTING 12/99

1.1 It is not really possible to draw up a complete list of all the errors which might be made by bookkeepers and accountants. Even if you tried, it is more than likely that as soon as you finished, someone would commit a completely new error that you had never even dreamed of! However, it is possible to describe five *types* of error which cover most of the errors which might occur. They are as follows.

(a) Errors of transposition
(b) Errors of omission
(c) Errors of principle
(d) Errors of commission
(e) Compensating errors

1.2 Once an error has been detected, it needs to be put right.

(a) If the correction involves a double entry in the ledger accounts, then it is done by using a journal entry in the journal.

(b) When the error breaks the rule of double entry, then it is corrected by the use of a suspense account as well as a journal entry.

1.3 In this chapter we will:

(a) Look at the five common types of error.
(b) Review journal entries (which we briefly looked at earlier in this text).
(c) Define a suspense account, and describe how it is used.

Errors of transposition

1.4 An error of transposition is when two digits in an amount are accidentally recorded the wrong way round. For example, suppose that a sale is recorded in the sales account as £6,843, but it has been incorrectly recorded in the total debtors account as £6,483. The error is the transposition of the 4 and the 8. The consequence is that total debits will not be equal to total credits. You can often detect a transposition error by checking whether the difference between debits and credits can be divided exactly by 9. For example, £6,843 – £6,483 = £360; £360 ÷ 9 = 40.

Errors of omission

1.5 An error of omission means failing to record a transaction at all, or making a debit or credit entry, but not the corresponding double entry.

(a) If a business receives an invoice from a supplier for £250, the transaction might be omitted from the books entirely. As a result, both the total debits and the total credits of the business will be out by £250.

(b) If a business receives an invoice from a supplier for £300, the purchase ledger control account might be credited, but the debit entry in the purchases account might be omitted. In this case, the total credits would not equal total debits (because total debits are £300 less than they ought to be).

Errors of principle

1.6 An error of principle involves making a double entry in the belief that the transaction is being entered in the correct accounts, but subsequently finding out that the accounting entry breaks the 'rules' of an accounting principle or concept. A typical example of such an error is to treat certain revenue expenditure incorrectly as capital expenditure.

(a) For example, repairs to a machine costing £150 should be treated as revenue expenditure, and debited to a repairs account. If, instead, the repair costs are added to the cost of the fixed asset (capital expenditure) an error of principle would have occurred. As a result, although total debits still equal total credits, the repairs account is £150 less than it should be and the cost of the fixed asset is £150 greater than it should be.

(b) Similarly, suppose that the proprietor of the business sometimes takes cash out of the till for his personal use and during a certain year these drawings amount to £280. The book-keeper states that he has reduced cash sales by £280 so that the cash book could be made to balance. This would be an error of principle, and the result of it would be that the drawings account is understated by £280, and so is the total value of sales in the sales account.

Errors of commission

1.7 Errors of commission are where the bookkeeper makes a mistake in carrying out his or her task of recording transactions in the accounts.

(a) *Putting a debit entry or a credit entry in the wrong account.* For example, if telephone expenses of £540 are debited to the electricity expenses account, an error of commission would have occurred. The result is that although total debits and total credits balance, telephone expenses are understated by £540 and electricity expenses are overstated by the same amount.

(b) *Errors of casting (adding up).* Suppose for example that the total daily credit sales in the sales day book of a business should add up to £28,425, but are incorrectly added up as £28,825. The total sales in the sales day book are then used to credit total sales and debit total debtors in the ledger accounts, so that total debits and total credits are still equal, although incorrect.

Compensating errors

1.8 Compensating errors are errors which are, coincidentally, equal and opposite to one another.

1.9 For example, two transposition errors of £540 might occur in extracting ledger balances, one on each side of the double entry. In the administration expenses account, £2,282 might be written instead of £2,822, while in the sundry income account, £8,391 might be written instead of £8,931. Both the debits and the credits would be £540 too low, and the mistake would not be apparent when the trial balance is cast. Consequently, compensating errors hide the fact that there are errors in the trial balance.

2 THE CORRECTION OF ERRORS 6/97

Journal entries

2.1 Some errors can be corrected by journal entries. To remind you, the format of a journal entry is:

Date	*Folio*	*Debit*	*Credit*
		£	£
Account to be debited		X	
Account to be credited			X
(Narrative to explain the transaction)			

2.2 The journal requires a debit and an equal credit entry for each 'transaction' - ie for each correction. This means that if total debits equal total credits before a journal entry is made then they will still be equal after the journal entry is made. This would be the case if, for example, the original error was a debit wrongly posted as a credit or vice versa.

2.3 Similarly, if total debits and total credits are unequal before a journal entry is made, then they will still be unequal (by the same amount) after it is made.

2.4 For example, suppose a bookkeeper accidentally posts a bill for £40 to the rates account instead of to the electricity account. A trial balance is drawn up, and total debits are £40,000 and total credits are £40,000. A journal entry is made to correct the misposting error as follows.

1.7.20X7

DEBIT	Electricity account	£40	
CREDIT	Rates account		£40

To correct a misposting of £40 from the rates account to electricity account.

2.5 After the journal has been posted, total debits will still be £40,000 and total credits will be £40,000. Total debits and totals credits are still equal.

2.6 Now suppose that, because of some error which has not yet been detected, total debits were originally £40,000 but total credits were £39,900. If the same journal correcting the £40 is put through, total debits will remain £40,000 and total credits will remain £39,900. Total debits were different by £100 *before* the journal, and they are still different by £100 *after* the journal.

2.7 This means that journals can only be used to correct errors which require both a credit and (an equal) debit adjustment.

Example: journal entries

2.8 Listed below are five errors which were used as examples earlier in this chapter. Write out the journal entries which would correct these errors.

(a) A business receives an invoice for £250 from a supplier which was omitted from the books entirely.

(b) Repairs worth £150 were incorrectly debited to the fixed asset (machinery) account instead of the repairs account.

(c) The bookkeeper of a business reduces cash sales by £280 because he was not sure what the £280 represented. In fact, it was drawings.

(d) Telephone expenses of £540 are incorrectly debited to the electricity account.

(e) A page in the sales day book has been added up to £28,425 instead of £28,825.

Solution

2.9 (a)

DEBIT	Purchases	£250	
CREDIT	Creditors		£250

A transaction previously omitted.

(b)

DEBIT	Repairs account	£150	
CREDIT	Fixed asset (machinery) a/c		£150

The correction of an error of principle. Repairs costs incorrectly added to fixed asset costs.

(c)

DEBIT	Drawings account	£280	
CREDIT	Sales		£280

An error of principle, in which sales were reduced to compensate for cash drawings not accounted for.

(d)

DEBIT	Telephone expenses	£540	
CREDIT	Electricity expenses		£540

Correction of an error of commission. Telephone expenses wrongly charged to the electricity account.

(e)

DEBIT	Debtors	£400	
CREDIT	Sales		£400

The correction of a casting error in the sales day book.
(£28,825 – £28,425 = £400)

Use of journal entries in examinations

2.10 Occasionally an examination question might ask you to 'journalise' a transaction (ie write it out in the form of a journal entry), even though the transaction is perfectly normal and nothing to do with an error. This is just the examiner's way of finding out whether you know your debits and credits. For example:

Question: A business sells £500 of goods on credit. Journalise the transaction.

Answer:

DEBIT	Debtors	£500	
CREDIT	Sales		£500

Goods to the value of £500 sold on credit.

2.11 No error has occurred here, just a normal credit sale of £500. By asking you to put it in the form of a journal, the examiner can see that you understand the double-entry bookkeeping involved.

Suspense accounts

6/98, 12/99

2.12 A suspense account is a *temporary* account which can be opened for a number of reasons. The most common reasons are as follows.

(a) A trial balance is drawn up which does not balance (ie total debits do not equal total credits).

(b) The bookkeeper of a business knows where to post the credit side of a transaction, but does not know where to post the debit (or vice versa). For example, a cash payment might be made and must obviously be credited to cash. The bookkeeper may not know what the payment is for, and so will not know which account to debit.

2.13 In both these cases, a temporary suspense account is opened up until the problem is sorted out. The next few paragraphs explain exactly how this works.

Use of suspense account: when the trial balance does not balance

2.14 When an error has occurred which results in an imbalance between total debits and total credits in the ledger accounts, the first step is to open a suspense account. For example, suppose an accountant draws up a trial balance and finds that, for some reason he cannot immediately discover, total debits exceed total credits by £162.

2.15 He knows that there is an error somewhere, but for the time being he opens a suspense account and enters a credit of £162 in it. This serves two purposes.

(a) Because the suspense account now exists, the accountant will not forget that there is an error (of £162) to be sorted out.

(b) Now that there is a credit of £162 in the suspense account, the trial balance balances.

2.16 When the cause of the £162 discrepancy is tracked down, it is corrected by means of a journal entry. For example, suppose it turned out that the accountant had accidentally failed to make a credit of £162 to purchases. The journal entry would be:

DEBIT	Suspense a/c	£162	
CREDIT	Purchases		£162

To close off suspense a/c and correct error.

2.17 Whenever an error occurs which results in total debits not being equal to total credits, the first step an accountant makes is to open up a suspense account. Three more examples are given below.

Example: transposition error

2.18 The bookkeeper of Mixem Gladly Ltd made a transposition error when entering an amount for sales in the sales account. Instead of entering the correct amount of £37,453.60 he entered £37,543.60, transposing the 4 and 5. The debtors were posted correctly, and so when total debits and credits on the ledger accounts were compared, it was found that credits exceeded debits by £(37,543.60 – 37,453.60) = £90.

2.19 The initial step is to equalise the total debits and credits by posting a debit of £90 to a suspense account.

2.20 When the cause of the error is discovered, the double entry to correct it should be logged in the journal as:

DEBIT	Sales	£90	
CREDIT	Suspense a/c		£90

To close off suspense a/c and correct transposition error.

Example: error of omission

2.21 When Guttersnipe Builders paid the monthly salary cheques to its office staff, the payment of £5,250 was correctly entered in the cash account, but the bookkeeper omitted to debit the office salaries account. As a consequence, the total debit and credit balances on the ledger accounts were not equal, and credits exceeded debits by £5,250.

2.22 The initial step in correcting the situation is to debit £5,250 to a suspense account, to equalise the total debits and total credits.

2.23 When the cause of the error is discovered, the double entry to correct it should be logged in the journal as:

DEBIT	Office salaries account	£5,250	
CREDIT	Suspense account		£5,250

To close off suspense account and correct error of omission.

Example: error of commission

2.24 A bookkeeper might make a mistake by entering what should be a debit entry as a credit, or vice versa. For example, suppose that a credit customer pays £460 of the £660 he owes to Ashdown Tree Felling Contractors, but Ashdown's bookkeeper has debited £460 on the debtors account in the nominal ledger by mistake instead of crediting the payment received.

2.25 The total debit balances in Ashdown's ledger accounts would now exceed the total credits by 2 × £460 = £920. The initial step in correcting the error would be to make a credit entry of £920 in a suspense account. When the cause of the error is discovered, it should be corrected as follows.

DEBIT	Suspense account	£920	
CREDIT	Debtors		£920

To close off suspense account and correct error of commission.

2.26 In the debtors account in the nominal ledger, the correction would appear therefore as follows.

DEBTORS ACCOUNT

	£		£
Balance b/f	660	Suspense account: error corrected	920
Payment incorrectly debited	460	Balance c/f	200
	1,120		1,120

Use of suspense account: not knowing where to post a transaction

2.27 Another use of suspense accounts occurs when a bookkeeper does not know in which account to post one side of a transaction. Until the mystery is sorted out, the credit entry can be recorded in a suspense account. A typical example is when the business receives cash through the post from a source which cannot be determined. The double entry in the accounts would be a debit in the cash book, and a credit to a suspense account.

2.28 Similarly, when the bookkeeper knows in which account to make one entry, but for some reason does not know where to make the corresponding entry, this can be posted to a suspense account. A very common example is to credit proceeds on disposal of fixed assets to the suspense account instead of working out the profit or loss on disposal.

Example: not knowing where to post a transaction

2.29 Windfall Garments received a cheque in the post for £620. The name on the cheque is R J Beasley Esq, but Windfall Garments have no idea who this person is, nor why he should be sending £620. The bookkeeper decides to open a suspense account, so that the double entry for the transaction is:

DEBIT	Cash	£620	
CREDIT	Suspense account		£620

2.30 Eventually, it transpires that the cheque was in payment for a debt owed by the Haute Couture Corner Shop and paid out of the proprietor's personal bank account. The suspense account can now be cleared, as follows.

DEBIT	Suspense account	£620	
CREDIT	Debtors		£620

Suspense accounts might contain several items

2.31 If more than one error or unidentifiable posting to a ledger account arises during an accounting period, they will all be merged together in the same suspense account. Indeed, until the causes of the errors are discovered, the bookkeepers are unlikely to know exactly how many errors there are. An examination question might give you a balance on a suspense account, together with enough information to make the necessary corrections, leaving a nil balance on the suspense account and correct balances on various other accounts. In practice, of course, finding these errors is far from easy!

Suspense accounts are temporary

2.32 It must be stressed that a suspense account can only be temporary. Postings to a suspense account are only made when the bookkeeper doesn't know yet what to do, or when an error has occurred. Mysteries must be solved, and errors must be corrected. Under no circumstances should there still be a suspense account when it comes to preparing the balance sheet of a business. The suspense account must be cleared and all the correcting entries made before the final accounts are drawn up.

3 PREPARATION OF FINAL ACCOUNTS 6/96 - 6/97, 12/98

3.1 You have already had practice at preparing a profit and loss account and balance sheet from a simple trial balance. Now see if you can do the same thing but at a more advanced level, taking account of adjustments for depreciation, stock, accruals, prepayments and bad and doubtful debts. Have a go at the following exercise.

Exercise

The following trial balance was extracted from the ledger of Stephen Chee, a sole trader, as at 31 May 20X1 - the end of his financial year.

STEPHEN CHEE
TRIAL BALANCE AS AT 31 MAY 20X1

	Dr	*Cr*
	£	£
Property, at cost	120,000	
Equipment, at cost	80,000	
Provisions for depreciation (as at 1 June 20X0)		
- on property		20,000
- on equipment		38,000
Purchases	250,000	
Sales		402,200
Stock, as at 1 June 20X0	50,000	
Discounts allowed	18,000	
Discounts received		4,800
Returns out		15,000
Wages and salaries	58,800	
Bad debts	4,600	
Loan interest	5,100	
Other operating expenses	17,700	
Trade creditors		36,000
Trade debtors	38,000	
Cash in hand	300	
Bank	1,300	
Drawings	24,000	
Provision for bad debts		500
17% long term loan		30,000
Capital, as at 1 June 20X0		121,300
	667,800	667,800

The following additional information as at 31 May 20X1 is available.

(a) Stock as at the close of business has been valued at cost at £42,000.
(b) Wages and salaries need to be accrued by £800.
(c) Other operating expenses are prepaid by £300.
(d) The provision for bad debts is to be adjusted so that it is 2% of trade debtors.
(e) Depreciation for the year ended 31 May 20X1 has still to be provided for as follows:

Property: 1.5% per annum using the straight line method.
Equipment: 25% per annum using the diminishing balance method.

Required

Prepare Stephen Chee's trading and profit and loss account for the year ended 31 May 20X1 and his balance sheet as at that date.

Solution

STEPHEN CHEE
TRADING AND PROFIT AND LOSS ACCOUNT
FOR THE YEAR ENDED 31 MAY 20X1

	£	£
Sales		
Cost of sales		402,200
Opening stock	50,000	
Purchases	250,000	
Purchases returns	(15,000)	
	285,000	
Closing stock	42,000	
		243,000
Gross profit		159,200
Other income - discounts received		4,800
		164,000
Expenses		
Operating expenses		
Wages and salaries (£58,800 + £800)	59,600	
Discounts allowed	18,000	
Bad debts (W1)	4,860	
Loan interest	5,100	
Depreciation	12,300	
Other operating expenses (£17,700 - £300)	17,400	
		117,260
Net profit for the year		46,740

STEPHEN CHEE
BALANCE SHEET AS AT 31 MAY 20X1

	Cost	*Accumu-lated depn.*	*Net book value*
Fixed assets	£	£	£
Property	120,000	21,800	98,200
Equipment	80,000	48,500	31,500
	200,000	70,300	129,700
Current assets			
Stock		42,000	
Trade debtors net of provision for bad debts (£38,000 less 2%)		37,240	
Prepayments		300	
Bank		1,300	
Cash in hand		300	
		81,140	
Current liabilities			
Trade creditors		36,000	
Accruals		800	
		36,800	
Net current assets			44,340
Less 17% loan			(30,000)
Net assets			144,040
Capital			
Balance at 1 June 20X0			121,300
Net profit for the year			46,740
			168,040
Drawings			(24,000)
			144,040

Workings

		£
1	*Provision for bad debts*	
	Previous provision	500
	New provision (2% × 38,000)	760
	Increase	260
	Per trial balance	4,600
	Profit and loss account	4,860
2	*Depreciation*	
	Property	
	Opening provision	20,000
	Provision for the year (1.5% × 120,000)	1,800
	Closing provision	21,800
	Equipment	
	Opening provision	38,000
	Provision for the year (25% × 42,000)	10,500
	Closing provision	48,500

Chapter roundup

- There are five types of error.
  - Errors of transposition
  - Errors of omission
  - Errors of principle
  - Errors of commission
  - Compensating errors
- Errors which leave total debits and total credits on the ledger accounts in balance can be corrected by using journal entries. Otherwise, a suspense account has to be opened first (and a journal entry used later to record the correction of the error, clearing the suspense account in the process).
- Suspense accounts, as well as being used to correct some errors, are also opened when it is not known immediately where to post an amount. When the mystery is solved, the suspense account is closed and the amount correctly posted using a journal entry.
- Suspense accounts are only temporary. None should exist when it comes to drawing up the financial statements at the end of the accounting period.
- You should now be able to prepare a set of final accounts for a sole trader from a trial balance after incorporating period end adjustments for depreciation, stock, prepayments, accruals and bad and doubtful debts.

Test your knowledge

1 List five types of error made in accounting. (see para 1.1)

2 What is the format of a journal entry? (2.1)

3 Explain what a suspense account is. (2.12)

4 What must be done with a suspense account before preparing a balance sheet? (2.32)

Now try illustrative questions 19 to 22 at the end of the Study Text

Chapter 15

INCOMPLETE RECORDS

This chapter covers the following topics.

Introduction

So far in your work on preparing the final accounts for a sole trader we have assumed that a full set of records are kept. In practice many sole traders do not keep a full set of records and you must apply certain techniques to arrive at the necessary figures.

Incomplete records questions are a very good test of your understanding of the way in which a set of accounts is built up.

Limited companies are obliged by law to keep proper accounting records. They will be considered in Chapter 16.

1 INCOMPLETE RECORDS QUESTIONS

1.1 Incomplete records problems occur when a business does not have a full set of accounting records.

(a) The proprietor of the business does not keep a full set of accounts.
(b) Some of the business accounts are accidentally lost or destroyed.

1.2 The problem for the accountant is to prepare a set of year-end accounts for the business; ie a trading, profit and loss account, and a balance sheet. Since the business does not have a full set of accounts, preparing the final accounts is not a simple matter of closing off accounts and transferring balances to the trading, P&L account, or showing outstanding balances in the balance sheet. The task of preparing the final accounts involves establishing the following.

(a) Cost of purchases and other expenses.
(b) Total amount of sales.
(c) Amount of creditors, accruals, debtors and prepayments at the end of the year.

1.3 Examination questions often take incomplete records problems a stage further, by introducing an 'incident' - such as fire or burglary- which leaves the owner of the business uncertain about how much stock has been destroyed or stolen.

1.4 The great merit of incomplete records problems is that they focus attention on the relationship between cash received and paid, sales and debtors, purchases and creditors, and stocks, as well as calling for the preparation of final accounts from basic principles.

1.5 To understand what incomplete records are about, it will obviously be useful now to look at what exactly might be incomplete. The items we shall consider in turn are:

(a) The opening balance sheet.
(b) Credit sales and debtors.
(c) Purchases and trade creditors.
(d) Purchases, stocks and the cost of sales.
(e) Stolen goods or goods destroyed.
(f) The cash book.
(g) Accruals and prepayments.
(h) Drawings.

2 THE OPENING BALANCE SHEET

2.1 The opening balance sheet is often referred to as a 'statement of affairs'. In practice there should not be any missing item in the opening balance sheet of the business, because it should be available from the preparation of the previous year's final accounts. However, an examination problem might provide information about the assets and liabilities of the business at the beginning of the period under review, but then leave the balancing figure - ie the proprietor's business capital - unspecified.

Example: opening balance sheet

2.2 Suppose a business has the following assets and liabilities as at 1 January 20X3.

	£
Fixtures and fittings at cost	7,000
Provision for depreciation, fixtures and fittings	4,000
Motor vehicles at cost	12,000
Provision for depreciation, motor vehicles	6,800
Stock in trade	4,500
Trade debtors	5,200
Cash at bank and in hand	1,230
Trade creditors	3,700
Prepayment	450
Accrued rent	2,000

You are required to prepare a balance sheet for the business, inserting a balancing figure for proprietor's capital.

Solution

2.3 Balance sheet as at 1 January 20X3

	£	£
Fixed assets		
Fixtures and fittings at cost	7,000	
Less accumulated depreciation	4,000	
		3,000
Motor vehicles at cost	12,000	
Less accumulated depreciation	6,800	
		5,200
		8,200
Current assets		
Stock in trade	4,500	
Trade debtors	5,200	
Prepayment	450	
Cash	1,230	
	11,380	
Current liabilities		
Trade creditors	3,700	
Accrual	2,000	
	5,700	
Net current assets		5,680
		13,880
Proprietor's capital as at 1 January 20X3 (balancing figure)		13,880

3 CREDIT SALES AND DEBTORS

3.1 If a business does not keep a record of its sales on credit, the value of these sales can be derived from the opening balance of trade debtors, the closing balance of trade debtors, and the payments received from trade debtors during the period.

	£
Credit sales are:	
Payments received from trade debtors	X
Plus closing balance of trade debtors (since these represent sales in the current Period for which cash payment has not yet been received)	X
Less opening balance of trade debtors (unless these become bad debts, they will pay What they owe in the current period for sales in a previous period)	(X)
	X

3.2 For example, suppose that a business had trade debtors of £1,750 on 1 April 20X4 and trade debtors of £3,140 on 31 March 20X5. If payments received from trade debtors during the year to 31 March 20X5 were £28,490, and if there are no bad debts, then credit sales for the period would be:

	£
Cash received from debtors	28,490
Plus closing debtors	3,140
Less opening debtors	(1,750)
Credit sales	29,880

If there are bad debts during the period, the value of sales will be increased by the amount of bad debts written off, no matter whether they relate to opening debtors or credit sales during the current period.

3.3 The same calculation could be made in a T account, with credit sales being the balancing figure to complete the account.

DEBTORS

	£		£
Opening balance b/f	1,750	Cash received	28,490
Credit sales (balancing fig)	29,880	Closing balance c/f	3,140
	31,630		31,630

3.4 The same interrelationship between credit sales, cash from debtors, and opening and closing debtors balances can be used to derive a missing figure for cash from debtors, or opening or closing debtors, given the values for the three other items. For example, if we know that opening debtors are £6,700, closing debtors are £3,200 and credit sales for the period are £69,400, then cash received from debtors during the period would be:

DEBTORS

	£		£
Opening balance	6,700	Cash received (balancing figure)	72,900
Sales (on credit)	69,400	Closing balance c/f	3,200
	76,100		76,100

An alternative way of presenting the same calculation would be as follows.

	£
Opening balance of debtors	6,700
Credit sales during the period	69,400
Total money owed to the business	76,100
Less closing balance of debtors	3,200
Equals cash received during the period	72,900

4 PURCHASES AND TRADE CREDITORS

4.1 A similar relationship exists between purchases of stock during a period, the opening and closing balances for trade creditors, and amounts paid to trade creditors during the period.

If we wish to calculate an unknown amount for purchases, the amount would be derived as follows.

	£
Payments to trade creditors during the period	X
Plus closing balance of trade creditors	X
(since these represent purchases in the current period for which payment has not yet been made)	
Less opening balance of trade creditors	(X)
(these debts, paid in the current period, relate to purchases in a previous period)	
Purchases during the period	X

4.2 For example, suppose that a business had trade creditors of £3,728 on 1 October 20X5 and trade creditors of £2,645 on 30 September 20X6. If payments to trade creditors during the year to 30 September 20X6 were £31,479, then purchases during the year would be:

	£
Payments to trade creditors	31,479
Plus closing balance of trade creditors	2,645
Less opening balance of trade creditors	(3,728)
Purchases	30,396

4.3 The same calculation could be made in a T account, with purchases being the balancing figure to complete the account.

CREDITORS

	£		£
Cash payments	31,479	Opening balance b/f	3,728
Closing balance c/f	2,645	Purchases (balancing figure)	30,396
	34,124		34,124

5 ESTABLISHING COST OF SALES

5.1 When the value of purchases is not known, a different approach might be required to find out what they were, depending on the nature of the information given to you.

5.2 One approach would be to use information about the cost of sales, and opening and closing stocks, in other words, to use the trading account rather than the trade creditors account to find the cost of purchases.

		£
Since	opening stocks	X
	plus purchases	X
	less closing stocks	(X)
	equals the cost of goods sold	X
then	the cost of goods sold	X
	plus closing stocks	X
	less opening stocks	(X)
	equals purchases	X

5.3 Suppose that the stock in trade of a business on 1 July 20X6 has a balance sheet value of £8,400, and a stock taking exercise at 30 June 20X7 showed stock to be valued at £9,350. Sales for the year to 30 June 20X7 are £80,000, and the business makes a gross profit of $33^1/_3$% on cost for all the items that it sells. What were the purchases during the year?

5.4 The cost of goods sold can be derived from the value of sales, as follows.

		£
Sales	($133^1/_3$%)	80,000
Gross profit	($33^1/_3$%)	20,000
Cost of goods sold	(100%)	60,000

The cost of goods sold is 75% of sales value.

	£
Cost of goods sold	60,000
Plus closing stock	9,350
Less opening stocks	(8,400)
Purchases	60,950

6 STOLEN GOODS OR GOODS DESTROYED

6.1 A similar type of calculation might be required to derive the value of goods stolen or destroyed. When an unknown quantity of goods is lost, whether they are stolen, destroyed in a fire, or lost in any other way such that the quantity lost cannot be counted, then the cost of the goods lost is the difference between (a) and (b) below.

(a) The cost of goods sold.

(b) Opening stock of the goods (at cost) plus purchases less closing stock of the goods (at cost).

In theory (a) and (b) should be the same. However, if (b) is a larger amount than (a), it follows that the difference must be the cost of the goods purchased and neither sold nor remaining in stock - ie the cost of the goods lost.

Example: cost of goods destroyed

6.2 Orlean Flames is a shop which sells fashion clothes. On 1 January 20X5, it had stock in trade which cost £7,345. During the 9 months to 30 September 20X5, the business purchased goods from suppliers costing £106,420. Sales during the same period were £154,000. The shop makes a gross profit of 40% on cost for everything it sells. On 30

September 20X5, there was a fire in the shop which destroyed most of the stock in it. Only a small amount of stock, known to have cost £350, was undamaged and still fit for sale.

How much stock was lost in the fire?

Solution

6.3 (a)

	£
Sales (140%)	154,000
Gross profit (40%)	44,000
Cost of goods sold (100%)	110,000

(b)

	£
Opening stock, at cost	7,345
Plus purchases	106,420
	113,765
Less closing stock, at cost	350
Equals cost of goods sold and goods lost	113,415

(c)

	£
Cost of goods sold and lost	113,415
Cost of goods sold	110,000
Cost of goods lost	3,415

Example: cost of goods stolen

6.4 Beau Gullard runs a jewellery shop in the High Street. On 1 January 20X9, his stock in trade, at cost, amounted to £4,700 and his trade creditors were £3,950.

During the six months to 30 June 20X9, sales were £42,000. Beau Gullard makes a gross profit of $33^1/_3$% on the sales value of everything he sells.

On 30 June, there was a burglary at the shop, and all the stock was stolen.

In trying to establish how much stock had been taken, Beau Gullard was only able to say that:

(a) He knew from his bank statements that he had paid £28,400 to creditors in the 6 month period to 30 June 20X9.

(b) He currently owed creditors £5,550.

Required

(a) Calculate the amount of stock stolen.
(b) Prepare a trading account for the 6 months to 30 June 20X9.

Solution

6.5 (a) The first 'unknown' is the amount of purchases during the period. This is established by the method previously described in this chapter.

CREDITORS

	£		£
Payments to creditors	28,400	Opening balance b/f	3,950
Closing balance c/f	5,550	Purchases (balancing figure)	30,000
	33,950		33,950

(b) The cost of goods sold is also unknown, but this can be established from the gross profit margin and the sales for the period.

		£
Sales	(100%)	42,000
Gross profit	($33^1/_3$%)	14,000
Cost of goods sold	($66^2/_3$%)	28,000

(c) The cost of the goods stolen is:

	£
Opening stock at cost	4,700
Purchases	30,000
	34,700
Less closing stock (after burglary)	0
Cost of goods sold and goods stolen	34,700
Cost of goods sold (see (b) above)	28,000
Cost of goods stolen	6,700

(d) The cost of the goods stolen will not be a charge in the trading account, and so the trading account for the period is as follows:

BEAU GULLARD
TRADING ACCOUNT FOR THE SIX MONTHS TO 30 JUNE 20X9

	£	£
Sales		42,000
Less cost of goods sold		
Opening stock	4,700	
Purchases	30,000	
	34,700	
Less stock stolen	6,700	
		28,000
Gross profit		14,000

Accounting for stock destroyed, stolen or otherwise lost

6.6 When stock is stolen, destroyed or otherwise lost, the loss must be accounted for somehow. The procedure was described briefly in the earlier chapter on accounting for stocks. Since the loss is not a trading loss, the cost of the goods lost is not included in the trading account, as the previous example showed. The accounting double entry is therefore

DEBIT See below
CREDIT Trading account (although instead of showing the cost of the loss as a credit, it is usually shown as a deduction on the debit side of the trading account, which is the same as a 'plus' on the credit side).

6.7 The account that is to be debited is one of two possibilities, depending on whether or not the lost goods were insured against the loss.

(a) If the lost goods were not insured, the business must bear the loss, and the loss is shown in the P & L account: ie

DEBIT Profit and loss
CREDIT Trading account

(b) If the lost goods were insured, the business will not suffer a loss, because the insurance will pay back the cost of the lost goods. This means that there is no charge at all in the P&L account, and the appropriate double entry is:

DEBIT Insurance claim account (debtor account)
CREDIT Trading account

with the cost of the loss. The insurance claim will then be a current asset, and shown in the balance sheet of the business as such. When the claim is paid, the account is then closed by

DEBIT Cash
CREDIT Insurance claim account

7 THE CASH BOOK

7.1 The construction of a cash book, largely from bank statements showing receipts and payments of a business during a given period, is often an important feature of incomplete records problems. In an examination, the purpose of an incomplete records question is largely to test the understanding of candidates about how various items of receipts or payments relate to the preparation of a final set of accounts for a business.

7.2 We have already seen in this chapter that information about cash receipts or payments might be needed to establish the amount of:

(a) Purchases during a period.
(b) Credit sales during a period.

Other items of receipts or payments might be relevant to establishing the amount of:

(a) Cash sales.
(b) Certain expenses in the P & L account.
(c) Drawings by the business proprietor.

7.3 It might therefore be helpful, if a business does not keep a cash book day-to-day, to construct a cash book at the end of an accounting period. A business which typically might not keep a day-to-day cash book is a shop.

(a) Many sales, if not all sales, are cash sales (ie with payment by notes and coins, cheques, or credit cards at the time of sale).

(b) Some payments are made in notes and coins out of the till rather than by payment out of the business bank account by cheque.

7.4 Where there appears to be a sizeable volume of receipts and payments in cash (ie notes and coins), then it is also helpful to construct a two column cash book. This is a cash book with one column for receipts and payments, and one column for money paid into and out of the business bank account.

An example will illustrate the technique and the purpose of a two column cash book.

Example: two column cash book

7.5 Jonathan Slugg owns and runs a shop selling fishing tackle, making a gross profit of 25% on the cost of everything he sells. He does not keep a cash book.

On 1 January 20X7 the balance sheet of his business was as follows.

	£	£
Net fixed assets		20,000
Stock	10,000	
Cash in the bank	3,000	
Cash in the till	200	
	13,200	
Trade creditors	1,200	
		12,000
		32,000
Proprietor's capital		32,000

In the year to 31 December 20X7:

(a) There were no sales on credit.
(b) £41,750 in receipts were banked.
(c) The bank statements of the period show the payments:

		£
(i)	To trade creditors	36,000
(ii)	Sundry expenses	5,600
(iii)	In drawings	4,400

(d) Payments were also made in cash out of the till:

		£
(i)	To trade creditors	800
(ii)	Sundry expenses	1,500
(iii)	In drawings	3,700

At 31 December 20X7, the business had cash in the till of £450 and trade creditors of £1,400. The cash balance in the bank was not known and the value of closing stock has not yet been calculated. There were no accruals or prepayments. No further fixed assets were purchased during the year. The depreciation charge for the year is £900.

Required

(a) Prepare a two column cash book for the period.

(b) Prepare the trading, profit and loss account for the year to 31 December 20X7 and the balance sheet as at 31 December 20X7.

Discussion and solution

7.6 A two column cash book is completed as follows.

(a) Enter the opening cash balances.

(b) Enter the information given about cash payments (and any cash receipts, if there had been any such items given in the problem).

(c) The cash receipts banked are a 'contra' entry, being both a debit (bank column) and a credit (cash in hand column) in the same account.

(d) Enter the closing cash in hand (cash in the bank at the end of the period is not known).

CASH BOOK

	Cash in hand	*Bank*		*Cash in hand*	*Bank*
	£	£		£	£
Balance b/f	200	3,000	Trade creditors	800	36,000
Cash receipts banked			Sundry expenses		
(contra)		41,750		1,500	5,600
Sales*	48,000		Drawings	3,700	4,400
			Cash receipts banked		
			(contra)	41,750	
Balance c/f		*1,250	Balance c/f	450	
	48,200	46,000		48,200	46,000

* Balancing figure

(e) The closing balance of money in the bank is a balancing figure.

(f) Since all sales are for cash, a balancing figure that can be entered in the cash book is sales, in the cash in hand (debit) column.

7.7 It is important to notice that since not all receipts from cash sales are banked, the value of cash sales during the period is:

	£
Receipts banked	41,750
Plus expenses and drawings paid out of the till in cash £(800 + 1,500 + 3,700)	6,000
Plus any cash stolen (here there is none)	0
Plus the closing balance of cash in hand	450
	48,200
Less the opening balance of cash in hand	(200)
Equals cash sales	48,000

7.8 The cash book constructed in this way has enabled us to establish both the closing balance for cash in the bank and also the volume of cash sales. The trading, profit and loss account and the balance sheet can also be prepared, once a value for purchases has been calculated.

CREDITORS

	£		£
Cash book:		Balance b/f	1,200
Payments from bank	36,000	Purchases (balancing figure)	37,000
Cash book:			
Payments in cash	800		
Balance c/f	1,400		
	38,200		38,200

The gross profit margin of 25% on cost indicates that the cost of the goods sold is £38,400, ie:

	£
Sales (125%)	48,000
Gross profit (25%)	9,600
Cost of goods sold (100%)	38,400

The closing stock amount is now a balancing figure in the trading account.

JONATHAN SLUGG
TRADING, PROFIT AND LOSS ACCOUNT
FOR THE YEAR ENDED 31 DECEMBER 20X7

	£	£
Sales		48,000
Less cost of goods sold		
Opening stock	10,000	
Purchases	37,000	
	47,000	
Less closing stock (balancing figure)	8,600	
		38,400
Gross profit (25/125 × £48,000)		9,600
Expenses		
Sundry £(1,500 + 5,600)	7,100	
Depreciation	900	
		8,000
Net profit		1,600

JONATHAN SLUGG
BALANCE SHEET AS AT 31 DECEMBER 20X7

	£	£
Net fixed assets £(20,000 – 900)		19,100
Stock	8,600	
Cash in the till	450	
	9,050	
Bank overdraft	1,250	
Trade creditors	1,400	
	2,650	
Net current assets		6,400
		25,500
Proprietor's capital		
Balance b/f		32,000
Net profit for the year		1,600
		33,600
Drawings £(3,700 + 4,400)		(8,100)
Balance c/f		25,500

Theft of cash from the till

7.9 When cash is stolen from the till, the amount stolen will be a credit entry in the cash book, and a debit in either the P&L account or insurance claim account, depending on whether the business is insured. The missing figure for cash sales, if this has to be calculated, must not ignore cash received but later stolen - see above.

8 ACCRUALS AND PREPAYMENTS

8.1 Where there is an accrued expense or a prepayment, the charge to be made in the P&L account for the item concerned should be found from the opening balance b/f, the closing balance c/f, and cash payments for the item during the period. The charge in the P&L account is perhaps most easily found as the balancing figure in a T account.

8.2 For example, suppose that on 1 April 20X6 a business had prepaid rent of £700 which relates to the next accounting period. During the year to 31 March 20X7 it pays £9,300 in rent, and at 31 March 20X7 the prepayment of rent is £1,000. The cost of rent in the P&L account for the year to 31 March 20X7 would be the balancing figure in the following T account. (Remember that a prepayment is a current asset, and so is a debit balance b/f.)

RENT

	£		£
Prepayment: balance b/f	700	P & L account (balancing figure)	9,000
Cash	9,300	Prepayment: balance c/f	1,000
	10,000		10,000
Balance b/f	1,000		

8.3 Similarly, if a business has accrued telephone expenses as at 1 July 20X6 of £850, pays £6,720 in telephone bills during the year to 30 June 20X7, and has accrued telephone expenses of £1,140 as at 30 June 20X7, then the telephone expense to be shown in the P&L account for the year to 30 June 20X7 is the balancing figure in the following T account. (Remember that an accrual is a current liability, and so is a credit balance b/f.)

TELEPHONE EXPENSES

	£		£
Cash	6,720	Balance b/f (accrual)	850
Balance c/f (accrual)	1,140	P&L a/c (balancing figure)	7,010
	7,860		7,860
		Balance b/f	1,140

9 DRAWINGS

9.1 Drawings would normally represent no particular problem at all in preparing a set of final accounts from incomplete records, but it is not unusual for examination questions to introduce a situation in which:

(a) The business owner pays income into his bank account which has nothing whatever to do with the business operations. For example, the owner might pay dividend income, or other income from investments into the bank, from stocks and shares which he owns personally, separate from the business itself. (In other words, there are no investments in the business balance sheet, and so income from investments cannot possibly be income of the business).

(b) The business owner pays money out of the business bank account for items which are not business expenses, such as life insurance premiums or a payment for his family's holidays etc.

9.2 Where such personal items of receipts or payments are made:

(a) Receipts should be set off against drawings. For example, if a business owner receives £600 in dividend income and pays it into his business bank account, although the dividends are from investments not owned by the business, then the accounting entry is:

DEBIT Cash
CREDIT Drawings

(b) Payments should be charged to drawings; ie

DEBIT Drawings
CREDIT Cash

Drawings: beware of the wording in an examination question

9.3 You should note the following.

(a) If a question states that a proprietor's drawings during a given year are 'approximately £40 per week' then you should assume that drawings for the year are £40 × 52 weeks = £2,080.

(b) However, if a question states that drawings in the year are 'between £35 and £45 per week', do not assume that the drawings average £40 per week and so amount to £2,080 for the year. You could not be certain that the actual drawings did average £40, and so you should treat the drawings figure as a missing item that needs to be calculated.

10 DEALING WITH INCOMPLETE RECORDS PROBLEMS IN THE EXAMINATION

6/96, 6/97, 6/99

10.1 A suggested approach to dealing with incomplete records problems brings together the various points described so far in this chapter. The nature of the 'incompleteness' in the records will vary from problem to problem, but the approach, suitably applied, should be successful in arriving at the final accounts whatever the particular characteristics of the problem might be.

10.2 The approach is as follows.

(a) *Step 1.* If possible, and if it is not already known, establish the opening balance sheet and the proprietor's interest.

(b) *Step 2.* Open up four accounts.

(i) Trading account (if you wish, leave space underneath for entering the P&L account later)

(ii) A cash book, with two columns if cash sales are significant and there are payments in cash out of the till

(iii) A debtors account

(iv) A creditors account

(c) *Step 3.* Enter the opening balances in these accounts.

(d) *Step 4.* Work through the information you are given line by line; and each item should be entered into the appropriate account if it is relevant to one or more of these four accounts.

You should also try to recognise each item as a 'P&L account income or expense item' or a 'closing balance sheet item'.

It may be necessary to calculate an amount for drawings and an amount for fixed asset depreciation.

(e) *Step 5.* Look for the balancing figures in your accounts. In particular you might be looking for a value for credit sales, cash sales, purchases, the cost of goods sold, the cost of goods stolen or destroyed, or the closing bank balance. Calculate these missing figures, and make any necessary double entry (eg to the trading account from the creditors account for purchases, to the trading account from the cash book for cash sales, and to the trading account from the debtors account for credit sales).

(f) *Step 6.* Now complete the P&L account and balance sheet. Working T accounts might be needed where there are accruals or prepayments.

10.3 An example will illustrate this approach.

Example: an incomplete records problem

10.4 John Snow is the sole distribution agent in the Branton area for Diamond floor tiles. Under an agreement with the manufacturers, John Snow purchases the Diamond floor tiles at a trade discount of 20% off list price and annually in May receives an agency commission of 1% of his purchases for the year ended on the previous 31 March.

For several years, John Snow has obtained a gross profit of 40% on all sales. In a burglary in January 20X1 John Snow lost stock costing £4,000 as well as many of his accounting records. However, after careful investigations, the following information has been obtained covering the year ended 31 March 20X1.

(a) Assets and liabilities at 31 March 20X0 were as follows:

		£
Buildings:	at cost	10,000
	provision for depreciation	6,000
Motor vehicles:	at cost	5,000
	provision for depreciation	2,000
Stock: at cost		3,200
Trade debtors (for sales)		6,300
Agency commission due		300
Prepayments (trade expenses)		120
Balance at bank		4,310
Trade creditors		4,200
Accrued vehicle expenses		230

(b) John Snow has been notified that he will receive an agency commission of £440 on 1 May 20X1.

(c) Stock, at cost, at 31 March 20X1 was valued at an amount £3,000 more than a year previously.

(d) In October 20X0 stock costing £1,000 was damaged by damp and had to be scrapped as worthless.

(e) Trade creditors at 31 March 20X1 related entirely to goods received whose list prices totalled £9,500.

(f) Discounts allowed amounted to £1,620 whilst discounts received were £1,200.

(g) Trade expenses prepaid at 31 March 20X1 totalled £80.

(h) Vehicle expenses for the year ended 31 March 20X1 amounted to £7,020.

(i) Trade debtors (for sales) at 31 March 20X1 were £6,700.

(j) All receipts are passed through the bank account.

(k) Depreciation is provided annually at the following rates.

Buildings 5% on cost
Motor vehicles 20% on cost.

(l) Commissions received are paid directly to the bank account.

(m) In addition to the payments for purchases, the bank payments were:

	£
Vehicle expenses	6,720
Drawings	4,300
Trade expenses	7,360

(n) John Snow is not insured against loss of stock owing to burglary or damage to stock caused by damp.

Required

Prepare John Snow's trading and profit and loss account for the year ended 31 March 20X1 and a balance sheet on that date.

Discussion and solution

10.5 This is an incomplete records problem because we are told that John Snow has lost many of his accounting records. In particular we do not know sales for the year, purchases during the year, or all the cash receipts and payments.

10.6 The first step is to find the opening balance sheet, if possible. In this case, it is. The proprietor's capital is the balancing figure.

JOHN SNOW
BALANCE SHEET AS AT 31 MARCH 20X0

	Cost	*Dep'n*	*NBV*
	£	£	£
Fixed assets			
Buildings	10,000	6,000	4,000
Motor vehicles	5,000	2,000	3,000
	15,000	8,000	7,000
Current assets			
Stock		3,200	
Trade debtors		6,300	
Commission due		300	
Prepayments		120	
Balance at hand		4,310	
		14,230	
Current liabilities			
Trade creditors		4,200	
Accrued expenses		230	
		4,430	
			9,800
			16,800
Proprietor's capital as at 31 March 20X0			16,800

10.7 The next step is to open up a trading account, cash book, debtors account and creditors account and to insert the opening balances, if known. Cash sales and payments in cash are not a feature of the problem, and so a single column cash book is sufficient.

10.8 The problem should then be read line by line, identifying any transactions affecting those accounts.

TRADING ACCOUNT

	£	£
Sales (note (f))		60,000
Opening stock	3,200	
Purchases (note (a))	44,000	
	47,200	
Less: damaged stock written off (note (c))	(1,000)	
stock stolen (note (e))	(4,000)	
	42,200	
Less closing stock (note (b))	6,200	
Cost of goods sold		36,000
Gross profit (note (f))		24,000

CASH BOOK

	£		£
Opening balance	4,310	Trade creditors	
Trade debtors (see below)	57,980	(see creditors a/c)	39,400
Agency commission (note (g))	300	Trade expenses	7,360
		Vehicle expenses	6,720
		Drawings	4,300
		Balance c/f	4,810
	62,590		62,590

TRADE DEBTORS

	£		£
Opening balance b/f	6,300	Discounts allowed (note (d))	1,620
Sales (note (f))	60,000	Cash received (balancing figure)	57,980
		Closing balance c/f	6,700
	66,300		66,300

TRADE CREDITORS

	£		£
Discounts received (note (d))	1,200	Opening balance b/f	4,200
Cash paid (balancing figure)	39,400	Purchases (note (a))	44,000
Closing balance c/f	7,600		
(£9,500 – 20% trade discount)	48,200		48,200

VEHICLE EXPENSES

	£		£
Cash	6,720	Accrual b/f	230
Accrual c/f (balancing figure)	530	P & L account	7,020
	7,250		7,250

10.9 The trading account is complete already, but now the P&L account and balance sheet can be prepared. Remember not to forget items such as the stock losses, commission earned on purchases, discounts allowed and discounts received.

JOHN SNOW - TRADING, PROFIT AND LOSS ACCOUNT
FOR THE YEAR ENDED 31 MARCH 20X1

	£	£
Sales (note (f))		60,000
Opening stock	3,200	
Purchases (note (a))	44,000	
	47,200	
Less: damaged stock written off (note (c))	(1,000)	
stock stolen	(4,000)	
	42,200	
Less closing stock (note (b))	6,200	
Cost of goods sold		36,000
Gross profit (note (f))		24,000
Add: commission on purchases		440
discounts received		1,200
		25,640
Expenses		
Trade expenses (note (h))	7,400	
Stock damaged	1,000	
Stock stolen	4,000	
Vehicle expenses	7,020	
Discounts allowed	1,620	
Depreciation		
Buildings	500	
Motor vehicles	1,000	
		22,540
Net profit (to capital account)		3,100

JOHN SNOW
BALANCE SHEET AS AT 31 MARCH 20X1

	Cost	Dep'n	NBV
	£	£	£
Fixed assets			
Buildings	10,000	6,500	3,500
Motor vehicles	5,000	3,000	2,000
	15,000	9,500	5,500
Current assets			
Stock		6,200	
Trade debtors		6,700	
Commission due		440	
Prepayments (trade expenses)		80	
Balance at bank		4,810	
		18,230	
Current liabilities			
Trade creditors		7,600	
Accrued expenses		530	
		8,130	
			10,100
			15,600
Proprietor's capital			
As at 31 March 20X0			16,800
Net profit for year to 31 March 20X1		3,100	
Less drawings		(4,300)	
Retained deficit			(1,200)
As at 31 March 20X1			15,600

Notes

(a) The agency commission due on 1 May 20X1 indicates that purchases for the year to 31 March 20X1 were

$100\%/1\% \times £440 = £44{,}000$

(b) Closing stock at cost on 31 March 20X1 was £(3,200 + 3,000) = £6,200.

(c) Stock scrapped (£1,000) is accounted for by:

CREDIT Trading account
DEBIT P&L account

(d) Discounts allowed are accounted for by:

DEBIT Discounts allowed account
CREDIT Debtors

Similarly, discounts received are:

DEBIT Creditors
CREDIT Discounts received

Note. Discounts received represents settlement discounts, not *trade* discounts, which are not usually accounted for as they are given automatically at source.

(e) Stocks lost in the burglary are accounted for by:

CREDIT Trading account
DEBIT P&L account

(f) The trade discount of 20% has already been deducted in arriving at the value of the purchases. The gross profit is 40% on sales, so with cost of sales = £36,000

		£
Cost	(60%)	36,000
Profit	(40%)	24,000
Sales	(100%)	60,000

(It is assumed that trade expenses are not included in the trading account, and so should be ignored in this calculation.)

(g) The agency commission of £300 due on 1 May 20X0 would have been paid to John Snow at that date.

(h) The P&L account expenditure for trade expenses and closing balance on vehicle expenses account are as follows:

TRADE EXPENSES

	£		£
Prepayment	120	P&L account (balancing figure)	7,400
Cash	7,360	Prepayment c/f	80
	7,480		7,480

Using a debtors account to calculate both cash sales and credit sales

10.10 A final point which needs to be considered is how a missing value can be found for cash sales and credit sales, when a business has both, but takings banked by the business are not divided between takings from cash sales and takings from credit sales.

Example: using a debtors account

10.11 Suppose, for example, that a business had, on 1 January 20X8, trade debtors of £2,000, cash in the bank of £3,000, and cash in hand of £300.

During the year to 31 December 20X8 the business banked £95,000 in takings.

It also paid out the following expenses in cash from the till:

Drawings	£1,200
Sundry expenses	£800

On 29 August 20X8 a thief broke into the shop and stole £400 from the till.

At 31 December 20X8 trade debtors amounted to £3,500, cash in the bank £2,500 and cash in the till £150.

What was the value of sales during the year?

Solution

10.12 If we tried to prepare a debtors account and a two column cash book, we would have insufficient information, in particular about whether the takings which were banked related to cash sales or credit sales.

DEBTORS

	£		£
Balance b/f	2,000	Payments from debtors (credit sales)	*Unknown*
Credit sales	*Unknown*		
		Balance c/f	3,500

CASH BOOK

	Cash	*Bank*		*Cash*	*Bank*
	£	£		£	£
Balance b/f	300	3,000	Drawings	1,200	
			Sundry expenses	800	
Debtors-payments		*Unknown*	Cash stolen	400	
Cash sales	*Unknown*		Balance c/f	150	2,500

All we do know is that the combined sums from debtors and cash takings banked is £95,000.

The value of sales can be found instead by using the debtors account, which should be used to record cash takings banked as well as payments by debtors. The balancing figure in the debtors account will then be a combination of credit sales and some cash sales. The cash book only needs to be a single column.

DEBTORS

	£		£
Balance b/f	2,000	Cash banked	95,000
Sales-to trading account	96,500	Balance c/f	3,500
	98,500		98,500

CASH (EXTRACT)

	£		£
Balance in hand b/f	300	Payments in cash:	
Balance in bank b/f	3,000	Drawings	1,200
Debtors a/c	95,000	Expenses	800
		Other payments	?
		Cash stolen	400
		Balance in hand c/f	150
		Balance in bank c/f	2,500

The remaining 'undiscovered' amount of cash sales is now found as follows.

	£	£
Payments in cash out of the till		
Drawings	1,200	
Expenses	800	
		2,000
Cash stolen		400
Closing balance of cash in hand		150
		2,550
Less opening balance of cash in hand		(300)
Further cash sales		2,250

(This calculation is similar to the one described above for calculating cash sales.)

Total sales for the year are:

	£
From debtors account	96,500
From cash book	2,250
Total sales	98,750

Exercise

Mary Grimes, retail fruit and vegetable merchant, does not keep a full set of accounting records. However, the following information has been produced from the business's records.

(a) Summary of the bank account for the year ended 31 August 20X8

	£		£
1 Sept 20X7 balance brought forward	1,970	Payment to suppliers	72,000
		Purchase of motor van (E471 KBR)	13,000
Receipts from trade debtors	96,000	Rent and rates	2,600
Sale of private yacht	20,000	Wages	15,100
Sale of motor van (A123 BWA)	2,100	Motor vehicle expenses	3,350
		Postages and stationery	1,360
		Drawings	9,200
		Repairs and renewals	650
		Insurances	800
		31 August 20X8 balance c/fwd	2,010
	120,070		120,070
1 Sept 20X8 balance b/fwd	2,010		

(b) Assets and liabilities, other than balance at bank as at:

			1 Sept 20X7	*31 Aug 20X8*
			£	£
Trade creditors			4,700	2,590
Trade debtors			7,320	9,500
Rent and rates accruals			200	260
Motor vans:				
	A123 BWA:	At cost	10,000	-
		Provision for depreciation	8,000	-
	E471 KBR:	At cost	-	13,000
		Provision for depreciation	-	To be determined
Stock in trade			4,900	5,900
Insurance prepaid			160	200

(c) All receipts are banked and all payments are made from the business bank account.

(d) A trade debt of £300 owing by John Blunt and included in the trade debtors at 31 August 20X8 (see (b) above), is to be written off as a bad debt.

(e) It is Mary Grimes' policy to provide depreciation at the rate of 20% on the cost of motor vans held at the end of each financial year; no depreciation is provided in the year of sale or disposal of a motor van.

(f) Discounts received during the year ended 31 August 20X8 from trade creditors amounted to £1,100.

Required

(a) Prepare Mary Grimes' trading and profit and loss account for the year ended 31 August 20X8.

(b) Prepare Mary Grimes' balance sheet as at 31 August 20X8.

Solution

(a) TRADING AND PROFIT AND LOSS ACCOUNT
FOR THE YEAR ENDED 31 AUGUST 20X8

	£	£
Sales (W1)		98,180
Opening stock	4,900	
Purchases (W2)	70,990	
	75,890	
Less closing stock	5,900	
		69,990
Gross profit		28,190
Discounts received		1,100
Profit on sale of motor vehicle £2,100 - £(10,000 - 8,000)		100
		29,390
Rent and rates (W3)	2,660	
Wages	15,100	
Motor vehicle expenses	3,350	
Postages and stationery	1,360	
Repairs and renewals	650	
Insurances (W4)	760	
Bad debt	300	
Depreciation of van (20% × £13,000)	2,600	
		26,780
		2,610

(b) BALANCE SHEET AS AT 31 AUGUST 20X8

	£	£
Fixed assets		
Motor van: cost	13,000	
depreciation	2,600	
		10,400
Current assets		
Stock	5,900	
Debtors (£9,500 - £300 bad debt)	9,200	
Prepayment	200	
Cash at bank	2,010	
	17,310	
Current liabilities		
Creditors	2,590	
Accrual	260	
	2,850	
Net current assets		14,460
		24,860
Capital account		
Balance at 1 September 20X7 (W5)		11,450
Additional capital: proceeds on sale of yacht		20,000
Net profit for the year	2,610	
Less drawings	9,200	
Retained loss for the year		(6,590)
Balance at 31 August 20X8		24,860

Workings

1 *Sales*

	£
Cash received from customers	96,000
Add debtors balances at 31 August 20X8	9,500
	105,500
Less debtors balances at 1 September 20X7	7,320
Sales in year	98,180

2 *Purchases*

	£	£
Payments to suppliers		72,000
Add: creditors balances at 31 August 20X8	2,590	
discounts granted by creditors	1,100	
		3,690
		75,690
Less creditors balances at 1 September 20X7		4,700
		70,990

3 *Rent and rates*

	£
Cash paid in year	2,600
Add accrual at 31 August 20X8	260
	2,860
Less accrual at 1 September 20X7	200
Charge for the year	2,660

4 *Insurances*

	£
Cash paid in year	800
Add prepayment at 1 September 20X7	160
	960
Less prepayment at 31 August 20X8	200
	760

Workings 1-4 could also be presented in ledger account format as follows. (In the examination, either format is acceptable, so use whichever method you find easier.)

TOTAL DEBTORS

	£		£
Balance b/f	7,320	Bank	96,000
∴ Sales	98,180	Balance c/f	9,500
	105,500		105,500

TOTAL CREDITORS

	£		£
Bank	72,000	Balance b/f	4,700
Discounts received	1,100	∴ Purchases	70,990
Balance c/f	2,590		
	75,690		75,690

RENT AND RATES

	£		£
Bank	2,600	Balance b/f	200
Balance c/f	260	∴ P & L charge	2,660
	2,860		2,860

INSURANCES

	£		£
Balance b/f	160	∴ P & L charge	760
Bank	800	Balance c/f	200
	960		960

5 *Capital at 1 September 20X7*

	£	£
Assets		
Bank balance		1,970
Debtors		7,320
Motor van £(10,000 - 8,000)		2,000
Stock		4,900
Prepayment		160
		16,350
Liabilities		
Trade creditors	4,700	
Accrual	200	
		4,900
		11,450

Chapter roundup

- Incomplete records questions may test your ability to prepare accounts in the following situations.
  - A trader does not maintain a ledger and therefore has no continuous double entry record of transactions.
  - Accounting records are destroyed by accident, such as fire.
  - Some essential figure is unknown and must be calculated as a balancing figure. This may occur as a result of stock being damaged or destroyed, or because of misappropriation of assets.
- The approach to incomplete records questions is to build up the information given so as to complete the necessary double entry. This may involve reconstructing control accounts for:
  - Cash and bank (often in columnar format)
  - Debtors and creditors
- Where stock, sales or purchases is the unknown figure it will be necessary to use information on gross profit percentages so as to construct a trading account in which the unknown figure can be inserted as a balance.

Test your knowledge

1. In the absence of a sales account or sales day book, how can a figure of credit sales for the year be computed? (see para 3.1)
2. In the absence of a purchase account or purchases day book, how can a figure of purchases for the year be computed? (4.1)
3. What is the accounting double entry to record the loss of stock by fire or burglary? (6.6, 6.7)
4. If a business proprietor pays his personal income into the business bank account, what is the accounting double entry to record the transaction? (9.2)

Now try illustrative questions 23 and 24 at the end of the Study Text

Chapter 16

LIMITED COMPANIES

This chapter covers the following topics.

Introduction

So far, this Study Text has dealt mainly with the accounts of businesses in general. In this chapter we shall turn our attention to the accounts of *limited companies.* As we should expect, the accounting rules and conventions for recording the business transactions of limited companies and then preparing their final accounts, are much the same as for sole traders. For example, companies will have a cash book, sales day book, purchase day book, journal, sales ledger, purchase ledger and nominal ledger etc. They also prepare a profit and loss account annually, and a balance sheet at the end of the accounting year.

We shall see in this chapter that, in the balance sheet, the treatment of assets and liabilities is basically the same but the particular nature of limited companies calls for changes in the owners' equity section. Similarly, in the profit and loss account, the principal differences are found in the appropriation account - that part of the profit and loss account which shows how the profit or loss for the period has been allocated.

One important difference is the legal requirement that limited companies must publish their accounts. The relevant legislation specifies certain information which must be included in the published financial statements of a limited company.

It should be stressed that, while you do not have to learn the published accounts formats by heart at this stage, it is important for you to have an overall awareness of the form of company accounts.

1 THE STATUTORY FRAMEWORK OF LIMITED COMPANY ACCOUNTS

1.1 The following are the most significant differences between the accounts of limited companies and those of unincorporated organisations.

(a) The legislation governing the activities of limited companies is very extensive. Amongst other things, the Companies Acts define certain minimum accounting records which must be maintained by companies. Accounts must be filed with the Registrar of Companies, normally once a year. This is so accounts are available for public inspection. There are detailed requirements on the minimum information which must be disclosed in a company's accounts. Businesses which are not limited companies (non-incorporated businesses) enjoy comparative freedom from statutory regulation.

(b) The owners of a company (its *members or shareholders*) may be very numerous. Their capital is shown differently from that of a sole trader; and similarly the appropriation account of a company is different.

(c) In the case of a sole trader, day-to-day management of the business is usually in the hands of the owner. With companies, the owners (members or shareholders) appoint directors to be responsible for management. The fact that in small companies shareholders and directors are often the same people should not obscure the legal distinction between the two roles. If a director receives a salary it is an employee payroll cost chargeable as an expense against profit. If the director is also a shareholder and receives a *dividend* (see 2.4), that is an appropriation of profit, similar to *drawings* in a sole trader's accounts.

Limited liability

12/97

1.2 Limited companies offer *limited liability* to their owners. This means that the maximum amount that an owner stands to lose in the event that the company becomes insolvent and cannot pay off its debts, is the capital in the business. This limited liability is therefore a major advantage of turning a business into a limited company. For example, if a limited company becomes insolvent owing large sums of money to its creditors, the owners of the company will not be required to pay the company's debts from their own personal resources.

1.3 As a business grows, it needs more capital to finance its operations, and significantly more than the people currently managing the business can provide themselves. One way of obtaining more capital is to invite investors from outside the business to invest in the ownership or 'equity' of the business. These new co-owners would not usually be expected to help with managing the business. To such investors, limited liability is very attractive. Investments are always risky undertakings, but with limited liability the investor knows the maximum amount that he stands to lose when he puts some capital into a company.

1.4 There are two classes of limited company.

(a) *Private companies*. These have the word 'limited' at the end of their name. Being private, they cannot invite members of the public to invest in their equity (ownership).

(b) *Public companies*. These are much fewer in number than private companies, but are generally much larger in size. They have the words 'public limited company' - shortened to PLC or plc (or the Welsh language equivalent) at the end of their name. Public limited companies can invite members of the general public to invest in their equity, and the 'shares' of these companies are traded on the Stock Exchange.

2 SHARE CAPITAL, RESERVES AND DEBENTURES

The capital of limited companies

2.1 The proprietors' capital in a limited company consists of share capital. When a company is set up for the first time, it issues shares, which are paid for by investors, who then become shareholders of the company. Shares are denominated in units of 25 pence, 50 pence, £1 or whatever seems appropriate. The 'face value' of the shares is called their nominal value.

2.2 For example, when a company is set up with a *share capital* of, say, £100,000, it may be decided to issue it in any of the following ways.

(a) 100,000 shares of £1 each nominal value
(b) 200,000 shares of 50p each
(c) 400,000 shares of 25p each
(d) 250,000 shares of 40p each

The nominal value is not the same as the market value, which is the price someone is prepared to pay for the share.

2.3 A distinction is made between authorised, issued, called up and paid up share capital. This will be covered in detail in your later studies. For now you should note that the *authorised* share capital is the maximum amount of share capital that the company is empowered to issue. *Issued* share capital is the nominal amount of share capital that has been issued to shareholders. This cannot exceed the authorised share capital.

Dividends

2.4 Profits paid out to shareholders are called *dividends*. Dividends are appropriations of profit after tax. A company might pay dividends in two stages during the course of their accounting year.

(a) In mid year, after the half-year financial results are known, the company might pay an interim dividend.

(b) At the end of the year, the company might pay a further final dividend.

The total dividend for the year is the sum of the interim and the final dividends. (Not all companies pay an interim dividend. Interim dividends are, however, commonly paid out by public limited companies.)

At the end of an accounting year, a company's directors will have proposed a final dividend payment, but this will not yet have been paid. This means that the final dividend should be appropriated out of profits and shown as a current liability in the balance sheet.

2.5 The terminology of dividend payments can be confusing, since they may be expressed either in the form, as 'x pence per share' or as 'y per cent'. In the latter case, the meaning is always 'y per cent of the *nominal* value of the shares in issue'. For example, suppose a company's issued share capital consists of 100,000 50p ordinary shares. The company's balance sheet would include the following.

Called up share capital:	100,000 50p ordinary shares	£50,000

If the directors wish to pay a dividend of £5,000, they may propose either:

(a) A dividend of 5p per share (100,000 × 5p = £5,000).
(b) A dividend of 10% (10% × £50,000 = £5,000).

Ordinary shares and preference shares

2.6 At this stage it is relevant to distinguish between the two types of shares most often encountered, *preference shares* and *ordinary shares*.

2.7 *Preference shares* are now rather old-fashioned and are rarely issued, although they do have occasional resurgences of popularity.

2.8 They carry the right to a final dividend which is expressed as a percentage of their nominal value: eg a 6% £1 preference share carries a right to an annual dividend of 6p. Preference dividends have priority over ordinary dividends; in other words, if the directors of a company wish to pay a dividend (which they are not obliged to so) they must pay any preference dividend first. Otherwise, no ordinary dividend may be paid.

2.9 The rights attaching to preference shares are set out in the company's constitution. They may vary from company to company, but typically:

(a) Preference shareholders have a *priority right* over ordinary shareholders to a *return of their capital* if the company goes into liquidation.

(b) Preference shares do *not carry a right to vote.*

(c) If the preference shares are cumulative, it means that before a company can pay an ordinary dividend it must not only pay the current year's preference dividend, but must also make good any arrears of preference dividends unpaid in previous years.

2.10 *Ordinary shares* are by far the most common. They carry no right to a fixed dividend but are entitled to all profits left after payment of any preference dividend. Generally however, only a part of such remaining profits is distributed, the rest being kept in reserve (see below). The amount of ordinary dividends fluctuates although there is a general expectation that it will increase from year to year. Should the company be wound up, any surplus is shared between the ordinary shareholders. Ordinary shares normally carry voting rights, and in effect ordinary shareholders are the owners of the company.

Exercise 1

At the year-end, the trial balance for KT Ltd shows a debit balance of £20,000 in respect of dividends. The Share Capital account of £1m comprises 200,000 5% preference shares of £1 with the balance made up of 50p ordinary shares. The dividends account represents a half-year's preference dividend and an interim ordinary dividend. A final dividend of 5p per ordinary share is proposed.

Calculate the interim and final dividends for each category of share.

Solution

A full year's dividend on the preference shares is 200,000 @ 5% = £10,000, therefore a half-year's dividend was £5,000, with a final dividend of the same amount.

The interim ordinary dividend was therefore £15,000 (£20,000 - £5,000).

As the share capital account amounts to £1m, £800,000 (£1m - £200k) must relate to ordinary shares. However, the ordinary shares are only 50p each, meaning that there are 1.6 million of them. The final dividend is therefore £80,000 (1.6m x 5p)

Reserves

2.11 The ordinary shareholders' total investment in a limited company is called the *equity* and consists of share capital plus *reserves*. You will also meet the term *shareholders' funds*, which is used to describe the total of all share capital, both ordinary and preference, and the reserves. The important point to note is that all reserves are owned by the ordinary shareholders.

2.12 A distinction should be made between the two types of reserves.

(a) Statutory reserves are reserves which a company is required to set up by law and which are not available for the distribution of dividends.

(b) Non-statutory reserves are reserves consisting of profits which are distributable as dividends, if the company so wishes.

Profit and loss reserve (retained profits)

2.13 This is the most significant non-statutory reserve, and it is described in many different ways:

(a) Revenue reserve.
(b) Retained profits.
(c) Retained earnings.
(d) Undistributed profits.
(e) Profit and loss account.
(f) Unappropriated profits.

2.14 These are profits earned by the company and not appropriated by dividends, taxation or transfer to another reserve account. This reserve generally increases from year to year, as most companies do not distribute all their profits as dividends. Dividends can be paid from it: even if a loss is made in one particular year, a dividend can be paid from previous years' retained profits. For example, if a company makes a loss of £100,000 in one year, yet has unappropriated profits from previous years totalling £250,000, it can pay a dividend not exceeding £150,000. One reason for retaining some profit each year is to enable the company to pay dividends even when profits are low (or non-existent). Another reason is usually shortage of cash. Very occasionally, you might come across a debit balance on the profit and loss account. This would indicate that the company has accumulated losses.

Other non-statutory reserves

2.15 The company directors may choose to set up other reserves. These may have a specific purpose (for example plant and machinery replacement reserve) or not (for example general reserve). The creation of these reserves usually indicates a general intention not to distribute the profits involved at any future date, although legally any such reserves, being non-statutory, remain available for the payment of dividends. Therefore, these reserves are revenue reserves.

2.16 Profits are transferred to these reserves by making an appropriation out of profits, usually profits for the year. Typically, you might come across the following.

	£	£
Profit after taxation		100,000
Appropriations of profit		
Dividend	60,000	
Transfer to general reserve	10,000	
		70,000
Retained profits for the year		30,000
Profit and loss reserve b/f		250,000
Profit and loss reserve c/f		280,000

2.17 There is no real significance about the creation of separate non-statutory reserves. After all, there is little difference between the following two balance sheet extracts.

		£	£
(a)	Net assets		3,500
	Financed by		
	Share capital		2,000
	Reserves: general (distributable as dividend)	1,000	
	retained profits (distributable)	500	
			1,500
			3,500

		£
(b)	Net assets	3,500
	Financed by	
	Share capital	2,000
	Reserves: retained profit (distributable)	1,500
		3,500

2.18 The establishment of a 'plant and machinery replacement reserve' (or something similar) indicates an intention by a company to keep funds in the business to replace its plant and machinery. However, the reserve would still, legally, represent distributable profits, and the existence of such a reserve no more guarantees the company's ability to replace its fixed assets in the future than the depreciation charge in the P & L account, or accumulated provision for depreciation in the balance sheet.

The share premium account

2.19 There are a number of statutory (or capital) reserves, the most important of which at this stage is the share premium account. A share premium arises when a company sells shares for a price which is higher than their nominal value. By 'premium' is meant the difference between the issue price of the share and its nominal value. When a company is first incorporated (set up) the issue price of its shares will probably be the same as their nominal value and so there would be no share premium. If the company does well the market value of its shares will increase, but not the nominal value. The price of any new shares issued will be approximately their market value. The difference between cash received by the company and the nominal value of the new shares issued is transferred to the share premium account. For example, if X Ltd issues 1,000 £1 ordinary shares at £2.60 each the book entry will be as follows.

		£	£
DEBIT	Cash	2,600	
CREDIT	Ordinary share capital		1,000
CREDIT	Share premium account		1,600

A share premium account only comes into being when a company issues shares at a price in excess of their nominal value. The market price of the shares, once they have been issued, has no bearing at all on the company's accounts, and so if their market price goes up or down, the share premium account would remain unaltered.

Revaluation reserve

2.20 A revaluation reserve must be created when a company revalues one or more of its fixed assets. Revaluations frequently occur with freehold property, as the market value of property rises. The company's directors might wish to show a more 'reasonable' value of the asset in their balance sheet, to avoid giving a misleading impression about the financial position of the company.

2.21 When an asset is revalued the revaluation reserve is credited with the difference between the revalued amount of the asset, and its net book value before the revaluation took place. Depreciation is subsequently charged on the revalued amount.

Example: revaluation reserve

2.22 X Ltd bought freehold land and buildings for £20,000 ten years ago; their net book value (after depreciation of the buildings) is now £19,300. A professional valuation of £390,000 has been given, and the directors wish to reflect this in the accounts.

2.23 The revaluation surplus is £390,000 – £19,300 = £370,700. The entry to be made is thus:

		£	£
DEBIT	Freehold property	370,700	
CREDIT	Revaluation reserve		370,700

The balance sheet will then include the following.

Reserves	
Revaluation reserve	370,700
Fixed assets	
Freehold property (at valuation)	390,000

2.24 An unrealised capital profit (such as the £370,700 above) is generally not distributable, whereas a realised capital profit (ie if the property is actually sold for £390,000) usually is distributable.

Distinction between reserves and provisions

2.25 A reserve is an appropriation of distributable profits for a specific purpose (eg plant replacement) while a provision is an amount charged against revenue as an expense. A provision relates either to a diminution in the value of an asset (eg doubtful debtors) or a known liability (eg audit fees), the amount of which cannot be established with any accuracy. Provisions (for depreciation, doubtful debts etc) are dealt with in company accounts in the same way as in the accounts of other types of business.

Exercise 2

(a) How do the Companies Acts influence the contents of accounts?

(b) Name two differences between the accounts of a sole trader and the accounts of an owner-managed limited company.

(c) A public company has 10,000,000 25p shares in issue and their current value on the stock market is £4.97 per share. What is the value of share capital in the company's nominal ledger?

(d) Is the profit and loss reserve of a limited company the same thing as the trading account of a sole trader?

(e) When is a revaluation reserve created?

Solution

(a) See 1.1 (a).
(b) See Paragraph 1.1 (b) and (c).
(c) £2.5m (10m x 25p).
(d) No: the reserve is for *retained* profits, not profits of the current year only.
(e) See Paragraph 2.20.

Debenture loans

2.26 Limited companies may issue debenture stock ('debentures') or loan stock. These are long-term liabilities described on the balance sheet as loan capital. They are different from share capital for the following reasons.

(a) Shareholders are members of a company, while providers of loan capital are creditors.

(b) Shareholders receive dividends (appropriations of profit) whereas the holders of loan capital are entitled to a fixed rate of interest (an expense charged against revenue).

(c) Loan capital holders can take legal action against a company if their interest is not paid when due, whereas shareholders cannot enforce the payment of dividends.

(d) Debentures or loan stock are often secured on company assets, whereas shares are not.

2.27 Interest is calculated on the nominal value of loan capital, regardless of its market value. If a company has £700,000 (nominal value) 12% debentures in issue, interest of £84,000 will be charged in the profit and loss account per year. Interest is usually paid half-yearly and examination questions often require an accrual to be made for interest due at the year end. Accrued interest is shown as a current liability in the year-end balance sheet.

2.28 For example, if a company has £700,000 of 12% debentures in issue, pays interest on 30 June and 31 December each year, and ends its accounting year on 30 September, there would be an accrual of three months' unpaid interest (3/12 × £84,000) = £21,000 at the end of each accounting year that the debentures are still in issue.

3 THE FINAL ACCOUNTS OF LIMITED COMPANIES — 12/97, 12/98, 12/99, 6/00

3.1 The preparation and publication of the final accounts of limited companies in the UK are governed by the Companies Act 1985 as amended by the Companies Act 1989. At this stage in your studies, you do not have to learn the detailed regulations laid down by these Acts. However, the general format of the balance sheet and profit and loss account of a limited company will be shown with some simplifications, in order to introduce certain assets and liabilities which we have not come across before in earlier chapters of this Study Text.

3.2 TYPICAL COMPANY LIMITED BALANCE SHEET AS AT.....

Fixed assets	£	£	£
Intangible assets			
Development costs		X	
Concessions, patents, licences, trademarks		X	
Goodwill		X	
			X
Tangible assets			
Land and buildings		X	
Plant and machinery		X	
Fixtures, fittings, tools and equipment		X	
Motor vehicles		X	
			X
Investments			X
			X
Current assets			
Stocks		X	
Debtors and prepayments		X	
Investments		X	
Cash at bank and in hand		X	
		X	
Creditors: amounts falling due within one year (ie current liabilities)			
Debenture loans			
(nearing their redemption date)	X		
Bank loans and overdrafts	X		
Trade creditors	X		
Bills of exchange payable	X		
Taxation	X		
Accruals	X		
Proposed dividend	X		
		(X)	
Net current assets			X
Total assets less current liabilities			X
Creditors : amounts falling due after more than one year			
Debenture loans		X	
Taxation		X	
			(X)
			X

Capital and reserves		£	£
Called up share capital			
Ordinary shares		X	
Preference shares		X	
			X
Reserves			
Share premium account		X	
Revaluation reserve		X	
Other reserves		X	
Profit and loss account (retained profits)		X	
			X
			X

3.3 TYPICAL COMPANY LIMITED
PROFIT AND LOSS ACCOUNT FOR THE YEAR ENDED...

	£	£
Turnover		X
Cost of sales		(X)
Gross profit		X
Distribution costs	X	
Administrative expenses	X	
		(X)
		X
Other operating income	X	
Income from fixed asset investments	X	
Other interest receivable and similar income	X	
		X
		X
Interest payable		(X)
Profit before taxation		X
Tax		(X)
Profit after tax		X
Dividends: preference	X	
Ordinary	X	
		(X)
Retained profit for the year		X
Profit and loss account as at the beginning of the year		X
Profit and loss account as at the end of the year		X

Investments

3.4 Investments are fixed assets if the company intends to hold on to them for a long time, and current assets if they are only likely to be held for a short time before being sold.

Creditors: amounts falling due within one year

3.5 The term 'creditors: amounts falling due within one year' was introduced by the Companies Act 1981 as an alternative phrase meaning 'current liabilities'.

Profit and Loss Appropriation Account 6/99, 12/99, 6/00

3.6 You will notice that the profit and loss account for a limited company is somewhat more extended than that of a sole trader. Whereas previously we stopped at profit before taxation (formerly termed as net profit for the year), we now include a profit and loss appropriation account.

3.7 This shows those items which reduce profits but which are not expenses incurred in the day to day running of the business. In other words, it shows how profits are set apart for particular purposes.

3.8 Essentially, profits are set aside (appropriated) for three purposes - to:

(a) Pay tax.
(b) Pay dividends to shareholders.
(c) Reinvest in the business.

3.9 The amount reinvested in the business is the residual amount left after the tax and dividends have been paid. This residual amount is referred to as retained profit for the year.

3.10 The profit and loss account at the beginning of the year is the profit and loss reserve as described in paragraphs 2.13 and 2.14. The retained profit for the current year is added to this opening balance to give the profit and loss account balance at the end of the year. This will then appear in next year's profit and loss appropriation account as the profit and loss account at the beginning of the year.

Taxation

3.11 Companies pay *corporation tax* on the profits they earn. The charge for corporation tax on profits for the year is shown as a deduction from net profit, before other appropriations. In the balance sheet, tax payable to the government is generally shown as a current liability.

3.12 When corporation tax on profits is calculated for the profit and loss account the calculation is only an estimate of what the company thinks its tax liability will be. In subsequent dealings with the Inland Revenue, a different corporation tax charge might eventually be agreed. Any difference is adjusted in the estimated taxation charge for the following year.

Example: taxation

3.13 Urals Ltd made a profit before tax of £150,000 in the year to 30 September 20X3 and of £180,000 in the following year (to 30 September 20X4).

The estimated corporation tax for the first year was £60,000 and in the second year was £75,000. The actual tax charge in the year to 30 September 20X3 was finally agreed with the Inland Revenue at £55,000.

Required

Compute the charge for taxation in the year to 30 September 20X4.

Solution

3.14

	To 30 September	
	20X3	*20X4*
	£	£
Estimate of tax on profits	60,000	75,000
Actual tax charge	55,000	
Overestimate of tax in 20X3	5,000	
		(5,000)
Tax charge in year to 30 September 20X4		70,000

The effect of this adjustment will be to increase profits in 20X4 by £5,000, to correct the 'error' in 20X3 when profits were reduced by £5,000 because of the overestimate of the tax charge.

3.15 Most companies pay tax within 9 months of their accounting year end. However, the tax on profits in the P & L account and the tax payable in the balance sheet are not usually the same amount, for reasons which will be covered in your later studies.

Examination question on company accounts

3.16 We can now draw together several of the items described in this chapter into an illustrative example. Study it carefully because it is typical of the type of problems encountered in the examination.

3.17 The accountant of Wislon Ltd has prepared the following trial balance as at 31 December 20X7.

	£'000
50p ordinary shares (fully paid)	350
7% £1 preference shares (fully paid)	100
10% debentures (secured)	200
Retained profit 1 January 20X7	242
General reserve 1 January 20X7	171
Freehold land and buildings 1 January 20X7 (cost)	430
Plant and machinery 1 January 20X7 (cost)	830
Provision for depreciation	
Freehold buildings 1 January 20X7	20
Plant and machinery 1 January 20X7	222
Stock 1 January 20X7	190
Sales	2,695
Purchases	2,152
Preference dividend	7
Ordinary dividend (interim)	8
Debenture interest	10
Wages and salaries	254
Light and heat	31
Sundry expenses	113
Suspense account	135
Debtors	179
Creditors	195
Cash	126

Notes

(a) Sundry expenses include £9,000 paid in respect of insurance for the year ending 1 September 20X8. Light and heat does not include an invoice of £3,000 for electricity for the three months ending 2 January 20X8, which was paid in February 20X8. Light and heat also includes £20,000 relating to salesmen's commission.

(b) The suspense account is in respect of the following items.

	£'000
Proceeds from the issue of 100,000 ordinary shares	120
Proceeds from the sale of plant	300
	420
Less consideration for the acquisition of Mary & Co	285
	135

(c) The net assets of Mary & Co were purchased on 3 March 20X7. Assets were valued as follows.

	£'000
Investments	230
Stock	34
	264

All the stock acquired was sold during 20X7. The investments were still held by Wislon at 31 December 20X7.

(d) The freehold property was acquired some years ago. The buildings element of the cost was estimated at £100,000 and the estimated useful life of the assets was fifty years at the time of purchase. As at 31 December 20X7 the property is to be revalued at £800,000.

(e) The plant which was sold had cost £350,000 and had a net book value of £274,000 as on 1 January 20X7. £36,000 depreciation is to be charged on plant and machinery for 20X7.

(f) The debentures have been in issue for some years. The 50p ordinary shares all rank for dividends at the end of the year.

(g) The directors wish to provide for:

(i) Debenture interest due.
(ii) A final ordinary dividend of 2p per share.
(iii) A transfer to general reserve of £16,000.
(iv) Audit fees of £4,000.

(h) Stock as at 31 December 20X7 was valued at £220,000 (cost).

(i) Taxation is to be ignored.

Required

Prepare the final accounts of Wislon Ltd.

Approach and suggested solution

3.18 (a) The usual adjustments are needed for accruals and prepayments (insurance, light and heat, debenture interest and audit fees). The debenture interest accrued is calculated as follows.

	£'000
Charge needed in P & L account (10% × £200,000)	20
Amount paid so far, as shown in trial balance	10
Accrual - presumably six months' interest now payable	10

The accrued expenses to be shown in the balance sheet comprise:

	£'000
Debenture interest	10
Light and heat	3
Audit fee	4
	17

(b) The misposting of £20,000 to light and heat is also adjusted, by reducing the light and heat expense, but charging £20,000 to salesmen's commission.

(c) Depreciation on the freehold building is calculated as $\frac{£100{,}000}{50} = £2{,}000$.

The net book value of the freehold property is then £430,000 – £20,000 – £2,000 = £408,000 at the end of the year. When the property is revalued a reserve of £800,000 – £408,000 = £392,000 is then created.

(d) The profit on disposal of plant is calculated as proceeds £300,000 (per suspense account) less NBV £274,000 ie £26,000. The cost of the remaining plant is calculated at £830,000 – £350,000 = £480,000. The depreciation provision at the year end is made up of the following.

	£'000
Balance 1 January 20X7	222
Charge for 20X7	36
Less depreciation on disposals (350 – 274)	(76)
	182

(e) Goodwill arising on the purchase of Mary & Co is calculated as follows.

	£'000
Consideration (per suspense account)	285
Assets at valuation	264
Goodwill	21

In the absence of other instructions, this is shown as an asset on the balance sheet. The investments, being owned by Wislon at the year end, are also shown on the balance sheet, whereas Mary's stock, acquired and then sold, is added to the purchases figure for the year.

(f) The other item in the suspense account is dealt with as follows.

	£'000
Proceeds of issue of 100,000 ordinary shares	120
Less nominal value 100,000 × 50p	50
Excess of consideration over nominal value (= share premium)	70

(g) Appropriations of profit must be considered. The final ordinary dividend, shown as a current liability in the balance sheet, is calculated as follows.

(700,000 + 100,000 ordinary shares) × 2p = £16,000

(h) The transfer to general reserve increases that reserve to £171,000 + £16,000 = £187,000.

3.19 WISLON LIMITED
TRADING AND PROFIT AND LOSS ACCOUNT
FOR THE YEAR ENDING 31 DECEMBER 20X7

	£'000	£'000	£'000
Sales			2,695
Less cost of sales			
Opening stock		190	
Purchases		2,186	
		2,376	
Less closing stock		220	
			2,156
Gross profit			539
Profit on disposal of plant			26
			565
Less expenses			
Wages, salaries and commission		274	
Sundry expenses		107	
Light and heat		14	
Depreciation: freehold buildings		2	
plant		36	
Audit fees		4	
Debenture interest		20	
			457
Net profit			108
Appropriations			
Transfer to general reserve		16	
Dividends			
Preference (paid)	7		
Ordinary: interim (paid)	8		
final (proposed)	16		
		31	
			47
Retained profit for the year			61
Retained profit brought forward			242
Retained profit carried forward			303

3.20 WISLON LIMITED
BALANCE SHEET AS AT 31 DECEMBER 20X7

			£'000
Fixed assets			
Intangible assets			
Goodwill			21
Tangible assets	*Cost/ val'n*	*Dep'n*	
	£'000	£'000	
Freehold property	800	-	800
Plant and machinery	480	182	298
	1,280	182	
Investments			230
			1,349
Current assets			
Stock		220	
Debtors		179	
Prepayment		6	
Cash		126	
		531	
Creditors: amounts falling due within one year			
Creditors	195		
Accrued expenses	17		
Proposed dividend	16		
		228	
Net current assets			303
Total assets less current liabilities			1,652
Creditors: amounts falling due after more than one year			
10% debentures (secured)			(200)
			1,452
Capital and reserves			
Called up share capital			
50p ordinary shares		400	
7% £1 preference shares		100	
			500
Reserves			
Share premium		70	
Revaluation reserve		392	
General reserve		187	
Profit and loss account		303	
			952
			1,452

4 THE LEDGER ACCOUNTS OF LIMITED COMPANIES

4.1 Limited companies keep ledger accounts and the only difference between the ledger accounts of companies and sole traders is the nature of some of the accounts which need to be kept.

For example, there will be an account for each of the following items.

(a) *Taxation*

(i) Tax charged against profits will be accounted for as follows.

DEBIT P & L account
CREDIT Taxation account

(ii) The outstanding balance on the taxation account will be a liability in the balance sheet, until eventually paid, when the accounting entry would be as follows.

DEBIT	Taxation account
CREDIT	Cash

(b) *Dividends*

A separate account will be kept for the dividends for each different class of shares (eg preference, ordinary).

(i) Dividends declared out of profits will be accounted for as follows.

DEBIT	P & L appropriation account
CREDIT	Dividends payable account

Dividends payable (but not yet paid) are a current liability.

(ii) When dividends are paid the following entries would be made.

DEBIT	Dividends payable account
CREDIT	Cash

(c) *Debenture loans*

Debenture loans are a long term liability and will be shown as a credit balance in a debenture loan account. Interest payable on such loans is not credited to the loan account, but is credited to a separate creditors account for interest until it is eventually paid.

DEBIT	Interest account (an expense, chargeable against profits)
CREDIT	Interest payable (a current liability until eventually paid).

(d) *Share capital and reserves*

There will be a separate account for each different class of share capital and for each different type of reserve. The balance on the share capital account will always be a credit and the balance on the reserve account will nearly always be a credit.

Chapter roundup

- This chapter has explained some important differences between the accounts of a limited company and those of sole traders.
- The accounting records and financial statements of a limited company are strictly regulated by statute.
- A company is recognised in law as a person, with its own identity quite separate from that of its owners. One important consequence of this is the concept of limited liability: a company's shareholders have no liability for the company's debts, beyond what they have contributed as capital.
- To reflect the difference in ownership, the capital of companies is shown differently from that of sole traders.
- Profits paid out to shareholders are called *dividends.*
- *Preference shares* carry the right to a fixed dividend which is expressed as a percentage of their nominal value.
- *Ordinary shares* normally carry voting rights. They carry no right to a fixed dividend but are entitled to all profits left after payment of any preference dividend.
- *Debentures* differ from shares in many ways. A debentureholder is a creditor of the company.
- Statutory reserves are reserves which a company must set up by law. They are not distributable.
- Non statutory reserves are distributable.
- The difference between the price paid for a new issue of shares and their nominal value is the *premium,* which is credited to a share premium account.
- A revaluation reserve must be created when a company revalues one or more of its fixed assets.
- The preparation and publication of final accounts of limited companies is governed by the Companies Act 1985.

Test your knowledge

1 What is the meaning of limited liability? (see para 1.3)

2 What are the differences between ordinary shares and preference shares? (2.6 - 2.10)

3 How does a share premium account arise? (2.19)

4 What is the difference between a reserve and a provision? (2.25)

5 What are the differences between debentures and share capital? (2.26)

Now try illustrative questions 25 and 26 at the end of the Study Text

Chapter 17

CASH FLOW STATEMENTS

This chapter covers the following topics.

1 Profits and cash flow

2 Cash flow statements

Introduction

Another type of statement is introduced in this chapter: the cash flow statement.

In the long run, a profit will result in an increase in the company's cash balance but, as Keynes observed, 'in the long run we are all dead'. In the short run, the making of a profit will not necessarily result in an increased cash balance. The observation leads us to two questions. The first relates to the importance of the distinction between cash and profit. The second is concerned with the usefulness of the information provided by the balance sheet and profit and loss account in the problem of deciding whether the company has, or will be able to generate, sufficient cash to finance its operations.

The importance of the distinction between cash and profit and the scant attention paid to this by the profit and loss account has resulted in the development of cash flow statements.

1 PROFITS AND CASH FLOW

1.1 To be successful in business, an enterprise must make a profit. Profits are needed to pay dividends to shareholders (and shareholders expect to receive dividends as a return on their investment in ownership of the business) and to reward partners or proprietors. Some profits are retained within the business as reserves or as proprietor's funds, to finance the development and growth of the business. We can therefore say that although a firm may be able to bear occasional losses, it must be profitable in the long term. A loss means that the value of sales in a period is less than the value of resources used up in making the sales, so that a loss causes a reduction in the overall value of a business. Long-term losses will lead to the eventual collapse of a firm.

1.2 In addition to being *profitable* in order to survive and grow, it is also necessary for a firm to 'pay its way': to *pay in cash* for the goods and services and capital equipment it buys, the workforce it employs and the other expenses (such as rent, rates and taxation) that it incurs. If a firm does not pay its bills when they are due, it will first of all lose the goodwill of its suppliers or workforce and may then be driven into liquidation. It is therefore necessary to be not just profitable, but also capable of obtaining cash to meet demand for payment.

1.3 Profits and cash surpluses are not the same thing, for a number of reasons.

(a) Cash may be obtained from a transaction which has nothing to do with profit or loss. For example, an issue of shares or loan stock for cash has no effect on profit (except for subsequent interest charges on a loan) but is obviously a source of cash. Similarly, an increase in bank overdraft provides a source of cash for payments, but it is not reported in the profit and loss account.

(b) Cash may be paid for the purchase of fixed assets, but the charge in the profit and loss account is depreciation, which is only a part of an asset's cost. For example, a company may have existing fixed assets which originally cost £300,000. If it buys a new asset for £20,000 on 1 January and if depreciation is charged at a rate of 10% of cost:

(i) The charge for depreciation for the year to 31 December would be 10% of £320,000 or £32,000.

(ii) The cash payments during the year would be £20,000 - the purchase cost of the new asset.

(c) When a fixed asset is sold there is a profit or loss on sale equal to the difference between the sale proceeds and the 'net book value' of the asset in the balance sheet at the time it is sold. For example, if an asset originally cost £50,000 and depreciation of £35,000 has been charged since its purchase, its net book value will be £15,000. If it is now sold for £11,000, there will be a loss on disposal of £4,000. This loss would be recorded in the profit and loss account, but the effect of the sale would be to increase the firm's cash by £11,000 (the sale price).

(d) The profit and loss account reports the total value of sales in a year. If goods are sold on credit, the cash receipts will differ from the value of sales. The relationship between sales and receipts is as follows (excluding increases or decreases in the provision for doubtful debts and writing-off bad debts).

	£
Debtors owing money at the start of the year	X
Sales during the year	X
Total money due from customers	X
Less debtors owing money at the end of the year	(X)
Cash receipts from debtors during the year	X

(e) Similarly, the profit and loss account reports the cost of goods sold during the year.

(i) If materials are bought on credit, the cash payments to suppliers will be different from the value of materials purchased.

(ii) If some materials are bought and added to stocks rather than sold (ie if there is an increase in stocks during the year) total purchases will be different from the materials cost of sales. (In the same way, a firm may decide to run down its stocks and sell goods without making good the stocks used up by purchasing replacement items.)

The relationship between the cost of materials in the materials cost of sales and cash payments for materials purchased is as follows:

	£
Opening stocks (at the start of the year)	X
Add purchases during the year	X
	X
Less closing stocks at the end of the year	(X)
Equals materials cost in the cost of sales	Y
Payments still owing to creditors at the start of the year	X
Add materials cost in the cost of sales	Y
	X
Less payments still owing to creditors at the end of the year	(X)
Equals cash payments to creditors during the year	X

The need for information about cash flow

1.4 It has been suggested to you in the previous paragraphs that:

(a) A firm must not only be profitable, but must also obtain cash receipts (or an overdraft facility) to pay its way.

(b) Profits and cash surpluses are not the same.

Information about cash receipts and payments can therefore add to our understanding of a firm's operations and financial stability. Whereas a profit and loss statement reports on profitability, cash flow statements report on liquidity.

2 CASH FLOW STATEMENTS 6/97, 12/99, 6/00

2.1 It follows from the above discussion that 'profit' does not always give a useful or meaningful picture of a company's operations. Readers of a company's financial statements might even be misled by a reported profit figure.

(a) Shareholders might believe that if a company makes a profit after tax, of say, £100,000 then this is the amount which it could afford to pay as a dividend. Unless the company has sufficient cash available to stay in business and also to pay a dividend, the shareholders' expectations would be wrong.

(b) Employees might believe that if a company makes profits, it can afford to pay higher wages next year. This opinion may not be correct: the ability to pay wages depends on the availability of cash.

(c) Creditors might consider that a profitable company is a going concern.

  (i) If a company builds up large amounts of unsold stocks of goods, their cost would not be chargeable against profits, but cash would have been used up in making them, thus weakening the company's liquid resources.

  (ii) A company might capitalise large development costs, having spent considerable amounts of money on R & D, but only charge small amounts against current profits. As a result, the company might show reasonable profits, but get into severe difficulties with its liquidity position. (This is roughly the problem that led to the collapse of the old Rolls Royce company in 1971.)

(d) Management might suppose that if their company makes a profit, and reinvests some of those profits, then the company must be expanding. This is not the case: in a period of inflation, a company might have insufficient retained profits to prevent the operating capability of the firm from declining.

(e) Survival of a business entity depends not so much on profits as on its ability to pay its debts when they fall due. Such payments might include 'profit and loss' items such as material purchases, wages, interest and taxation etc, but also capital payments for new fixed assets and the repayment of loan capital when this falls due (eg on the redemption of debentures).

2.2 From these examples, it may be apparent that a company's performance and prospects depend not so much on the 'profits' earned in a period, but more realistically on liquidity: cash flows. A statement of cash flows is unambiguous and provides information which is additional to that provided in the rest of the accounts. It also lends itself to organisation by activity and not by balance sheet classification. The Accounting Standards Board (ASB) has published FRS 1 *Cash flow statements.* You do not need to know the prescribed format in detail, but you should know how to construct a cash flow statement and what its aims are.

2.3 The aim of a cashflow statement should be to assist users:

(a) To assess the enterprise's ability to generate positive net cash flows in the future.
(b) To assess its ability to meet its obligations to service loans, pay dividends etc.
(c) To assess the reasons for difference between reported profit and related cash flows.
(d) To assess the effect on its finances of major transactions in the year.

The statement should therefore show changes in cash and cash equivalents. The opening and closing figures given for cash etc should be those shown in the balance sheet. Receipts and payments should not be netted off. Non-cash transactions should be reported separately by note (eg purchasing an asset with lease finance) and a reconciliation of net income to net cash flow from operating activities should be given.

2.4 The statement should classify cash receipts and payments as resulting from investing, financing or operating activities. Examples of each follow.

(a) Investing: making loans, acquiring/disposing of fixed assets.

(b) Financing: borrowing/repaying money, making an issue of shares, paying dividends.

(c) Operating: receipts from customers, payments to employees and suppliers, any other cash flows from transactions not classified as investing or financing.

2.5 A cash flow statement can be a historical statement or a forecast. It shows the sources and uses of cash over a period of time, whereas a cash budget shows expected sources and uses of cash daily, weekly or monthly, to help in management of working capital.

Example: cash flow statement

2.6 Flail Ltd commenced trading on 1 January 20X1 with a medium-term loan of £21,000 and a share issue which raised £35,000. The company purchased fixed assets for £21,000 cash, and during the year to 31 December 20X1 entered into the following transactions.

(a) Purchases from suppliers were £19,500, of which £2,550 was unpaid at the year end.

(b) Wages and salaries amounted to £10,500, of which £750 was unpaid at the year end.

(c) Interest on the loan of £2,100 was fully paid in the year and a repayment of £5,250 was made.

(d) Sales turnover was £29,400, including £900 debtors at the year end.

(e) Interest on cash deposits at the bank amounted to £75.

(f) A dividend of £4,000 was proposed as at 31 December 20X1.

You are required to prepare a historical cash flow statement for the year ended 31 December 20X1.

Solution

2.7 FLAIL LIMITED
STATEMENT OF CASH FLOWS FOR
THE YEAR ENDED 31 DECEMBER 20X1

	£	£	£
Operating activities			
Cash received from customers (£29,400 – £900)	28,500		
Cash paid to suppliers (£19,500 – £2,550)	(16,950)		
Cash paid to and on behalf of employees (£10,500 – £750)	(9,750)		
Cash flow from operating activities			1,800
Returns on investment and servicing of finance			
Interest paid	(2,100)		
Interest received	75		
		(2,025)	(2,025)
Capital expenditure			
Purchase of fixed assets	(21,000)		
		(21,000)	
Cash flow from investing activities		-	(23,025)
Financing			
Issue of shares	35,000		
Proceeds from medium-term loan	21,000		
Repayment of medium-term loan	(5,250)		
Cash flow from financing activities			50,750
Net increase in cash			29,525
Cash at 1 January 20X1		-	-
Cash at 31 December 20X1		=	29,525

Note that the dividend is only proposed and so there is no related cash flow in 20X1.

Exercise 1

The directors of Flail Ltd obtain the following information in respect of projected cash flows for the year to 31 December 20X2.

(a) Fixed asset purchases for cash will be £3,000.

(b) Further expenses will be:

(i) Purchases from suppliers - £18,750 (£4,125 owed at the year end).
(ii) Wages and salaries - £11,250 (£600 owed at the year end).
(iii) Loan interest - £1,575.

(c) Turnover will be £36,000 (£450 debtors at the year end).

(d) Interest on bank deposits will be £150.

(e) A further capital repayment of £5,250 will be made on the loan.

(f) A dividend of £5,000 will be proposed and last year's final dividend paid.

(g) Corporation tax of £2,300 will be paid in respect of 20X1.

Prepare the cash flow forecast for the year to 31 December 20X2.

Solution

FLAIL LIMITED
STATEMENT OF FORECAST CASH FLOWS FOR
THE YEAR ENDING 31 DECEMBER 20X2

	£	£
Operating activities		
Cash received from customers (£36,000 + £900 – £450)	36,450	
Cash paid to suppliers (£18,750 + £2,550 – £4,125)	(17,175)	
Cash paid to and on behalf of employees (£11,250 + £750 – £600)	(11,400)	
Net cash flow from operating activities		7,875
Returns on investments and servicing of finance		
Interest paid	(1,575)	
Interest received	150	
		(1,425)
Taxation		(2,300)
Capital expenditure		
Purchase of fixed assets		(3,000)
		1,150
Equity dividends paid		(4,000)
Financing		
Repayment of medium-term loan		(5,250)
Forecast net decrease in cash at 31 December 20X2		(8,100)
Cash as at 31 December 20X1		29,525
Forecast cash as at 31 December 20X2		21,425

Indirect method

2.8 Another way of arriving at net cash flows from operating activities is to start from operating profit and adjust for non-cash items, such as depreciation, debtors etc. This is known as the *indirect method.* A proforma calculation is given below.

	£
Operating profit (P&L)	X
Add depreciation	X
Loss/(profit) on sale of fixed assets	X
(Increase)/decrease in stocks	(X)/X
(Increase)/decrease in debtors	(X)/X
Increase/(decrease) in creditors	X/(X)
Net cash flow from operating activities	X

2.9 It is important to understand why certain items are added and others subtracted. Note the following points.

(a) Depreciation is not a cash expense, but is deducted in arriving at the profit figure in the profit and loss account. It makes sense, therefore, to eliminate it by adding it back.

(b) By the same logic, a loss on a disposal of a fixed asset (arising through underprovision of depreciation) needs to be added back and a profit deducted.

(c) An increase in stocks means less cash - you have spent cash on buying stock.

(d) An increase in debtors means debtors have not paid as much, therefore less cash.

(e) If we pay off creditors, causing the figure to decrease, again we have less cash.

2.10 It is important that you familiarise yourself with the indirect method by practising illustrative question 27 at the end of the Study Text. It is the indirect method which will generally be needed, particularly in more advanced cash flow statements, where you will be required to follow the FRS 1 format.

2.11 Note that, in an examination question, you may not be given the profit figure; instead you may be required to calculate it by finding the difference between the capital figures in two consecutive years' balance sheets.

The advantages of cash flow accounting

2.12 The advantages of cash flow accounting are as follows.

(a) Survival in business depends on the ability to generate cash. Cash flow accounting directs attention towards this critical issue.

(b) Cash flow is more comprehensive than 'profit' which is dependent on accounting conventions and concepts.

(c) Creditors (long and short-term) are more interested in an entity's ability to repay them than in its profitability. Whereas 'profits' might indicate that cash is likely to be available, cash flow accounting is more direct with its message.

(d) Cash flow reporting provides a better means of comparing the results of different companies than traditional profit reporting.

(e) Cash flow reporting satisfies the needs of all users better.

   (i) For management, it provides the sort of information on which decisions should be taken (in management accounting, 'relevant costs' to a decision are future cash flows); traditional profit accounting does not help with decision-making.

   (ii) For shareholders and auditors, cash flow accounting can provide a satisfactory basis for stewardship accounting.

   (iii) As described previously, the information needs of creditors and employees will be better served by cash flow accounting.

(f) Cash flow forecasts are easier to prepare, as well as more useful, than profit forecasts.

Exercise 2

You should give some thought to the possible *disadvantages* of cashflow accounting which are essentially the advantages of accruals accounting. There is also the practical problem that few businesses keep historical cash flow information in the form needed to prepare a historical cash flow statement and so extra record keeping is likely to be necessary.

Chapter roundup

- Profit does not always give a useful or meaningful picture of a company's operations.
- Survival in business depends on the ability to generate cash. Cash flow accounting directs attention towards this critical issue.
- Cash flow statements concentrate on the sources and uses of cash, and are a useful indicator of a company's liquidity and solvency.

Test your knowledge

1 Why is it argued that users of accounts can be misled by the reported profit figure? (2.1)

2 Differentiate between a cash flow statement and a cash budget. (2.5)

3 How is net cash flow from operating activities calculated using the indirect method? (2.8)

4 What are the advantages of cash flow accounting? (2.12)

Now try illustrative question 27 at the end of the Study Text

Part D
Interpretation of financial information

Chapter 18

THE INTERPRETATION OF FINANCIAL STATEMENTS

Introduction

Having seen how to prepare financial statements, we will now turn our attention to the interpretation of financial information.

In this chapter we will take a fairly broad view of financial statements. In the next chapter we will look at working capital in detail.

1 ANALYSING FINANCIAL STATEMENTS 6/96 - 6/00

1.1 The profit and loss account and the balance sheet are both sources of useful information about the condition of a business. The analysis and interpretation of these statements can be done by calculating certain ratios and then using the ratios for comparison ('ratio analysis'), in one of the following ways.

(a) Between one year and the next for a particular business, in order to identify any trends, or significantly better or worse results than before.

(b) Between one business and another, to establish which business has performed better, and in what ways.

1.2 The most important ratios are described in this and the following chapters.

2 PROFIT MARGIN, ASSET TURNOVER AND RETURN ON CAPITAL EMPLOYED 12/98, 12/99, 6/00

2.1 There are three principal ratios which can be used to measure how efficiently the operations of a business have been managed, that is its *profitability*. These are:

(a) Profit margin.
(b) Asset turnover.
(c) Return on capital employed (ROCE).

Profit margin

2.2 *Profit margin* is the ratio of profit to sales, and may also be called 'profit percentage'. For example, if a company makes a profit of £20,000 on sales of £100,000 its profit percentage or profit margin is 20%. This also means that its costs are 80% of sales. A high profit margin indicates that one of the following may be true.

(a) Costs are being kept well under control because if the ratio of costs to sales goes down, the profit margin will automatically go up. For example, if the cost:sales ratio changes from 80% to 75%, the profit margin will go up from 20% to 25%.

(b) Sales prices are high. For example, if a company sells goods for £100,000 and makes a profit of £16,000 costs would be £84,000 and the profit margin 16%. Now if the company can raise selling prices by 20% to £120,000 without affecting the volume of goods sold or their cost, profits would rise by the amount of revenue increase (£20,000) to £36,000 and the profit margin would also rise (from 16% to 30%).

Asset turnover

2.3 *Asset turnover* is the ratio of sales in a year to the amount of capital employed. It indicates a business's level of *activity*. For example, if a company has sales of £720,000 and has assets of £360,000, the asset turnover will be:

$$\frac{£720,000}{£360,000} = 2 \text{ times}$$

This means that for every £1 of assets employed, the company can generate sales of £2 per annum. To use assets more efficiently, managers should try to create a higher volume of sales and a higher asset turnover ratio. For example, suppose that our firm with assets of £360,000 can increase its sales from £720,000 to £900,000 per annum. The asset turnover would improve to:

$$\frac{£900,000}{£360,000} = 2.5 \text{ times}$$

Return on capital employed (ROCE)

2.4 *Return on capital employed* (ROCE) is the amount of profit as a percentage of capital employed. If a company makes a profit of £30,000, we do not know how good or bad the result is until we look at the amount of capital which has been invested to achieve the profit. £30,000 might be a good sized profit for a small firm, but it would not be good enough for a 'giant' firm such as Marks and Spencer. For this reason, it is helpful to measure performance by relating profits to capital employed, and because this seems to be the only satisfactory ratio which judges profits in relation to the size of business, it is sometimes called the primary ratio in financial analysis.

2.5 You may already have realised that there is a mathematical connection between return on capital employed, profit margin and asset turnover:

$$\frac{\text{Profit}}{\text{Capital employed}} = \frac{\text{Profit}}{\text{Sales}} \times \frac{\text{Sales}}{\text{Capital employed}}$$

$$\text{ROCE} = \text{Profit margin} \times \text{Asset turnover}$$

This is important. If we accept that ROCE is the single most important measure of business performance, comparing profit with the amount of capital invested, we can go on to say that business performance is dependent on two separate 'subsidiary' factors, each of which contributes to ROCE:

(a) Profit margin.
(b) Asset turnover.

For this reason, just as ROCE is sometimes called the primary ratio, the profit margin and asset turnover ratios are sometimes called the secondary ratios.

2.6 The implications of this relationship must be understood. Suppose that a return on capital employed of 20% is thought to be a good level of business performance in the retail trade for electrical goods:

(a) Company A might decide to sell its products at a fairly high price and make a profit margin on sales of 10%. It would then need only an asset turnover of 2.0 times to achieve an ROCE of 20%.

(b) Company B might decide to cut its prices so that its profit margin is only 2½%. Provided that it can achieve an asset turnover of 8 times a year, attracting more customers with its lower prices, it will still make an ROCE of 2½% × 8 = 20%.

2.7 Company A might be a department store and company B a discount warehouse. Each will have a different selling price policy, but each, in its own way, can be effective in achieving a target ROCE. In this example, if we supposed that both companies had capital employed of £100,000 and a target return of 20% or £20,000:

(a) Company A would need annual sales of £200,000 to give a profit margin of 10% and an asset turnover of 2 times.

(b) Company B would need annual sales of £800,000 to give a profit margin of only 2½% but an asset turnover of 8 times.

The inter-relationship between profit margin and asset turnover

2.8 A higher return on capital employed can be obtained by increasing the profit margin or the asset turnover ratio. The profit margin can be increased by reducing costs or by raising selling prices.

However, if selling prices are raised, it is likely that demand will fall, with the possible consequences that the asset turnover will also decline. If higher prices mean lower sales, the increase in profit margin might be offset by the fall in asset turnover, so that total return on capital employed might not improve.

Whose return and whose capital employed?

2.9 Most of the providers of finance to a business expect some return on their investment.

(a) Trade creditors and other current liabilities merely expect to be paid what they are owed.

(b) A bank charges interest on overdrafts.

(c) Interest must be paid to the holders of loan stock and debentures.

(d) Preference shareholders expect a dividend at a fixed percentage rate of the nominal value of their shares.

(e) Ordinary shareholders also expect a dividend. However, any retained profits kept in the business also represent funds 'owned' or 'provided' by them.

2.10 So when we refer to 'return' we must be clear in our mind about which providers of finance we are concerned with, and we should relate the return earned for those providers of finance to the amount of capital they are providing.

(a) If 'return' is profit after tax, it is the return earned by ordinary and preference shareholders. The capital employed by these investors is:

(i) The nominal value of preference shares.

(ii) The nominal value of ordinary shares.

(iii) The amount in various reserves, because reserves are surpluses or profits retained in a business and 'owned' by the equity investors.

(b) If 'return' is profit after tax and preference dividend, it is the return earned by ordinary shareholders, and is called 'earnings'. The return on equity capital is:

$$\frac{\text{Earnings}}{\text{Ordinary share capital plus reserves}}$$

(c) If we prefer to consider the business as a whole, then the fixed assets and net current assets are financed by long-term capital which may include loan creditors as well as shareholders. The fund available to satisfy the claims of all these providers of finance is the profit before interest payments and taxation. In this case ROCE may be calculated as:

$$\frac{\text{Profit before interest and tax (PBIT)}}{\text{Loan capital plus share capital plus reserves}}$$

which equals

$$\frac{\text{PBIT}}{\text{Fixed assets plus net current assets}}$$

Example: return on capital employed

2.11 Suppose that Draught Ltd reports the following figures:

PROFIT AND LOSS ACCOUNT FOR 20X4 (EXTRACT)

	£
Profit before interest and tax	120,000
Interest	(20,000)
Profit before tax	100,000
Taxation	(40,000)
Profit after tax	60,000
Preference dividend	(1,000)
Profit available for ordinary shareholders (= earnings)	59,000
Ordinary dividend	(49,000)
Retained profits	10,000

BALANCE SHEET AT 31 DECEMBER 20X4

	£	£
Fixed assets: tangible assets		350,000
Current assets	400,000	
Less current liabilities	150,000	
Net current assets		250,000
Total assets less current liabilities		600,000
Creditors: amounts falling due after more than one year:		
10% debenture loans		200,000
		400,000
Capital and reserves:		
Called up share capital:		
5% preference shares	20,000	
£1 ordinary shares	80,000	
		100,000
Profit and loss account		300,000
		400,000

2.12 Using the three alternatives described above, ROCE might be calculated in any of the following ways.

(a) *Return on shareholders' capital*

$$\frac{\text{Profit after tax}}{\text{Share capital plus reserves}} = \frac{£60{,}000}{£400{,}000} = 15\%$$

(b) *Return on equity capital*

$$\frac{\text{Profit after tax and preference dividend (earnings)}}{\text{Ordinary share capital plus reserves}} = \frac{£59{,}000}{£380{,}000} = 15.5\%$$

(c) *Return on total long-term capital*

$$\frac{\text{Profit before interest and tax}}{\text{Loan capital plus share capital plus reserves}} = \frac{£120{,}000}{£600{,}000} = 20\%$$

3 EARNINGS PER SHARE 6/00

3.1 In the previous example it is possible to calculate the return on each ordinary share in the year. This is the earnings per share (EPS). Earnings are profits after tax, preference dividend and 'extraordinary items' (large, extremely rare items), which can either be paid out as a dividend to ordinary shareholders or retained in the business. Earnings are the total return for ordinary shareholders and for Draught Ltd in 20X4, the EPS is:

$$\frac{£59{,}000}{80{,}000\text{shares}} = 73.7 \text{ pence}$$

4 GEARING 6/00

4.1 We have now seen that a company is financed by different types of capital and that each type expects a return in the form of interest or dividend.

Gearing is a method of comparing how much of the long-term capital of a business is provided by equity (ordinary shares and reserves) and how much is provided by investors who are entitled to interest or dividend before ordinary shareholders can have a dividend themselves. These sources of capital are loans and preference shares, and are sometimes known collectively as 'prior charge capital'.

4.2 The two most usual methods of measuring gearing are as follows.

(a) $$\frac{\text{Prior charge capital (long - term loans and preference shares)}}{\text{Equity (ordinary shares plus reserves)}} \times 100\%$$

(i) A business is low-geared if the gearing is less than 100%.
(ii) It is neutrally-geared if the gearing is exactly 100%.
(iii) It is high-geared if the gearing is more than 100%.

(b) $$\frac{\text{Prior charge capital (long - term loans and preference shares)}}{\text{Total long - term capital}} \times 100\%$$

With this method, a business is low-geared if gearing is less than 50%, neutrally-geared if gearing is exactly 50% and high-geared if it exceeds 50%.

4.3 Low gearing means that there is more equity finance in the business than there is prior charge capital. High gearing means the opposite: prior charge capital exceeds the amount of equity.

4.4 Draught Ltd, the company in Paragraph 2.11, has a gearing of:

(a) $\frac{£220{,}000 \text{ (debenture loans plus preference shares)}}{£380{,}000 \text{ (ordinary shares plus reserves)}} \times 100\% = 57.9\%$ or

(b) $\frac{£220{,}000 \text{ (debenture loans plus preference shares)}}{£600{,}000 \text{ (total long-term capital)}} \times 100\% = 36.7\%$

Why is gearing important?

4.5 Gearing can be important when a company wants to raise extra capital, because if its gearing is already too high, the company might find that it is difficult to raise a loan. Would-be lenders might take the view that ordinary shareholders should provide a fair proportion of the total capital for the business and that at the moment they are not doing so. Unless ordinary shareholders are prepared to put in more money themselves (either by issuing new shares or by retaining more profits), the company might be viewed as a bad business risk.

4.6 One of the reasons why high gearing might be considered risky for lenders is that the more loan capital a business has, the bigger becomes the size of profit before interest and tax (PBIT) needed to meet demands for interest payments.

4.7 If excessive gearing indicates that more loans should not be made to a company, we must now ask the question 'what is excessive gearing?'

Unfortunately, there is no hard and fast answer to this question. The 'acceptable' level of gearing varies according to the country (thus average gearing is higher among companies in Japan than in Britain), the industry and the size and status of the individual company within the industry. The more stable the company is, the safer higher gearing should be.

4.8 The advantages of gearing (ie of using prior charge capital) are as follows.

(a) Prior charge capital is cheaper.

(i) The reward (interest or preference dividend) is fixed permanently, and therefore diminishes in real terms if there is inflation. Ordinary shareholders, on the other hand, usually expect dividend growth.

(ii) The reward required by debt-holders is usually lower than that required by equity holders, because debt capital is often secured on company assets, whereas share capital is a more risky investment.

(iii) Payments of interest attract tax relief, whereas ordinary (or preference) dividends do not.

(b) Debt capital does not normally carry voting rights, but ordinary shares usually do. The issue of debt capital therefore leaves pre-existing voting rights unchanged.

(c) If profits are rising, ordinary shareholders will benefit from gearing (see example below).

4.9 The main disadvantage of gearing is that if profits before interest and tax fall, the profit available to shareholders will fall at a greater rate.

Example: gearing and earnings per share

4.10 Suppose that there are two companies, Nogear Ltd and Highgear Ltd, which have the following long-term capital structures.

	Nogear Ltd	*Highgear Ltd*
	£	£
Ordinary shares of £1	10,000	4,000
10% loans	0	6,000
Total long-term capital	10,000	10,000

Required

Calculate the earnings per share for each company if profits before interest and tax are:

(a) £500.
(b) £1,000.
(c) £1,500.

Assume that taxation on profits (after deducting interest) is 50%.

Solution

4.11

		Nogear Ltd	*Highgear Ltd*
		£	£
(a)	*PBIT = £500*		
	PBIT	500	500
	Interest	0	600
	Profit/(loss) before tax	500	(100)
	Tax (50%)	250	0
	Earnings	250	0
	Number of shares	10,000	4,000
	Earnings per share	2.5p	0

		Nogear Ltd	Highgear Ltd
(b)	*PBIT = £1,000*	£	£
	PBIT	1,000	1,000
	Interest	0	600
	Profit before tax	1,000	400
	Tax (50%)	500	200
	Earnings	500	200
	Number of shares	10,000	4,000
	Earnings per share	5p	5p
(c)	*PBIT = £1,500*	£	£
	PBIT	1,500	1,500
	Interest	0	600
	Profit before tax	1,500	900
	Tax (50%)	750	450
	Earnings	750	450
	Number of shares	10,000	4,000
	Earnings per share	7.5p	11.25p

4.12 In a high-geared company, profits before interest and tax might be insufficient to pay interest charges. However, once profits get larger the earnings per share grow at a much faster rate than in a low-geared company.

4.13 In our example, when PBIT is £500, Highgear makes a loss, whereas Nogear makes earnings of 2.5p per share. When profits double to £1,000 before interest and tax, the earnings per share in Highgear have caught up and are equal to the earnings per share in Nogear. With PBIT in excess of £1,000, the earnings per share of Highgear overtake those of Nogear, and the difference gets bigger as profits go up.

Chapter roundup

- In this chapter, we have looked at the primary accounting ratio, ROCE, and at ratios analysing profitability and asset turnover, and the significance of the ratios has been explained.
- Gearing as a feature of capital structure has also been introduced.
- A number of ratios important to investment analysis have been explained.

Test your knowledge

1 Define 'profit margin' and 'asset turnover'. (see paras 2.2, 2.3)

2 What is the relationship which links ROCE, profit margin and asset turnover? (2.5)

3 How is the ratio 'return on total long-term capital' calculated? (2.10(c))

4 Describe two methods of calculating a gearing ratio. (4.2)

5 List three advantages of prior charge capital over equity capital. (4.8)

Now try illustrative question 28 at the end of the Study Text

Chapter 19

THE OPERATING CYCLE AND WORKING CAPITAL RATIOS

This chapter covers the following topics.

1 Working capital

2 The operating cycle or cash cycle

3 Liquidity ratios

4 Working capital and cash

Introduction

In this chapter, we will look in detail at what can be learnt about a business from the current assets and current liabilities sections of its balance sheet.

We will also look at how current assets and current liabilities flow through a business: remember that a balance sheet is only a still 'photograph' of a dynamic business.

1 WORKING CAPITAL

1.1 Working capital is the difference between current assets (mainly stocks, debtors and cash) and current liabilities (such as trade creditors and a bank overdraft).

(a) *Current assets* are items which are either cash already, or which will soon lead to the receipt of cash. Stocks will be sold to customers and create debtors; and debtors will soon pay in cash for their purchases.

(b) *Current liabilities* are items which will soon have to be paid for with cash. Trade creditors will have to be paid and bank overdraft is usually regarded as short-term borrowing which may need to be repaid fairly quickly.

1.2 Current assets and current liabilities are a necessary feature of a firm's trading operations. There is a repeated cycle of buying and selling which is carried on all the time. For example, suppose that on 1 April a firm has the following items.

	£
Stocks	3,000
Debtors	0
Cash	2,000
	5,000
Creditors	0
Working capital	5,000

1.3 It might sell all the stocks for £4,500, and at the same time obtain more stock from suppliers at a cost of £3,500. The balance sheet items would now be:

	£
Stocks	3,500
Debtors	4,500
Cash	2,000
	10,000
Creditors	3,500
Working capital	6,500

(The increase in working capital to £6,500 from £5,000 is caused by the profit of £1,500 on the sale of the stocks.)

1.4 The debtors for £4,500 will eventually pay in cash and the creditors for £3,500 must also be paid. This would give us:

	£
Stocks	3,500
Debtors	0
Cash (2,000 + 4,500 – 3,500)	3,000
	6,500
Creditors	0
Working capital	6,500

1.5 However, if the stocks are sold on credit for £5,500 and further purchases of stock costing £6,000 are made, the cycle of trading will continue as follows

	£
Stocks	6,000
Debtors	5,500
Cash	3,000
	14,500
Creditors	6,000
Working capital (increased by further profit of £2,000)	8,500

From this example you can see that working capital items are part of a continuous flow of trading operations. Purchases add to stocks and creditors at the same time, creditors must be paid and debtors will pay for their goods. The cycle of operations always eventually comes back to cash receipts and cash payments.

2 THE OPERATING CYCLE OR CASH CYCLE 6/96 - 6/00

2.1 The operating cycle (or cash cycle) is a term used to describe the connection between working capital and cash movements in and out. The cycle is usually measured in days or months.

2.2 A firm buys raw materials, probably on credit. The raw materials might be held for some time in stores before being issued to the production department and turned into an item of finished goods. The finished goods might be kept in a warehouse for some time before they are eventually sold to customers. By this time, the firm will probably have paid for the raw materials purchased. If customers buy the goods on credit, it will be some time before the cash from the sales is eventually received.

2.3 (a) The operating cycle measures the period of time between the purchase of raw materials and the receipt of cash from debtors for goods sold.

(b) The cash cycle measures the period between the time cash is paid out for raw materials and the time cash is received from debtors.

2.4 This cycle of repeating events may be shown as follows.

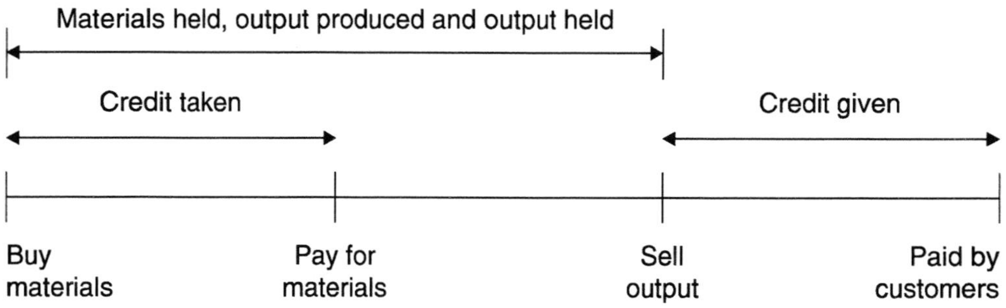

The horizontal line represents the passage of time. The operating cycle starts with the purchase of materials and ends with the receipt of cash from debtors. Cash is not paid when materials are bought because credit is taken from suppliers.

2.5 Suppose that a firm buys raw materials on 1½ months' credit, holds them in store for 1 month and then issues them to the production department. Production time is very short, but finished goods are held for 1 month before they are sold. Debtors take two months' credit. The cash cycle would be:

	months
Raw material stock turnover period	1.0
Less credit taken from suppliers	(1.5)
Finished goods stock turnover period	1.0
Debtors payment period	2.0
Cash cycle	2.5

There would be a gap of 2½ months between paying cash for raw materials and receiving cash from debtors.

Turnover periods

2.6 A turnover period is an (average) length of time.

(a) Stock turnover is the length of time an item of stock is held in stores before it is used (raw materials) or sold (finished goods).

(b) The debtors turnover period, or debt collection period, is the length of the credit period taken by customers.

(c) Similarly, the creditors turnover period is the length of time between the purchase of materials and the payment to suppliers.

2.7 Turnover periods can be calculated from information in a firm's profit and loss account and balance sheet.

Stock turnover periods are calculated as follows:

(a) Raw materials: $\dfrac{\text{(Average) raw material stocks held}}{\text{Total raw materials consumed in one year}} \times 12 \text{ months}$

(b) Work in progress (the length of the production period):

$$\frac{\text{(Average) finished goods stocks held}}{\text{Total cost of production in the year}} \times 12 \text{ months}$$

(c) Finished goods: $\dfrac{\text{(Average) stocks}}{\text{Total cost of goods sold in one year}} \times 12 \text{ months}$

(d) Stocks of items bought for re-sale:

$$\frac{\text{(Average) stocks}}{\text{Total (materials) cost of goods bought and sold in one year}} \times 12 \text{ months}$$

The word 'average' is put in brackets because although it is strictly correct to use average values, it is more common to use the value of stocks shown in a balance sheet (at one point in time) to estimate the turnover periods.

2.8 For example, if a company buys goods costing £620,000 in one year but uses goods costing £600,000 in production (in regular monthly quantities) and the cost of material in stock at 1 January is £100,000, the stock turnover period could be calculated as:

$$\frac{£100{,}000}{£600{,}000} \times 12 \text{ months} = 2 \text{ months}$$

In other words, stocks are bought two months before they are eventually sold.

2.9 The debt collection period is calculated as:

$$\frac{\text{Average debtors}}{\text{Annual credit sales}} \times 12 \text{ months}$$

For example, if a company sells goods for £1,200,000 per annum in regular monthly quantities, and if debtors in the balance sheet are £150,000, the debt collection period is:

$$\frac{£150{,}000}{£1{,}200{,}000} \times 12 \text{ months} = 1.5 \text{ months}$$

In other words, debtors will pay for goods 1½ months on average after the time of sale.

2.10 The period of credit taken from suppliers is calculated as:

$$\frac{\text{Average trade creditors}}{\text{Total purchases in one year}} \times 12 \text{ months}$$

(Notice that the creditors are compared with materials bought whereas for raw material stock turnover, raw material stocks are compared with materials used in production.)

For example, if a company sells goods for £600,000 and makes a gross profit of 40% on sales, and if the amount of trade creditors in the balance sheet is £30,000, the period of credit taken from the suppliers is:

$$\frac{£30{,}000}{(60\% \text{ of } £600{,}000)} \times 12 \text{ months} = 1 \text{ month}$$

In other words, suppliers are paid in the month following the purchase of goods.

Exercise

The profit and loss account of Legion Ltd for the year to 30 June 20X4 and the balance sheet of the company as at 30 June 20X4 are as follows:

PROFIT AND LOSS ACCOUNT

	£	£
Sales		360,000
Cost of goods sold	180,000	
Wages and salaries	80,000	
Depreciation	20,000	
Other expenses	60,000	
		340,000
Profit		20,000

BALANCE SHEET

	£	£
Fixed assets at cost less depreciation		180,000
Stocks	30,000	
Debtors	75,000	
Cash	10,000	
	115,000	
Trade creditors	45,000	
		70,000
		250,000
Share capital and reserves		250,000

Calculate the length of the cash cycle.

Solution

Stock turnover	*Debt collection period*	*Credit taken from suppliers*
$\frac{30,000}{180,000} \times 12$	$\frac{75,000}{360,000} \times 12$	$\frac{45,000}{180,000} \times 12$
= 2 months	= 2½ months	= 3 months

The cash cycle is:

	months	
Stock turnover period	2.0	
Credit taken from suppliers	(3.0)	
Debt collection period	2.5	
Cash cycle	1.5	Months

Turnover periods and the total amount of working capital

2.11 If the stock turnover period gets longer or if the debt collection period gets longer, the total amount of stocks held or of debtors will increase. Similarly, if the period of credit taken from suppliers gets shorter, the amount of creditors will become smaller. The effect of these changes would be to increase the size of working capital (ignoring bank balances or overdrafts).

2.12 Suppose that a company has annual sales of £480,000 (in regular monthly quantities, all on credit) and a cost of sales of £300,000. A 'materials cost of sales' is the cost of materials in the cost of sales.

(a) If the stock turnover period is 2 months, the debt collection period is 1 month and the period of credit taken from suppliers is 2 months, the company's working capital (ignoring cash) would be:

		£
Stocks	(2/12 × £300,000)	50,000
Debtors	(1/12 × £480,000)	40,000
		90,000
Creditors	(2/12 × £300,000)	(50,000)
		40,000

The cash cycle would be (2 + 1 – 2) = 1 month.

(b) Now if the stock turnover period is extended to 3 months and the debt collection period to 2 months, and if the payment period for purchases from suppliers is reduced to one month, the company's working capital (ignoring cash) would be:

		£
Stocks	(3/12 × £300,000)	75,000
Debtors	(2/12 × £480,000)	80,000
		155,000
Creditors	(1/12 × £300,000)	(25,000)
		130,000

and the cash cycle would be $(3 + 2 - 1) = 4$ months.

2.13 We can see that a lengthening of the cash cycle will result in a larger volume of working capital.

2.14 If the volume of working capital required by a business varies with the length of the cash cycle, it is worth asking the question: 'Is there an ideal length of cash cycle and an ideal volume of working capital?'

2.15 Obviously, stocks, debtors and creditors should be managed efficiently, and:

(a) Stocks should be sufficiently large to meet the demand for stock items when they are needed, but they should not be allowed to become excessive.

(b) Debtors should be allowed a reasonable credit period, but late payers should be pursued.

(c) Suppliers should be asked to allow a reasonable period of credit and the firm should make use of the credit period offered.

3 LIQUIDITY RATIOS 6/96 - 6/98, 6/99, 12/99, 6/00

3.1 The word 'liquid' means 'readily convertible into cash' and a firm's liquidity is its ability to convert its assets into cash to meet all the demands for payments when they fall due.

3.2 The most liquid asset, of course, is cash itself (or a bank balance). The next most liquid assets are short-term investments (stocks and shares) because these can be sold quickly for cash should this be necessary. Debtors are fairly liquid assets because they can be expected to pay their bills in the near future. Stocks are the least liquid current asset because they must first be sold and the customers given a credit period in which to pay before they can be converted into cash.

3.3 Current liabilities are items which must be paid for in the near future. When payment becomes due, enough cash must be available. The managers of a business must therefore make sure that a regular supply of cash comes in (from current assets) at all times to meet the regular flow of payments (current liabilities) it is necessary to provide for.

Liquidity ratios

3.4 There are two common liquidity ratios:

(a) The current ratio or working capital ratio.
(b) The quick ratio or acid test ratio, also known as the liquid ratio.

3.5 The *current ratio* or *working capital ratio* is the more commonly used and is the ratio of current assets to current liabilities.

A 'prudent' current ratio is sometimes said to be 2:1. In other words, current assets should be twice the size of current liabilities. This is a rather simplistic view of the matter, because particular attention needs to be paid to:

(a) Bank overdrafts: these are technically repayable on demand, and therefore must be classified as current liabilities. However, many companies have semi-permanent overdrafts in which case the likelihood of their having to be repaid in the near future is remote. It would also often be relevant to know a company's overdraft limit - this may give a truer indication of liquidity than a current or quick ratio.

(b) Whether the year-end figures are typical of the year as a whole. This is particularly relevant in the case of seasonal businesses. For example, many large retail companies choose an accounting year end following soon after the January sales and their balance sheets show a higher level of cash than would be usual at any other time in the year.

3.6 In practice, many businesses operate with a much lower current ratio and in these cases, the best way to judge their liquidity would be to look at the current ratio at different dates over a period of time. If the trend is towards a lower current ratio, we would judge that the liquidity position is getting steadily worse.

3.7 The *quick ratio* or *acid test* ratio is used when we take the view that stocks may take a long time to sell, so that they are not particularly liquid assets. If this is the case, a firm's liquidity depends more heavily on the amount of debtors, short-term investments and cash that it has to match its current liabilities. The quick ratio is the ratio of current assets excluding stocks to current liabilities.

3.8 A 'prudent' quick ratio is 1:1. In practice, many businesses have a lower quick ratio (eg 0.5:1), and the best way of judging a firm's liquidity would be to look at the trend in the quick ratio over a period of time.

4 WORKING CAPITAL AND CASH

4.1 An increase in stocks and debtors, or a decrease in creditors, will have the effect of reducing the cash balance we would otherwise expect. An example will illustrate this point.

4.2 At 1 January, Cottontail had stocks of £2,000, no debtors or cash, and creditors of £1,000. During the month, stocks costing £15,000 were purchased and goods costing £14,000 were sold for £20,000. At 31 January, creditors were £500, and debtors £3,000.

The gross profit in January was £6,000, ie:

	£
Sales	20,000
Cost of sales	14,000
Gross profit	6,000

4.3 Cottontail should expect a cash surplus of £6,000 from these sales, but the cash balance at 31 January will not be as high as £6,000. This is because Cottontail has increased the investment in items of working capital other than cash.

	£
Increase in stocks held (15,000 – 14,000)	1,000
Increase in debtors (3,000 – 0)	3,000
Decrease in creditors (1,000 – 500)	500
Increase in other items of working capital	4,500
Profit in January	6,000
Increase in cash (balance)	1,500

4.4 This can be proved as follows:

	£	£
Creditors at 1 January	1,000	
Purchases	15,000	
	16,000	
Creditors at 31 January	(500)	
Payments to creditors in January		15,500
Debtors at 1 January	0	
Sales in January	20,000	
	20,000	
Debtors at 31 January	(3,000)	
Receipts from debtors in January		17,000
Net receipts of cash in January		1,500

4.5 This example shows that an increase in stocks and debtors or a decrease in creditors will use up cash, so that cash receipts during a period of time will be less than the profits earned.

Similarly, a decrease in stocks and debtors or an increase in creditors will have the opposite effect of releasing cash, so that cash receipts during a period will exceed the profits earned.

Example: working capital and cash

4.6 The cash balance of Wing Ltd has declined significantly over the last 12 months. The following financial information is provided:

	Year to 31 December	
	20X2	*20X3*
	£	£
Sales	573,000	643,000
Purchases of raw materials	215,000	264,000
Raw materials consumed	210,000	256,400
Cost of goods manufactured	435,000	515,000
Cost of goods sold	420,000	460,000

	Balance at 31 December	
	20X2	*20X3*
	£	£
Debtors	97,100	121,500
Creditors	23,900	32,500
Stocks: raw materials	22,400	30,000
work in progress	29,000	34,300
finished goods	70,000	125,000

All purchases and sales were made on credit.

Required

(a) Prepare an analysis of the above information, which should include calculations of the cash operating cycle (ie the time lag between making payment to suppliers and collecting cash from customers) for 20X2 and 20X3.

(b) Write a brief report on the implications of the changes which have occurred between 20X2 and 20X3.

Notes

1 Assume a 360 day year for the purpose of your calculations and that all transactions take place at an even rate.

2 All calculations are to be made to the nearest day.

Solution

4.7 (a) The information should be analysed in as many ways as possible. The relevant calculations would seem to be as follows.

(i)

	20X2	*20X3*
	£	£
Sales	573,000	643,000
Cost of goods sold	420,000	460,000
Gross profit	153,000	183,000

(ii) Size of working capital and liquidity ratios, ignoring cash/bank overdrafts:

	£	£
Debtors	97,100	121,500
Stocks: raw materials	22,400	30,000
work in progress	29,000	34,300
finished goods	70,000	125,000
	218,500	310,800
Creditors	23,900	32,500
Working capital (ignoring cash or overdraft)	194,600	278,300

Current ratio	$\frac{218{,}500}{23{,}900}$	$\frac{310{,}800}{32{,}500}$
	= 9.1:1	= 9.6:1
Quick ratio	$\frac{97{,}100}{23{,}900}$	$\frac{121{,}500}{32{,}500}$
	= 4.7:1	= 3.7:1

(iii) Turnover periods:

	20X2			Days	*20X3*			Days
Raw materials in stock	$\frac{22{,}400}{210{,}000}$	× 360	=	38	$\frac{30{,}000}{256{,}400}$	× 360	=	42
Work in progress	$\frac{29{,}000}{435{,}000}$	× 360	=	24	$\frac{34{,}300}{515{,}000}$	× 360	=	24
Finished goods stock	$\frac{70{,}000}{420{,}000}$	× 360	=	60	$\frac{125{,}000}{460{,}000}$	× 360	=	98
Debtors' collection period	$\frac{97{,}100}{573{,}000}$	× 360	=	61	$\frac{121{,}500}{643{,}000}$	× 360	=	68
Creditors' payment period	$\frac{23{,}900}{215{,}000}$	× 360	=	(40)	$\frac{32{,}500}{264{,}000}$	× 360	=	(44)
Cash cycle				143				188

(b) Sales were about 12% higher in 20X3 than in 20X2 and the cost of sales was about 10% higher. The investments in stocks and debtors minus creditors rose from £194,600 to £278,300 ie by £83,700 or 43%. This is completely out of proportion to the volume of increase in trade, which indicates that working capital turnover periods are not being properly controlled.

The increase in working capital of £83,700 means that the net cash receipts from profits in 20X3 were £83,700 less than they would have been if there had been no increase at all in stocks and debtors (less creditors) during 20X3. The company might therefore have an unnecessary bank overdraft, although we are not given enough information to comment on this point fully.

Current assets must be financed by a combination of long-term funds and current liabilities. Working capital (current assets minus current liabilities) is the amount of this finance provided by long-term funds. A large and unnecessary increase in working capital will mean that too many long-term funds are invested in current assets (and they are obviously being invested wastefully if trading operations can be sustained with less working capital). A current ratio (ignoring cash and bank overdraft) of over 9:1 in both years would appear to be excessive. The quick ratio is also very high in both years, although it is falling.

The causes of the increase in working capital in 20X3 are:

(i) The increase in sales.
(ii) The increased length of turnover periods.

Raw materials stock turnover has risen from 38 to 42 days, although this increase was cancelled out by an extension of the credit taken from suppliers, from 40 to 44 days. Debtors, already allowed 61 days to pay in 20X2, were allowed 68 days in 20X3 and this would seem to be an excessive length of time. The most serious change, however, is the increase in the finished goods stock turnover period from 60 days (2 months) to 98 days (over 3 months) and it is difficult to see an obvious reason why this should have occurred.

Chapter roundup

- The cash cycle is the time which elapses between paying suppliers for goods purchased and receiving cash from debtors in respect of those goods. This period can be calculated as:
  - Stock turnover period; plus
  - Debtor collection period; less
  - Creditors' payment period.
- The greater the amount of a business's investment in stocks and debtors (less creditors) the less cash it will have available. For this reason, it is unwise to allow the levels of stock and debtors to rise too high and turnover periods should be monitored carefully. At the same time, a business must ensure that it has enough stock on hand to meet customer demands.
- Two important liquidity ratios are the current ratio and the quick ratio.

Test your knowledge

1 What is the 'cash cycle'? (see para 2.3)

2 What is:

(a) a stock turnover period (2.6(a));
(b) a debtors turnover period? (2.6(b))

How are they calculated? (2.7, 2.9)

3 A lengthening of the cash cycle will result in a smaller volume of working capital. True or false? (2.13)

4 Define:

(a) the current ratio. (3.5)
(b) the quick ratio. (3.7)

5 A decrease in creditors has the effect of increasing the cash balance. True or false? (4.1)

Now try illustrative question 29 at the end of the Study Text

Part E
Management accounting

Chapter 20

THE MANAGEMENT ACCOUNTANT. CLASSIFYING COSTS

This chapter covers the following topics.

Introduction

The emphasis so far has been on reporting and analysing the past performance of a business.

In this part of the text we will study management accounting, which aims to make a contribution to decision making by looking at the past in order to predict the future.

1 FINANCIAL ACCOUNTING AND MANAGEMENT ACCOUNTING

1.1 So far in this text we have been concerned with the preparation of *financial* accounts. Financial accounting is mainly a method of reporting the results and financial position of a business; it is not primarily concerned with providing information as a guide to the more efficient conduct of the business. Although financial accounts may be of interest to management, their principal function is to satisfy the information needs of persons not involved in the day-to-day running of the business.

1.2 The information needs of management go far beyond those of other users of accounts. Shareholders, for example, are content if they can see that profits and dividends are rising strongly; the Inland Revenue is satisfied if the amount of the company's taxable profits can be calculated. However, management must plan and control the resources of the business. To do this they need much more detailed information than the financial accounts disclose.

1.3 *Management accounting* (also called *cost accounting*) is a management information system which analyses data to provide information as a basis for managerial action. The concern of a management accountant is to present accounting information in the form most helpful to management.

1.4 Since the management accounting system and the financial accounting system have different purposes, they are often kept separately in two sets of books. Each set records the same income and expenditure, but the two sets analyse them in different ways. However, it is possible to maintain a single integrated set of books containing both management and financial accounting information.

2 THE ROLE OF THE MANAGEMENT ACCOUNTANT

2.1 The management accountant is interested in the following questions.

(a) What has been the cost of goods produced or services provided, or what has been the cost of a department or work section? What have revenues been? Knowing about costs and revenues enables management:

(i) To assess the profitability of a product, a service, a department or the organisation in total.

(ii) To set selling prices with some regard to the costs of sale.

(iii) To put a value to stocks of goods that are still held in store at the end of a period so as to prepare a balance sheet.

(b) What are future costs likely to be? Costing is an integral part of budgeting (planning) for the future.

(c) How do actual costs compare with budgeted costs? If an organisation plans for its revenues and costs to be a certain amount, but they actually turn out differently, the differences can be measured and reported. Management can use these reports as a guide to whether corrective action is needed to sort out a problem revealed by these differences. This system of control is often referred to as *budgetary control.*

2.2 An important first step is the *cost classification*, so that costs can be dealt with in appropriate ways.

3 TOTAL COSTS OF A PRODUCT OR SERVICE

3.1 Total costs of a product or service consist of:

(a) The cost of materials consumed in making the product or providing the service.

(b) The cost of the wages and salaries of employees of the organisation, who are directly or indirectly involved in producing the product or providing the service.

(c) The cost of other expenses, apart from materials and labour costs. These include expense items such as rent and rates, electricity bills, gas bills, depreciation, interest charges, the cost of contractors' services (eg sub-contractors and office cleaners) and telephone bills.

3.2 So one way of classifying the total costs of a product or service is under the three headings 'materials costs', 'costs of wages and salaries' and 'other expenses'.

4 DIRECT AND INDIRECT COSTS

4.1 Materials, labour costs and other expenses can be classified as direct costs or indirect costs.

(a) A *direct* cost is a cost that can be traced in full to the product or service that is being costed.

(i) Direct materials costs are the costs of materials that are known to have been used in making and selling a product (or providing a service).

(ii) Direct labour costs are the costs of the workforce used to make a product or provide a service. Direct labour costs are established by measuring the time taken for a job. Traditionally, direct labour costs have been restricted to wage-earning factory workers, but in recent years, with the development of systems for costing services, the costs of some salaried staff might also be treated as a direct labour cost.

(iii) Other direct expenses are those expenses that have been incurred in full as a direct consequence of making a product or providing a service.

(b) An *indirect* cost is a cost which cannot be traced directly and in full to a product or service.

(i) Indirect materials costs might include coolants and cleaning materials.
(ii) Indirect labour costs might include a supervisor's salary.
(iii) Indirect expenses might include building insurance and water rates.

4.2 Total expenditure may therefore be analysed as follows:

£		£		£
Material cost	=	Direct material cost	+	Indirect material cost
+		+		+
Wages	=	Direct wages	+	Indirect wages
+		+		+
Expenses	=	Direct expenses	+	Indirect expenses
Total cost	=	Prime cost	+	Overhead

Prime cost is the aggregate of all direct costs and overhead is the aggregate of all indirect costs. Total cost is the sum of prime cost and overhead.

4.3 Another definition of direct and indirect costs, that you might find useful later, is this.

(a) A direct cost is a cost which can be identified with and allocated to a cost centre (eg a department) or cost unit (eg a product).

(b) An indirect cost is a cost which cannot be directly *allocated*, but which can be *apportioned* to cost centres or cost units. Indirect costs are commonly referred to as overheads.

Many costs are both direct and indirect

4.4 A cost may be a direct cost in one cost analysis and an indirect cost in another. Here is an example.

4.5 The Donkey Oater Racing Stables trains and races two horses, Sancho Panza and Rosinante. Costs for a recent month are as follows.

		£
Salary of the stable manager		1,000
Wages		
Special groom to Sancho Panza		80
General stable boy		80
Jockey for both horses:	retainer	200
	race fees	200
Race entrance fees:	Sancho Panza (3 races)	150
	Rosinante (2 races)	100
Hay and straw		600
Depreciation on stables and riding equipment		200
Rent and rates		300
Heating and lighting		100

4.6 All of the costs listed are direct costs of operating the stable, with the exception of the various race fees (which are only incurred as and when horses are entered for races).

4.7 The direct costs of keeping one of the horses, Sancho Panza, in the month are the costs of the special groom and race fees. All other costs are either:

(a) Costs shared with Rosinante: the stable manager's salary, wages of the stable boy, the jockey's retainer, hay and straw, depreciation, rent, rates, heating and lighting. Some of these costs could be charged directly (eg hay and straw consumed, stable boy's time) if a system for recording the material issues to each horse or time spent with each horse were used.

(b) Direct costs of Ronsinante (race fees).

4.8 The direct costs of a race are the entrance fee (£50) and the jockey's fee (£40). Indirect costs would be not only the jockey's retainer, but also the other costs of running the stable.

4.9 What you should be able to see from this example is that deciding whether a cost is direct or indirect (an overhead) must depend on what it is that the cost accountant is attempting to establish the cost of.

5 FUNCTIONAL COSTS

5.1 In a traditional management accounting system for a manufacturing organisation, costs are classified as:

(a) Production costs.
(b) Administration costs.
(c) Selling and distribution costs.

5.2 Many expenses fall comfortably into one of other of these three broad classifications. Production costs are associated with the factory, selling and distribution costs with the sales, marketing, warehousing and transport departments and administration costs with general office departments (such as accounting and personnel).

5.3 Other expenses that do not fall fully into one of these classifications might be categorised as 'general overheads' or even classified separately (eg research and development costs).

5.4 In costing a small product made by a manufacturing organisation, direct costs are usually restricted to some of the production costs (although it is not uncommon to find a salesman's commission for selling the product as a direct selling cost). A commonly found build-up of costs is therefore as follows.

	£
Production cost	
Direct materials	10
Direct wages	12
Direct expenses (if any)	8
Prime cost	30
Production overheads	5
Full factory cost	35
Administration overheads	3
Selling and distribution overheads	3
Full cost of sales	41

Functional costs in more detail

5.5 (a) *Production costs:* the costs which are incurred by the sequence of operations beginning with the supply of raw materials and ending with the completion of the product ready for warehousing as a finished goods item.

(b) *Administration costs:* the costs of managing an organisation, that is planning and controlling its operations, but only insofar as such administration costs are not related specifically to the production, sales, distribution or research and development functions.

(c) *Selling costs:* sometimes known as marketing costs are the costs of creating demand for products and securing firm orders from customers.

(d) *Distribution costs:* the costs of the sequence of operations beginning with the receipt of finished goods from the production department and making them ready for dispatch and ending with the reconditioning for re-use of returned empty containers.

(e) *Research and development costs:*

(i) Research costs are the costs of searching for new or improved products.

(ii) Development costs are the costs incurred between the decision to produce a new or improved product and the start of full manufacture of the product.

5.6 We will now give some specific examples of costs of each type.

5.7 *Direct material cost:* all material becoming part of the product (unless used in negligible amounts and having negligible costs) is direct material, the cost of which is part of the prime cost. Material used in negligible amounts and/or having negligible cost can be grouped under indirect materials as part of overhead. Examples of direct materials are:

(a) Materials, including component parts, specially purchased for a particular job, order or process.

(b) Materials passing from one operation to another. For example, if a product is made in two departments, when part-finished work is transferred from department 1 to department 2 it becomes finished work of department 1 and a direct material cost in department 2.

(c) Primary packing materials, such as cartons and boxes.

5.8 *Direct labour or direct wages:* all wages paid for labour expended in altering the condition, conformation or composition of the product are direct wages, the cost of which is charged to the product as part of the prime cost. Some indirect wages (those paid to foremen, inspectors and so on) which can be accurately identified with the product may be included as direct wages.

5.9 *Direct expenses:* all expenses incurred on a specific product other than direct material cost and direct wages are direct expenses. Examples of direct expenses are:

(a) Cost of special designs, drawings or layouts.
(b) Hire of tools or equipment for a particular job.
(c) Maintenance costs of tools.

5.10 *Production overhead:* all indirect materials cost, indirect wages and indirect expenses incurred in the factory from receipt of the order until its completion are included in production (or factory) overhead. Examples are:

(a) Indirect materials which cannot be traced in the finished product, such as consumable stores (eg lubricants) or minor items of material used in negligible amounts or amounts which it is uneconomical to allocate to a particular product (eg the cost of glue in box-making).

(b) Indirect wages. Generally these include salaries and wages of non-productive personnel in the production department, such as foremen, inspectors, general labourers, maintenance staff and stores staff.

(c) Indirect expenses (other than material and labour) not charged directly to production. Expenses included under this heading could be:

(i) Rent, rates and insurance of a factory.

(ii) Depreciation, fuel, power, repairs and maintenance of plant, machinery and factory buildings.

Production overhead is also referred to as factory overhead.

5.11 *Administration overhead:* all indirect material costs, wages and expenses incurred in the direction, control and administration of an undertaking. Examples of this are:

(a) Depreciation of office machines.

(b) Office salaries, including salaries of administrative directors, secretaries and accountants.

(c) Rent, rates, insurance of general offices, lighting, cleaning and heating of general offices, telephone and postal charges, bank charges, legal charges, audit fees, depreciation and repairs of office buildings and machinery.

5.12 *Selling overhead:* all indirect materials costs, wages and expenses incurred in promoting sales and retaining customers. Examples of selling overhead are:

(a) Printing and stationery, such as catalogues, price lists and order forms.

(b) Salaries and commission of sales representatives and sales department staff.

(c) Advertising, sales promotion and market research.

(d) Rent, rates and insurance of sales offices and showrooms, bad debts and debt collection charges, cash discounts allowed and the cost of after-sales services.

5.13 *Distribution overhead:* all indirect materials, costs, wages and expenses incurred in making the packed product ready for despatch and delivering it to the customer.

Examples of distribution overhead are:

(a) The cost of packing cases; materials (eg oil, spare parts) used in the upkeep of delivery vehicles; the cost of reconditioning returned packing cases ready for re-use.

(b) Wages of packers, drivers and despatch clerks.

(c) Freight and insurance charges, rent, rates, insurance and depreciation of warehouses and depreciation and running expenses of delivery vehicles.

5.14 The following exercise will demonstrate that the distinction between direct and indirect costs is not always clear, and that judgement may need to be exercised.

Exercise

A direct labour employee's wage in week 5 consists of:

		£
(a)	basic pay for normal hours worked, 36 hours at £8 per hour	288
(b)	pay at the basic rate for overtime hours worked, 6 hours at £8 per hour	48
(c)	overtime shift premium, with overtime paid at time-and-a-quarter ¼ x 6 hours x £8 per hour	12
(d)	a bonus payment for the month under a group bonus scheme	50
Total gross wages in week 5 for 42 hours of work		398

Which costs are direct? Are any indirect?

Solution

Items (a) and (b) are direct labour costs of the items produced in the 42 hours worked in week 5.

Overtime premium, item (c) is usually regarded as an overhead expense, because it is 'unfair' to charge the items produced in overtime hours with the premium. Why should an item made in overtime be more costly just because, by chance, it was made after the employee normally clocks off for the day? But the difficulties of cost classification can be seen by considering the case of a company that accepts a large, special order which it cannot meet in normal working hours. If employees are asked to work long hours specifically to produce the special order then it is arguable that all their wages, including overtime premium, are a direct cost of the items produced.

Group bonus scheme payments, item (d), are usually overhead costs, because they cannot normally be traced directly to individual products or jobs.

In this example, the direct labour employee costs were £336 in direct costs and £62 in indirect costs.

6 FIXED COSTS AND VARIABLE COSTS

6.1. A different way of analysing and classifying costs is into:

(a) Fixed costs.
(b) Variable costs.

Some items of expenditure are part-fixed and part-variable or 'mixed' costs, but in cost accounting, mixed costs are divided into their fixed and their variable elements.

6.2 The distinction between fixed and variable costs lies in whether the amount of costs incurred will go up as the volume of activity goes up, or whether the costs will remain the same, regardless of the volume of activity. For example:

(a) Direct material costs will rise as more units of a product are manufactured, and so they are variable costs, varying with the volume of production.

(b) Sales commission is often a fixed percentage of sales turnover, and so is a variable cost that varies with the level of sales (but not with the level of production).

(c) Telephone call charges are likely to increase if the volume of business expands, and so they are a variable overhead cost, varying with the volume of production and sales.

(d) The rental charge for a telephone line is a fixed cost, which is unaffected by the volume of activity.

(e) Combining (c) and (d), the total telephone expense is a mixed cost, with a fixed element (the rental) and a variable element (the call charges).

(f) The rental cost of business premises is a constant amount, and so it is a fixed cost that does not vary with the level of activity conducted on the premises.

7 COSTS FOR DECISION MAKING 12/96, 6/00

7.1 A *relevant cost* is a future cash flow arising as a direct consequence of the decision under review. Only relevant costs should be considered in decision-making, because they are the costs affected by the decision.

Costs which are not *relevant* include:

(a) Past costs, or money already spent (sunk costs).

(b) Future spending already committed by previous decisions.

(c) Costs which are not of a cash nature, such as depreciation. In the long term, profits are affected by what assets cost and what they can be sold for when they are worn out.

The relevant cost of a unit of production is the variable cost of making that unit. Costs which are the same whether or not it is produced are irrelevant.

7.2 The assumption used, quite correctly, is that in the end, profits earn cash. Reported profits and cash flow are not the same in any one period, for reasons discussed in the chapter on cash flow statements. In the end, however, at some time or another, a profit that is earned will produce a net inflow of an equal amount of cash. Hence, accounting for decision-making looks at cash flow as a means of measuring profits.

7.3 A *differential cost* is the difference in cost of alternative choices. If option A will cost £300 and option B will cost £360, the differential cost is £60, with option B being more expensive. A differential cost is the difference between the *relevant costs* of each option.

The differential cost of an extra unit of production is the increase in total costs caused by making that unit. This type of cost is also called an *incremental cost.* Incremental costs are relevant costs.

7.4 An *opportunity cost* is the benefit foregone by selecting one course of action in preference to the most profitable alternative. Suppose for example, that there are three mutually exclusive options, A, B and C. The net profit from each would be £80, £100 and £70 respectively.

Since only one option can be selected option B would be chosen because it offers the biggest benefit.

	£
Profit from option B	100
Less opportunity cost (the benefit from the most profitable alternative, A)	80
Differential benefit of option B	20

The decision to choose option B would not be made because it offers a profit of £100, but because it offers a differential profit of £20 in excess of the best alternative.

7.5 The principle underlying decision making is that 'bygones are bygones'. What has happened in the past cannot be altered. Management decisions can only affect the future. In decision-making, managers therefore require information about future costs and revenues which would be affected by the decision under review, and they must not be misled by events, costs and revenues in the past, about which they can do nothing. Past expenditures (or future expenditures to which the business is already committed) are *sunk costs*.

7.6 In contrast, relevant costs are future costs resulting from choosing one option, and they include the benefits which could have been earned by choosing another option but which have been given up. Opportunity costs will never appear in a set of double entry cost accounts, but they often appear in reports to help decision makers.

7.7 An *avoidable cost* is, quite simply, a cost which a business could avoid altogether if it wanted to. A good example of an avoidable cost is the cost of advertising: if a business advertises something, then it will incur advertising costs, but if it chooses not to advertise, then no such cost will arise.

Chapter roundup

- Management accounting and financial accounting differ both in their purposes and in the persons to whom they are addressed. Financial accounts provide a report on the results and financial position of a business to persons not involved in day-to-day management. Management accounts are designed to assist managers in the efficient conduct of the business.
- Costs can be analysed in many different ways. Important analyses are into direct and indirect costs, and by function.

Test your knowledge

1 Why does management need management accounts? (see para 1.2)

2 What sort of matters are the subject of management accounting? (2.1)

3 Distinguish between direct and indirect costs. (4.1)

4 What is prime cost? (4.2)

5 List five types of functional cost. (5.5)

6 Give some examples of distribution overheads. (5.13)

7 Why is a sunk cost not a relevant cost? (7.5)

Now try illustrative question 30 at the end of the Study Text

Chapter 21

ABSORPTION COSTING

This chapter covers the following topics.

1 Attributing overheads to products and services

2 Absorption costing

3 Overhead allocation

4 Overhead apportionment

5 Overhead absorption

Introduction

In the last chapter we distinguished between direct costs and indirect costs (overheads).

In this chapter we will look at one possible treatment of overheads, absorbing them into units of production.

In the next chapter we will look at an alternative approach, marginal costing, which keeps overheads separate from units of production.

1 ATTRIBUTING OVERHEADS TO PRODUCTS AND SERVICES

1.1 A manufacturing company has the objective of producing a product which can be sold so as to generate a profit for the company; similarly, the main objective of a service company is to provide a particular service at a price which will more than cover the costs incurred. The problem is that many of the costs incurred by companies are indirect costs, which are not directly attributable to the product or service provided. This makes it difficult to compare the revenue earned from a product or service with the costs of providing it.

1.2 One of the reasons why overheads are difficult to attribute to products or services is that they often relate to periods of time rather than output levels. For instance, rates are charged per year. This is quite different from variable costs, which vary with the level of output.

1.3 A company must pay money to cover overhead costs, and this must somehow be reflected in the calculation of profit earned. Two main methods are in use to do this.

(a) In *marginal costing*, overheads are deducted as a total sum to arrive at a profit figure. We will look in more detail at marginal costing in the next chapter.

(b) In *absorption costing*, an attempt is made to allocate overhead costs to individual units of output. To calculate the cost of a unit of output we add to its prime cost a proportion of the total overheads incurred by the company. (This process is referred to as absorbing overheads into units of output, and the system is consequently known as absorption costing.)

1.4 The main practical problem is that of estimation: to absorb overheads correctly, management needs to know the total overheads incurred and the number of units of output to which they should be allocated. Neither is known for certain until the end of an accounting period, and in the meantime estimates must be made. In calculating net profit, adjustments will need to be made in respect of differences (*variances*) between overheads actually incurred and overheads absorbed.

2 ABSORPTION COSTING 6/97, 12/97, 12/98, 6/99, 12/99

2.1 Suppose that a company makes and sells 100 units of a product each week. The prime cost per unit is £6 and the unit sales price is £10. Production overhead costs £200 per week, and administration, selling and distribution overhead costs £150 per week. The weekly profit could be calculated as follows.

	£	£
Sales (100 units × £10)		1,000
Prime costs (100 × £6)	600	
Production overheads	200	
Administration, selling and distribution costs	150	
		950
Profit		50

2.2 There has been no 'absorption' used in drawing up this profit statement. Prime costs and overheads are shown as two separate figures.

2.3 Now suppose that production overheads are absorbed into the product cost. In other words, production overheads are added to prime costs, in order to arrive at a 'full factory cost'. The calculation of the full factory cost per unit is:

	£
Prime cost per unit	6
Production overhead (£200 per week ÷ 100 units)	2
Full factory cost	8

Using the figure of £8 for full factory cost per unit, the weekly profit statement would be:

	£
Sales	1,000
Less factory cost of sales (100 units × £8)	800
Gross profit	200
Less administration, selling and distribution costs	150
Net profit	50

The net profit still works out at £50.

2.4 Now we will take the absorption a stage further, and suppose that administration, selling and distribution overheads are absorbed into the product cost, as well as production overheads (this is a perfectly valid procedure, although not common). The calculation of full cost per unit is now:

	£
Prime cost per unit	6.00
Factory overhead cost per unit	2.00
Administration etc cost per unit (£150 ÷ 100)	1.50
Full cost of sales	9.50

Using the new figure of £9.50 for the full unit cost of sales, the weekly profit statement would be:

	£
Sales	1,000
Less full cost of sales (100 × £9.50)	950
Profit	50

Yet again, net profit has worked out at £50.

2.5 The weekly profit is £50 no matter how the figures have been presented. This being so, how does absorption costing serve any useful purpose in accounting?

2.6 Two reasons for using absorption costing have traditionally been identified as follows.

(a) It provides, according to many accountants, a superior basis for valuing stock.
(b) It is a useful guide in taking pricing decisions.

Closing stock valuations

2.7 When there is closing stock at the end of an accounting period (and opening stock at the beginning of the next period) the stock must have a valuation:

(a) For the balance sheet.
(b) To calculate the cost of stocks sold in the period so as to arrive at a figure of profit.

In our example, closing stocks might be valued at prime cost (£6 per unit), but in absorption costing, they would be valued at the full factory cost of £8 per unit. (They would not be valued at £9.50, the full cost of sales, because the only costs incurred in producing goods for finished stock are factory costs.)

Pricing decisions

2.8 Many companies attempt to fix prices by calculating the full cost of each product, and then adding a margin for profit. In our example, the company might have fixed a gross profit margin at 25% on factory cost, or 20% of the sales price, in order to establish the unit sales price of £10. 'Full cost plus pricing' can be particularly useful for companies which do jobbing work or contract work, where each job or contract is different, so that a standard unit sales price cannot be fixed.

2.9 Of these two arguments, the problem of valuing closing stocks is perhaps the more significant because absorption costing is recommended in financial accounting by SSAP 9 *Stocks and long-term contracts*. SSAP 9 deals with *financial* accounting systems and not with management accounting systems. The management accountant is (in theory) free to value closing stocks by whatever method seems best, but where companies integrate their financial accounting and management accounting systems into a single system of accounting records, the valuation of closing stocks will be determined by SSAP 9.

2.10 SSAP 9 states that the cost of stock should comprise the costs which have been incurred in the normal course of business in bringing the product to its present location and condition. These costs incurred will include all related production overheads. In other words, in financial accounting, closing stocks should be valued at full factory cost, and it may therefore be convenient and appropriate to value stocks by the same method in the management accounting system.

2.11 Despite the fact that *absorption costing* is the required basis for stock valuation in financial accounts, for management accounting purposes *marginal costing* has many advantages. Particularly in the context of decision making, consideration of fixed costs is often misleading. Marginal costs are usually the relevant costs for decision making.

Costing procedures

2.12 Ultimately, the objective of an absorption costing system is to attribute all production overheads (and possibly administration, selling and distribution overheads as well) to units of output. But it is not possible to allocate overhead costs in this way the moment they are incurred. We must first allocate overhead costs to *cost centres*. These are departments, functions or items of equipment which costs can be (at least temporarily) attributed to.

2.13 Examples of cost centres include the following.

(a) A production department (such as the machining department in a factory).

(b) A service department (stores, repairs and maintenance) within the factory area.

(c) An administrative department (such as personnel).

(d) A selling or distribution department (such as a warehouse).

(e) 'Functional' cost centres for items of expense which are shared by several departments (such as rent, rates, heating and lighting, insurance or a canteen).

2.14 As overheads are incurred they are initially allocated to appropriate cost centre such as those identified above. The next step after allocation is *apportionment*. This is the process by which costs originally allocated to service department or functional cost centres are apportioned between other cost centres, so that all overheads are eventually charged to production, administration and selling and distribution departments.

2.15 Finally, overheads are absorbed into the cost of finished units, jobs or processes. Overhead absorption is sometimes called overhead recovery.

2.16 So the three steps in absorption costing are:

(a) Allocation.
(b) Apportionment.
(c) Absorption.

3 OVERHEAD ALLOCATION

3.1 As an example of overhead allocation, the costs of a company might include:

	£
Wages of the foreman of department A	200
Wages of the foreman of department B	150
Indirect materials consumed in department A	50
Rent of the factory premises shared by departments A and B	300

The management accounting system might include three overhead cost centres:

101	Department A
102	Department B
201	Rent

Overhead costs would be allocated directly to each cost centre: £200 + £50 to cost centre 101, £150 to cost centre 102 and £300 to cost centre 201. The rent of the factory will be subsequently apportioned (shared) between the two production departments, but for the purpose of day-to-day cost recording, the rent would first of all be charged in full to a separate cost centre.

4 OVERHEAD APPORTIONMENT

4.1 Overhead apportionment follows on from overhead allocation. The first stage of overhead apportionment is to identify all overhead costs as production department, production service department, administration or selling and distribution overhead. This means that the item (e) costs in Paragraph 2.13 must be shared out between the other cost centres.

4.2 In the example in Paragraph 3.1, the rent would be shared out between the two production departments.

Bases of apportionment

4.3 Overhead costs should be shared out on a fair basis. The bases of apportionment for the most usual cases are given below.

Overhead	*Basis*
Rent, rates, lighting, repairs and depreciation of buildings	Floor area occupied by each Department
Depreciation, and insurance of equipment	Cost or book value of equipment
Personnel office, canteen, welfare, wages and cost offices, first aid	Number of employees, or labour hours worked in each department
Heating	Volume of space occupied by each Department
Carriage inwards (costs paid for the delivery of raw materials)	Value of materials issued to each cost centre/department.

4.4 An examination question may be set which calls for the apportionment of overhead items. In the majority of cases the basis to be used is obvious, but you may encounter one or two items for which two (or more) bases may appear to be equally acceptable. In such circumstances, do not waste time trying to weigh up the merits of each; use the method you prefer. Always indicate the basis of apportionment you have chosen, and in any case of doubt explain why you chose one basis in preference to another.

4.5 Some overhead costs can be directly allocated to user departments, for example indirect wages and consumable supplies.

Example: bases of apportionment

4.6 Fire Bases Ltd incurred the following overhead costs:

	£
Depreciation of factory	1,000
Factory repairs and maintenance	600
Factory office costs (treat as production overhead)	1,500
Depreciation of equipment	800
Insurance of equipment	200
Heating	390
Lighting	100
Canteen	900
	5,490

Information relating to the production and service departments in the factory is:

	Department			
	Production *A*	*Production* *B*	*Service* *X*	*Service* *Y*
Floor area (sq. metres)	1,200	1,600	800	400
Volume (cubic metres)	3,000	6,000	2,400	1,600
Number of employees	30	30	15	15
Book value of equipment	£30,000	£20,000	£10,000	£20,000

How should the overhead costs be apportioned between the four departments?

Solution

4.7

Item of cost and basis of apportionment	Total cost	A	B	X	Y
			To department		
	£	£	£	£	£
Factory depreciation (floor area)	1,000	300	400	200	100
Factory repairs (floor area)	600	180	240	120	60
Factory office (no. of employees)	1,500	500	500	250	250
Equipment depreciation (book value)	800	300	200	100	200
Equipment insurance (book value)	200	75	50	25	50
Heating (volume)	390	90	180	72	48
Lighting (floor area)	100	30	40	20	10
Canteen (no. of employees)	900	300	300	150	150
Total	5,490	1,775	1,910	937	868

Apportionment of service department costs

4.8 The second stage of overhead apportionment concerns the treatment of service department overheads. A factory is divided into several production departments and also many service departments, but only the production departments are directly involved in the manufacture of the units. In order to be able to add service department overheads to unit costs, it is necessary to have all the overheads charged to (or located in) the production departments. The next stage is, therefore, to apportion the costs of service departments to the production departments.

4.9 The basis of apportionment must be fair and a different apportionment basis may be applied for each service department. For example:

Service department	*Possible basis of apportionment*
Stores	Number or cost value of material requisitions
Maintenance	Hours of maintenance and repair work done for each department
Production planning	Labour hours worked in each production department

Example: apportioning service department costs directly to production departments

4.10 Gervaise Allotments Ltd incurred the following overhead costs:

	Production departments A	B	*Stores department*	*Maintenance department*
	£	£	£	£
Allocated costs	6,000	4,000	1,000	2,000
Apportioned costs	2,000	1,000	1,000	500
	8,000	5,000	2,000	2,500

Production department A worked 5,000 direct labour hours and requisitioned materials to the value of £12,000. Department B worked 7,500 labour hours and requisitioned £8,000 of materials. What are the total production overhead costs of departments A and B?

Solution

4.11

Service department	*Basis of apportionment*	*Total cost*	*Dept A*	*Dept B*
		£	£	£
Stores	Value of requisitions	2,000	1,200	800
Maintenance	Direct labour hours	2,500	1,000	1,500
		4,500	2,200	2,300
Previously allocated and apportioned costs		13,000	8,000	5,000
Total overhead		17,500	10,200	7,300

4.12 Overhead apportionment is also called *overhead analysis*, and if the examiner asks you for an overhead analysis sheet you should prepare a table showing how overheads are apportioned, like the one in Paragraph 4.7 (and if necessary a further table like the one in Paragraph 4.11).

5 OVERHEAD ABSORPTION

6/98

5.1 Having allocated and/or apportioned overheads, the next stage is to absorb them into the cost of production.

Use of a predetermined absorption rate

5.2 It is inappropriate to collect data about actual costs and to absorb overheads on the basis of actual costs.

(a) Goods are produced and sold throughout the year, but actual overheads are not known until the end of the year. It would be inconvenient to wait until the year end in order to decide what overhead costs should be.

(b) An attempt to calculate overhead costs more regularly (eg each month) is possible, although estimated costs must be added for occasional expenditures such as rent and rates (incurred once or twice a year). The difficulty with this approach is that actual overheads from month to month fluctuate randomly; therefore, overhead costs charged to production would depend to a certain extent on random changes. A unit made in one week might be charged with £4 of overhead, in a subsequent week with £5, and in a third week with £4.50. Such changes are:

(i) Misleading for costing purposes.
(ii) Administratively and clerically inconvenient to deal with.

5.3 Overheads are therefore usually added to cost using a predetermined overhead absorption rate, which is calculated from the budget, and businesses establish their overhead absorption for the forthcoming accounting year by:

(a) Estimating the overhead likely to be incurred during the coming year.

(b) Estimating the total hours, units or direct costs on which the overhead absorption rates are to be based (the activity level).

(c) Dividing the estimated overhead by the estimated activity level.

Over or under absorption of overheads

5.4 Because the rate of overhead absorption is based on estimates, it is almost inevitable that at the end of the accounting year there will have been an over-absorption or under-absorption of the overhead actually incurred.

5.5 Suppose that the budgeted overhead in a production department is £80,000 and the budgeted activity is 40,000 direct labour hours. The overhead recovery rate would be £2 per direct labour hour.

Actual overheads in the period are, say £84,000, and 45,000 direct labour hours are worked:

	£
Overhead incurred (actual)	84,000
Overhead absorbed (45,000 × £2)	90,000
Over-absorption of overhead	6,000

5.6 In this example, the cost of produced units or jobs has been charged with £6,000 more than was actually spent. An adjustment to reconcile the overheads charged to the actual overhead is necessary, and the over-absorbed overhead will appear as an addition to profit in the profit and loss account for the accounting period.

Absorption of production overheads into factory cost

5.7 The different bases of absorption which can be used are as follows.

(a) Percentage of direct materials cost.
(b) Percentage of direct labour cost.
(c) Percentage of prime cost.
(d) Rate per machine hour.
(e) Rate per direct labour hour.
(f) Rate per unit.

5.8 Which basis should be used for production overhead depends largely on the organisation concerned. Percentages of materials cost, wages or prime cost should be adopted only where the value of the materials and/or wages is considered to have some relationship with the overhead.

5.9 For example, it is safe to assume that the indirect costs for producing brass screws are similar to those for producing steel screws, but the cost of brass is very much greater than that of steel. Consequently, the overhead charge for brass screws would be too high and that for steel screws too low, if a percentage of cost of materials rate were to be used.

5.10 Again, if the overhead actually attributable to units was incurred on a time basis, but one skilled (and consequently highly paid) employee was engaged on producing one item, while a less skilled (and low paid) employee was producing another item, the overhead charged to the first job using the percentage of wages rate might be too high while the amount absorbed by the second job might be too low. A rate per direct labour hour might be considered fairer.

5.11 It is for this reason that many factories use the direct labour hour rate or machine hour rate in preference to a rate based on a percentage of direct materials cost, wages or prime cost.

Example of absorption

5.12 The budgeted production overheads and other budget data of Hairy Mammoth Ltd are as follows:

Budget	
Overhead cost	£36,000
Direct materials cost	£32,000
Direct labour cost	£40,000
Machine hours	10,000
Direct labour hours	18,000

What would the absorption rate be using the various bases of apportionment?

Solution

5.13

(a) Percentage of direct materials cost $\frac{£36,000}{£32,000} \times 100\% = 112.5\%$

(b) Percentage of direct labour cost $\frac{£36,000}{£40,000} \times 100\% = 90\%$

(c) Percentage of prime cost $\frac{£36,000}{£72,000} \times 100\% = 50\%$

(d) Rate per machine hour $\frac{£36,000}{10,000 \text{ hrs}}$ = £3.60 per machine hour

(e) Rate per direct labour hour $\frac{£36,000}{18,000 \text{ hrs}}$ = £2 per direct labour hour

5.14 The choice of the basis of apportionment is significant in determining the cost per unit of different products. Using the previous example, suppose that an individual product has a material cost of £80, a labour cost of £85, and requires 23 machine hours and 36 labour hours to complete. The overhead cost of the product would vary, depending on the basis of absorption used by the company for overhead recovery.

(a)	As a percentage of direct material cost, the overhead cost would be 112.5% × £80 =	£90
(b)	As a percentage of direct labour cost, the overhead cost would be 90% × £85 =	£76.50
(c)	As a percentage of prime cost, the overhead cost would be 50% × £165 =	£82.50
(d)	Using a machine hour basis of absorption, the overhead cost would be 23 hrs × £3.60 =	£82.80
(e)	Using a labour hour basis, the overhead cost would be 36 hrs × £2 =	£72

Exercise

Strictly Ltd is a manufacturing company which produces three types of burglar alarms, model 1, model 2 and model 3, all of which pass through three production departments, A, B and C. During the third quarter of 20X8, Strictly Ltd budgets for the following overhead costs.

	£
Depreciation (factory)	800
Repairs and maintenance (factory)	250
Office costs	1,000
Depreciation (equipment)	450
Insurance costs (equipment)	150
Heating	200
Lighting	250
	3,100

Strictly Ltd comprises the three production departments (A, B and C), and one service department. Information relating to these departments is as follows.

	Production department			*Service*
	A	*B*	*C*	*department*
Floor area (sq metres)	1,000	1,000	1,500	750
Volume (cubic metres)	3,150	3,350	4,500	2,250
Number of employees	25	25	32	13
Book value of equipment (£)	10,000	12,000	17,000	11,000

The service department spends 40% of its time working for production department C, 35% for production department B, and only 25% for production department A.

Other budgeted figures for the third quarter are as follows.

			Production department	
		A	*B*	*C*
Machine hours		330	440	460
Machine hours per unit:	Model 1	1	3	2
	Model 2	2	1	2
	Model 3	1	2	2

	Model 1	*Model 2*	*Model 3*
	£	£	£
Direct materials	15.00	19.00	33.00
Direct labour	16.00	18.00	14.00

In the quarter, output will be 80 units of model 1, 100 units of model 2 and 50 units of model 3.

Required

Calculate the full cost of each unit, absorbing overheads on a machine hour basis.

Solution

The first step is to apportion the various overheads to the four departments:

Item of cost	Basis of apportionment	Total cost	Department A	Department B	Department C	Service
		£	£	£	£	£
Factory depreciation	Floor area	800	188	188	282	142
Factory repairs and maintenance	Floor area	250	59	59	88	44
Office costs	Number of employees	1,000	263	263	337	137
Equipment depreciation	Book value	450	90	108	153	99
Insurance costs	Book value	150	30	36	51	33
Heating	Volume	200	48	51	68	33
Lighting	Floor area	250	59	59	88	44
		3,100	737	764	1,067	532

The second step is to apportion the service department overheads to the production departments in the ratio 25 : 35 : 40

Production department	Previously apportioned overheads	Apportioned from Service department	Total	Per machine hour
	£	£	£	£
A	737	133	870	2.64
B	764	186	950	2.16
C	1,067	213	1,280	2.78
	2,568	532	3,100	

The final step is to absorb the total apportioned overheads for each of the departments, and add the results to the direct costs, to reach the full cost for each unit produced.

	Model 1	Model 2	Model 3
	£	£	£
Direct materials per unit	15.00	19.00	33.00
Direct labour per unit	16.00	18.00	14.00
Absorbed overhead per unit	16.68	13.00	12.52
Full cost	14.68	50.00	59.52

*Example: model 1: 1 × £2.64 + 3 × £2.16 + 2 × £2.78.

Chapter roundup

- In absorption costing, overheads are added into product costs by applying a pre-determined overhead absorption rate.
- The absorption rate is calculated by dividing budgeted overhead for the department by the budgeted level of activity. For production overheads, the level of activity is often budgeted direct labour hours or budgeted machine hours.
- At the end of the accounting period (year) actual overheads are compared with the overheads which have been absorbed using the pre-determined rates. Any discrepancy must be adjusted for.

Test your knowledge

1 What is meant by 'absorbing' overheads? (see paras 2.1 - 2.4)

2 Why is absorption costing used? (2.6- 2.8)

3 What effect do the provisions of SSAP 9 have on a company's choice of stock valuation system? (2.9)

4 What is a cost centre? (2.12)

5 How may service department costs be allocated to production departments? (4.9)

6 Why is a predetermined absorption rate usually used? (5.2)

Now try illustrative question 31 at the end of the Study Text

Chapter 22

MARGINAL COSTING. PRICING

This chapter covers the following topics.

Introduction

In this chapter we will look at marginal costing, which is quite different from absorption costing.

In marginal costing, all fixed overheads are charged in the profit and loss account as lump sums. They are not shared between units of output, and therefore do not affect closing stock valuations.

1 WHAT IS MARGINAL COSTING? 12/97, 6/99

1.1 Marginal costing is an alternative method of costing to absorption costing. Whereas in absorption costing an attempt is made to apportion all overhead costs to units of production, in marginal costing only costs which vary directly with production are allocated to units of production.

1.2 The marginal cost per unit of production of an item usually consists of:

(a) Direct materials.
(b) Direct labour.
(c) Variable production overheads.

1.3 The basic idea of marginal costing is that if an extra item is produced, then the costs in the above paragraph will all go up slightly. It therefore makes sense to identify those costs as the costs of production: the marginal costs. On the other hand, overheads such as rent, rates, and heating will remain the same even if an extra item is produced. They are fixed costs, and are not linked directly to the level of production.

2 CONTRIBUTION

2.1 Contribution is the difference between selling price and the marginal cost of sales. It is of fundamental importance in marginal costing, and the term 'contribution' is really short for 'contribution towards covering fixed overheads and making a profit'.

Example: contribution

2.2 Suppose that an organisation does not use marginal costing. All the fixed costs incurred by the organisation are absorbed into the production costs. The organisation is made up of two departments X and Y, and for one particular period of six months, the profit statement drawn up by the organisation is as follows:

		Departments		*Total*
		X	*Y*	
		£	£	£
Sales		10,000	12,000	22,000
Less production costs:	fixed	(2,000)	(2,000)	(4,000)
	variable	(4,000)	(7,000)	(11,000)
Gross profit		4,000	3,000	7,000
Less administrative, selling and distribution costs (fixed)		(2,000)	(4,000)	(6,000)
Net profit/(loss)		2,000	(1,000)	1,000

2.3 The organisation as a whole is making a profit, but department Y is making a loss. On the face of it, therefore, it looks as though department Y should be closed. So let's draw up a statement with department Y closed - which means, of course, that department X has to bear *all of* the fixed costs.

		Department X
		£
Sales		10,000
Less production costs:	fixed	(4,000)
	variable	(4,000)
Gross profit		2,000
Less administrative, selling and distribution costs (fixed)		(6,000)
		(4,000)

2.4 Although it was the apparently weak department which was axed, the organisation as a whole now makes a loss. Why should that be? It is because previously, department Y was contributing something towards covering the organisation's fixed costs, and therefore contributing something towards profit. It is this amount which is referred to as the 'contribution'.

2.5 The exact amount of contribution made by a product or department can be seen by isolating the fixed costs from variable costs. Shown below is the profit statement for our example organisation, this time drawn up using marginal costing principles.

		Departments		*Total*
		X	*Y*	
		£	£	£
Sales		10,000	12,000	
Less variable production costs		(4,000)	(7,000)	
Contribution		6,000	5,000	11,000
Less fixed costs:	production			(4,000)
	administration, selling and distribution			(6,000)
				1,000

2.6 The original absorption costing statement showed department Y making a loss. But the marginal costing statement shows that Department Y does make a contribution of £5,000 towards the organisation's fixed costs, which in turn contributes towards the organisation's overall profit. By closing down department Y, the organisation makes no saving in fixed costs, but loses £5,000 in contribution. It is therefore £5,000 worse off: a profit of £1,000 overall becomes a loss of £4,000.

2.7 If management had been presented with the original absorption costing statement, it might have closed department Y and then wondered why the organisation started to make a loss.

The marginal costing statement is more useful for decision making: if department Y had been making a negative contribution, then it probably should have been closed.

3 STOCK VALUATION

3.1 You might think that marginal costing and absorption costing always give the same final profit figures, even if they reach those figures in different ways. In fact the two costing systems arrive at different profit figures when stock is carried forward from one period to the next.

3.2 When stock is valued under absorption costing, overheads are considered as a product cost rather than as a period cost. As a result, if not all of the production of a period is sold in that period, some of the overheads absorbed in the period are carried forward to the *next* period, as part of the value of closing stocks. This does not happen with marginal costing.

Example: stock valuation

3.3 Evergreen Ltd manufactures artificial Christmas trees. Selling and production figures for the first quarter of 20X8 are:

Opening stock	:	None
Variable costs	:	£2 per tree
Fixed costs	:	£40,000 per quarter
Output	:	40,000 trees
Sales	:	30,000 trees
Selling price	:	£5 per tree

3.4 Under the method of absorption costing, the value of closing stock includes the variable production costs and the absorbed fixed costs. Fixed costs per unit are £40,000/40,000 = £1.

Closing stock = value of 10,000 trees in stock
= 10,000 × (variable cost per unit + fixed cost per unit)
= 10,000 × (£2 + £1)
= £30,000

EVERGREEN LIMITED
TRADING, PROFIT AND LOSS ACCOUNT FOR THE PERIOD
(absorption costing)

	£	£
Sales		150,000
Less full cost of sales		
Opening stock	0	
Costs of production £3 × 40,000	120,000	
	120,000	
Less closing stock £3 × 10,000	30,000	
		90,000
Net profit		60,000

3.5 Under the method of marginal costing, the value of closing stock does not include any element of absorbed fixed cost.

Closing stock = value of 10,000 trees in stock
= 10,000 × variable cost per unit
= 10,000 × £2
= £20,000

EVERGREEN LIMITED
TRADING, PROFIT AND LOSS ACCOUNT FOR THE PERIOD
(marginal costing)

	£	£
Sales		150,000
Less marginal cost of sales		
Opening stock	0	
Production costs £2 × 40,000	80,000	
	80,000	
Less closing stock	20,000	
		60,000
Contribution		90,000
Less fixed costs		40,000
Net profit		50,000

3.6 The results of Evergreen Ltd are therefore shown in a more favourable light if absorption rather than marginal costing is used. The difference in profits, £(60,000 − 50,000) = £10,000, equals the fixed overheads in closing stock, £1 × 10,000 = £10,000.

Example continued

3.7 In the second quarter of the year the company made no more trees but sold all its outstanding stock. In fact, it closed down production so there were no fixed costs either.

EVERGREEN LIMITED
TRADING, PROFIT AND LOSS ACCOUNT FOR THE PERIOD
(absorption costing)

	£	£
Sales		50,000
Less full cost of sales		
Opening stock	30,000	
Production costs	0	
	30,000	
Less closing stock	0	
		30,000
Net profit		20,000

EVERGREEN LIMITED
TRADING, PROFIT AND LOSS ACCOUNT FOR THE PERIOD
(marginal costing)

	£	£
Sales		50,000
Less marginal cost of sales		
Opening stock	20,000	
Production costs	0	
	20,000	
Less closing stock	0	
		20,000
Contribution		30,000
Less fixed costs		0
Net profit		30,000

3.8 In this second quarter, marginal costing gives a profit of £30,000 whereas absorption costing only gives £20,000. The difference is that the part of the previous quarter's fixed cost carried forward in stock is deducted as part of cost of sales when absorption costing is used, thereby reducing profit.

3.9 You should note that, now a complete production cycle has finished, total profit is the same for both costing methods.

	Absorption costing	Marginal costing
	£	£
Quarter 1	60,000	50,000
Quarter 2	20,000	30,000
Total	80,000	80,000

4 MARGINAL AND ABSORPTION COSTING COMPARED 6/96, 6/97, 12/98, 12/99

4.1 Marginal costing as a cost accounting system is significantly different from absorption costing.

Marginal costing	*Absorption costing*
(a) Closing stock valued at *marginal* production cost.	(a) Closing stock valued at full production cost, including a share of fixed production costs.
(b) Fixed costs are charged in full against the profit for the period in which they are incurred: they are treated as *period costs.*	(b) Fixed costs are charged against profit in the period of sale of the stock units into whose value they have been absorbed. So in any period: (i) cost of sales *includes* some fixed overhead from a previous period (in opening stock) (ii) cost of sales *excludes* some fixed overhead of the current period (in closing stock)

Marginal costing versus absorption costing

4.2 *Arguments in favour of absorption costing*

(a) Fixed production costs are incurred in order to make output; it is therefore *fair* to charge all output with a share of these costs.

(b) *Closing stock values*, by including a share of fixed production overhead, will be valued on the principle required by SSAP 9 for the valuation of stocks in financial accounts.

(c) A problem with calculating the contribution of various products made by a company is that it may not be clear whether the contribution earned by each product is enough to cover that product's share of fixed costs, whereas by charging fixed overhead to a product we can decide whether it is *profitable* or not.

4.3 *Arguments in favour of marginal costing*

(a) Fixed costs will be the same regardless of the volume of output, because they are *period* costs. It makes sense, therefore, to charge them in full as a cost to the period.

(b) The cost to produce an extra unit is the variable production cost. It is *realistic* to value closing stock items at this directly attributable cost.

(c) As we have seen, the size of total contribution varies directly with sales volume at a constant rate per unit. For management purposes, *better information* about expected profit is obtained from the use of variable costs and contribution in the accounting system.

(d) As marginal costing yields better management information about expected profit, it is a better tool for *planning* purposes. In particular, the following points can be made.

   (i) If total contribution exceeds fixed costs, a profit is made.

   (ii) If total contribution exactly equals fixed costs, no profit and no loss is made: ie *breakeven point* is reached.

   (iii) If total contribution is less than the fixed costs, there will be a loss.

(e) No adjustments for under-absorbed or over-absorbed overheads can arise, because overheads are not absorbed.

Exercise

A company makes and sells a single product. At the beginning of period 1, there are no opening stocks of the product, for which the variable production cost is £4 and the sales price £6 per unit. Fixed costs are £2,000 per period, of which £1,500 are fixed production costs.

	Period 1	*Period 2*
Sales	1,200 units	1,800 units
Production	1,500 units	1,500 units

(a) Calculate the profit in each period using:

(i) Absorption costing (assume that normal output is 1,500 units per period).
(ii) Marginal costing.

(b) Comment on the result of your calculations.

Solution

(a) (i) *Absorption costing*

The absorption rate for fixed production overhead is $\frac{£1,500}{1,500 \text{ units}}$ = £1 per unit

	Period 1		*Period 2*		*Period 3*	
	£	£	£	£	£	£
Sales		7,200		10,800		18,000
Production costs:						
Variable	6,000		6,000		12,000	
Fixed	1,500		1,500		3,000	
	7,500		7,500		15,000	
Add opening stock	0		1,500		0	
	7,500		9,000		15,000	
Less closing stock						
(£7,500 × 300/1,500)	1,500		0		0	
Production cost of						
sales	6,000		9,000		15,000	
Other costs	500		500		1,000	
Total cost of sales		6,500		9,500		16,000
Profit		700		1,300		2,000

(ii) *Marginal costing*

	Period 1		*Period 2*		*Total*	
	£	£	£	£	£	£
Sales		7,200		10,800		18,000
Variable production						
cost	6,000		6,000		12,000	
Add opening stock	0		1,200		0	
	6,000		7,200		12,000	
Less closing stock						
(£6,000 × 300/1,500)	1,200		0		0	
Variable production						
cost of sales		4,800		7,200		12,000
Contribution		2,400		3,600		6,000
Fixed costs		2,000		2,000		4,000
Profit		400		1,600		2,000

(b) (i) The total profit over the two periods is the same for each method of costing, but the profit in each period is different.

(ii) In absorption costing, fixed production overhead of £300 is carried forward from period 1 into period 2 in stock values, and becomes a charge to profit in period 2. In marginal costing all fixed costs are charged in the period they are incurred. This is why the profit in period 1 is £300 lower and in period 2 is £300 higher than the absorption costing profit.

5 LIMITING FACTOR

12/96

5.1 One of the more common decision-making problems is a situation where there are not enough resources to meet the potential sales demand, and so a decision has to be made about what mix of products to produce, using what resources there are as effectively as possible. The *scarce resource* is known as a *limiting factor* or a *key factor* since it limits the organisation's activities. There might be just one limiting factor (other than maximum sales demand) but there might also be several scarce resources, with two or more of them acting as limiting factors by putting an effective limit on the level of activity that can be achieved. We will be concentrating on single limiting factor problems and a technique for resolving these, however.

5.2 A limiting factor could be sales if there is a limit to sales demand but any one of the organisation's resources (labour, materials, manufacturing capacity, financial resources and so on) may be insufficient to meet the level of production demanded. If sales demand is the factor which restricts greater production output, profit will be maximised by making exactly the amount required for sales (and no more) provided that each product sold earns a positive contribution. If labour supply, materials availability, machine capacity or cash availability limits production to less than the volume which could be sold, management is faced with the problem of deciding what products to produce because there are insufficient resources to make everything.

5.3 It is assumed in limiting factor accounting that management wishes to maximise profit and that profit will be maximised when contribution is maximised (given no change in fixed cost expenditure incurred). In other words, marginal costing ideas are applied.

Contribution will be maximised by earning the biggest possible contribution from each unit of limiting factor. Thus if grade A labour is the limiting factor, contribution will be maximised by earning the biggest contribution from each hour of grade A labour worked. Similarly, if machine time is in short supply, profit will be maximised by earning the biggest contribution from each machine hour worked.

The limiting factor decision therefore involves the determination of the contribution earned by each different product from each unit of the limiting factor. In limiting factor decisions, we generally assume that fixed costs are the same whatever production mix is selected, so that the only relevant costs are variable costs.

Example: limiting factor

5.4 AB Ltd makes two products, the Ay and the Be. Unit variable costs are as follows.

	Ay	*Be*
	£	£
Direct materials	1	3
Direct labour (£3 per hour)	6	3
Variable overhead	1	1
	8	7

The sales price per unit is £14 per Ay and £11 per Be. During July 20X2 the available direct labour is limited to 8,000 hours. Sales demand in July is expected to be 3,000 units for Ays and 5,000 units for Bes.

Required

Determine the profit-maximising production mix, assuming that monthly fixed costs are £20,000, and that opening stocks of finished goods and work in progress are nil.

Solution

5.5 (a) The first step in the solution is to confirm that the limiting factor is something other than sales demand.

	Ays	Bes	Total
Labour hours per unit	2 hrs	1 hr	
Sales demand	3,000 units	5,000 units	
Labour hours needed	6,000 hrs	5,000 hrs	11,000 hrs
Labour hours available			8,000 hrs
Shortfall			3,000 hrs

Labour is the limiting factor on production.

(b) The second step is to identify the contribution earned by each product per unit of limiting factor, that is per labour hour worked.

	Ays	Bes
	£	£
Sales price	14	11
Variable cost	8	7
Unit contribution	6	4
Labour hours per unit	2 hrs	1 hr
Contribution per labour hour (= unit of limiting factor)	£3	£4

Although Ays have a higher unit contribution than Bes, two Bes can be made in the time it takes to make one Ay. Because labour is in short supply it is more profitable to make Bes than Ays.

5.6 The final stage in the solution is to work out the budgeted production and sales mix. Sufficient Bes will be made to meet the full sales demand, and the remaining labour hours available will then be used to make Ays.

(a)

Product	*Demand*	*Hours required*	*Hours available*	*Priority of manufacture*
Bes	5,000	5,000	5,000	1st
Ays	3,000	6,000	3,000 (bal)	2nd
		11,000	8,000	

(b)

Product	*Units*	*Hours needed*	*Contribution per unit*	*Total*
			£	£
Bes	5,000	5,000	4	20,000
Ays	1,500	3,000	6	9,000
		8,000		29,000
Less fixed costs				20,000
Profit				9,000

Note that it is *not* more profitable to begin by making as many units as possible with the bigger unit contribution. We could make 3,000 units of Ay in 6,000 hours and 2,000 units of Be in the remaining 2,000 hours but profit would be only £6,000. Unit contribution is not the correct way to decide priorities, because it takes two hours to earn £6 from a Ay and one hour to earn £4 from a Be. Bes make more profitable use of the scarce resource, labour hours.

Other considerations regarding limiting factors

5.7 The following points should also be borne in mind when making a decision which involves limiting factors.

(a) In the long run management should seek to remove the limiting factor.

(b) In the short term management may be able to find ways around the limiting factors (such as overtime working and sub-contracting).

(c) It may not be easy to identify the limiting factor.

6 PRICING

6.1 A company selling a product must decide on a selling price. There are several ways of doing this, which take account of costs in different ways.

6.2 A traditional approach to pricing is *full cost-plus pricing*, whereby the sales price is determined by calculating the full cost of the product and then adding a percentage mark-up for profit. The 'full cost' may be a fully absorbed production cost only, or it may include some absorbed administration, selling and distribution overhead.

6.3 A business might have an idea of the percentage profit margin it would like to earn, and so might decide on an average profit mark-up as a general guideline for pricing decisions. This would be particularly useful for businesses that carry out a large amount of contract work or jobbing work, for which individual job or contract prices must be quoted regularly to prospective customers.

6.4 However, the percentage profit mark-up does not have to be fixed, but can be varied to suit the circumstances. In particular, the percentage mark-up can be varied to suit demand conditions in the market.

Example: full cost-plus pricing

6.5 Markup Ltd has begun to produce a new product, Product X, for which the following cost estimates have been made.

	£
Direct materials	27
Direct labour: 4 hours at £5 per hour	20
Variable production overheads: machining, 1 hr at £6 per hour	3
	50

Fixed production overheads are budgeted at £300,000 per month and because of the shortage of available machining capacity, the company will be restricted to 10,000 hours of machine time per month. The absorption rate will be a direct labour rate, however, and budgeted direct labour hours are 25,000 per month.

The company wishes to make a profit of 20% on full production cost from product X. What should the full cost-plus price be?

Solution

6.6

	£
Direct materials	27.00
Direct labour (4 hours)	20.00
Variable production overheads	3.00
Fixed production overheads	
(at $\frac{£300,000}{25,000}$ = £12 per direct labour hour)	48.00
Full production cost	98.00
Profit mark-up (20%)	19.60
Selling price per unit of product X	117.60

6.7 You might also notice in this example that the company uses a direct labour hour absorption rate for its overheads. If it had used a machine hour rate of

$$\frac{£300,000}{10,000} = £30 \text{ per machine hour}$$

the fixed production overhead cost per unit would be ½ hr × £30 = £15 per unit of product X instead of the £48 per unit fixed overhead cost given by a direct labour hour absorption rate.

Problems with full cost-plus pricing

6.8 There are several serious problems with relying on a full cost approach to pricing. These are as follows.

(a) The need to adjust prices to market and demand conditions.

(b) Budgeting what output volume is gong to be. Output volume is a key factor in the overhead absorption rate.

(c) Selecting a suitable basis for overhead absorption, especially where a business produces more than one product.

(d) Perhaps the most important criticism of full cost-plus pricing is that it fails to recognise that since sales demand may be determined by the sales price, there will be a profit-maximising combination of price and demand. A full cost-plus based approach to pricing will be most unlikely to arrive at the profit-maximising price. In contrast, a marginal costing approach to looking at costs and prices would be more likely to help with identifying a profit-maximising price, because profit is maximised when total contribution is maximised.

Marginal cost-plus pricing

6.9 Instead of pricing products or services by adding a profit margin onto full cost, a business might add a profit margin onto the marginal cost (either the marginal cost of production or the marginal cost of sales). This is called *marginal cost-plus pricing* or (sometimes) *mark-up pricing.*

6.10 For example, if a company budgets to make 10,000 units of a product for which the variable cost of production is £3 per unit and the fixed production costs £60,000 per annum, it might decide to fix a price by adding, say, 33.33% to full production cost, to give a price of £9 × 1.3333 = £12 per unit. Alternatively, it might decide to add a profit margin of, say, 300% to the variable production cost, to give a price of £3 × 400% = £12. In this example, the sales price happens to be £12 by both methods, given the profit mark-ups selected, but of course there is no reason at all why both approaches to pricing need arrive at the same price. Nevertheless, we should expect the typical mark-up on variable cost to be higher than the typical profit margin on full cost, so as to lead to comparable profit levels.

6.11 Whereas a full cost-plus approach to pricing draws attention to net profit and the net profit margin, a marginal cost-plus approach to pricing draws attention to *gross profit* and the *gross profit margin* or contribution.

6.12 The advantages of a marginal cost-plus approach to pricing are as follows.

(a) It is a simple and easy method to use.

(b) The mark-up percentage can be varied, and so provided that a rigid mark-up is not used, prices can be adjusted to reflect demand conditions.

(c) It draws management attention to contribution, and the effects of higher or lower sales volumes on profit. In this way, it helps to create a better awareness of the concepts and implications of marginal costing. For example, if a product costs £10 per unit and a mark-up of 150% is added to reach a price of £25 per unit, management should be clearly aware that every additional £1 of sales revenue would add 60 pence to contribution and profit.

6.13 In practice, the method is used in businesses where there is a readily-identifiable basic variable cost. Retail industries are the most obvious example, and it is quite common for the prices of goods in shops to be fixed by adding a mark-up (20% or 33.3%, say) to the purchase cost. For example, a department store might buy in items of pottery at £3 each, add a mark-up of one-third and resell the items at £4.

6.14 There are, of course, drawbacks to marginal cost plus pricing, in particular the following.

(a) Although the size of the mark-up can be varied in accordance with demand conditions, it is not a method of pricing which *ensures* that sufficient attention is paid to demand conditions and competitors' prices.

(b) It ignores fixed overheads in the pricing decision, but the sales price must be high enough to ensure that a profit is made after covering fixed costs. Pricing decisions cannot ignore fixed costs altogether.

Chapter roundup

- Marginal costing and absorption costing are different techniques for assessing profit in a period.
- Marginal cost is the variable cost of one unit of product or service.
- Contribution is an important measure in marginal costing and it is calculated as the difference between sales value and marginal or variable cost.
- In marginal costing, fixed production costs are treated as period costs and written off as they are incurred. In absorption costing, fixed production costs are absorbed into the cost of units, and are carried forward in stock to be charged against sales for the next period.
- If there are changes in stocks during a period, so that opening stock or closing stock values are different, marginal costing and absorption costing give different results for profit.
- In a limiting factor situation, contribution will be maximised by earning the biggest possible contribution per unit of limiting factor.

Test your knowledge

1 What does the marginal cost per unit of production usually consist of? (see para 1.2)

2 Define contribution. (2.1)

3 What is the effect on profit if marginal costing is used to value closing stock, rather than absorption costing? (3.3-3.6)

4 If a company has opening (but not closing) stock, which costing system will produce the higher profit figure? Why? (3.7-3.9)

5 Give three arguments in favour of absorption costing. (4.2)

6 What is breakeven point? (4.3(d))

7 What is the general rule for maximising contribution in a limiting factor decision? (5.3)

Now try illustrative questions 32 and 33 at the end of the Study Text

Chapter 23

BUDGETS AND BUDGETARY CONTROL

This chapter covers the following topics.

Introduction

So far our study of management accounting has concentrated on analysing costs and on different ways of taking costs into account in computing profits.

In this chapter, we will concentrate on predicting what a company will achieve, and on comparing actual achievements with budgets.

1 MASTER BUDGETS AND FUNCTIONAL BUDGETS 6/00

1.1 A budget is a financial or quantitative plan of operations for a forthcoming accounting period. The purposes of making a budget ('budgeting') are:

(a) To coordinate the activities of different departments towards a single plan.

(b) To communicate targets to the managers responsible for achieving them.

(c) To establish a system of control by having a plan against which actual results can be compared.

(d) To compel planning.

1.2 A *master* budget is usually prepared by amalgamating many *functional* budgets (sales budgets, production budgets, direct labour budgets and so on). Each functional budget should ideally be prepared by the manager responsible for that function; for example, the sales manager should draft the sales budget. The master budget may well include a budgeted profit and loss account and closing balance sheet.

1.3 An example will illustrate below how a particular functional budget, the material purchases budget, may be prepared.

Example: material purchases budget

1.4 Earthquake Ltd manufactures two products, S and T, which use the same raw materials D and E. One unit of S uses 3 litres of D and 4 kgs of E. One unit of T uses 5 litres of D and 2 kg of E. A litre of D is expected to cost £3 and a kg of E £7.

Budgeted sales for 20X2 are 8,000 units of S and 6,000 units of T; finished goods in stock on 1 January 20X2 are 1,500 units of S and 300 units of T, and the company plans to hold stocks of 600 units of each product on 31 December 20X2.

Stocks of raw material on 1 January 20X2 are 6,000 litres of D and 2,800 kg of E and the company plans to hold 5,000 litres of D and 3,500 kg of E on 31 December 20X2.

The warehouse and stores managers have suggested that a provision should be made for damage and deterioration of items held in store, as follows.

Product S :	loss of 50 units
Product T :	loss of 100 units
Material D :	loss of 500 litres
Material E :	loss of 200 kg

Prepare a material purchases budget for the year 20X2.

Solution

1.5 To calculate material purchase requirements it is first necessary to calculate the material usage requirements. That in turn depends on calculating the budgeted production volumes.

	Product S	*Product T*
	Units	Units
Production required		
To meet sales demand	8,000	6,000
To provide for stock loss	50	100
For closing stock	600	600
	8,650	6,700
Less stock already in hand	1,500	300
Budgeted production volume	7,150	6,400
	Material D	*Material E*
	litres	kg
Usage requirements		
To produce 7,150 units of S	21,450	28,600
To produce 6,400 units of T	32,000	12,800
To provide for stock loss	500	200
For closing stock	5,000	3,500
	58,950	45,100
Less stock already in hand	6,000	2,800
Budgeted material purchases	52,950	42,300
Unit cost	£3	£7
Cost of material purchases	£158,850	£296,100
Total	£454,950	

2 FLEXIBLE BUDGETS 6/99

2.1 The materials purchase budget in the example above is based on estimated volumes of production but does not include any provision for the event that actual volumes may differ from the budget. It is a fixed budget.

2.2 A *flexible* budget is designed to change so as to relate to actual volumes achieved. This has two advantages.

(a) At the planning stage, it may be helpful to know what the effects would be if the actual outcome differs from the prediction. For example, a company may budget to sell 10,000 units of its product, but may prepare flexible budgets based on sales of, say 8,000 and 12,000 units. This would enable contingency plans to be drawn up if necessary.

(b) At the end of each month or year, actual results may be compared with the flexible budget as a control procedure.

2.3 Flexible budgeting uses the principles of marginal costing. In estimating future costs it is often necessary to begin by looking at cost behaviour in the past. For costs which are wholly fixed or wholly variable no problem arises. But you may be presented with a cost which appears to have behaved in the past as a mixed cost (partly fixed and partly variable). A technique for estimating the level of the cost for the future is called the high/low technique.

Example: the high/low technique

2.4 Suppose that the cost of factory power has behaved as follows in past years:

	Units of output produced	*Cost of factory power*
		£
20X1	7,900	38,700
20X2	7,700	38,100
20X3	9,800	44,400
20X4	9,100	42,300

Budgeted production for 20X5 is 10,200 units. Estimate the cost of factory power which will be incurred.

Solution

2.5 The high/low technique involves selecting from the historical data the figures for the two years when production was respectively highest and lowest. We assume that the level of fixed cost was the same in each year and therefore the difference in total costs incurred must represent the variable cost of the difference in output levels.

Here we have:

			£
20X3 (highest output)	9,800	units cost	44,400
20X2 (lowest output)	7,700	units cost	38,100
Variable cost of	2,100	units =	6,300

The variable cost per unit is therefore £6,300/2,100 = £3.

The level of fixed cost can be calculated by looking at the highest output level:

	£
Total cost of factory power in 20X3	44,400
Less variable cost of factory power (9,800 × £3)	29,400
Fixed cost of factory power	15,000

The high/low technique has enabled us to calculate that factory power is partly a fixed cost (£15,000 per year) and partly a variable cost (£3 per unit produced). Our estimate of costs in 20X5 will be:

	£
Fixed cost	15,000
Variable cost of budgeted production (10,200 × £3)	30,600
Total budgeted cost of factory power	45,600

Example: flexible budget

2.6 (a) Prepare a budget for 20X6 for the costs of a production department at the activity levels of 80%, 90% and 100%, using the information listed below.

(i) The direct labour hourly rate is expected to be £3.75.

(ii) 100% activity represents 60,000 direct labour hours.

(iii) Variable costs:

Indirect labour	£0.75 per direct labour hour
Consumable supplies	£0.375 per direct labour hour
Canteen and other welfare services	6% of direct and indirect labour costs

(iv) Semi-variable costs are expected to correlate with the direct labour hours in the same manner as for the last five years, as follows.

Year	*Direct labour hours*	*Semi-variable costs*
		£
20X1	64,000	20,800
20X2	59,000	19,800
20X3	53,000	18,600
20X4	49,000	17,800
20X5	40,000 (estimate)	16,000 (estimate)

(v) Fixed costs:

	£
Depreciation	18,000
Maintenance	10,000
Insurance	4,000
Rates	15,000
Management salaries	25,000

(vi) Inflation is to be ignored.

(b) Calculate the budgeted costs for 20X6 assuming that 57,000 direct labour hours are worked.

Solution

2.7 (a)

	80% level 48,000 hrs	*90% level 54,000 hrs*	*100% level 60,000 hrs*
	£'000	£'000	£'000
Direct labour	180.00	202.50	225.00
Other variable costs			
Indirect labour	36.00	40.50	45.00
Consumable supplies	18.00	20.25	22.50
Canteen etc	12.96	14.58	16.20
Total variable costs (£5.145 per hour)	246.96	277.83	308.70
Semi-variable costs (see below)	17.60	18.80	20.00
Fixed costs			
Depreciation	18.00	18.00	18.00
Maintenance	10.00	10.00	10.00
Insurance	4.00	4.00	4.00
Rates	15.00	15.00	15.00
Management salaries	25.00	25.00	25.00
Budgeted costs	336.56	368.63	400.70

Note: semi-variable costs

Using the high-low method:

	£
Total cost of 64,000 hours	20,800
Total cost of 40,000 hours	16,000
Variable cost of 24,000 hours	4,800
Variable cost per hour	£0.20

	£
Total cost of 64,000 hours	20,800
Variable cost of 64,000 hours (× 0.2)	12,800
Fixed costs	8,000

Semi-variable costs for:

60,000 hours	(60,000 × 20p)	+	£8,000	=	£20,000
54,000 hours	(54,000 × 20p)	+	£8,000	=	£18,800
48,000 hours	(48,000 × 20p)	+	£8,000	=	£17,600

(b) The budgeted costs for 57,000 direct labour hours of work would be:

		£
Variable costs	(57,000 × £5.145)	293,265
Semi-variable costs	(8,000 + 57,000 × 0.2)	19,400
Fixed costs		72,000
		384,665

3 CASH BUDGETS

12/96, 6/98

3.1 A cash budget is a statement in which estimated future cash receipts and payments are tabulated in such a way as to show the forecast cash balance of a business at defined intervals. For example, in December 20X5 an accounts department might wish to estimate the cash position of the business during the three following months, January to March 20X6. A cash budget might be drawn up in the following format.

	Jan	*Feb*	*Mar*
	£	£	£
Estimated cash receipts			
From credit customers	14,000	16,500	17,000
From cash sales	3,000	4,000	4,500
Proceeds on disposal of fixed assets		2,200	
Total cash receipts	17,000	22,700	21,500
Estimated cash payments			
To suppliers of goods	8,000	7,800	10,500
To employees (wages)	3,000	3,500	3,500
Purchase of fixed assets		16,000	
Rent and rates			1,000
Other overheads	1,200	1,200	1,200
Repayment of loan	2,500		
Total cash payments	14,700	28,500	16,200
Net surplus/(deficit) for month	2,300	(5,800)	5,300
Opening cash balance	1,200	3,500	(2,300)
Closing cash balance	3,500	(2,300)	3,000

3.2 In the example above the accounts department has calculated that the cash balance at the beginning of the budget period, 1 January, will be £1,200. Estimates have been made of the cash which is likely to be received by the business (from cash and credit sales, and from a planned disposal of fixed assets in February). Similar estimates have been made of cash due to be paid out by the business (payments to suppliers and employees, payments for rent, rates and other overheads, payment for a planned purchase of fixed assets and a loan repayment due in January).

3.3 From these estimates it is a simple step to calculate the excess of cash receipts over cash payments in each month. In some months cash payments may exceed cash receipts and there will be a deficit for the month; this occurs during February in the above example because of the large investment in fixed assets in that month.

3.4 The last part of the cash budget above shows how the business's estimated cash balance can then be rolled along from month to month. Starting with the opening balance of £1,200 at 1 January a cash surplus of £2,300 is generated in January. This leads to a closing January balance of £3,500 which becomes the opening balance for February. The deficit of £5,800 in February throws the business's cash position into overdraft and the overdrawn balance of £2,300 becomes the opening balance for March. Finally, the healthy cash surplus of £5,300 in March leaves the business with £3,000 cash at the end of the budget period.

3.5 The usefulness of cash budgets is that they enable management to make any forward planning decisions that may be needed, such as advising their bank of estimated overdraft requirements or strengthening their credit control procedures to ensure that debtors pay more quickly. In our example, management might well be advised to discuss with the bank the estimated need for an overdraft facility in February.

How are cash budgets constructed?

3.6 Constructing a cash budget in practice is a complex job because a great many assumptions need to be formulated first.

(a) The sales or marketing department might produce estimates of the level of sales.

(b) The credit control department might be able to supply information on how quickly debtors pay and what proportion of debts go bad.

(c) The production or purchasing department might estimate the level of purchases required and the credit period to be taken from suppliers.

(d) Other assumptions would need to be made about the dates and amounts of, for example, purchases and disposals of fixed assets.

3.7 In the examination, you will not be asked to formulate this kind of assumption. Instead you will be presented with a list of assumptions already made and you will be required to calculate the cash flows which follow from them.

3.8 To avoid confusion it may be useful to set out some differences between a cash budget and a profit and loss account. The differences arise from the fact that cash budgets show movements of cash only, while a profit and loss account is prepared on an accruals basis.

(a) Sales and cost of sales are recognised in a profit and loss account as soon as they are incurred; the cash budget does not show a figure for sales or cost of sales. It is concerned with cash actually received from customers or paid to suppliers.

(b) A profit and loss account may include accrued amounts for rates, insurance and other expenses. In the cash budget such amounts will appear in full in the month in which they are paid. There is no attempt to apportion the payments over the period to which they relate.

(c) Similarly, a profit and loss account may show a charge for depreciation. This is not a cash expense and will never appear in a cash budget. The cash budget will show a purchase of a fixed asset as a payment in the month when it is paid for, and may also show the proceeds on disposal of a fixed asset as a receipt of cash. No attempt is made to allocate purchase cost over the life of the asset.

Example: cash budget

3.9 Peter Blair has worked for some years as a sales representative, but has recently been made redundant. He intends to start up in business on his own account, using £15,000 which he currently has invested with a building society. Peter maintains a bank account showing a small credit balance, and he plans to approach his bank for the necessary additional finance. Peter asks you for advice and provides the following additional information:

(a) Arrangements have been made to purchase fixed assets costing £8,000. These will be paid for at the end of September 20X3 and are expected to have a five year life, at the end of which they will possess a nil residual value.

(b) Stocks costing £5,000 will be acquired on 28 September and subsequent monthly purchases will be at a level sufficient to replace forecast sales for the month.

(c) Forecast monthly sales are £3,000 for October, £6,000 for November and December, and £10,500 from January 20X4 onwards.

(d) Selling price is fixed at the cost of stock plus 50%.

(e) Two months' credit will be allowed to customers but only one month's credit will be received from suppliers of stock.

(f) Running expenses, including rent but excluding depreciation of fixed assets, are estimated at £1,600 per month.

(g) Blair intends to make monthly cash drawings of £1,000.

Prepare a cash budget for the six months to 31 March 20X4.

Solution

3.10 The opening cash balance at 1 October will consist of Peter's initial £15,000 less the £8,000 expended on fixed assets purchased in September, so the opening balance is £7,000. Cash receipts from credit customers arise two months after the relevant sales.

Payments to suppliers are a little more tricky. We are told that cost of sales is 100/150 × sales. Thus for October cost of sales is 100/150 × £3,000 = £2,000. These goods will be purchased in October but not paid for until November. Similar calculations can be made for later months. The initial stock of £5,000 is purchased in September and consequently paid for in October.

The cash budget can now be constructed.

CASH BUDGET FOR THE SIX MONTHS ENDING 31 MARCH 20X4

	Oct	*Nov*	*Dec*	*Jan*	*Feb*	*Mar*
	£	£	£	£	£	£
Payments						
Suppliers	5,000	2,000	4,000	4,000	7,000	7,000
Running expenses	1,600	1,600	1,600	1,600	1,600	1,600
Drawings	1,000	1,000	1,000	1,000	1,000	1,000
	7,600	4,600	6,600	6,600	9,600	9,600
Receipts						
Debtors	-	-	3,000	6,000	6,000	10,500
Surplus/(shortfall)	(7,600)	(4,600)	(3,600)	(600)	(3,600)	900
Opening balance	7,000	(600)	(5,200)	(8,800)	(9,400)	(13,000)
Closing balance	(600)	(5,200)	(8,800)	(9,400)	(13,000)	(12,100)

Exercise

Cash budgets for months 1,2 and 3 are given.

You are required to prepare, using the information supplied, cash budgets for months 4,5 and 6 in the format shown.

CASH BOOK

	Month					
	1	*2*	*3*	*4*	*5*	*6*
	£	£	£	£	£	£
Balance b/f	(12,705)	(10,215)	100			
Receipts						
Debtors	15,700	16,000	6,000			
Issue of ordinary shares						
Sale of plant						
	2,995	5,785	6,100			
Payments						
Creditors for materials	12,000	4,500	4,350			
Wages	600	575	595			
Overhead	610	610	615			
Debenture interest						
Taxation						
Dividends						
Purchase of plant						
Repayment of debentures						
	13,210	5,685	5,560			
Balance c/f	(10,215)	100	540			
	2,995	5,785	6,100			

(a) Material cost is expected to be 75% of invoiced sales.

(b) Debtors are given two months' credit.

(c) Creditors for materials allow the company one month's credit.

(d) Three quarters of wages earned each month are paid in that month and the remaining quarter in the following month.

(e) Overhead expenses are paid, half in the month in which they are incurred and half in the following month.

(f) Items other than above are dealt with completely in the month shown in the table of data below.

	Month					
	1	*2*	*3*	*4*	*5*	*6*
	£	£	£	£	£	£
Invoiced sales	6,000	6,200	6,800	7,200	8,400	12,000
Material stocks						
Increase					700	
Decrease		300	100			
Wages earned	560	580	600	640	700	960
Overhead incurred	600	620	610	630	630	640
Debenture interest paid						1,000
Taxation paid				10,000		
Dividends paid						500
Plant purchased						1,945
Ordinary shares issued at par						35,000
Plant sold				200		
Debentures repaid						20,000

Solution

CASH BUDGET

	Month 4	Month 5	Month 6
	£	£	£
Balance b/f	540	(9,310)	(9,225)
Receipts			
Debtors	6,200	6,800	7,200
Issue of ordinary shares			35,000
Sale of plant	200	-	-
	6,940	(2,510)	32,975
Payments			
Creditors for materials	5,000	5,400	7,000
Wages paid	630	685	895
Overhead paid	620	630	635
Debenture interest paid			1,000
Taxation paid	10,000		
Dividends paid			500
Purchase of plant			1,945
Repayment of debentures			20,000
	16,250	6,715	31,975
Balance c/f	(9,310)	(9,225)	1,000
	6,940	(2,510)	32,975

There is a cash balance of £1,000 at the end of month 6, although there will be overdrafts in excess of £9,000 at the end of both month 4 and month 5.

Workings

		Month					
		1	*2*	*3*	*4*	*5*	*6*
		£	£	£	£	£	£
1	Sales		6,200	6,800	7,200	8,400	
2	Receipts from debtors (2 months credit)				6,200	6,800	7,200
3	Materials cost of sales (75% of sales)			5,100	5,400	6,300	
4	Increase(decrease) in stocks			(100)	-	700	
5	Materials purchased (item 3 + item 4)			5,000	5,400	7,000	
6	Payments to creditors				5,000	5,400	7,000
7	Wages: ¾ of current month				480	525	720
	¼ of previous month				150	160	175
	Total wages paid				630	685	895
8	Overhead expenses (presumably all cash expenses)						
	½ of current month				315	315	320
	½ of previous month				305	315	315
	Total paid				620	630	635

4 BUDGETED PROFIT AND LOSS ACCOUNT AND BALANCE SHEET 6/96,12/99

4.1 As well as wishing to forecast its cash position, a business might want to estimate its profitability and its financial position for a coming period. This would involve the preparation of a forecast profit and loss account and balance sheet.

4.2 Just like historical financial statements, budgeted accounts are based on the accruals concept. If you keep this point in mind you will often be able to cut through the deliberately confusing detail of examination questions to prepare an answer very quickly. The example of Peter Blair (see Paragraph 3.9 above) will be used to illustrate the procedure.

Example: budgeted profit and loss account and balance sheet

4.3 Using the information in Paragraph 3.9, you are required to prepare Peter Blair's forecast profit and loss account for the six months ending on 31 March 20X4 and a forecast balance sheet as at that date.

Solution

4.4 The profit and loss account is straightforward. The first figure is sales, which can be computed very easily from the information in Paragraph 3.9(c). It is sufficient to add up the monthly sales figures given there; for the profit and loss account there is no need to worry about any closing debtor. Similarly, cost of sales is calculated directly from the information on gross margin contained in Paragraph 3.9(d).

FORECAST TRADING AND PROFIT AND LOSS ACCOUNT
FOR THE SIX MONTHS ENDING 31 MARCH 20X4

	£	£
Sales (3,000 + (2 × 6,000) + (3 × 10,500))		46,500
Cost of sales (2/3 × £46,500)		31,000
Gross profit		15,500
Expenses		
Running expenses (6 × £1,600)	9,600	
Depreciation (£8,000 × 20% × 6/12)	800	
		10,400
Net profit		5,100

4.5 In the balance sheet:

(a) Stock will comprise the initial purchases of £5,000.

(b) Debtors will comprise sales made in February and March (not paid until April and May respectively).

(c) Creditors will comprise purchases made in March (not paid for until April).

(d) The bank overdraft is the closing cash figure computed in the cash budget.

FORECAST BALANCE SHEET AT 31 MARCH 20X4

	£	£
Fixed assets £(8,000 – £800)		7,200
Current assets		
Stocks	5,000	
Debtors (2 × £10,500)	21,000	
	26,000	
Current liabilities		
Bank overdraft	12,100	
Trade creditors (March purchases)	7,000	
	19,100	
Net current assets		6,900
		14,100
Proprietor's interest		
Capital introduced		15,000
Profit for the period	5,100	
Less drawings	6,000	
Deficit		(900)
		14,100

5 BUDGETARY CONTROL

5.1 Budgetary control is the practice of establishing budgets which identify areas of responsibility for individual managers (such as production managers or purchasing managers) and of regularly comparing actual results against expected results. The most important method of budgetary control is variance analysis, which involves the comparison of actual results achieved during a control period (such as a month) with a flexible budget. The differences between actual results and expected results are called variances and these are used to provide a guideline for control action.

The wrong approach to budgetary control

5.2 The wrong approach to budgetary control is to compare actual results with a fixed budget. Consider the following example.

Sidewinder Ltd manufactures a single product. Budgeted results and actual results for June 20X2 are shown below.

	Budget	*Actual results*	*Variance*	
Production and sales (units)	2,000	3,000		
	£	£	£	
Sales revenue (a)	20,000	30,000	10,000	(F)
Direct materials	6,000	8,500	2,500	(A)
Direct labour	4,000	4,500	500	(A)
Maintenance	1,000	1,400	400	(A)
Depreciation	2,000	2,200	200	(A)
Rent and rates	1,500	1,600	100	(A)
Other costs	3,600	5,000	1,400	(A)
Total costs (b)	18,100	23,200	5,100	
Profit (a) – (b)	1,900	6,800	4,900	(F)

(F) stand for 'favourable' (revenue high, or costs low) and (A) for 'adverse (revenue low, or costs high). Adverse variances are sometimes called 'unfavourable'.

5.3 (a) In this example, the variances are meaningless for the purposes of control. Costs were higher than budget because the volume of output was also higher; variable costs would be expected to increase above the budgeted costs. There is no information to show whether control action is needed for any aspect of costs or revenue.

(b) For control purposes, we need to know:

(i) Whether actual costs were higher than they should have been to produce and sell 3,000 units.

(ii) Whether actual revenue was satisfactory from the sale of 3,000 units.

(iii) Whether the volume of units made and sold has varied from the budget in a good or a bad way.

The correct approach to budgetary control

5.4 The correct approach to budgetary control is to:

(a) Identify fixed and variable costs.
(b) Produce a flexible budget.

5.5 In the previous example of Sidewinder Ltd, let us suppose that we have the following estimates of cost behaviour:

(a) Direct materials and maintenance costs are variable.

(b) Although basic wages are a fixed cost, direct labour is regarded as variable in order to measure efficiency.

(c) Rent and rates and depreciation are fixed costs.

(d) Other costs should consist of fixed costs of £1,600 plus a variable cost of £1 per unit made and sold.

5.6 The budgetary control (variance) analysis should be:

	Fixed budget (a)	Flexible budget (b)	Actual results (c)	Variance (b) – (c)	
Production & sales (units)	2,000	3,000	3,000		
	£	£	£	£	
Sales revenue	20,000	30,000	30,000	-	
Variable costs:					
direct materials	6,000	9,000	8,500	500	(F)
direct labour	4,000	6,000	4,500	1,500	(F)
maintenance	1,000	1,500	1,400	100	(F)
Semi-variable costs:					
other costs	3,600	4,600	5,000	400	(A)
Fixed costs:					
depreciation	2,000	2,000	2,200	200	(A)
rent and rates	1,500	1,500	1,600	100	(A)
Total costs	18,100	24,600	23,200	1,400	(F)
Profit	1,900	5,400	6,800	1,400	(F)

Analysis

(a) In selling 3,000 units, the expected profit should have been, not the fixed budget profit of £1,900 but the flexible budget profit of £5,400. Instead, actual profit was £6,800, £1,400 more than we should have expected. The reasons for this improvement is that, given output and sales of 3,000 units, costs are lower than expected (and sales revenue exactly as expected), as shown by the variance column.

	£	
Direct materials cost variance	500	(F)
Direct labour cost variance	1,500	(F)
Maintenance cost variance	100	(F)
'Other costs' cost variance	400	(A)
Fixed cost expenditure variances:		
rent and rates	100	(A)
depreciation	200	(A)
	1,400	(F)

(b) Another reason for the improvement in profit above the fixed budget profit is the sales volume. Sidewinder Ltd sold 3,000 units of varmint instead of 2,000 units, with the following results.

		£	£
(i)	Budgeted sales revenue increased by		10,000
(ii)	Budgeted variable costs increased by:		
	direct materials	3,000	
	direct labour	2,000	
	maintenance	500	
	variable element of other costs	1,000	
			6,500
(iv)	Budgeted profit increased by		3,500

The sales volume variance of £3,900 is the difference between the extra revenue and the extra variable costs as a result of selling more units than in the fixed budget.

(c) The budgeted contribution earned per unit sold is:

	£	£
Sales price per unit		10.00
Variable cost per unit:		
direct materials	3.00	
direct labour	2.00	
maintenance	0.50	
other costs	1.00	
Total variable costs		6.50
Contribution per unit		3.50

The sales volume variance was 1,000 units favourable (3,000 – 2,000). The difference between the profit in the fixed budget and the flexible budget = 1,000 units (F) × £3.50 per unit = £3,500 (F).

(d) A full variance analysis statement would be:

	£		£	
Fixed budget profit			1,900	
Variances:				
Sales volume	3,500	(F)		
Direct materials cost	500	(F)		
Direct labour cost	1,500	(F)		
Maintenance cost	100	(F)		
Other costs	400	(A)		
Rent and rates expenditure	100	(A)		
Depreciation expenditure	200	(A)		
			4,900	(F)
Actual profit			6,800	

5.7 If management believes that these variances are large enough to justify action, they will investigate the reasons for them to see what corrective action is appropriate.

Chapter roundup

- Cash budgets are concerned solely with cash received and paid out by the business. No question of accruals accounting arises; thus there is no attempt to spread the cost of fixed assets or of expenses such as rates. Such expenditure is recorded in full in the month when the cash receipt or payment arises.
- Budgeted profit and loss accounts and balance sheets are prepared on normal accruals principles.
- Fixed budgets remain unchanged regardless of the level of activity; flexible budgets are designed to flex with the level of activity.
- Comparison of a fixed budget with the actual results for a different activity level is meaningless. Flexible budgets should be used for control purposes if activity levels change.

Test your knowledge

1 What is the relationship between the master budget and functional budgets? (see para 1.2)

2 What is a flexible budget? (2.2-2.3)

3 What is the purpose of preparing cash budgets? (3.5)

4 Budgeted financial statements are prepared under the accruals concept. True or false? (4.2)

5 How does variance analysis work? (5.1)

6 If a product has a unit selling price of £12 and a unit variable cost of £7, what will the sales volume variance be if actual sales exceed budget by 25,000 units? (5.6(c))

Now try illustrative questions 34 and 35 at the end of the Study Text

Illustrative questions and suggested answers

1 **ROLE OF ACCOUNTING (10 marks)**

Why does a business keep accounts?

2 **DEFINITIONS (20 marks)**

The observance of the following concepts is presumed in financial statements unless otherwise stated.

(a) Going concern
(b) Accruals
(c) Consistency
(d) Prudence

Required

Explain each of the above concepts giving examples of how each is observed in conventional financial statements.

3 **THE ACCOUNTING EQUATION (10 marks)**

Peter Reid decides he is going to open a bookshop called Easyread, which he does by investing £5,000 on 1 January 20X7. During the first month of Easyread's existence, the following transactions occur.

(a) Bookshelves are purchased for £1,800.
(b) Books are purchased for £2,000.
(c) Half of the books are sold for £1,500 cash.
(d) Peter draws £200 out of the business for himself.
(e) Peter's brother John loans £500 to the business.
(f) Carpets are purchased for £1,000 on credit (to be paid in two months time).
(g) A bulk order of books worth £400 is sold on credit (to be paid in one month's time) for £600.

Required

Write down the accounting equation after each transaction has occurred.

4 **FINANCIAL STATEMENTS (20 marks)**

What is the difference between the balance sheet and the trading, profit and loss account? What is the difference between capital and revenue expenditure? Which of the following transactions is capital expenditure and which revenue expenditure?

(a) A bookseller buys a car for its director for £9,000.
(b) In the first year, the car is depreciated by £900.
(c) The business buys books for £1,500.
(d) The business builds an extension for £7,600.
(e) The original building is repainted, a job costing £1,200.
(f) A new sales assistant is taken on and his salary in the first year is £10,000.

5 **IVOR WILLOW (10 marks)**

Ivor Willow opened up a shop selling cricket bats and accessories on 1 April 20X7. During the year:

(a) His purchases of stock cost £10,000.

(b) He still owed £800 to suppliers at the end of the year.

(c) Sales during the year were £28,000 (after which he had no stocks left). Half of the sales were on credit.

(d) Rent on his premises came to £1,800.

(e) He borrowed £5,000 from the bank, and interest on the loan came to £50 per month.

(f) He employed a sales assistant, and paid him £8,300 for the year.

(g) Other expenses were:

	£
telephone	162
electricity	304
postage	24

(h) Ivor paid himself £3,000.

Required

Prepare a trading, profit and loss account for the year ended 31 March 20X8.

6 J OCKEY (10 marks)

Mr J Ockey commenced trading as a wholesale stationer on 1 May 20X4 with a capital of £5,000 with which he opened a bank account for his business.

During May the following transactions took place.

May	1	Bought shop fittings and fixtures for cash from Store Fitments Ltd for £2,000
	2	Purchased goods on credit from Abel £650
	4	Sold goods on credit to Bruce £700
	9	Purchased goods on credit from Green £300
	11	Sold goods on credit to Hill £580
	13	Cash sales paid intact into bank £200
	16	Received cheque from Bruce in settlement of his account
	17	Purchased goods on credit from Kaye £800
	18	Sold goods on credit to Nailor £360
	19	Sent cheque to Abel in settlement of his account
	20	Paid rent by cheque £200
	21	Paid delivery expenses by cheque £50
	24	Received from Hill £200 on account
	30	Drew cheques for personal expenses £200 and assistant's wages £320
	31	Settled the account of Green.

Required

Record the foregoing in appropriate books of prime entry.

7 JOCKFIELD (15 marks)

The following is a summary of the petty cash transactions of Jockfield Ltd for May 20X2.

May	1	Received from cashier £300 as petty cash float	
			£
	2	Postages	18
	3	Travelling	12
	4	Cleaning	15
	7	Petrol for delivery van	22
	8	Travelling	25
	9	Stationery	17
	11	Cleaning	18
	14	Postage	5
	15	Travelling	8
	18	Stationery	9
		Cleaning	23
	20	Postage	13
	24	Delivery van 5,000 miles service	43
	26	Petrol	18
	27	Cleaning	21
	29	Postage	5
	30	Petrol	14

Required

(a) Rule up a suitable petty cash book with analysis columns for expenditure on cleaning, motor expenses, postage, stationery, travelling.

(b) Enter the month's transactions.

(c) Enter the receipt of the amount necessary to restore the imprest and carry down the balance for the commencement of the following month.

(d) State how the double entry for the expenditure is completed.

8 OMEGA (15 marks)

At 1 May 20X3 amounts owing to Omega by his customers in respect of their April purchases were:

	£
Alpha	210
Beta	1,040
Gamma	1,286
Delta	279
Epsilon	823

The amounts owing by Omega to his suppliers at 1 May were:

	£
Zeta	2,173
Eta	187
Theta	318

Sales made by Omega during May were as follows:

	£
Gamma	432
Epsilon	129
Beta	314
Epsilon	269
Alpha	88
Delta	417
Epsilon	228

Purchases during May:

	£
Eta	423
Zeta	268
Eta	741

Returns inwards: (ie sales returns)

	£
Epsilon	88

Cash payments:

	£
Eta	187
Theta	318
Zeta	1,000

Cash receipts:

	£
Beta	1,040
Delta	279
Gamma	826
Epsilon	823

Required

(a) Open personal accounts for Omega's customers and suppliers and record therein the 1 May balances.

(b) Record the transactions in the appropriate personal *and* impersonal accounts.

(c) Balance the personal accounts where necessary.

(d) Extract a list of debtors at 31 May showing in separate columns:

   (i) The total amounts owing.
   (ii) Amounts owing in respect of May.
   (iii) Amounts owing in respect of April.

Note. You need not enter dates or narrative in the accounts.

9 HUBBLE (15 marks)

On 28.2.20X8, which is one month before the end of his financial year, the ledger accounts of A Hubble were as follows.

CASH

	£		£
Capital	9,500	Rent	2,750
Bank loan	3,000	Creditors	700
Sales	11,200	Interest	350
Debtors	400	Electricity	400
		Telephone	180
		Drawings	1,300

CAPITAL

	£		£
		Cash	9,500

BANK LOAN

	£		£
		Cash	3,000

SALES

	£		£
		Cash	11,200
		Debtors	4,600

DEBTORS

	£		£
Sales	4,600	Cash	400

RENT

	£		£
Cash	2,750		

PURCHASES

	£		£
Creditors	2,100		

CREDITORS

	£		£
Cash	700	Purchases	2,100

INTEREST

	£		£
Cash	350		

ELECTRICITY

	£		£
Cash	400		

TELEPHONE

	£		£
Cash	180		

DRAWINGS

	£		£
Cash	1,300		

During the last month of his financial year, A Hubble recorded the following transactions.

(a) He bought goods for £2,000, half for credit and half for cash.

(b) He paid the following:

(i) Interest £20.
(ii) Electricity £25.
(iii) Telephone £12.

(c) He made sales of £3,500 of which £500 were for cash.

(d) He received £220 from debtors

Required

(a) Post the transactions for March 20X8 into the ledger accounts.

(b) Balance off the ledger accounts and draw up a trial balance.

(c) Prepare a balance sheet as at 31.3.20X8 and a trading, profit and loss account for the year ended 31.3.20X8.

10 RENT, RATES AND INSURANCE (10 marks)

From the information given below you are required:

(a) To calculate the charge to the profit and loss account for the year ended 30 June 20X6 in respect of rent, rates and insurance.

(b) To state the amount of accrual or prepayment for rent, rates and insurance as at 30 June 20X6.

The accruals and prepayments as at 30 June 20X5 were as follows.

	£
Rent accrued	2,000
Rates prepaid	1,500
Insurance prepaid	1,800

Payments made during the year ended 30 June 20X6 were as follows.

		£
20X5		
10 August	Rent, three months to 31 July 20X5	3,000
26 October	Insurance, one year to 31 October 20X6	6,000
2 November	Rates, six months to 31 March 20X6	3,500
12 December	Rent, four months to 30 November 20X5	4,000
20X6		
17 April	Rent, four months to 31 March 20X6	4,000
9 May	Rates, six months to 30 September 20X6	3,500

11 BAD AND DOUBTFUL DEBTS (10 marks)

The Lax Company began trading in 20X7 and makes all its sales on credit. The company suffers from a high level of bad debts and a provision for doubtful debts of 3% of outstanding debtors is made at the end of each year.

Information for 20X7, 20X8 and 20X9 is as follows.

	Year to 31 December		
	20X7	*20X8*	*20X9*
	£	£	£
Outstanding debtors at 31 December	44,000	55,000	47,000
Bad debts written off during year	7,000	10,000	8,000

Required

(a) State the amount to be shown in the profit and loss account for bad debts and provision for doubtful debts for the years ended 31 December 20X7, 20X8 and 20X9. (6 marks)

(b) State the value of debtors which would be shown in the balance sheet as at 31 December each year. (4 marks)

12 MEGALOT (15 marks)

Megalot Ltd made the following purchases and sales of stock item C4321 during May 20X6.

May 10 Purchased 3,000 units at £6.00 each
May 15 Sold 2,500 units at £9.00 each
May 16 Purchased 1,000 units at £6.60 each
May 23 Sold 900 units at £9.70 each

There were no units of stock item C4321 in stock on 1 May 20X6.

Required

(a) Compute the values for sales and purchases of stock item C4321 for May. (4 marks)

(b) How many units should there be in stock on 31 May 20X6? (3 marks)

(c) Compute the value of closing stock on each of the following bases:

(i) FIFO.
(ii) LIFO. (6 marks)

(d) Calculate the gross profit earned on this item during May if closing stock were to be valued under each of the two bases in (c) above. (2 marks)

13 L MERVIN (20 marks)

L Mervin is a retail ironmonger whose sales are mainly for cash although he has a few customers to whom he allows credit. The whole of his cash takings are paid intact into the bank each day and all payments are made by cheque.

A summary of Mervin's bank account is shown below.

	£		£
Balance 1 November 20X3	1,470	Personal drawings	14,250
Cash takings	233,870	Trade creditors	186,750
		Trade expenses	27,240
		Fixtures and fittings	2,400
		Painting and decorating	2,850

Mervin estimates that of the £2,850 paid for painting and decorating one third applies to his private residence, which has also had the benefit of goods value £1,250 taken from the shop stock.

Relevant figures as at 31 October were as follows.

	20X3	*20X4*
	£	£
Stock	11,430	14,160
Debtors	720	510
Trade creditors	10,100	6,500
Trade expenses owing	1,260	1,840
Fixtures and fittings (cost in previous years £14,200)	7,100	?
Delivery van (cost in previous years £12,000)	4,320	?
Freehold premises, at cost	50,000	50,000

Mervin charges depreciation on his fixtures and fittings at 10% per annum on cost, and on his delivery van, at 40% on the reducing balance. A full year's depreciation is charged during the year of acquisition, irrespective of the date.

Required

Prepare Mervin's trading and profit and loss account for the year ended 31 October 20X4 and his balance sheet at that date.

14 ASPLEY (20 marks)

The following information has been extracted from the machine register of R Aspley as at 31 October 20X6.

(a)

Machine number	*Date of purchase*	*Original cost*	*Expected life*
		£	Years
10	1.11.X2	1,000	10
12	1. 4.X4	6,300	7
14	31.10.X5	5,000	20
16	1. 8.X6	10,000	5

(b) The company operates a straight line method of depreciation based on the original cost of each machine. It is assumed that at the end of its life each machine will have a scrap value equivalent to 10% of its original cost.

(c) A full year's depreciation is charged in the year of acquisition (irrespective of the date of purchase), but no depreciation is charged in the year of disposal.

(d) Separate ledger accounts are not kept for each machine.

(e) During the year to 31 October 20X7 the following transactions occurred.

   (i) On 1 April 20X7 machine number 10 was sold for £600 in cash.

   (ii) On 1 June 20X7 machine number 17 was purchased for £15,000 in part exchange for machine number 14. It was agreed that machine number 14 had a part exchange value of £4,600, the balance of £10,400 being paid in cash. Machine number 17's expected life is ten years.

   (iii) On 1 August 20X7 machine number 18 was purchased for £7,000 and was paid for in cash; its expected life is five years.

Required

(a) Write up the following accounts for the year to 31 October 20X7.

   (i) Machines account.
   (ii) Accumulated depreciation on machines account.
   (iii) Disposal of machines account. (16 marks)

(b) Show how the figures from the machines account and the accumulated depreciation on machines account would appear in Aspley's balance sheet at 31 October 20X7. (4 marks)

15 DEPRECIATION (20 marks)

(a) Explain what is meant in accounting by the term 'depreciation'. State the main factors which should be taken into account when choosing a method of depreciation and the appropriate rate of depreciation to apply. (5 marks)

(b) Discuss the problems involved in providing for depreciation in the following situations.

   (i) Revision of the estimated useful life of an asset.
   (ii) A change from one method of depreciation to another in respect of a depreciable asset.
   (iii) An asset revaluation for balance sheet purposes. (10 marks)

(c) In the balance sheet of Cherry Ltd at 30 June 20X5, the freehold properties are shown as follows.

	£	£
Freehold properties at cost	95,000	
Less accumulated depreciation (on buildings)	16,000	
		79,000

On 1 August 20X5, the freehold properties were revalued on the basis of a professional valuation as follows.

	£
Freehold land (original cost £25,000)	130,000
Building (original cost £70,000)	210,000
	340,000

These revaluations were written into the books of account.

Required

State the effects of the revaluation on the financial statements. (5 marks)

16 INTANGIBLE (15 marks)

The accounts of Intangible Ltd at 1 January 20X6 include deferred development costs of £26,500. During the year ended 31 December 20X6 Intangible Ltd purchased a new business. The consideration paid to the proprietor included £4,800 in respect of goodwill. The company also spent £7,900 on research and £3,500 on development activities.

The directors of Intangible Ltd intend to write off goodwill evenly over its estimated economic life of four years. They believe that £22,600 of development costs should be carried forward at 31 December 20X6.

Required

Show the ledger accounts for goodwill and research and development in the books of Intangible Ltd.

17 RECTIFY (20 marks)

A summary of the cash book of Rectify Ltd for the year to 31 May 20X5 is as follows.

CASH BOOK

	£		£
Balance b/d	805	Payments	146,203
Receipts	145,720	Balance c/d	322
	146,525		146,525

After some investigation of the cash book and vouchers you discover the following facts.

(a) Bank charges of £143 shown on the bank statement have not yet been entered in the cash book.

(b) A cheque drawn for £98 has been entered in the cash book as £89, and another drawn at £230 has been entered as a receipt.

(c) A cheque received from a customer for £180 has been returned by the bank marked 'refer to drawer', but it has not yet been written back in the cash book.

(d) An error of transposition has occurred in that the opening balance of the cash book should have been brought down as £850.

(e) Cheques paid to suppliers totalling £630 have not yet been presented at the bank, whilst payments in to the bank of £580 on 31 May 20X5 have not yet been credited to the company's account.

(f) A cheque for £82 has been debited to the company's account in error by the bank.

(g) The company owes £430 to an electricity company.

(h) The following items appearing on the bank statement have not yet been entered in the cash book:

(i) Interest for the half year to 31 March on a loan of £20,000 at 11% pa.
(ii) Hire purchase payments on the managing director's car - 12 months at £55 per month.
(iii) Dividend received on a trade investment - £1,147.

(i) A page of the receipts side of the cash book has been undercast by £200.

(j) The bank statement shows a balance overdrawn of £870.

Required

(a) Adjust the cash book in the light of the above discoveries. (10 marks)

(b) Produce a statement reconciling the bank statement balance to the cash book balance. (10 marks)

18 HANDILE (20 marks)

The financial year of Handile plc ended on 31 March 20X6. A trial balance extracted as at that date reveals a difference of £100 in the books. It is decided to draw up a sales ledger control account and a purchases ledger control account to help locate any errors. The trial balance figures for debtors and creditors were £16,940 and £23,188 respectively. These represent the totals of the balances on the individual debtors and creditors accounts in the sales and purchase ledgers.

The following information is obtained from the books of prime entry.

	£
Cash book	
Discounts allowed	3,112
Cash and cheques from customers	124,819
Discounts received	2,097
Cash and cheques paid to suppliers	139,830
Customers' cheques dishonoured	55
Journal	
Balances in the purchase ledger set off against	
Balances in the sales ledger	460
Bad debts written off	661
Decrease in the provision for bad debts	51
Sales day book	130,411
Purchases day book	155,603
Returns in day book	3,150
Returns out day book	3,227

According to the audited accounts for the previous year debtors and creditors as at 1 April 20X5 were £18,776 and £13,199 respectively.

Required

(a) Draw up the relevant control accounts. (15 marks)
(b) Suggest where an error might have been made. (5 marks)

19 DEBBIE BROWN (20 marks)

When Debbie Brown extracted her trial balance at 31 March 20X2 she found it did not agree. She opened a suspense account, prepared her trading and profit and loss account and drew up the following balance sheet.

	Cost	*Dep'n*	*NBV*
	£	£	£
Fixed assets			
Shop fittings	1,500	300	1,200
Van	3,200	800	2,400
	4,700	1,100	3,600
Current assets			
Stock		2,917	
Debtors		2,154	
Bank		1,095	
Cash		128	
		6,294	
Current liabilities			
Creditors		1,888	
Suspense account		9	
		1,897	
Net current assets			4,397
			7,997
Capital			
As at 1 April 20X1			7,500
Profit for the year			5,497
			12,997
Less drawings			5,000
As at 31 March 20X2			7,997

Subsequent checking of her records revealed the following errors which when corrected eliminated the suspense account.

(a) A cheque for £260 for the purchase of a new display stand on 31 March had been entered correctly in the cash book but had been entered in shop fitting account as £200.

(b) A credit note from XY Suppliers Ltd for £60 had been entered correctly in the returns outwards book but had been posted to XY's account as £66.

(c) Bank charges of £21 appeared in the cash book but had not been posted to the ledger.

(d) An invoice for £139 for goods sold to Thompson had been correctly entered in the sales day book but had been posted to Thompson's account as £193.

(e) The debit balance of £223 on Smith's account at 31 March 20X2 had been carried down as £253 and included in the trial balance at that figure.

Required

(a) Write up the suspense account showing therein the necessary correcting entries. (10 marks)
(b) Prepare a statement showing the revised profit for the year. (5 marks)
(c) Prepare a corrected balance sheet. (5 marks)

20 DONALD BROWN (20 marks)

Donald Brown, a sole trader, extracted the following trial balance on 31 December 20X0.

TRIAL BALANCE AS AT 31 DECEMBER 20X0

	Debit	*Credit*
	£	£
Capital at 1 January 20X0		26,094
Debtors	42,737	
Cash in hand	1,411	
Creditors		35,404
Fixtures and fittings at cost	42,200	
Discounts allowed	1,304	
Discounts received		1,175
Stock at 1 January 20X0	18,460	
Sales		491,620
Purchases	387,936	
Motor vehicles at cost	45,730	
Lighting and heating	6,184	
Motor expenses	2,862	
Rent	8,841	
General expenses	7,413	
Balance at bank		19,861
Provision for deprecation		
Fixtures and fitting		2,200
Motor vehicles		15,292
Drawings	26,568	
	591,646	591,646

The following information as at 31 December is also available.

(a) £218 is owing for motor expenses.

(b) £680 has been prepaid for rent.

(c) Depreciation is to be provided for the year as follows.

Motor vehicles: 20% on cost
Fixtures and fittings: 10% reducing balance method

(d) Stock at the close of business was valued at £19,926.

Required

Prepare Donald Brown's trading and profit and loss account for the year ended 31 December 20X0 and his balance sheet at that date.

21 HERBERT HOWELL (20 marks)

The following trial balance has been extracted from the ledger of Herbert Howell, a sole trader, as at 31 May 20X9, the end of his most recent financial year.

HERBERT HOWELL
TRIAL BALANCE AS AT 31 MAY 20X9

	Dr	*Cr*
	£	£
Property, at cost	90,000	
Equipment, at cost	57,500	
Provisions for depreciation (as at 1 June 20X8)		
- property		12,500
- equipment		32,500
Stock, as at 1 June 20X8	27,400	
Purchases	259,600	
Sales		405,000
Discounts allowed	3,370	
Discounts received		4,420
Wages and salaries	52,360	
Bad debts	1,720	
Loan interest	1,560	
Carriage out	5,310	
Other operating expenses	38,800	
Trade debtors	46,200	
Trade creditors		33,600
Provision for bad debts		280
Cash on hand	151	
Bank overdraft		14,500
Drawings	28,930	
13% Loan		12,000
Capital, as at 1 June 20X8		98,101
	612,901	612,901

The following additional information as at 31 May 20X9 is available:

(a) Stock as at the close of business was valued at £25,900.

(b) Depreciation for the year ended 31 May 20X9 has yet to be provided as follows:

property - 1% using the straight line method;
equipment - 15% using the straight line method;

(c) Wages and salaries are accrued by £140.

(d) 'Other operating expenses' includes certain expenses prepaid by £500. Other expenses included under this heading are accrued by £200.

(e) The provision for bad debts is to be adjusted so that it is 0.5% of trade debtors as at 31 May 20X9.

(f) 'Purchases' includes goods valued at £1,040 which were withdrawn by Mr Howell for his own personal use.

Required

Prepare Mr Howell's trading and profit and loss account for the year ended 31 May 20X9 and his balance sheet as at 31 May 20X9.

22 BRENDA BAILEY (25 marks)

The following trial balance has been extracted from the accounts of Brenda Bailey, a sole trader.

BRENDA BAILEY
TRIAL BALANCE AS AT 30 JUNE 20X9

	Dr	*Cr*
	£	£
Sales		427,726
Purchases	302,419	
Carriage inwards	476	
Carriage outwards	829	
Wages and salaries	64,210	
Rent and rates	12,466	
Heat and light	4,757	
Stock at 1 July 20X8	15,310	
Drawings	21,600	
Equipment at cost	102,000	
Motor vehicles at cost	43,270	
Provision for depreciation:		
Equipment		22,250
Motor vehicles		8,920
Debtors	50,633	
Creditors		41,792
Bank		3,295
Sundry expenses	8,426	
Cash	477	
Capital		122,890
	626,873	626,873

The following information as at 30 June 20X9 is also available.

(a) £350 is owing for heat and light.

(b) £620 has been prepaid for rent and rates.

(c) Depreciation is to be provided for the year as follows:

Equipment - 10% on cost
Motor vehicles - 20% on cost.

(d) Stock at the close of business was valued at £16,480.

Required

Prepare Brenda Bailey's trading and profit and loss account for the year ended 30 June 20X9 and her balance sheet at that date.

23 HIGHTON (25 marks) *45 mins*

A Highton is in business as a general retailer. He does not keep a full set of accounting records; however it has been possible to extract the following details from the few records that are available.

		1 April 20X1	*31 March 20X2*
		£	£
Freehold land and buildings at cost		10,000	10,000
Motor vehicle (cost £3,000)		2,250	
Stock, at cost		3,500	4,000
Trade debtors		500	1,000
Prepayments:	motor vehicle expenses	200	300
	property insurance	50	100
Cash at bank		550	950
Cash in hand		100	450
Loan from Highton's father		10,000	
Trade creditors:	accruals	1,500	1,800
	electricity	200	400
	motor vehicle expenses	200	100

Extract from a rough cash book for the year to 31 March 20X2

	£
Receipts	
Cash sales	80,400
Payments	£
Cash purchases	17,000
Drawings	7,000
General shop expenses	100
Telephone	100
Wages	3,000

Extract from the bank pass sheets for the year to 31 March 20X2

	£
Receipts	
Cash banked	52,850
Cheques from trade debtors	8,750
	£
Payments	
Cheques to suppliers	47,200
Loan repayment (including interest)	10,100
Electricity	400
Motor vehicle expenses	1,000
Property insurance	150
Rates	300
Telephone	300
Drawings	1,750

Note. Depreciation is to be provided on the motor vehicle at a rate of 25% per annum on cost.

You are required to prepare a trading and profit and loss account for the year to 31 March 20X2, and a balance sheet as at that date.

24 CHURCH (25 marks)

The summarised balance sheet of Richard Church, photographic retailer, as at 31 March 20X2, is as follows.

	Cost	*Dep'n*	*NBV*
	£	£	£
Fixed assets			
Shop equipment and fittings	15,000	3,000	12,000
Motor vehicles	6,000	1,500	4,500
	21,000	4,500	16,500
Current assets			
Stock		10,420	
Debtors		6,260	
Rent prepaid		650	
Bank		6,690	
		24,020	
Current liabilities			
Trade creditors		4,740	
Accrued expenses: heating and lighting		380	
		5,120	
Net current assets			18,900
			35,400
Long term liabilities			
Loan from S Chappell			3,000
			32,400
Capital			32,400

Despite professional advice, Richard Church has not maintained an accounting system, but produces the following information regarding the financial year ended 31 March 20X3.

(a) Total sales and sales returns were £152,600 and £3,500 respectively. An average gross profit to sales ratio of 30 per cent is maintained during the year.

(b) The trade debtors figure at 31 March 20X3 was £5,620, on which figure it has been decided to make a provision for doubtful debts of 5 per cent at the year end. During the course of the year trade debts amounting to £470 had been written off.

(c) The trade creditors figure at 31 March 20X3 was £6,390. Discounts received from suppliers amounted to £760.

(d) Stock at 31 March 20X3 indicates an increased investment of £4,000 in stock over that one year earlier. Drawings from stock by Richard Church during the year amounted to £600 and were included in payments made to suppliers; otherwise no records of these drawings were made.

(e) Payments for shop salaries for the year were £15,840, and for heating, lighting, rent and rates and other administration expenses amounted to £3,460. At 31 March 20X3 rent paid in advance amounted to £480, and heating bills outstanding were £310.

(f) Shop fittings acquired during the year, and paid for, amounted to £2,000. Depreciation on shop equipment and fittings is provided annually at the rate of 10 per cent on the original cost of assets held at the year end. Similarly, depreciation on the motor vehicle is to be provided at the rate of 25% on original cost.

(g) On 31 March 20X3 the loan from S Chappell was repaid.

(h) Cash drawings by Richard Church amounted to £9,000.

Required

(a) Prepare a trading, profit and loss account for the year ended 31 March 20X3. (15 marks)
(b) Prepare a balance sheet as at 31 March 20X3. (10 marks)

25 NEWGALE (15 marks)

You are presented with the following draft balance sheet of Newgale Ltd as at 31 December 20X5.

	Cost	*Dep'n*	*NBV*
	£	£	£
Fixed assets			
Freehold premises	108,000	36,000	72,000
Plant	60,000	16,260	43,740
	168,000	52,260	115,740
Current assets			
Stock		27,450	
Debtors		22,200	
Bank		3,360	
		53,010	
Current liabilities			
Creditors		33,750	
Net current assets			19,260
			135,000
Capital and reserves			
Ordinary shares of £1 each			75,000
Retained profits			60,000
			135,000

Additional information relevant to the year to 31 December 20X5 is as follows.

(a) A dividend of 10p per share has been proposed by the directors in respect of the year to 31 December 20X5 and payable on all ordinary shares in issue on that date.

(b) When taking stock on 31 December 20X5, one of the stock sheets was undercast by £1,100. Investigations have also shown that the opening stock at 1 January 20X5 was understated by £4,200.

(c) Cheques totalling £2,600 were despatched to creditors on 31 December 20X5 but had not been recorded in the books.

(d) All of the plant in the above draft balance sheet had been purchased in 20X3. It is the policy of the company to make provision for depreciation at the rate of 10% per annum on the cost of all plant held at the end of each financial year. This policy had been misinterpreted as indicating that the reducing balance method should be applied in respect of depreciation provisions, when the intention was to apply the straight line method when making these provisions.

(e) A new item of plant purchased in October 20X5 at a cost of £12,000 had been recorded in the goods purchased account.

(f) Ordinary shares in issue in the above draft balance sheet were called up and fully paid.

Required

Prepare a revised balance sheet of the company at 31 December 20X5.

26 EXCEL (25 marks)

The following balances were extracted from the accounting records of Excel Ltd, a car hire and taxi service company in respect of the year ended 30th November 20X5.

	£
Motor cars	111,200
Depreciation - motor cars to 30th November 20X4	46,320
Revenue from business operations	510,500
Ordinary shares - 200,000 of £1 each, allotted and fully paid	200,000
Retained profits at 30th November 20X4	127,200
Drivers' wages and expenses	245,200
Motor vehicle expenses	
Licence and insurance	7,500
Repairs etc.	35,460
Petrol and oil	45,310
Trade debtors	62,530
Administration expenses	30,460
Advertising expenses	12,540
Directors' remuneration	40,000
12% Debentures issued 1st September 20X5 (interest payable January and July)	120,000
Interim dividend on ordinary shares	12,000
Freehold premises at cost	420,000
Stock at 30th November 20X4	
Petrol and oil	1,200
Vehicle spares	700
Share premium	40,000
Cash at bank	19,920

Additional information relevant to the year ended 30th November 20X5 is as follows.

(a) Trade debtors include bad debts of £890; in addition, it is considered necessary to make a provision for doubtful debts of 3% of debtors.

(b) The following expenses were outstanding at 30th November 20X5:

	£
Advertising	800
Auditor's fee	2,000
Repairs	1,450

(c) Prepayments in respect of licences and insurance amounted to £1,500.

(d) Stocks at 30th November 20X5 were:

	£
Petrol and oil	1,640
Vehicle spares	3,170

(e) All the motor vehicles were bought after 1st December 20X1. The depreciation of the vehicles is provided from the date of purchase to the date of sale at the rate of 25% per annum on the straight line method. The motor vehicles figure is made up as follows:

	£
Cost to 30th November 20X4	85,200
Additions - 1 September 20X5	32,000
Sale proceeds 1 September 20X5 (cost £24,000 on 1 December 20X2)	6,000

(f) A final ordinary share dividend of 12p per share is proposed for the year ended 30th November 20X5.

Required

(a) Prepare the profit and loss appropriation accounts for the year ended 30 November 20X5. (13 marks)

(b) Prepare the balance sheet as on the above date. (12 marks)

27 MATTHEWS (15 marks)

The financial details which follow are in respect of Matthews Ltd.

PROFIT AND LOSS ACCOUNT EXTRACT FOR THE YEAR ENDED 31 MAY 20X4

	£'000
Sales	1,284
Cost of goods sold	708
Operating profit	88
Interest payable	(23)
Net profit	65
Corporation tax	(20)
Dividends	(17)
Retained profit	28

BALANCE SHEETS AS AT 31 MAY

	20X3	*20X4*
	£'000	£'000
Fixed assets at cost	780	812
Cumulative depreciation	(485)	(546)
	295	266
Stock	118	154
Debtors	96	167
Cash in hand	12	-
Trade creditors	179	210
Bank overdraft	-	23
Proposed dividends	17	17
Corporation tax	14	18
12% debenture	200	180
	111	139
Ordinary shares @ £1	40	40
Retained profits	71	99
	111	139

Note. No fixed assets were sold between 31 May 20X3 and 31 May 20X4.

Required

Prepare a cash flow statement in respect of Matthews Ltd for the year ended 31 May 20X4.

28 MAXIM (20 marks)

You have been approached by the financial director of Maxim plc for a loan at a competitive rate of interest for increased investment in trading stock. In support of his request he makes available the latest financial statements as follows:

PROFIT AND LOSS ACCOUNT FOR YEAR ENDED 31 OCTOBER 20X5

	£
Sales	780,000
Less operating expenses	670,000
	110,000
Debenture interest	26,000
Profit before taxation	84,000
Company taxation	32,000
Profit after taxation	52,000
Losses brought forward from previous year	36,000
Retained profit carried forward	16,000

BALANCE SHEET AT 31 OCTOBER 20X5

	Cost	*Depreciation*	*Net*
Fixed assets	£	£	£
Goodwill	80,000	-	80,000
Machinery	624,000	402,000	222,000
Motor vehicles	24,000	18,000	6,000
	728,000	420,000	308,000
Current assets			
Stock at or below cost		236,000	
Debtors		188,000	
		424,000	
Current liabilities			
Bank overdraft		74,000	
Creditors		300,000	
Company taxation		32,000	
Net current assets		406,000	
			18,000
			326,000
Long-term liabilities			
10% debentures (secured)			260,000
			66,000
Capital and reserves:			
Share capital: authorised, allocated and fully paid ordinary shares (£1)			50,000
Retained profits			16,000
			66,000

Required

Prepare a report, incorporating appropriate accounting ratios, on the overall financial position as revealed by the above accounts, giving reasons whether or not you would approve such a loan.

29 BLOW (15 marks)

Your client Mr Blow has been in business for several years now and you have just prepared his accounts for the year ended 30 June 20X9. It appears to you that he is less than happy with the state of affairs and a friend has told him that his liquidity seems to be declining and that he ought to manage his working capital more efficiently.

The two most recent sets of accounts are summarised below.

Required

(a) Calculate the current and quick ratios for both years, indicating the purpose of the ratios and any reservations which you have about them. (10 marks)

(b) Comment on the movement in debtors over the year. Use any other ratios which you feel are relevant. (5 marks)

TRADING, PROFIT AND LOSS ACCOUNTS
FOR THE YEARS ENDING 30 JUNE

	20X9		*20X8*	
	£	£	£	£
Sales (all on credit)		91,000		83,000
Less cost of sales				
Opening stock	3,100		2,800	
Purchases	82,640		75,460	
	85,740		78,260	
Less closing stock	4,500		3,100	
		81,240		75,160
Gross profit		9,760		7,840
Less expenses		2,300		1,900
Net profit		7,460		5,940

BALANCE SHEETS AS AT 30 JUNE

	20X9		20X8	
	£	£	£	£
Fixed assets				
Cost		23,000		18,000
Accumulated depreciation		11,000		10,000
Net book value		12,000		8,000
Current assets				
Stock	4,500		3,100	
Debtors	5,900		3,200	
Prepayments	240		190	
Cash at bank	0		500	
	10,640		6,990	
Less current liabilities				
Trade creditors	(4,100)		(4,700)	
Accruals	(350)		(260)	
Bank overdraft	(4,500)		0	
		1,690		2,030
		13,690		10,030
Proprietor's interest				
Capital brought forward		10,030		6,990
Profit for the year	7,460		5,940	
Less drawings	3,800		2,900	
Retained profit for the year		3,660		3,040
Capital carried forward		13,690		10,030

30 DIRECT/INDIRECT (10 marks)

(a) Distinguish between, and give an example each of:

(i) Direct costs.

(ii) Indirect costs. (4 marks)

(b) Give a list of headings and sub-headings under which costs may be analysed by function and indicate which headings or sub-headings correspond to direct costs. (6 marks)

31 APPORTIONMENT (20 marks)

A company manufactures and sells two products, X and Y, whose selling prices are £100 and £300 respectively, and each product passes through two manufacturing processes, A and B. In process A, product X takes two hours per unit and product Y takes four hours. In process B, product X takes one hour per unit, and product Y takes three hours. Labour in process A is paid £4 per hour, and in process B £5 per hour.

The two products are made out of materials P,Q and R and the quantities of each material used in making one unit of each product is as follows.

	Product X	*Product Y*
Material P	37 kg	93 kg
Material Q	10 units	240 units
Material R	20 m	75 m

Material prices are £1 per kg for P, £2.40 per dozen units for Q and £0.20 per metre for R.

Salesmen are paid a commission of 5% of sales. The packing materials cost £1 for X and £4 for Y. Costs of transporting the goods to the customer are £2 for X and £5 for Y.

Other annual costs are as follows.

		£	£
Indirect wages:	process A	25,000	
	process B	40,000	
	stores	20,000	
	canteen	10,000	
			95,000
Indirect materials:	process A	51,510	
	process B	58,505	
	stores	1,310	
	canteen	8,425	
			119,750
Rent and rates			450,000
Depreciation of plant and machinery			140,000
Power			50,000
Insurance:	fire on buildings		3,750
	workmen's compensation at 2% of wages		12,000
Heating and lighting			4,500
Advertising			90,000

A royalty of £1 is payable on product X. The annual quantities sold are 15,000 units of X and 10,000 units of Y.

Other relevant information is as follows.

Cost centre	*Area in square metres*	*Book value of plant and machinery*	*Power of machinery*	*Direct labour hours*	*Number of employees*	*Number of stores issue notes*
		£	%			
Process A	10,000	1,000,000	80	70,000	40	10,000
Process B	5,000	200,000	20	45,000	30	5,000
Stores	10,000	150,000			10	
Canteen	5,000	50,000			5	
	30,000	1,400,000	100	115,000	85	15,000

Required

(a) Prepare a production overhead analysis and apportionment sheet, showing clearly the bases of apportionment used. (10 marks)

(b) Calculate appropriate rates of overhead recovery for processes A and B. (2 marks)

(c) Calculate the full (absorption) cost of making and selling one unit of each product. (5 marks)

(d) Calculate the unit profit or loss for each product. (3 marks)

32 ABSORPTION AND MARGINAL COSTING (20 marks)

The data below relate to a company which makes and sells one product. There was no stock at the beginning of March.

	March	*April*
	Units	Units
Sales	4,000	6,000
Production	8,000	2,000
	£	£
Selling price per unit	80	80
Variable production costs per unit	40	40
Fixed production overhead incurred	96,000	96,000
Fixed production overhead cost per unit, being the predetermined overhead absorption rate	12	12
Selling, distribution and administration costs (all fixed)	40,000	40,000

Required

(a) Present comparative profit statements for each month using:

(i) Absorption costing.
(ii) Marginal costing. (15 marks)

(b) Comment on the following statement using, for purposes of illustration, if you wish, figures contained in your answer to (a).

'Marginal costing rewards sales whereas absorption costing rewards production.' (5 marks)

33 ESTIMATED COSTS (20 marks)

A company which manufactures and sells a single product has estimated its costs for the forthcoming year as follows:

	Unit cost	
	100,000 units	*200,000 units*
	£	£
Direct wages	10	10.00
Direct materials	40	40.00
Manufacturing overheads	20	12.50
Administration cost	10	5.00
Marketing and selling costs	10	7.50
	90	75.00

The marketing manager estimates that 100,000 units could be sold annually if the unit selling price were £100, and 200,000 if the selling price were £84. Fixed costs will be unaffected by the level of output adopted.

Assume that the number of units manufactured and sold is the same.

(a) Calculate the annual net profit if the company sells:

(i) 100,000 units.
(ii) 200,000 units. (10 marks)

(b) Calculate the number of units that the company must sell annually to break even (make no profit and no loss) when the unit selling price is:

(i) £100.
(ii) £84. (7 marks)

(c) State, with reasons, which of the two unit selling prices you would advise the company to adopt. (3 marks)

34 POSTHORN (25 marks)

The balance sheet of Posthorn Ltd at 30 September 20X5 includes the following balances.

	£'000
Ordinary shares of £1: allotted and paid up	450
Retained profits	180
10% Debentures	270
Fixed assets (net)	405
Working capital	495

The company's operational activities for the year to 30 September 20X6 are forecast to be as follows.

(a) Revenue from sales of £180,000 per calendar month (£135,000 in the year ended 30 September 20X5), based on a gross profit margin of 25% on selling prices.

(b) Purchases of goods for resale at the rate of £139,500 per calendar month (£112,500 per calendar month in the year ended 30 September 20X5): stocks are planned to rise to £324,000 at the end of the forecast period.

(c) Credit terms of two months are applied to all customers. Suppliers are paid one month after the goods are delivered.

(d) No disposals of fixed assets are planned, but additional fixed assets will be purchased for £135,000 and paid for in the forecast year.

(e) Overhead expenses (excluding depreciation and debenture interest) of £207,000 will be incurred, of which £45,000 will remain unpaid on 30 September 20X6 (£36,000 on 30 September 20X5).

(f) The provision for depreciation will be increased from the accumulated figure of £270,000 at 30 September 20X5 to £351,000 on 30 September 20X6.

(g) The ordinary share dividend of 15p per share proposed on 30 September 20X5 will be paid in the year, and the dividend for the year ending 30 September 20X6 is forecast at 25p per share.

Required

(a) Forecast the company's cash flow for the year ending 30 September 20X6, showing any cash deficiency or surplus for the year. (10 marks)

(b) Prepare a forecast trading, profit and loss account for the year ending 30 September 20X6. (10 marks)

(c) Prepare a forecast balance sheet as at 30 September 20X6. (5 marks)

35 FLEXIBLE BUDGET (20 marks)

(a) Explain what is meant by the terms 'fixed budget' and 'flexible budget' and state the main objective of preparing flexible budgets. (5 marks)

(b) Prepare a flexible budget for 20X6 for the overhead expenses of a production department at the activity levels of 80% and 100%, using the information below.

(i) 100% activity represents 100,000 direct labour hours. Direct labour is paid £5 per hour.

(ii) Variable costs:

Indirect labour	30% of direct labour cost
Consumable supplies	40% of direct labour cost
Canteen and other welfare services	10% of direct and indirect labour costs

(iii) Fixed cost absorption rates per direct labour hour based on 100% capacity.

	£
Depreciation	2.00
Maintenance	1.30
Insurance	0.35
Rates	0.50

(15 marks)

Suggested answers

1 ROLE OF ACCOUNTING

A business keeps accounts for the following reasons.

(a) It helps the business keep track of what it is doing, and also enables the business to analyse what it has been doing, so that it can see how it is getting on.

(b) There are a number of people who want financial information about the business.

(i) *Owners* of the business will want to know whether the business is doing well, so they know how much money they can extract from it.

(ii) *Managers* running the business on behalf of the owners will want information to help them make decisions (and then will want information so that they can see how the decisions worked out).

(iii) The *Inland Revenue* will want financial information so that they can assess how much tax the business should pay.

(c) There are legal requirements to keep and prepare financial information for all companies and for businesses registered for VAT.

2 DEFINITIONS

(a) The *going concern* concept is the assumption that, when preparing accounts, the business will continue trading for the foreseeable future, without closing down or even running down its activities to a significant extent.

If a business is to be closed down, for example, then any stock on hand will have to be valued at the amount it will realise in a forced sale. But if the business is regarded as a going concern, then the value (usually at cost) of any unsold stock at the end of an accounting period will be carried forward to the next period and will eventually be matched against income earned in that period.

(b) The *accruals* concept is that, when profit is being calculated, revenue earned must be matched against the expenditure incurred in earning it. For example, suppose you were calculating profit for the year ended 31 December 20X8 and had got as far as working out that gross profit was £12,000. To calculate net profit, expenses must be deducted. Suppose that rent paid in 20X8 was £700. Then only that part of the £700 relating to 20X8 should be deducted from the gross profit. If £200 was actually a prepayment for rent in 20X9, then that £200 must be matched against next year's income, not against the £12,000 gross profit for 20X8.

(c) The *consistency* concept states that in preparing accounts consistency should be observed in two respects.

(i) Similar items within a single set of accounts should be given similar accounting treatments.

(ii) The same treatment should be applied from one period to another in accounting for similar items. This enables valid comparisons to be made from one period to the next.

For example, suppose a business owns a fleet of cars. Then the consistency concept rules that each car should be depreciated in the same way (by whatever method the business deems most appropriate) and once that depreciation policy has been set, it should be applied consistently from one year to the next.

A business can change its accounting methods, but it should explain clearly why it is doing so, and it should show the effects of the change on the profits for the relevant year in its financial statements.

(d) The *prudence* concept is that where alternative procedures, or alternative valuations, are possible, the one selected should be the one which gives the most cautious presentation of the business's financial position or results. For example, stocks should be stated in the balance sheet at the lower of cost or net realisable value rather than at their selling price: to value the stock at selling price would be to anticipate making a profit before the profit had been earned, and would not be prudent.

The other aspect of the prudence concept is that where a loss is foreseen, it should be anticipated and taken into account immediately. If a business purchases stock for £1,200 but because of a sudden slump in the market only £900 is likely to be realised when the stock is sold, the prudence concept dictates that the stock should be valued at £900. It is not acceptable to wait until the stock is sold, and then recognise the £300 loss. It must be recognised as soon as it is foreseen.

3 THE ACCOUNTING EQUATION

Transaction	*Assets*		=	*Capital*		+	*Liabilities*	
		£			£			£
Start of business	Cash	5,000	=		5,000	+		0
(a)	Cash	3,200	=		5,000	+		0
	Shelves	1,800						
		5,000						
(b)	Cash	1,200	=		5,000	+		0
	Shelves	1,800						
	Books	2,000						
		5,000						
(c)	Cash	2,700	=		5,000	+		0
	Shelves	1,800		Profit	500			
	Books	1,000						
		5,500			5,500			
(d)	Cash	2,500	=		5,000	+		0
	Shelves	1,800		Profit	500			
	Books	1,000		Drawings	(200)			
		5,300			5,300			
(e)	Cash	3,000	=		5,000	+	Loan	500
	Shelves	1,800		Profit	500			
	Books	1,000		Drawings	(200)			
		5,800			5,300			500
(f)	Cash	3,000	=		5,000	+	Loan	500
	Shelves	1,800		Profit	500		Creditor	1,000
	Books	1,000		Drawings	(200)			
	Carpets	1,000			5,300			1,500
		6,800						
(g)	Cash	3,000	=		5,000	+	Loan	500
	Shelves	1,800		Profit	700		Creditor	1,000
	Books	600		Drawings	(200)			
	Carpets	1,000			5,500			1,500
	Debtor	600						
		7,000						

4 FINANCIAL STATEMENTS

A balance sheet is a 'snapshot' of the financial position of a business. It is a statement of the liabilities, assets and capital of the business at a given moment in time. It is basically the same as the accounting equation, but written out in more detail.

The trading profit and loss account is not a static picture like the balance sheet, but is a record of income generated and expenditure incurred over the relevant accounting period.

Capital expenditure is expenditure which results in the acquisition of fixed assets (or an improvement in their earning capacity). It is not charged as an expense in the trading, profit and loss account.

Revenue expenditure is any other expenditure such as purchase of goods and expenses incurred to keep the business running (for example repairs, wages, electricity and so on). It is accounted for in the trading, profit and loss account.

Capital expenditure: (a), (d)
Revenue expenditure: (b), (c), (e), (f)

(Note that the value of the transactions is irrelevant.)

5 IVOR WILLOW

IVOR WILLOW
TRADING, PROFIT AND LOSS ACCOUNT FOR THE YEAR ENDED 31 MARCH 20X8

	£	£
Sales		28,000
Less cost of sales		10,000
Gross profit		18,000
Less other expenses		
Rent	1,800	
Interest	600	
Wages	8,300	
Telephone	162	
Electricity	304	
Postage	24	
		11,190
Net profit		6,810

6 J OCKEY

The relevant books of prime entry are the cash book, the sales day book, the purchase day book.

CASH BOOK (RECEIPTS)

Date	*Narrative*	*Total*	*Capital*	*Sales*	*Debtors*
		£	£	£	£
May 1	Capital	5,000	5,000		
May 13	Sales	200		200	
May 16	Bruce	700			700
May 24	Hill	200			200
		6,100	5,000	200	900

CASH BOOK (PAYMENTS)

Date	*Narrative*	*Total*	*Fixtures and fittings*	*Creditors*	*Rent*	*Delivery expenses*	*Drawings*	*Wages*
May		£	£	£	£	£	£	£
1	Store Fitments Ltd	2,000	2,000					
19	Abel	650		650				
20	Rent	200			200			
21	Delivery expenses	50				50		
30	Drawings	200					200	
30	Wages	320						320
31	Green	300		300				
		3,720	2,000	950	200	50	200	320

SALES DAY BOOK

Date	*Customer*	*Amount*
		£
May 4	Bruce	700
May 11	Hill	580
Mat 18	Nailor	360
		1,640

PURCHASE DAY BOOK

Date	*Customer*	*Amount*
		£
May 2	Abel	650
May 9	Green	300
May 17	Kaye	800
		1,750

7 JOCKFIELD

(a),(b),(c)

PETTY CASH BOOK

Receipts	*Date*	*Narrative*	*Total*	*Postage*	*Travelling*	*Cleaning*	*Stationery*	*Motor*
£			£	£	£	£	£	£
300	May 1	Cash						
	May 2	Postage	18	18				
	May 3	Travelling	12		12			
	May 5	Cleaning	15			15		
	May 7	Petrol	22					22
	May 8	Travelling	25		25			
	May 9	Stationery	17				17	
	May 11	Cleaning	18			18		
	May 14	Postage	5	5				
	May 15	Travelling	8		8			
	May 18	Stationery	9				9	
	May 18	Cleaning	23			23		
	May 20	Postage	13	13				
	May 24	Van service	43					43
	May 26	Petrol	18					18
	May 27	Cleaning	21			21		
	May 29	Postage	5	5				
	May 30	Petrol	14					14
			286	41	45	77	26	97
286	May 31	Cash						
		Balance c/d	300					
586			586					
300	June 1	Balance b/d						

(d) The totals in the analysis column are posted to the relevant ledger accounts (the cash account will be CR £286, the relevant accounts will be debited the analysed amounts).

8 OMEGA

(a),(b),(c)

ALPHA

	£		£
Opening balance	210		
May sales	88	Balance c/d	298
	298		298

BETA

	£		£
Opening balance	1,040	Cash	1,040
May sales	314	Balance c/d	314
	1,354		1,354

GAMMA

	£		£
Opening balance	1,286	Cash	826
May sales	432	Balance c/d	892
	1,718		1,718

DELTA

	£		£
Opening balance	279	Cash	279
May sales	417	Balance c/d	417
	696		696

EPSILON

	£		£
Opening balance	823	Cash	823
May sales	129	Returns	88
May sales	269	Balance c/d	538
May sales	228		
	1,449		1,449

ZETA

	£		£
Cash	1,000	Opening balance	2,173
Balance c/d	1,441	May purchases	268
	2,441		2,441

ETA

	£		£
Cash	187	Opening balance	187
Balance c/d	1,164	May purchases	423
		May purchases	741
	1,351		1,351

THETA

	£		£
Cash	318	Opening balance	318

SALES ACCOUNT

	£		£
		May sales	1,877

PURCHASES ACCOUNT

	£		£
May purchases	1,432		

RETURNS ACCOUNT

	£		£
May returns	88		

CASH ACCOUNT

	£		£
May receipts	2,968	May payments	1,505

(d) DEBTORS AS AT 31 MAY

	April	*May*	*Total*
	£	£	£
Alpha	210	88	298
Beta	-	314	314
Gamma	460	432	892
Delta	-	417	417
Epsilon	-	538	538
	670	1,789	2,459

9 HUBBLE

Rather than write out the ledger accounts all over again, the question may be answered as follows.

(a) The postings necessary for each transaction are:

		£	£
DEBIT	Purchases	2,000	
CREDIT	Cash		1,000
CREDIT	Creditors		1,000
DEBIT	Interest	20	
CREDIT	Cash		20
DEBIT	Electricity	25	
CREDIT	Cash		25
DEBIT	Telephone	12	
CREDIT	Cash		12
DEBIT	Cash	500	
DEBIT	Debtors	3,000	
CREDIT	Sales		3,500
DEBIT	Cash	220	
CREDIT	Debtors		220

(b) Once these have been posted and the accounts balanced off, the trial balance is:

Account	*Dr*	Cr
	£	£
Cash	18,083	
Capital		9,500
Bank loan		3,000
Sales		19,300
Debtors	6,980	
Rent	2,750	
Purchases	4,100	
Creditors		2,400
Interest	370	
Electricity	425	
Telephone	192	
Drawings	1,300	
	34,200	34,200

(*Note.* If you are not confident of your arithmetic, you may find it safer to write out and balance off all the ledger accounts individually.)

PROFIT AND LOSS (LEDGER) ACCOUNT

	£		£
Rent	2,750	Sales	19,300
Purchases	4,100		
Interest	370		
Electricity	425		
Telephone	192		
Balance (net profit taken to balance sheet)	11,463		
	19,300		19,300

(c) A HUBBLE BALANCE SHEET AS AT 31 MARCH 20X8

	£	£
Assets		
Cash	18,083	
Debtors	6,980	
	25,063	
Current liabilities		
Creditors	(2,400)	
		22,663
Long-term liabilities		
Loan		(3,000)
		19,663
Capital		
Capital as at 1.4.20X7		9,500
Add profit for year		11,463
Less drawings		(1,300)
Capital as at 31.3.20X8		19,663

A HUBBLE
TRADING, PROFIT AND LOSS ACCOUNT
FOR THE YEAR ENDED 31 MARCH 20X8

	£	£
Sales		19,300
Less cost of sales		4,100
Gross profit		15,200
Less other expenses		
Rent	2,750	
Interest	370	
Electricity	425	
Telephone	192	
		3,737
Net profit		11,463

10 RENT, RATES AND INSURANCE

(a) *Rent for the year ending 30 June 20X6*

	£
1 July 20X5 to 31 July 20X5 = £3,000/3	1,000
1 August 20X5 to 30 November 20X5	4,000
1 December 20X5 to 31 March 20X6	4,000
Accrued, 1 April 20X6 to 30 June 20X6 = 3/4 × £4,000	3,000
Charge to profit and loss for year ending 30 June 20X6	12,000

Rates for the year ending 30 June 20X6

	£	£
Rates prepaid last year, relating to this year		1,500
1 October 20X5 to 31 March 20X6		3,500
1 April 20X6 to 30 September 20X6	3,500	
Less prepaid July to September (3/6)	1,750	
April to June 20X6		1,750
Charge to profit and loss for year ending 30 June 20X6		6,750

Insurance for the year ending 30 June 20X6

	£	£
Insurance prepaid last year, relating to this year		1,800
1 November 20X5 to 31 October 20X6	6,000	
Less prepaid July to October (4/12)	2,000	
		4,000
Charge to profit and loss for year ending 30 June 20X6		5,800

(b) The accrual or prepayment for each expense can be summarised from the workings in part (a).

As at 30 June 20X6	£
Rent accrued	3,000
Rates prepaid	1,750
Insurance prepaid	2,000

11 BAD AND DOUBTFUL DEBTS

(a) *Initial working: provision for doubtful debts*

			£	£
31 December				
20X7	Provision required	= £44,000 × 3%	1,320	
20X8	Provision required	= £55,000 × 3%	1,650	
Increase in provision - charge to profit and loss				330
20X9	Provision required	= £47,000 × 3%	1,410	
Decrease in provision - credit to profit and loss				(240)

Profit and loss account charge
Year ended 31 December

	20X7	*20X8*	*20X9*
	£	£	£
Bad debts	7,000	10,000	8,000
Provision for doubtful debts	1,320	330	(240) credit

(b)

Balance sheet extracts
as at 31 December

	20X7	*20X8*	*20X9*
	£	£	£
Debtors	44,000	55,000	47,000
Less provision for doubtful debts	1,320	1,650	1,410
Balance sheet value	42,680	53,350	45,590

12 MEGALOT

(a)

Purchases	=	(3,000 × £6) + (1,000 × £6.60)
	=	£18,000 + £6,600
	=	£24,600
Sales	=	(2,500 × £9) + (900 × £9.70)
	=	£22,500 + £8,730
	=	£31,230

(b)

Purchases	=	4,000 items
Sales	=	3,400 items

600 items remain in stock

(c) Using FIFO: 3,400 items were sold. All of the stock bought for £6 per item has been sold. All remaining stock is valued at £6.60 per item.

Closing stock value = 600 × £6.60 = £3,960

Using LIFO: 3,400 items were sold, 2,500 from the first consignment received and 900 from the second consignment.

Balance of stock:

	£
500 × £6	3,000
100 × £6.60	660
	3,660

(d) Using FIFO:

	£	£
Sales		31,230
Less cost of goods sold:		
Purchases	24,600	
Closing stock	(3,960)	
		20,640
Gross profit		10,590

Using LIFO:

	£	£
Sales		31,230
Less cost of goods sold:		
Purchases	24,600	
Closing stock	(3,660)	
		20,940
		10,290

13 L MERVIN

Before the trading, profit and loss account and the balance sheet can be prepared, we need some workings.

(a)

Sales	£
Cash takings	233,870
Less debtors at 31.10.X3	(720)
Add debtors at 31.10.X4	510
	233,660

(b)

Purchases	£
Payments	186,750
Less creditors at 31.10.X3	(10,100)
Add creditors at 31.10.X4	6,500
Less drawings	(1,250)
	181,900

(c)

Trade expenses	£
Payments	27,240
Less owed at 31.10.X3	(1,260)
Add owed at 31.10.X4	1,840
	27,820

(d) The painting and decorating expense should be reduced by the £950 spent on the private residence.

Painting and decorating expense = £2,850 – £950
= £1,900

(e) Total drawings are:

	£
Cash	14,250
Painting and decorating	950
Goods	1,250
	16,450

(f) Depreciation to be charged is:

	£
Fixtures and fittings	
(£14,200 + £2,400) × 10%	1,660
Delivery van	
£4,320 × 40%	1,728
	3,388

L MERVIN
TRADING, PROFIT AND LOSS ACCOUNT
FOR THE YEAR ENDED 31 OCTOBER 20X4

	£	£
Sales		233,660
Less cost of goods sold:		
Opening stock	11,430	
Purchases	181,900	
	193,330	
Closing stock	(14,160)	
		179,170
Gross profit		54,490
Less other expenses:		
Trade expenses	27,820	
Painting and decorating	1,900	
Depreciation	3,388	
		33,108
Net profit		21,382

BALANCE SHEET AS AT 31 OCTOBER 20X4

	Cost	*Accumulated dep'n*	*Net book value*
	£	£	£
Fixed assets			
Freehold premises	50,000	0	50,000
Fixtures and fittings	16,600	8,760	7,840
Delivery van	12,000	9,408	2,592
	78,600	18,168	60,432
Current assets			
Stock		14,160	
Debtors		510	
Bank		1,850	
		16,520	
Current liabilities			
Creditors and accruals		8,340	
Net current assets			8,180
			68,612
Capital			
Capital as at 1.11.X3 *			63,680
Add profit for year			21,382
			85,062
Less drawings			16,450
Capital as at 31.10.X4			68,612

* Calculated using the accounting equation in the form capital = assets - liabilities from the 1 November 20X3 balances in the question.

14 ASPLEY

(a) (i)

MACHINES

			£			£
1.11.X6	Balance b/d		22,300	1.4.X7	Disposal a/c - machine 10	1,000
1. 6.X7	Machine 17:			1.6.X7	Disposal a/c - machine 14	5,000
	Cash	10,400		31.10.X7	Balance c/d	38,300
	Disposals a/c	4,600				
			15,000			
1.8.X7	Cash-machine 18		7,000			
			44,300			44,300
1.11.X7	Balance b/d		38,300			

(ii)

ACCUMULATED DEPRECIATION ON MACHINES

		£				£
1.4.X7	Disposal a/c: machine 10	360	1.11.X6	Balance b/d (W)		5,040
1.6.X7	Disposal a/c: machine 14	450	31.10.X7	Profit and loss a/c:		
31.10.X7	Balance c/d (W)	9,450		12	810	
				16	1,800	
				17	1,350	
				18	1,260	
						5,220
		10,260				10,260
			1.11.X7	Balance b/d		9,450

(iii)

DISPOSAL OF MACHINES

		£			£
1.3.X7	Machines a/c: 10	1,000	1.4.X7	Depreciation a/c-10	360
				Cash	600
1.6.X7	Machines a/c: 14	5,000	1.6.X7	Depreciation a/c-14	450
30.10.X7	P & L a/c - profit on disposals	10		Machine a/c - part exchange proceeds	4,600
		6,010			6,010

(b)

BALANCE SHEET (EXTRACT)
AS AT 31 OCTOBER 20X7

	£
Fixed assets	
Machines at cost	38,300
Less accumulated depreciation	9,450
	28,850

Working

Depreciation on machines

Machine No.	*10*	*12*	*14*	*16*	*17*	*18*
Year ending 31 October	£	£	£	£	£	£
20X3	90					
20X4	90	810				
20X5	90	810	225			
20X6	90	810	225	1,800		
Accumulated at 31.10.X6	360	2,430	450	1,800		
20X7						
Disposals	(360)		(450)			
Charge for year		810		1,800	1,350	1,260
Accumulated at 31.10.X7	0	3,240	0	3,600	1,350	1,260

15 DEPRECIATION

(a) With the exception of land held freehold, every tangible fixed asset acquired by a business will eventually wear out. But that 'wearing out' will usually be over a period of time, not all at once in the period when the asset was purchased. Depreciation is a measure of the cost to a business of that wearing out over time, so that it can be reflected in the financial statements of the business

There is more than one method of depreciation, and the method adopted by a business for a particular category of asset depends on several factors. Three main methods of depreciation are:

(i) *Straight-line*, where the asset is depreciated by a constant percentage of cost each year.

(ii) *Reducing balance*, where the asset is depreciated by a constant percentage of the balance as at the end of the previous accounting period.

(iii) The *machine hour method*, where depreciation is calculated according to how much an asset is used in an accounting period.

The following guidelines should be used in selecting the most suitable method.

(i) A fair charge to each accounting period will be one which allocates cost in proportion to the amount of benefits, profits or revenues earned during each accounting period by the asset. These 'profits' almost certainly cannot be calculated exactly, but the business should be able to decide whether:

(1) The asset provides greater benefits in the earliest years of its life (in which case the reducing balance method would be suitable).

(2) The asset provides equal benefits to each period throughout its life (in which case the straight line method would be suitable).

(3) The asset wears out with use, not with time (in which case the machine hour method would be suitable).

(ii) The costs of using an asset include both depreciation and also repairs and maintenance. If an asset provides equal benefits in each accounting period throughout its life, but has significantly increasing repairs and maintenance costs as it gets older, it might be appropriate to use the reducing balance method of depreciation, in order to even out the combined annual costs of depreciation, repairs and maintenance.

For example, the reducing balance method might be used for company cars, since car repair costs increase as cars get older.

(iii) The method of depreciation used by a business for any fixed asset should be the same as the method used for similar assets.

(iv) The method of depreciation used should be one which is easy to apply in practice. There is no point in creating unnecessary complexities.

The straight-line method is by far the most common method used is practice. It is easy to use, and it is generally fair to assume that all periods benefit more or less equally from the use of a fixed asset throughout its useful life.

(b) (i) Regardless of which method of depreciation is used, a key element when calculating annual depreciation is the estimated useful life of the asset. This is because the useful life of the asset is the period over which the cost of the asset (less its residual value) will be depreciated.

For example, suppose a car is bought for £8,000, had an estimated useful life of five year, and had estimated residual value of £2,000. It is to be depreciated using the straight-line method. The initial calculation of annual depreciation is:

$$\frac{£8,000 - £2,000}{5} = £1,200$$

Now suppose that after a year has gone by, management decide that the total useful life of the case is only going to be three years. Now there are two problems to consider.

(1) Three years' depreciation at £1,200 only comes to £3,600 and not the required £6,000.

(2) One year's depreciation has already been accounted for.

The solution to these problems is quite simple. The net book value of the car should be depreciated according to the new estimate of its useful life. Using the figures from the example:

Annual depreciation (for the next two years)

$$= \frac{(£8,000 - £1,200) - £2,000}{2}$$

$= £2,400$

The effect of this adjustment is that the car will eventually be depreciated as follows.

	£
In year 1	1,200
In year 2	2,400
In year 3	2,400
	6,000

(ii) If a business decides to change its depreciation policy in regard to a particular type of asset, it faces problems similar to those described in (i) above. The asset will already be partly depreciated according to the old method; what the business has to do is to take the net book value of the asset, and calculate a new rate of depreciation (according to the new method to be used), over the remaining useful life of the asset. For the purposes of the calculation, it is as if the net book value of the asset is its cost, and the business is working out the rate of depreciation from scratch.

Any change in depreciation policy should be disclosed in the accounts of the business.

(iii) When an asset is revalued, it will affect the amount of depreciation that needs to be charged annually in the profit and loss account. What the business should do is to take the new asset value and use that figure as a basis for calculating depreciation over the remaining useful life of the asset.

For example, suppose that a building cost £150,000 and was being depreciated by 5% each year (straight-line) over a period of 20 years. This goes smoothly for the first six years, so the building is depreciated by 6 × £7,500 = £45,000 and has a net book value of £105,000. Now the building is revalued at £219,800. What happens to depreciation?

The new asset value is £219,800, and is estimated useful life is now 14 years. So he annual depreciation charge becomes £219,800 ÷ 14 = £15,700.

(c) The results of the revaluations are as follows.

(i) The land and buildings will be shown in the balance sheet at their new value.

(ii) A revaluation reserve will be created of £340,000 – £79,000 = £261,000, the amount of the revaluation.

(iii) The annual depreciation charge on buildings will increase. For example with a 2% depreciation rate, the charge will increase by £2,800, from 2% × £70,000 = £1,400 to 2% × £210,000 = £4,200.

16 INTANGIBLE

PURCHASED GOODWILL

	£		£
Cash	4,800	Profit and loss	1,200
		Balance c/d	3,600
	4,800		4,800
Balance b/d	3,600		

RESEARCH AND DEVELOPMENT EXPENDITURE

	£		£
Balance b/d	26,500	Profit and loss (balancing figure)	15,300
Cash: research	7,900	Development expenditure c/d	22,600
development	3,500		
	37,900		37,900
Balance b/d	22,600		

17 RECTIFY

(a)

CASH BOOK

	£		£
Balance b/d	322	Bank charges	143
		Cheque drawn entered as £89	9
		Cheque drawn entered as receipt (2 × £230)	460
Error in opening balance	45	Cheque returned written back	180
Dividend received	1,147	Loan interest	1,100
Undercast	200	HP payments	660
Balance c/d	838		
	2,552		2,552

(b) BANK RECONCILIATION STATEMENT

	£	
Balance per bank statement (31 May 20X5)	870	o/d
Cheque debited in error by bank	82	
Corrected balance per bank statement	788	o/d
Cheques not yet presented	630	
	1,418	o/d
Receipts not yet credited	580	
Balance per cash book (31 May 20X5)	838	o/d

Note. Item (g) in the question is irrelevant.

18 HANDILE

(a)

SALES LEDGER CONTROL

	£		£
Balance b/d	18,776	Returns	3,150
Bad cheques	55	Discounts	3,112
Sales	130,411	Bad debts	661
		Cash	124,819
		Purchase ledger control	460
		Balance c/d	17,040
	149,242		149,242

PURCHASE LEDGER CONTROL

	£		£
Cash payments	139,830	Balance b/d	13,199
Returns	3,227	Purchases	155,603
Discounts	2,097		
Sales ledger control	460		
Balance c/d	23,188		
	168,802		168,802

(b)

	£
Total of debtors from trial balance	16,940
Total of debtors from control account	17,040
Difference	100
Total of creditors from trial balance	23,188
Total of creditors from control account	23,188
Difference	0

It therefore looks as though the £100 difference discovered in drawing up the trial balance is related to the figure for trade debtors. The balances in the sales ledger might have been undercast by £100 for example.

19 DEBBIE BROWN

(a)

SUSPENSE

	£		£
XY Suppliers Ltd	6	Trial balance difference	9
Smith	30	Shop fittings	60
Thompson	54	Bank charges	21
	90		90

(b)

PROFIT AND LOSS

	£		£
Bank charges	21	Balance b/d	5,497
Balance c/d	5,476		
	5,497		5,497

(c) CORRECTED BALANCE SHEET

	Cost	*Dep'n*	*NBV*
	£	£	£
Fixed assets			
Shop fittings	1,560	300	1,260
Van	3,200	800	2,400
	4,760	1,100	3,660
Current assets			
Stock	2,917		
Debtors	2,070		
Bank	1,095		
Cash	128		
		6,210	
Current liabilities			
Creditors		1,894	
Net current assets			4,316
			7,976
Capital			
As at 1 April 20X1			7,500
Profit for year			5,476
			12,976
Less drawings			5,000
As at 31 March 20X2			7,976

20 DONALD BROWN

Tutorial note. You should note these points.

(a) Discounts allowed are an expense of the business and should be shown as a deduction from gross profit. Similarly, discounts received is a revenue item and should be added to gross profit.

(b) The figure for depreciation in the trial balance represents accumulated depreciation up to and including 20W9. You have to calculate the charge for the year 20X0 for the profit and loss account and add this to the trial balance figure to arrive at the accumulated depreciation figure to be included in the balance sheet.

DONALD BROWN
TRADING AND PROFIT AND LOSS ACCOUNT
FOR THE YEAR ENDED 31 DECEMBER 20X0

	£	£
Sales		491,620
Less cost of sales		
Opening stock	18,460	
Purchases	387,936	
	406,396	
Closing stock	19,926	
		386,470
Gross profit		105,150
Discounts received		1,175
		106,325
Less expenses		
Discounts allowed	1,304	
Lighting and heating	6,184	
Motor expenses	3,080	
Rent	8,161	
General expenses	7,413	
Depreciation (W)	13,146	
		39,288
Net profit		67,037

Working: depreciation charge

Motor vehicles: £45,730 × 20% = £9,146
Fixtures and fittings: 10% × £(42,200 – 2,200) = £4,000
Total: £4,000 + £9,146 = £13,146.

DONALD BROWN
BALANCE SHEET AS AT 31 DECEMBER 20X0

	Cost	*Depreciation*	*Net*
	£	£	£
Fixed assets			
Fixtures and fittings	42,200	6,200	36,000
Motor vehicles	45,730	24,438	21,292
	87,930	30,638	57,292
Current assets			
Stock		19,926	
Debtors		42,737	
Prepayments		680	
Cash in hand		1,411	
		64,754	
Current liabilities			
Creditors	35,404		
Accruals	218		
Bank overdraft	19,861		
		55,483	
Net current assets			9,271
Net assets			66,563
Represented by:			
Capital			26,094
Net profit for year			67,037
			93,131
Less drawings			26,568
			66,563

21 HERBERT HOWELL

HERBERT HOWELL
TRADING AND PROFIT AND LOSS ACCOUNT
FOR THE YEAR ENDED 31 MAY 20X9

	£	£
Sales		405,000
Cost of sales:		
Opening stock	27,400	
Purchases (£259,600 - £1,040)	258,560	
	285,960	
Closing stock	25,900	
		260,060
Gross profit		144,940
Discounts received		4,420
		149,360
Discounts allowed	3,370	
Loan interest	1,560	
Bad and doubtful debts (W1)	1,671	
Carriage out	5,310	
Wages and salaries	52,500	
Depreciation (W2)	9,525	
Other operating expenses (W3)	38,500	
		112,436
Net profit		36,924

HERBERT HOWELL
BALANCE SHEET AS AT 31 MAY 20X9

	Cost £	*Dep'n* £	*Net book value* £
Fixed assets			
Property (W4)	90,000	13,400	76,600
Equipment (W4)	57,500	41,125	16,375
	147,500	54,525	92,975
Current assets			
Stock		25,900	
Trade debtors	46,200		
Less provision for doubtful debts (W1)	231		
		45,969	
Prepayment		500	
Cash on hand		151	
		72,520	
Current liabilities			
Bank overdraft		14,500	
Trade creditors		33,600	
Accruals (140 + 200)		340	
		48,440	
Net current assets			24,080
Total assets less current liabilities			117,055
Long-term liabilities			
13% loan			12,000
			105,055
Capital			
Balance at 1 June 20X8			98,101
Net profit for the year			36,924
Drawings (£28,930 + £1,040)			(29,970)
Balance at 31 May 20X9			105,055

Workings

1 *Bad debts*

	£
Provision required: 0.5% x £46,200	231
Provision b/f	280
Decrease required	(49)
Add bad debts	1,720
Bad and doubtful debts expense for the year	1,671

2 *Depreciation*

	£
Property: 1% x £90,000	900
Equipment: 15% x £57,500	8,625
	9,525

3 *Other operating expenses*

	£
As trial balance	38,800
Less prepayment	(500)
Add accrual	200
	38,500

4 *Provision for depreciation*

	Property	*Equipment*
	£	£
Balance b/f	12,500	32,500
Charge for the year (W2)	900	8,625
Balance c/f	13,400	41,125

22 BRENDA BAILEY

TRADING AND PROFIT AND LOSS ACCOUNT
FOR THE YEAR ENDED 30 JUNE 20X9

	£	£
Sales		427,726
Opening stock	15,310	
Purchases	302,419	
Carriage inwards	476	
	318,205	
Less closing stock	16,480	
Cost of sales		301,725
Gross profit		126,001
Carriage outwards	829	
Wages and salaries	64,210	
Rent and rates (12,466 - 620)	11,846	
Heat and light (4,757 + 350)	5,107	
Depreciation - equipment	10,200	
- motor vehicles	8,654	
Sundry expenses	8,426	
		109,272
Net profit for the year		16,729

BRENDA BAILEY
BALANCE SHEET AS AT 30 JUNE 20X9

	Cost	Dep'n	Net book value
	£	£	£
Fixed assets			
Equipment	102,000	32,450	69,550
Motor vehicles	43,270	17,574	25,696
	145,270	50,024	95,246
Current assets			
Stock		16,480	
Debtors		50,633	
Prepayments		620	
Cash		477	
		68,210	
Current liabilities			
Bank overdraft		3,295	
Creditors		41,792	
Accruals		350	
		45,437	
Net current assets			22,773
			118,019
Capital			
Balance at 1 July 20X8			122,890
Add profit for the year			16,729
			139,619
Less drawings			21,600
Balance at 30 June 20X9			118,019

23 HIGHTON

TRADING PROFIT AND LOSS ACCOUNT
FOR THE YEAR ENDED 31 MARCH 20X2

	£	£
Sales: cash	80,400	
credit (W1)	9,250	
		89,650
Cost of sales		
Opening stock	3,500	
Purchases: cash	17,000	
credit (W2)	47,500	
	68,000	
Less closing stock	4,000	
		64,000
Gross profit		25,650
Expenses		
Depreciation of motor vehicle (25% × £3,000)	750	
Motor vehicle expenses (W3)	800	
Property insurance £(50 + 150 – 100)	100	
Loan interest	100	
Electricity £(400 + 400 – 200)	600	
General shop expenses	100	
Telephone £(100 + 300)	400	
Wages	3,000	
Rates	300	
		6,150
Net profit		19,500

BALANCE SHEET AS AT 31 MARCH 20X2

	£	£
Fixed assets		
Freehold land and buildings at cost		10,000
Motor vehicle: cost	3,000	
accumulated depreciation	1,500	
		1,500
		11,500
Current assets		
Stock	4,000	
Trade debtors	1,000	
Prepayments	400	
Cash at bank	950	
Cash in hand	450	
	6,800	
Current liabilities		
Trade creditors	1,800	
Accruals	500	
	2,300	
Net current assets		4,500
		16,000
Proprietor's capital		
At 1 April 20X1 (W4)*		5,250
Net profit for the year	19,500	
Less drawings £(7,000 + 1,750)	8,750	
Profit retained in business		10,750
		16,000

*The opening capital could be inserted as a balancing figure; W4 is included merely to prove the figure.

Workings

1 DEBTORS CONTROL ACCOUNT

	£		£
Opening balance	500	Bank	8,750
∴ Credit sales	9,250	Closing balance	1,000
	9,750		9,750

2 CREDITORS CONTROL ACCOUNT

	£		£
Bank	47,200	Opening balance	1,500
Closing balance	1,800	∴ Credit purchases	47,500
	49,000		49,000

3 MOTOR VEHICLE EXPENSES

	£		£
Prepayment b/f	200	Accrual b/f	200
Bank	1,000	∴ P & L account	800
Accrual b/f	100	Prepayment c/f	300
	1,300		1,300

4 PROPRIETOR'S CAPITAL AT 1 APRIL 20X1

	£	£
Assets		
Freehold land and buildings	10,000	
Motor vehicle	2,250	
Stock	3,500	
Debtors and prepayments	750	
Cash at bank and in hand	650	
		17,150
Liabilities		
Loan	10,000	
Creditors and accruals	1,900	
		11,900
		5,250

24 CHURCH

(a) TRADING PROFIT AND LOSS ACCOUNT
FOR THE YEAR ENDED 31 MARCH 20X3

	£	£
Sales (less returns)		149,100
Opening stock	10,420	
Purchases (balancing figure)	108,370	
	118,790	
Closing stock £(10,420 + 4,000)	14,420	
Cost of goods sold		104,370
Gross profit (30% × £149,100)		44,730
Add discounts received		760
		45,490
Expenses		
Bad debts	470	
Provision for doubtful debts (5% × £5,620)	281	
Salaries	15,840	
Heat, light etc (W5)	3,560	
Depreciation:		
shop fittings 10% × £(15,000 + 2,000)	1,700	
motor vehicle 25% × £6,000	1,500	
		23,351
Net profit		22,139

(b) BALANCE SHEET AS AT 31 MARCH 20X3

	Cost	*Depreciation*	*Net*
	£	£	£
Fixed assets			
Shop equipment and fittings	17,000	4,700	12,300
Motor vehicle	6,000	3,000	3,000
	23,000	7,700	15,300
Current assets			
Stock		14,420	
Trade debtors less provision		5,339	
Rent paid in advance		480	
Bank		16,100	
		36,339	
Current liabilities			
Trade creditors		6,390	
Accrued expenses		310	
		6,700	
Net current assets			29,639
			44,939
Proprietor's capital			
Balance at 1 April 20X2			32,400
Profit for year		22,139	
Less drawings £(9,000 + 600)		9,600	
			12,539
			44,939

Workings

Note. No distinction is made in the question between cash transactions and bank transactions. A 'total cash account' must therefore be constructed instead of the more usual columnar bank and cash account.

1 TOTAL CASH ACCOUNT

	£		£
Balance b/f	6,690	Creditors (Working 3)	106,560
Debtors (W2)	149,270	Salaries	15,840
		Heat, light etc	3,460
		Shop fittings	2,000
		Loan - repayment	3,000
		Drawings	9,000
		Balance c/d	16,100
	155,960		155,960
Balance b/d	16,100		

2 TOTAL DEBTORS ACCOUNT

	£		£
Balance b/f	6,260	Bad debts	470
Sales	152,600	Returns inwards	3,500
		Cash (balancing figure)	149,270
		Balance c/d	5,620
	158,860		158,860
Balance b/d	5,620		

3 TOTAL CREDITORS ACCOUNT

	£		£
Discounts received	760	Balance b/f	4,740
Cash (balancing figure)	106,560	Purchases (W4)	108,970
Balance c/d	6,390		
	113,710		113,710
		Balance b/d	6,390

4 PURCHASES ACCOUNT

	£		£
Creditors	108,970	Trading account	108,370
		Drawings	600
	108,970		108,970

5 *Heat, light etc*

	£	£
Amounts paid in year		3,460
Add: rent prepayment at 31 March 20X2	650	
heating accrual at 31 March 20X3	310	
		960
		4,420
Less: rent prepayment at 31 March 20X3	480	
heating accrual at 31 March 20X2	380	
		860
P & L charge for year		3,560

25 NEWGALE

NEWGALE LIMITED
BALANCE SHEET AS AT 31 DECEMBER 20X5

	Cost	*Depreciation*	*NBV*
Fixed assets	£	£	£
Freehold premises	108,000	36,000	72,000
Plant	72,000	19,200	52,800
	180,000	55,200	124,800
Current assets			
Stock		28,550	
Debtors		22,200	
Bank		760	
		51,510	
Creditors: amounts falling due within one year			
Creditors		31,150	
Accrual (proposed dividend)		7,500	
		38,650	
Net current assets			12,860
			137,660
Capital and reserves			
£1 ordinary shares			75,000
Retained profits			62,660
			137,660

Workings

1 *Proposed dividend*

Shares in issue = 75,000
Proposed dividend = 10p × 75,000 = £7,500

Adjustment required: decrease retained profits
insert accrual as current liability

2 *Stocks*

Adjustment required for undercast of £1,100:

increase stocks
increase retained profits (because cost of sales is decreased)

No adjustment is required for the £4,200 understatement. The adjustments, which should have been made last year, have no net effect on the retained profits for the current year: the retained profit brought forward should have been larger, but then so should 'opening stock' in the cost of sales figure for the current year.

3 *Despatched cheques*

Adjustment required for the cheques totalling £2,600:

decrease bank
decrease creditors

4 *Depreciation of plant*

Using the straight-line method of depreciation, the plant should have been depreciated by a total of 3 × 10% × £60,000 = £18,000. A difference of £18,000 – £16,260 = £1,740 has therefore arisen.

Adjustment required: increase accumulated depreciation
decrease retained profits

5 *New item of plant*

The new item of plant should have been recorded as a fixed asset, not as goods purchased

Adjustment required: increase plant at cost
increase retained profits

In addition, depreciation of 10% × £12,000 = £1,200 should be charged on the new plant.

Adjustment required: increase accumulated depreciation
decrease retained profits

26 EXCEL

(a) EXCEL LIMITED
PROFIT AND LOSS ACCOUNT
FOR THE YEAR ENDED 30 NOVEMBER 20X5

	£	£
Revenue		510,500
Less loss on vehicle disposal		1,500
		509,000
Less expenses		
Wages and expenses	245,200	
Licences and insurance	6,000	
Repairs	34,440	
Petrol and oil	44,870	
Administration expenses	30,460	
Advertising expenses	13,340	
Directors' remuneration	40,000	
Bad debts	890	
Provision for doubtful debts	1,849	
Auditor's fees	2,000	
Debenture interest	3,600	
Depreciation	21,800	
		444,449
		64,551
Appropriations		
Interim share dividend	12,000	
Final proposal dividend	24,000	
		36,000
Retained profit		28,551
Retained profit 30/11/X4		127,200
Retained profit 30/11/X5		155,751

(b) EXCEL LIMITED
BALANCE SHEET AS AT 30 NOVEMBER 20X5

	Cost	Depreciation	NBV
Fixed assets	£	£	£
Premises	420,000	-	420,000
Vehicles	93,200	51,620	41,580
	513,200	51,620	461,580
Current assets			
Stocks: petrol and oil	1,640		
spares	3,170		
		4,810	
Debtors	61,640		
Provision for doubtful debts	(1,849)		
		59,791	
Prepayments		1,500	
Cash		19,920	
		86,021	
Creditors: amounts falling due within one year:			
Debenture interest		3,600	
Final share dividend		24,000	
Advertising accrual		800	
Auditors fee		2,000	
Repairs		1,450	
		31,850	
Net current assets			54,171
Total assets less current liabilities			515,751
Creditors: amounts falling due after more than one year			
12% debentures			(120,000)
			395,751
Capital and reserves			£
Shares (200,000 at £1, fully paid)			200,000
Share premium			40,000
Profit and loss account			155,751
			395,751

Workings

1 *Provision for doubtful debts*

Provision = 3% × £(62,530 – 890) = £1,849

2 *Accounting treatment for stocks*

Because of the nature of the business, it is difficult to come to a 'cost of sales' figure for Excel Ltd. Consequently no attempt has been made to arrive at a gross profit figure. Stocks figures have therefore been incorporated into the relevant expense figures as follows.

	Petrol and oil	Vehicle spares (repairs)
	£	£
Charge shown in list of balances	45,310	35,460
Add opening stock	1,200	700
	46,510	36,160
Less closing stock	1,640	3,170
Charge to P & L account	44,870	32,990 *

* There is also a repairs accrual of £1,450, so the P & L charge for repairs is £32,990 + £1,450 = £34,440

3 *Motor vehicles and depreciation*

The motor vehicles figure of £111,200 is incorrect, as it has been made up incorrectly. The sales proceeds should not be shown in the motor vehicles account, but the £24,000 original cost disposed of should be. Journal entries to correct these errors are:

		£	£
DEBIT	Motor vehicles	6,000	
CREDIT	Motor vehicles disposals		6,000
DEBIT	Motor vehicle disposals	24,000	
CREDIT	Motor vehicles		24,000

In addition, depreciation in respect of the vehicle disposed of should be debited to depreciation account, and credited to disposals account (25% × £24,000 × 2 5 years = £16,500). Also, depreciation for the year should be calculated on the motor vehicles account balance.

The effect of all these adjustments is:

MOTOR VEHICLES

	£		£
Balance b/f	85,200	Sale proceeds	6,000
Additions	32,000	Disposals	24,000
Sales proceeds correction	6,000	Balance c/f	93,200
	123,200		123,200

DISPOSALS

	£		£
Motor vehicles	24,000	Sale proceeds	6,000
		Depreciation	16,500
		P & L account	1,500
	24,000		24,000

DEPRECIATION

	£		£
Disposals	16,500	Balance b/f	46,320
Balance c/f	51,620	P & L account	21,800 *
	68,120		68,120

		£
* £85,200 × 25% × 9/12	=	15,975
£93,200 × 25% × 3/12	=	5,825
		21,800

4 *Debenture interest*

Accrued debenture interest = 12% × £120,000 × 3 months
= £3,600

27 MATTHEWS

MATTHEWS LIMITED
CASH FLOW STATEMENT FOR THE YEAR ENDED 31 MAY 20X4

	£'000
Net cash inflow from operating activities (W)	73
Returns on investments and servicing of finance	
Interest paid	(23)
Taxation	
Corporation tax (14 + 20 — 18)	(16)
Tax paid	
Capital expenditure	
Purchase of tangible fixed assets (812 – 780)	(32)
	2
Equity dividends paid	(17)
	(15)
Financing	
Repayment of debentures	(20)
Decrease in cash	(35)

Working

	£'000
Operating profit	88
Depreciation charge (546 – 485)	61
Increase in stocks	(36)
Increase in debtors	(71)
Increase in creditors	31
Net cash inflow for operating activities	73

28 MAXIM

Schedule of ratios

Return on capital employed $= \dfrac{\text{net profit before interest and tax}}{\text{fixed assets + net current assets}}$

$= \dfrac{£110,000}{£308,000 + £18,000}$

$= 33.7\%$

Net profit percentage $= \dfrac{\text{net profit before interest and tax}}{\text{sales}}$

$= \dfrac{£110,000}{£780,000}$

$= 14.1\%$

Current ratio $= \dfrac{\text{current assets}}{\text{current liabilities}}$

$= \dfrac{£424,000}{£406,000}$

$= 1.04$

Quick ratio $= \dfrac{\text{current assets less stock}}{\text{current liabilities}}$

$= \dfrac{£188,000}{£406,000}$

$= 0.46$

Stock turnover period $= \dfrac{\text{stock}}{\text{cost of sales}} \times 365 \text{ days}$

$= \dfrac{£236,000}{£670,000 \, *} \times 365 \text{ days}$

$= 129 \text{ days}$

Gearing $= \dfrac{\text{long term loans and preference shares}}{\text{ordinary shares plus reserves}}$

$= \dfrac{£260,000}{£66,000}$

$= 394\%$

* Strictly, the stock turnover period should be calculated using a cost of sales figure. This information is not available for Maxim plc, so the operating expenses figure has been used instead. Cost of sales would in fact be less than £670,000, and so would give a stock turnover period greater than 129 days.

Report

This report considers whether or not a loan should be made to Maxim plc. The conclusions can only be tentative, because the ratios calculated do not mean very much by themselves. They ought to be compared with previous years' ratios, and if possible, with ratios based on the accounts of a business similar to Maxim plc.

The return on capital employed (33.7%) and net profit percentage (14.1%) do not give any apparent cause for concern. Both figures imply that the *profitability* of Maxim plc is satisfactory.

The current ratio of 1.04 is not unreasonable, but the quick ratio of 0.46 is low. The reason for this lies in the slow stock turnover (129 days). It is surprising that Maxim plc wishes to increase the investment in trading stock, when stock turnover is so slow. Maxim plc currently holds stock sufficient for at least 129 days. Whether or not the quick ratio and stock turnover figures are poor depends on:

(a) The nature of the business carried out by Maxim plc.
(b) Whether these ratios are improving or worsening over time.

More information is needed, therefore, before any judgement on the *liquidity* of the business can be made.

The gearing of Maxim plc is 394%, which is high. It is therefore possible that Maxim plc is in a risky business, because the capital put forward by shareholders is relatively low. If this is the case, making a loan to Maxim plc might not be a good idea. Again, more information on the nature of the business is needed.

Conclusion

On the basis of the information to hand, I would not approve a loan to Maxim plc. However, more information about the nature of the business should be sought before a final decision is made.

29 BLOW

(a) *Current ratio*

$$20X8 \quad \frac{6{,}990}{4{,}960} = 1.41$$

$$20X9 \quad \frac{10{,}640}{8{,}950} = 1.19$$

Quick ratio

$$20X8 \quad \frac{6{,}990 - 3{,}100}{4{,}960} = 0.78$$

$$20X9 \quad \frac{10{,}640 - 4{,}500}{8{,}950} = 0.69$$

The current ratio indicates the extent to which liabilities due to be met soon are covered by assets due to be converted into cash soon.

The rationale behind the quick ratio is similar, but shorter-term. Since stock may take months to convert into cash it is excluded.

Reservations

(i) Year end figures may not be typical of the rest of the year.

(ii) One needs to know more about the bank overdraft, for example:

(1) is it to be semi-permanent?
(2) is there an agreed overdraft limit?

(b) *Debtors' turnover ratio*

20X8	*20X9*
$\frac{83{,}000}{3{,}200}$	$\frac{91{,}000}{5{,}900}$
= 25.9	= 15.4

Debtors' collection period

$\frac{365}{25.9}$	$\frac{365}{15.4}$
= 14 days	= 24 days

The 20X9 debtors figure is significantly greater than the 20X8 figure, even allowing for the increase in sales. If one assumes that year-end figures are typical of the rest of the year then it would seem that the management of debtors may have been rather lax during the past year. If the 20X8 collection period (14 days) still applied then 20X9 debtors would be

$$\frac{91,000}{25.9} = £3,514$$

which would be a reduction of £2,386 in year-end debtors.

It is possible that inadequate attention has been given to chasing overdue debts. It is equally likely that in order to attract new customers, or to compete effectively, a longer credit period has been granted.

30 DIRECT/INDIRECT

(a) (i) Direct costs are costs which can be separately identified with a specific product or service. Direct materials costs, for example, are costs relating to the actual material from which a product is made. Direct labour costs are costs incurred in the form of wages for workers directly involved in the production process.

(ii) Indirect costs are costs which are not charged directly to a product or service, or cannot be separately identified with it. Examples are costs of coolants, cleaning materials, supervision of labour and water rates.

(b) (i) *Production costs*

Direct material*
Direct labour*
Direct expenses*
Production overhead

(ii) *Administration costs*

(iii) *Selling costs*

(iv) *Distribution costs*

(v) *Research and development costs*

Items marked * are direct costs.

31 APPORTIONMENT

(a) PRODUCTION OVERHEAD ANALYSIS AND APPORTIONMENT SHEET

	Production depts		*Service depts*		
	Process A	*Process B*	*Stores*	*Canteen*	*Total*
	£	£	£	£	£
Directly allocated o'heads					
Indirect wages	25,000	40,000	20,000	10,000	95,000
Indirect materials	51,510	58,505	1,310	8,425	119,750
Apportionment of other o'heads					
Rent and rates (i)	150,000	75,000	150,000	75,000	450,000
Depreciation of P & M (ii)	100,000	20,000	15,000	5,000	140,000
Power (iii)	40,000	10,000	-	-	50,000
Insurance: fire (i)	1,250	625	1,250	625	3,750
compensation (iv)	6,100	5,300	400	200	12,000
Heat and light (i)	1,500	750	1,500	750	4,500
	375,360	210,180	189,460	100,000	875,000
Canteen (v)	50,000	37,500	12,500	(100,000)	
	425,360	247,680	201,960	-	
Stores (vi)	134,640	67,320	(201,960)		
	560,000	315,000	-	-	875,000

Bases of apportionment

(i) Floor area
(ii) Book value of plant and machinery
(iii) Power of machinery
(iv) 2% of wages (see working 1 below)
(v) Number of employees
(vi) Number of stores issue notes.

(b) An overhead recovery rate can be calculated based on the number of direct hours worked in each process (see working 1 for details).

$$\text{Process A rate} = \frac{£560{,}000}{70{,}000 \text{ hrs}} = £8 \text{ per hour}$$

$$\text{Process B rate} = \frac{£315{,}000}{45,000 \text{ hrs}} = £7 \text{ per hour}$$

(c) and (d)

	Product X		Product Y	
Unit cost of production	£	£	£	£
Material P	37		93	
Material Q	2		48	
Material R	4		15	
		43		156
Process A labour	8		16	
Process B labour	5		15	
		13		31
Production overheads				
Process A	16		32	
Process B	7		21	
		23		53
Salesmen's commission		5		15
Packing		1		4
Transport		2		5
Royalties		1		0
Advertising (W2)		2		6
Total costs per unit		90		270
Selling price per unit		100		300
Profit per unit		10		30

Workings

1 *Wages incurred in year*

		£	£
Process A:	product X (15,000 × 2 × £4)	120,000	
	product Y (10,000 × 4 × £4)	160,000	
	indirect	25,000	
			305,000
Process B:	product X (15,000 × 1 × £5)	75,000	
	product Y (10,000 × 3 × £5)	150,000	
	indirect	40,000	
			265,000
Stores			20,000
Canteen			10,000
			600,000

2 *Allocation of advertising costs*

Allocated in proportion to sales revenue

	£
Revenue from product X	1,500,000
Revenue from product Y	3,000,000
	4,500,000

Allocated to product X: £90,000 × 15/45	=	£30,000
	=	£2 per unit
Allocated to product Y: £90,000 × 30/45	=	£60,000
	=	£6 per unit

32 ABSORPTION AND MARGINAL COSTING

(a) (i) *Profit statement under absorption costing*

	March		*April*	
	£'000	£'000	£'000	£'000
Sales		320		480
Cost of goods sold				
Opening stock	-		208	
Variable production costs	320		80	
Fixed production overhead	96		24	
Under-absorbed production overhead	-		72	
	416		384	
Less closing stock	208		-	
		208		384
Gross profit		112		96
Less selling, distribution and administration costs		40		40
Net profit		72		56

Workings

Sales:	March	= 4,000 × £80
	April	= 6,000 × £80
Variable production costs:	March	= 8,000 × £40
	April	= 2,000 × £40
Fixed production overhead:	March	= 8,000 × £12
	April	= 2,000 × £12
Under-absorbed production overhead:	April	= £96,000 – £24,000
Closing stock:	March	= 4,000 × £52

(ii) *Profit statement under marginal costing*

	March		*April*	
	£'000	£'000	£'000	£'000
Sales		320		480
Cost of goods sold				
Opening stock	-		160	
Variable production costs	320		80	
	320		240	
Less closing stock	160		-	
		160		240
Contribution		160		240
Fixed costs				
Production overhead	96		96	
Selling, distribution and Administration costs	40		40	
		136		136
Net profit		24		104

Working

Closing stock: March = 4,000 × £40

(b) In marginal costing:

(i) Closing stocks are valued at marginal production cost.

(ii) Fixed costs are charged in full against the profit for the period in which they are incurred.

In absorption costing:

(i) Closing stocks are valued at full production cost, and include a share of fixed production cost.

(ii) This means that the cost of sales in a period will include some fixed overhead incurred in a previous period (ie in opening stock values) and will exclude some fixed overhead incurred in the current period but carried forward in closing stock values as a charge to a subsequent accounting period.

When sales exceed production, a higher profit results from marginal costing. 'Marginal costing rewards sales', as the statement puts it. For example, in part (a) of this question, April sales are 6,000 units whereas production is only 2,000 units. Under marginal costing profit is £104,000, but under absorption costing profit it is only £56,000.

On the other hand, when production exceeds sales, a higher profit results from absorption costing. 'Absorption costing rewards production', as the statement puts it. For example, in part (a) of this question, March production was 8,000 units whereas sales were only 4,000 units. Absorption costing gives a profit of £72,000 but marginal costing only gives a profit of £24,000.

33 ESTIMATED COSTS

(a) (i) *100,000 units sold*

	£'000	£'000
Sales (100,000 × £100)		10,000
Less		
Direct wages	1,000	
Direct materials	4,000	
Manufacturing overheads	2,000	
Administration cost	1,000	
Marketing and selling costs	1,000	
		9,000
Net profit		1,000

Net profit is therefore £1m. An alternative method of reaching the same result is:

Net profit = 100,000 × unit profit
= 100,000 × (£100 - £90)
= £1m

(ii) *200,000 units sold*

	£'000	£'000
Sales (200,000 × £84)		16,800
Less		
Direct wages	2,000	
Direct materials	8,000	
Manufacturing overheads	2,500	
Administration cost	1,000	
Marketing and selling costs	1,500	
		15,000
Net profit		1,800

Net profit is therefore £1.8m. Alternatively:

Net profit = 200,000 × unit profit
= 200,000 × (£84 – £75)
= £1.8m

(b) Breakeven point means that fixed costs are exactly equalled by contribution (ie sale price less variable costs). To answer this part of the question, it is therefore necessary to calculate fixed costs as a preliminary step (using the high-low method).

Direct wages and direct materials are variable costs.

Manufacturing overheads

	Units produced	*Cost* (£)
High	200,000	2,500,000
Low	100,000	2,000,000
	100,000	500,000

Variable manufacturing overheads for producing 100,000 units amounts to £500,000. Fixed manufacturing overheads are therefore £1.5m.

Administration cost

	Units produced	*Cost* (£)
High	200,000	1,000,000
Low	100,000	1,000,000
	100,000	-

Administration cost is therefore entirely a fixed cost of £1m.

Marketing and selling costs

	Units produced	*Cost* (£)
High	200,000	1,500,000
Low	100,000	1,000,000
	100,000	500,000

Variable marketing and selling costs for producing 100,000 units amounts to £500,000. Fixed marketing and selling costs are therefore £500,000.

Total fixed costs

	£m
Manufacturing overheads	1.5
Administrative costs	1.0
Marketing and selling costs	0.5
	3.0

(i)

	£	£
Unit selling price		100
Variable costs:		
Direct wages	10	
Direct materials	40	
Manufacturing overheads	5	
Marketing and selling costs	5	
		60
Contribution/unit		40

Breakeven point in units = £3m ÷ £40
= 75,000 units

(ii)

	£	£
Unit selling price		84
Variable costs		
Direct wages	10.0	
Direct materials	40.0	
Manufacturing overheads	5.0	
Marketing and selling costs	5.0	
		60
		24

Breakeven point in units = £3m ÷ £24
= 125,000 units

(c) The company should adopt the selling price of £84, because it yields a higher profit (£1.8m as against £1m).

34 POSTHORN

(a) FORECAST CASH FLOW FOR THE YEAR ENDING 30 SEPTEMBER 20X6

	£	£
Inflow		
Paid by debtors		
(2 × £135,000) + (10 × £180,000)		2,070,000
		2,070,000
Outflows		
Paid to creditors		
(1 × £112,500) + (11 × £139,500)	1,647,000	
Purchase of fixed assets	135,000	
Overheads		
£(36,000 + 207,000 – 45,000)	198,000	
Payment of dividends		
(15p × 450,000)	67,500	
Payment of debenture interest		
(10% × £270,000)	27,000	
		2,074,500
Net cash deficiency		4,500

(b) FORECAST PROFIT AND LOSS ACCOUNT FOR THE YEAR ENDING 30 SEPTEMBER 20X6

	£	£
Sales (12 × £180,000)		2,160,000
Less cost of sales (75% × sales)		1,620,000
Gross profit (25% × sales)		540,000
Less expenses		
Overheads	207,000	
Debenture interest	27,000	
Depreciation £(351,000 – 270,000)	81,000	
		315,000
Net profit for the year		225,000
Less dividend		112,500
Retained profit for the year		112,500
Retained profits as at 30 September 20X5		180,000
Retained profits as at 30 September 20X6		292,500

(c) FORECAST BALANCE SHEET AS AT 30 SEPTEMBER 20X6

	Cost	*Dep'n*	*NBV*
	£	£	£
Fixed assets (W1)	810,000	351,000	459,000
Current assets			
Stock		324,000	
Debtors (W2)		360,000	
Cash (W3)		166,500	
		850,500	
Current liabilities			
Creditors (W4)		139,500	
Proposed dividend		112,500	
Expenses accrued		45,000	
		297,000	
Net current assets			553,500
			1,012,500
Long-term liabilities			
Debentures			270,000
			742,500
Capital and reserves			
Ordinary shares of £1, allotted and paid up			450,000
Retained profits			292,500
			742,500

Workings

1 Fixed assets at cost = NBV as at 30 September 20X5 plus depreciation as at 30 September 20X5 + acquisitions = £405,000 + £270,000 + £135,000 = £810,000.

2 Debtors = 2 × £180,000 = £360,000.

3 In order to calculate the cash figure, several other figures have to be derived.

Step 1 *Opening stock*

Cost of sales	=	opening stock + purchases – closing stock
Opening stock	=	cost of sales – purchases + closing stock
	=	£1,620,000 – £(12 × 139,500) + £324,000
	=	£270,000

Step 2 *Opening cash*

Working capital	=	stocks + debtors + cash – creditors - proposed dividend – accruals
Opening cash		working capital – stocks – debtors + creditors + proposed dividend + accruals
	=	£495,000 – £270,000 – £(2 × 135,000) + £112,500 + £67,500 + £36,000
	=	£171,000

Step 3 Closing cash

Closing cash	=	opening cash adjusted for cash inflow/outflow for year
	=	£171,000 – £4,500
	=	£166,500

4 Creditors = 1 × £139,500

35 FLEXIBLE BUDGET

(a) *Fixed* budgets are based on estimated volumes of production and sales but do not include any provision for the event that actual volumes may differ from the budgeted volumes.

A *flexible* budget is designed to change so as to relate to actual volumes achieved. This has two advantages.

(i) At the planning stage, it may be helpful to know what the effects would be if the actual outcome differs from the prediction. This would enable contingency plans to be drawn up if necessary.

(ii) At the end of each month or year, actual results may be compared with the flexible budget as a control procedure.

(b) FLEXIBLE BUDGET

	80%	*100%*
	£	£
Variable costs		
Indirect labour	120,000	150,000
Consumable supplies	160,000	200,500
Canteen and other welfare services	52,000	65,000
	332,000	415,000
Fixed costs		
Depreciation	200,000	200,000
Maintenance	130,000	130,000
Insurance	35,000	35,000
Rates	50,000	50,000
	747,000	830,000

Glossary and Index

Absorption costing The procedure which charges fixed as well as variable overhead to cost units. (CIMA *Official Terminology*)

Absorption rate A rate charged to a cost unit intended to account for the overhead at a predetermined level of activity. (CIMA *Official Terminology*)

Account A record in the bookkeeping ledger in which is kept details of all the financial transactions relating to one individual supplier, customer, asset, liability or type of expense or receipt.

Accounting The recording of financial transactions and the preparation of accounting reports and financial statements from bookkeeping records in accordance with acknowledged methods and conventions.

Accounting equation Assets = Capital + Liabilities

Accrual Expense (usually) or revenue outstanding at the end of a trading period which needs to be *accrued* for inclusion with the accounting records for the period.

Accruals concept Revenue and costs are accrued, that is, recognised as they are earned or incurred, not as money is received or paid, matched with one another so far as their relationship can be established or justifiably assumed and dealt with in the profit and loss account of the period to which they relate (SSAP 2).

Acid test ratio Also known as *quick ratio*. This is a measure of a company's ability to meet its short term debts. It is a more stringent test of liquidity than the *current ratio*, because it assumes that stocks cannot necessarily be readily converted into liquid funds.

$$\text{Acid test ratio} = \frac{\text{Current assets - stock}}{\text{Current liabities}}$$

Amortisation This is similar to *depreciation*, but is generally applied either to leasehold buildings, or to intangible fixed assets such as *research and development* or *goodwill*, rather than to machinery and equipment.

Applied research Original or critical investigation undertaken primarily to acquire new scientific or technical knowledge and directed towards a specific practical aim or objective.

Appropriation account The record of how the profit or loss has been allocated to distributions or reserves.

Asset Resource *owned* by a business and of value to that business. Assets are classified as *fixed* or *current*.

Asset turnover The ratio of sales in a year to the amount of net assets (capital employed).

Audit A systematic examination of the activities and status of an entity based primarily on investigation and analysis of its systems, controls, and records (CIMA *Official Terminology*). It is important to distinguish between *internal audit* and *external audit*.

Average cost A method of stock valuation whereby an average price is calculated for all material in stock and this average price is used to charge issues to production.

Bad debt A debtor who fails to pay his outstanding debt to a company within a reasonable time, after which the balance is written off.

Balance The difference between the totals of the debit and credit entries in an account.

Balance sheet A statement of the *liabilities*, *capital* and *assets* of a business at a given moment in time. It is like a 'snapshot' photograph since it captures on paper a still image of something which is constantly changing.

Bank reconciliation A comparison of a bank statement with the cash book. Differences between the balance on the bank statement - and the balance in the cashbook will be errors or timing differences, and they should be identified and explored.

Basis of apportionment A physical or financial unit used to apportion costs equitably to cost centres. (CIMA *Official Terminology*)

Bin card A record of receipts, issues and balances of the quantity of an item of stock handled by a store. (CIMA *Official Terminology*)

Bookkeeping The recording of monetary transactions.

Budget A plan expressed in money. It is prepared and approved prior to the budget period and may show income, expenditure, and the capital to be employed. May be drawn up showing incremental effects on former budgeted or actual figures, or be compiled by zero-based budgeting. (CIMA *Official Terminology*)

Budgetary control The practice of establishing budgets which identify areas of responsibility for individual managers and of regularly comparing actual results against expected results.

Business equation $P = I + D - C_i$

where P represents profit
I represents the increase in net assets after drawings have been taken out by the proprietor
D represents drawings

Ci represents the amount of extra capital introduced into the business during the period.

Capital employed The total funds invested in a business made up of shareholders' funds and loan capital. It is equivalent in value to a company's net assets.

Capital expenditure Expenditure on fixed assets, the net cost of which is to be 'capitalised' and depreciated over the anticipated useful working life of the assets.

Capital Money put into a business by its owner(s) with the intention of earning a profit.

Cash account A record of receipts and payments of cash or cheques.

Cash budget A statement in which estimated future cash receipts and payments are tabulated in such a way as to show the forecast cash balance of a business at defined intervals.

Cash cycle See *operating cycle*.

Cash flow The amount of money flowing into and out of a business during a period of time. It does not necessarily equate to costs and revenues over the same period.

Cash flow statement A statement produced either for management or for external reporting purposes showing, by broad category cash receipts and payments in a period. The term may also refer to a forecast for future period.

Company A company is a business which is separate legal entity formed by registration under the Companies Act.

Consistency concept The principle that there is uniformity of accounting treatment of like items whether each accounting period and from one period to the next. (SSAP 2)

Contribution Sales value less variable cost of sales. (CIMA *Official Terminology*)

Cost accounting An internal reporting system for an organisation's own management.

Cost behaviour The way in which costs of output are affected by fluctuations in the level of activity. (CIMA *Official Terminology*)

Cost centre A production or service location, function, activity or item of equipment whose costs may be attributed to cost units. (CIMA *Official Terminology*)

Cost department The department responsible for keeping cost accounting records.

Cost unit A unit of product or service in relation to which costs are ascertained. (CIMA *Official Terminology*)

Credit An entry recorded on the right hand side of the account which represents a decrease in the value of a company's assets or expenses or an increase in the value of its liabilities or revenues.

Creditor A person to whom a business owes money. A trade creditor is a person to whom a business owes money for debts incurred in the course of trading operations.

Creditors' turnover period This is the period of credit taken from suppliers. It is the length of time between the purchase of materials and the payment to suppliers. It may be calculated as:

$$\frac{\text{Average (or year end) trade creditors}}{\text{Purchases}} \times 365$$

Cumulative weighted average pricing A pricing method which calculates a weighted average price for all units in stock. Issues are priced at this average cost and the balance of stock remaining would have the same unit valuation.

Current asset Current assets are either:

(a) items owned by the business with the intention of turning them into cash within one year; or

(b) cash, including money in the bank, owned by the business.

These assets are current in the sense that they are continually flowing through the business.

Current liabilities Debts of the business which must be paid within a fairly short period of time, by convention one year.

Current ratio A ratio which measures a company's liquidity by comparing its short term liabilities with the current assets out of which these liabilities will be met.

$$\text{Current ratio} = \frac{\text{current assets}}{\text{current liabilities}}$$

Debit An entry made on the left hand side of the account which represents an increase in the value of a business' assets or expenses or a decrease in the value of its liabilities or revenue.

Debt collection period This is the length of the credit period taken by the customer - it is the time between the sale of an item and the receipt of cash from the customer. It may be calculated as:

$$\frac{\text{Average debtors (or year - end debtors)}}{\text{Credit sales}} \times 365$$

Debtor A person who owes the business money. A trade debtor is a customer who buys goods without paying cash for them straight away.

Debtors' turnover See *debt collection period.*

Depreciation The measure of the wearing out, using up or other reduction in value of a fixed asset whether arising from use, effluxion (passing) of time, or obsolescence through technology and market changes (FRS 15).

Development cost The cost of use of scientific or technical knowledge in order to produce new or substantially improved materials, devices, products or services; to install new processes or systems prior to the commencement of commercial production or commercial applications; or to improve substantially those already produced or installed. (SSAP 13)

Direct cost Expenditure which can be economically identified with a specific saleable cost unit. (CIMA *Official Terminology*)

Distribution cost The cost of warehousing products for sale and of delivering them to customers.

Dividend A distribution to shareholders out of profits, usually in the form of cash, in proportion to the number of shares that they hold in the business.

Double entry (bookkeeping) The method by which a business records financial transactions. An account is maintained for every supplier, customer, asset, liability, and income and expense. Every transaction is recorded twice so that every *debit* is balanced by a *credit.*

Doubtful debts An amount charged against profit which allows for the fact that a proportion of debts may not be recovered. The amount is also deducted from debtors.

External audit A periodic examination of the books of account and records of an entity carried out by an independent third party (the auditor), to ensure that they have been properly maintained, are accurate and comply with established concepts, principles, accounting standards, legal requirements and give a true and fair view of the financial state of the entity. (CIMA *Official Terminology*)

Financial accounting The classification and recording of monetary transactions of an entity in accordance with established concepts, principles, accounting standards and legal requirements and presentation of a view of the effect of those transactions during and at the end of an accounting period. (CIMA *Official Terminology*)

First in first out (FIFO) A method of stock valuation in which it is assumed that the first goods into stock will be the first to be issued for use or sale. Compare *LIFO* and *average cost.*

Fixed asset A fixed asset is an asset acquired for continuing use within the business with a view to earning income or making profits from its use either directly or indirectly. A fixed asset is not acquired for sale to a customer.

Fixed assets register A record showing details of individual fixed assets.

Fixed budget A budget which does not include any provision for the event that actual volumes of production may differ from those budgeted.

Fixed cost/fixed overhead/period cost The cost which is incurred for a period, and which, within certain output and turnover limits, tends to be unaffected by fluctuations in levels of activity (output or turnover). Examples are rent, rates, insurance and executive salaries. (CIMA *Official Terminology*)

Flexible budget A budget which, by recognising different cost behaviour patterns, is designed to change as volume of output changes. (CIMA *Official Terminology*)

Fundamental accounting concepts The basic assumptions which underlie the periodic financial accounts of an entity.

Gearing The proportion of a company's capital employed that is tied up in loan capital. There are various ways of calculating the ratio, which may be found in the chapter on ratio analysis.

Going concern concept The assumption that the entity will continue in operational existence for the foreseeable future. (SSAP 2)

Goods received note A record of goods at the point of receipt. (CIMA *Official Terminology*)

Goodwill The excess of the price paid for a business over the fair market value of the individual assets and liabilities acquired.

High/low method A technique for determining the fixed and variable components of a total cost that uses actual observations of total cost at the highest and lowest levels of activity and calculates the change in both activity and cost.

Idle time The period for which a work station is available for production but is not used due to a shortage of tooling, material or operators. (CIMA *Official Terminology*)

Imprest system A method of controlling cash or stock. When the cash or stock has been reduced by disbursements or issues it is restored to its original level.

Income and expenditure account The *profit and loss account* of a non-trading organisation.

Indirect cost/overhead Expenditure on labour, materials or services which cannot be economically identified with a specific saleable cost unit. (CIMA *Official Terminology*)

Intangible assets Assets which do not have a physical identity (such as *goodwill*, patents, trade marks unamortised research and development costs). They are classified as *fixed assets* because they cannot readily be converted into cash.

Last in first out (LIFO) A method of stock valuation which is the opposite of *FIFO.* Materials are charged to production in the reverse order of their receipt.

Ledger A collection of accounts eg a collection of suppliers' accounts is the purchase ledger.

Liabilities An amount *owed* to a business.

Loan capital Money that has been loaned to the company on a long-term basis at a pre-agreed rate of interest. The lenders of loan capital do not (normally) share in the profits of a business.

Long term liabilities Debts which are not payable within the *short term* and so any liability which is not current must be long-term.

Management accounting A management information system which analyses data to provide information as a basis for management action. The concern of a management accountant is to present accounting information in the form most helpful to management.

Marginal cost The cost of one unit of product or service which would be avoided if that unit were not produced or provided. (CIMA *Official Terminology*)

Marginal costing The accounting system in which variable costs are charged to cost units and fixed costs of the period are written off in full against the aggregate contribution. Its special value is in decision making. (CIMA *Official Terminology*)

Mark-up The addition to the cost of goods to arrive at a selling price. Mark-up is often expressed as a percentage.

Materiality concept The principle that financial statements should separately disclose terms which are significant enough to affect evaluation or decisions.

Net assets The value of a company's total assets less its current liabilities, equivalent in value to its *capital employed.*

Net book value The historical cost of an asset less accumulated depreciation or other write down.

Net realisable value The price at which goods in stock could be currently sold less any costs which would be incurred to complete the sale. (SSAP 9)

Operating cycle This is a term used to describe the connection between working capital and cash movements in and out. The cycle is usually measured in days or months. It is also called the *cash cycle.*

Opportunity cost The value of a benefit sacrificed in favour of an alternative course of action. (CIMA *Official Terminology*)

Over-absorbed overhead See under-absorbed overhead.

Overhead See indirect cost.

Overhead absorption rate A means of attributing overhead to a product or service based, for example, on direct labour hours, direct hour cost or machine hours. (CIMA *Official Terminology*)

Period cost See fixed cost.

Periodic stocktaking A process whereby all stock items are physically counted and then valued. (CIMA *Official Terminology*)

Prepayments Amounts of money already paid by the business for benefits which have not yet been enjoyed but will be enjoyed within the next accounting period.

Profit and loss account A record of income earned and expenditure incurred over a given period.

Profit margin This is ratio of profit to sales and may also be called profit percentage. For example, if a company makes a profit of £20,000 on sales of £100,000 its profit margin is 20%.

Prudence concept The principle that revenue and profits are not anticipated, but are included in the profit and loss account only when realised in the form either of cash or of other assets, the ultimate cash realisation of which can be assessed with reasonable certainty; provision is made for all known liabilities (expense and losses) whether the amount of these is known with certainty or is a best estimate in the light of the information available (SSAP 2).

Pure research Experimental or theoretical work undertaken primarily to acquire new scientific or technical knowledge for its own sake rather than directed towards any specific aim or application (SSAP 13).

Receipts and payments account A record of cash paid and received used by some (usually small) non-trading organisations.

Replacement cost Cost incurred as a result of hiring new employee(s).

Reserves Profit which has been re-invested in the business.

Return on capital employed (ROCE) The amount of profit as a percentage of capital employed. In your CIMA examination it should be calculated as:

$$\frac{\text{Net profit before tax and interest}}{\text{Average capital employed}}$$

Revenue expenditure Expenditure incurred for the purpose of the trade of the business or to maintain the existing earning capacity of fixed assets.

Scrap Discarded material having some value. (CIMA *Official Terminology*)

Semi-fixed cost See semi-variable cost.

Semi-variable cost/semi-fixed cost/mixed cost A cost containing both fixed and variable components and which is thus partly affected by fluctuations in the level of activity. (CIMA *Official Terminology*)

Share capital The amount of money invested in a company by its risk-taking shareholders.

Share premium The excess of the share price over the nominal value of the share.

Shareholders funds The amount of part of a company's capital owned by its shareholders. It is made up of share capital plus profits not distributed by the business.

Short term investments Stocks and shares of other businesses currently owned but with the intention of selling them in the near future.

Sole trader A person who carries on a business with sole legal responsibility. A sole trader's business is *not* a separate *legal* entity from the owner, but it is a separate accounting entity.

Spreadsheet A term for a microcomputer modelling package, being loosely derived from the likeness to a spreadsheet of paper divided into rows and columns.

Standard cost A standard expressed in money. It is built up from an assessment of the value of cost elements. Its main uses are providing bases for performance measurement, control by exception reporting, valuing stock and establishing selling prices. (CIMA *Official Terminology*)

Standard cost pricing A materials issues pricing method whereby all issues are at a predetermined standard price.

Standard costing A control technique which compares standard costs and revenues with actual results to obtain variances which are used to stimulate improved performance. (CIMA *Official Terminology*)

Step cost A cost which is fixed in nature but only within certain levels of activity.

Stock control The systematic regulation of stock levels. (CIMA *Official Terminology*)

Stocktaking/physical inventory See continuous stocktaking and periodic stocktaking.

Stock turnover This is the length of time an item is held in stores before it is used. It may be calculated as:

$$\frac{\text{Average stocks held (or year end stocks held)}}{\text{Cost of sales}}$$

Suspense account A temporary account opened for a number of reasons of which the most common are:

(a) the trial balance does not balance
(b) the bookkeeper of a business does not know where to post one side of a transaction.

Tangible asset An asset having a physical identity, eg plant and machinery.

Trial balance A list of all the balances in a company's ledger accounts. Such a listing is generally used as the first step in the preparation of the final accounts and is used to prove that the total of all the debit balances is equal to the total of all the credit balances.

Under-/over-absorbed overhead The difference between overhead incurred and overhead absorbed in a given period. (CIMA *Official Terminology*)

Variable cost Cost which tends to vary with the level of activity. (CIMA *Official Terminology*)

Variance Difference between planned, budgeted or standard cost and actual cost; and similarly for revenue. (CIMA *Official Terminology*)

Variance analysis The analysis of performance by means of variances. Used to promote management action at the earliest possible stages. (CIMA *Official Terminology*)

Work-in-progress Any material component, product or contract at an intermediate stage of completion.

Working capital The difference between current assets and current liabilities.